Bush's Law

Bush's Law

*The Remaking
of American Justice*

Eric Lichtblau

PANTHEON BOOKS • NEW YORK

Copyright © 2008 by Eric Lichtblau

All rights reserved. Published in the United States by Pantheon Books,
a division of Random House, Inc., New York, and in Canada by
Random House of Canada Limited, Toronto.

Pantheon Books and colophon are registered trademarks of
Random House, Inc.

Library of Congress Cataloging-in-Publication Data

Lichtblau, Eric.
Bush's law : the remaking of American justice after 9/11 / Eric Lichtblau.
p. cm.
Includes bibliographical references and index.
ISBN 978-0-375-42492-2
1. Terrorism—United States—Prevention—History.
2. National security—Law and legislation—United States—History.
3. Criminal justice, Administration of —United States—History.
4. War on Terrorism, 2001–   I. Title.
KF4850.L53 2008
973.931—dc22   2007049372

www.pantheonbooks.com

Printed in the United States of America

First Edition

2 4 6 8 9 7 5 3 1

In memory of my father, Myron,
who taught a love of language and of learning

CONTENTS

PROLOGUE

STEP BY RICKETY STEP, the Justice Department prosecutor and the FBI agent climbed the beat-up ladder toward the roof of the old Turkish warehouse. They had been waiting weeks for this trip, all for the chance to get a glimpse of what lay across the sprawling field to the north of the warehouse. They needed a way up on the roof, so an American military officer and a translator accompanying them had slipped a few lira to a baker who occupied the floor below, getting him to let them up to the top via a side balcony. They used a rope and an old drainpipe to begin hoisting their way to the top. But they hadn't counted on that rickety old ladder. A bolt clamping it to the wall was missing, and the ladder grew more wobbly with each step they took.

"If this falls, we're both going down," Rick Convertino, a pit bull of a prosecutor in Detroit, yelled to the FBI agent on the case, Mike Thomas, who was climbing a few rungs above him. Finally, they reached the top and stepped out onto the tar roof. Perched on the edge, they looked across a dirt road to survey their target off in the distance: a massive Turkish air base, launching pad for American and British fighter planes in the heart of one of the world's biggest Muslim nations. This was Incirlik Air Base, and this was what had brought them 5,700 miles in an improbable trek from an abandoned, run-down apartment in southwest Detroit to the fig-rich fields of Turkey.

From his pocket, Convertino pulled out his copy of their map to the Holy Grail: a lined page from a day-planner filled with what, at first glance, could pass for a child's idle scribbling. The markings were random, almost unintelligible—three sets of parallel lines, stick figures, arrows, a crude airplane, and some circles, or maybe it was a peace symbol; who could really tell? The doodling had been found in that run-down Detroit apartment a few months earlier, less than a week after the September 11 attacks, as Thomas and five other federal agents had descended on the place in search of a Muslim man named Nabil al-Marabh. A onetime Boston cabbie, al-Marabh had once roomed with a known al Qaeda operative, and he himself was now number 27 on the FBI's terrorist watch list. For years, the FBI had taken a wait-and-see attitude with hundreds of people like al-Marabh suspected of terrorist links, putting them on lists, compiling dossiers, occasionally monitoring their activities and wiretapping their phone calls, but rarely acting against them. Now, there was no longer time to wait. All leads, promising and improbable, had to be dusted off and scrubbed.

The problem was that al-Marabh no longer lived at the apartment; his name was still on the mailbox on the duplex at 2653 Norman Street, but he was long gone to Chicago. Instead, the agents were greeted at the front door by a Moroccan man, Karim Koubriti, wearing just boxer shorts and a T-shirt. Thomas showed Koubriti a photo of al-Marabh. "He doesn't live here," Koubriti, an Arabic speaker, said in halting English. No, he'd never seen him before. Thomas asked to see some ID. Koubriti had left it upstairs in the apartment. As he turned to go upstairs, Thomas and another agent asked to go upstairs with him. There, they found two other apparent transients sleeping on the floor. The men had little in the way of furniture—no beds, a few coffee tables and an old TV, some clothes strewn in garbage bags on the floor—but what they did have alarmed the FBI. Scattered through the place, Thomas and his colleagues found fraudulent IDs, two Sky Chef employee badges for access to the Detroit airport, dozens and dozens of audiotapes featuring fundamentalist Islamic teachings, a videotape with American landmarks like Disneyland and Las Vegas, and, inside a suitcase in a back closet, that small, mysterious day-planner with the odd markings inside it. One sketch bore writing in Arabic at the top, later translated as "The American Air Base in Turkey Under the Leadership of Defense Minister," and another said simply: "Queen Alia, Jordan."

What did it all mean? The Muslim men themselves, quickly handcuffed and facing criminal charges for document fraud, had no clear links to any known terrorist groups, but investigators were soon convinced they had stumbled onto what amounted to a terrorist sleeper cell. The hardest evidence linking the men to any real plot seemed to be the sketches themselves. Military intelligence officials were brought in to help decipher them. Some Air Force officers in Turkey were convinced: one sketch, they said, must be a blueprint for a possible attack on the air base. They could even guess which rooftop had served as the vantage point for the drawing. So serious was the threat that there was talk of changing the American flight patterns at the Turkish air base. Other military and intelligence analysts weren't so sure; some doubters considered the drawings unprofessional at best, a joke at worst. Now, Convertino and Thomas were there on the roof of the Turkish warehouse to find out for themselves.

An Air Force intelligence officer accompanying them drew out his own copy of the sketch and peered into his binoculars. It was a bright, clear day, and fighter planes were readying for take-off in the distance. Whoever had drawn the sketch, the officer surmised, could have stood right here at this spot. Convertino and Thomas gathered around him at rapt attention. "Look, here," the officer said, gesturing to a rectangular figure in the bottom left-hand corner of the page with what looked like a crudely drawn airplane coming out of it. "That's the hardened bunker." The dotted lines were the runway, and the plane-like figures in the drawing were the AWACS, the military refueling tankers and fighter jets readying for take-off in sequence. "There's the flight pattern," he said. As if to prove the theory, a jet took off from the air base as he spoke. Someone remarked how easy it would be for a terrorist to get a clean shot at a plane using a SAM—a shoulder-fired, surface-to-air missile popular among militant groups. Just a year before, Islamists in a tiny dinghy had managed to kill seventeen sailors on the USS *Cole* off the coast of Yemen. Were they now looking at the plans for another attack on another unprotected target?

Convertino grabbed the binoculars to look for himself. Just a few months earlier, before the attacks of 9/11, he was setting his sights on a University of Michigan basketball booster in a straightforward graft-and-corruption case that would ultimately net NBA star Chris Webber on perjury charges. Now, Convertino was chasing al Qaeda on a Turkish rooftop. As he gazed through the binoculars, he shook his head at the similarities between the air base in front of him and the drawing that appeared to mimic it so closely. Then Thomas took a turn. "Holy shit, this is it," the FBI agent finally remarked as he put down the binoculars. "This is a terrorist sketch. This is a case sketch."

This wasn't the kind of stuff they taught at the Case Western Law School, where Convertino first cut his teeth on the law, or even at Justice Department training seminars. There were no courses on deciphering suspected terrorist case sketchings or stopping the next big al Qaeda attack. Prosecutors didn't usually fly off to foreign countries with military escorts to divine the motives and targets of would-be terrorists. Then again, this was a new style of American justice—more agile, more aggressive, more muscular—and everyone had new roles to learn, and quickly. President George W. Bush and his generals in this new war at the White House, the Justice Department, and the Pentagon envisioned a wholly new approach to defeating the grave threat of terrorism. No longer, they believed, could America afford to wait on its heels for another terrorist attack to occur, and no longer could they be bound by the arcane customs that they believed had paralyzed counterterrorism agents for so long. They were now on a wartime footing, a permanent state of emergency. The government had to strike first as part of what Bush and his trusted White House counsel, Alberto Gonzales, liked to call "the new paradigm" of the global war on terror. This was a new kind of war, and Convertino and Thomas were among its many foot soldiers.

This war would require different tactics, different tools, and a different mindset in what would amount to the most radical remaking of America's notion of justice in generations. What Woodrow Wilson did in going after the socialists and anarchists, what J. Edgar Hoover did in going after communists, what Bobby Kennedy did in going after organized crime mob figures, Bush and his inner circle would now do in training the sights of the American government on those suspected of aiding the enemy known as al Qaeda. There was a new ethos at work, and it relied at its core on smashing walls—walls that had failed to stop the enemy from storming the country on 9/11; walls that had been erected in a bygone "don't tread on me" era to protect the American people from the powerful reach of its own government. Now, counterterrorism agents from the National Security Agency, the CIA, and the FBI would be allowed to go places and do things they had never done before in the quest to stop the next attack. Lawyers would give legal sanction to covert programs and secret interrogation tactics unimaginable just a few months earlier. And the drift net of government would sweep up thousands of suspects—some real, many imagined—in its tide. The walls had come crashing down.

As they stood on the rooftop scouring the case sketching, Convertino and Thomas knew nothing about many of the bold and audacious new tactics at play in attacking terrorism. This was a war planned in secret at the highest reaches of the Bush administration, with a go-it-alone muscularity that relied at its core on a broad, omnipotent reading of the president's wartime authority. There was little room for the checks and balances so inherent in American government, and many of the key decisions and strategies were hidden not only from Congress, the courts, the American public, and international allies, but even from many of the senior counterterrorism officials in Bush's administration who were charged with carrying out the new plan.

What the prosecutor did know as he and his colleagues tried to piece together the mystery of the rooftop etchings was that the stakes in this case were enormous. This was to be the first terrorism prosecution after the September 11 attacks, the first real test of how and whether the "new paradigm" fit into the constraints of the old legal system. This was a case already garnering attention from the highest levels. Bush himself had already hailed the arrests of the North African men in Detroit as one of several critical busts that had "thwarted terrorists," and his powerful and press-savvy attorney general, John Ashcroft, had told reporters, to the head-shaking of even his own befuddled investigators, that the men were suspected of having advance knowledge of the attacks on 9/11. Indeed, within a few months of the rooftop trip, with the vague outlines of the mysterious sketch now seemingly becoming clearer to the government, the Justice Department would announce major terrorism indictments against the three apartment-dwellers and a fourth Muslim man, producing a flood of headlines around the country about a major break in the war on terror. Policy-makers in Washington took proud notice. "For what it's worth," a Justice Department supervisor in Washington e-mailed the prosecution team in Detroit after the national publicity blitz, "the higher-ups in D.C. are pleased."

But soon enough, the afterglow of the headlines would turn dark. The court case collapsed, becoming so rife with problems that the Justice Department itself took the unheard-of step of moving to have its own prosecution against the "terror cell" thrown out of court. In a justice system designed at its best to produce clarity and finality, the case did just the opposite: what began in the view of Bush and Ashcroft as a slam dunk case against a terrorist sleeper cell ended with only lingering questions and doubts. The sketch showing a hardened bunker at the Turkish air base? The Justice Department was forced to conclude that it might just as easily have been a crude map of the Middle East doodled by a mentally ill man. The anti-American hate speech found on some of the audiotapes? Possibly just an old children's song in Arabic about a duck. And that videotape showing terrorist targets in Las Vegas and Disneyland might have been filmed by a tourist from Tunisia who wanted a cheery reminder of his travels.

Some agents at the FBI remained convinced: a real plot had been scuttled, and legitimate terrorists had gotten away. The terrorist case sketches, they insisted, were just that: case sketches. But in the end, the only thing certain about the muddled case was this: the system of justice that Americans had come to expect had broken down badly. The new "preemptive" intelligence mindset and the old, time-tested judicial one had collided with disastrous results. Just who was to blame would be hotly debated for years. Ashcroft himself was reprimanded for unfairly coloring the case through his improper public comments, not once but twice. Officials in Washington had lifted language for the indictment straight from a scholarly article on Islamic radicalism. The Air Force officer who led the rooftop expedition began to have doubts about what the supposed terrorist sketch actually represented. Photographs and evidence that the judge said should have been handed over to the defense—evidence that might have cast doubt on their guilt and that pointed up divisions with the government about the strength of the evidence—were never turned over, and the rights of the defendants to get a fair trial were cast in grave jeopardy.

Convertino, the star prosecutor, and a State Department witness would be indicted on perjury charges, facing prison time over allegations that they had intentionally concealed evidence from the jury and lied about it. In a prosecution that everyone from the White House on down wanted so badly to win, Convertino was depicted as a rogue prosecutor who pushed too hard to win and cut too many corners. His indictment, Convertino charged in a lawsuit of his own against the government, was the Bush administration's bitter payback against him for bucking up against his supervisors in Washington and exposing just how badly this new war on terror was being mismanaged. There was blame to go around. The government had turned on itself, with the prosecutor now the prosecuted. And a case that began on a wobbly ladder on the side of a Turkish warehouse had become, in the words of the Justice Department itself, "a three-legged stool" resting precariously on suspect assumptions and even more suspect tactics.

"This," the judge declared as the case began to unravel, "is a fine kettle of fish."

THIS WAS NEW TERRAIN for all of us; reporters too. As a beat reporter covering the Justice Department for a big-city newspaper, I was among the legions of journalists forced to become instant experts on al Qaeda and all things terrorism that moment at 9:03 a.m. on September 11, 2001. Horrified by what we'd witnessed and hungry for answers, we would chase leads from Islamabad to Lackawanna, scrambling from one figurative rooftop to the next ourselves in search of that next big story in this new war on terror. Everyone wanted to know: how could this have happened, and what could be done to prevent it from happening again.

For me, the Detroit sleeper cell case always held a special place of fascination, if only for the spectacular collapse of a case that had begun with such Rose Garden prominence. It came to embody, in my mind, the real dangers that lurked and the pitfalls of overzealously pursuing them. Long before the Detroit case began to implode, there were officials within the Bush administration itself who began to question whether the case was as rock-solid as the president and his attorney general had made it out to be. But the doubts were held to a whisper.

This was a war that would be waged on George Bush's own terms, and to raise questions about the rules of engagement was tantamount to career suicide for any government official. The casualties littered about Washington were evidence enough of that. The senior administration lawyers who dared to question privately whether the president had the power to wiretap suspects without a court warrant or to authorize interrogation tactics that bordered on torture. The junior ethics lawyer at the Justice Department who suggested that an American citizen captured in Afghanistan should be read his Miranda rights before he was interrogated, blindfolded, and strapped to a stretcher. The immigration officials who challenged whether hundreds of illegal immigrants rounded up after 9/11 could be locked up incommunicado for many months as terrorist suspects even though they had no known ties to al Qaeda or any other terrorist group. The FBI agent who thought the bureau was ill-equipped to handle its new mission against al Qaeda, or another who warned that the looming war in Iraq would only escalate the risk of another terrorist attack on American soil. All of them raised uncomfortable questions, and all did so at their own peril. Often, they were ignored, sometimes marginalized and silenced, occasionally even retaliated against. This was a time for action, not division, and to raise questions was to risk being cast on the "wrong side" of the war on terror.

Nor was there any safe harbor for the journalists who covered Bush's war. Reporters, by temperament and by training, are cynics. We are, as Gay Talese once described us, the "restless voyeurs who see the warts on the world, the imperfection in people and places." Like any reporter, I got into journalism because I wanted to tell people something that they didn't know the day before; I wanted to ask those in power the pesky, sometimes unpopular questions that they didn't want to be asked. But in this new war on terror, to raise difficult questions and to provoke debate was to invite charges of disloyalty. In the months and years after 9/11, I wrote my share of front-page stories that played up the threat of the next big attack from terrorists both real and illusory. No one at the White House remembered those stories. The ones they remembered—indeed, the ones that would lead to criminal investigations and vitriolic attacks on my own patriotism— were the ones that raised difficult but important questions about the secret, extralegal intelligence tools the Bush administration was willing to use in waging this new war. These were the stories that President Bush and Vice President Dick Cheney would denounce as disgraceful. These were the stories that would lead the FBI to interrogate government people I didn't even know, sometimes armed with subpoenas, in search of "leakers" who had supposedly said too much. These were the stories that would lead one of my closest friends to be pressured out of government service for the remarkable crime, in the administration's eyes, of simply knowing me. These were the stories the public wasn't supposed to know.

Inevitably, my partner at *The New York Times*, Jim Risen, and I were cast as either heroes or villains, intrepid reporters or treasonous turn-coats. I didn't recognize myself in either outsized caricature. But in the polarized, take-no-prisoners climate of post-9/11 Washington, there was no longer any middle ground, no room for discourse or debate. You were either for the war on terror, or you were against it.

Our notoriety grew so quickly that the librarian in the *Times'* Washington bureau began keeping a file with all the political cartoons she'd clipped showing *The New York Times* pitted against the Bush White House. The file grew fatter with each story Jim and I wrote. "You'll like this one," Barclay said one morning as she walked up to my desk with a fresh clipping that played off two of the stories Jim and I had written about once-secret terrorism programs. "The Bush White House Dream Scenario," read the caption on the cartoon. In it, two bedraggled prisoners were shown hanging in handcuffs from the rafters of a prison cell. "I got caught up in the secret domestic wiretapping and financial monitoring programs," one unshaven prisoner says to another. "What are you in for?" His cell mate, with a notepad jutting out of his pocket and a newspaper bag slung around his shoulder, answers back: "Reporting on it." Somehow, I could relate.

Bush's Law

"This Thing Called the Constitution"

WASHINGTON is a town in love with its acronyms. In the days of bedlam that followed the attacks of September 11, 2001, none was more important than SIOC, the emergency command center at the FBI's headquarters. It was there, amid a tangled web of sixty miles of fiber-optic cables, 225 computer terminals, and enough secure video monitors to stage an episode of the TV thriller *24*, that the Bush administration's top intelligence and law enforcement officials collected minute-by-minute updates and steeled themselves for what all in the room thought certain would be a "second wave" of terrorist attacks. But it was there too that a onetime Wall Street executive who ran the nation's immigration service was the first to ask an unpopular question that day that would resonate for years to come inside the Bush White House and out: How far are we willing to stretch and bend the Constitution in hopes of deterring another attack? And at what cost to the fabric of the country?

Even before the last legs had given out on the World Trade Center's Twin Towers on that horrific day, the FBI had begun the monumental task of piecing together what had happened. Who were the jihadists who had carried out the audacious attacks? How had they operated so invisibly, and with such impunity, on American soil? Who had helped them? And, most urgently, what other plots were already underway? There was no better law enforcement agency in the world than the FBI at solving a crime, and this investigation—code-named Penttbom—would be the biggest in its history. Thousands of agents, working more mundane tasks like drug seizures and white-collar crime on September 10, were now dispatched to the case as newly deputized counterterrorism sleuths. Investigators would be helped by a few early breaks: a piece of Mohamed Atta's luggage that didn't make it onto Flight 11 held a treasure trove of detailed preparations for the hijackings, and a search of a rental car parked at Logan Airport produced flight manuals and other potentially important bits of evidence. With 4,400 planes rerouted within hours, FBI agents were already scouring leads and eyeing other possible plotters. President Bush had made it clear to his war team: there could not be another attack, not on his watch. "Don't ever let this happen again," Bush told his attorney general, John Ashcroft, at an emergency White House meeting the day after the attacks.

For Ashcroft, an unlikely general in the war on terrorism who had once railed against the abusive reach of Big Brother government in his days in the Senate, the edict would become a guiding mantra. The rules of engagement had changed, Ashcroft told his aides, and that meant no lead, no possible plot, no strand of intelligence, however tangential or improbable it might seem, could go unchecked. The two suspicious Muslims found on the train to Texas with $5,000 in cash and box cutters; those immigrants in the dilapidated Detroit apartment found with the odd scribbling in the day-planner; the Saudi radiologist in San Antonio with the same last name as one of the hijackers; the homeless Egyptian man arrested for trespassing at a 7-Eleven in Baltimore—all were eyed as the next possible Mohamed Atta in the days and weeks immediately after 9/11. With planes grounded for days and the country shaken to its core, the investigation was playing out in the most public of ways, each step chronicled on CNN. The public manhunt was on.

Sub rosa, however, investigators were already employing unorthodox, push-the-limits tactics in those early days that would not become publicly known, even in the exhaustive, 567-page report of the 9/11 Commission three years later. The National Security Agency, in what amounted to a pilot project for a much bigger and more controversial exercise, would begin intercepting American calls and e-mails to and from Afghanistan, home of the Taliban, in an effort to identify al

Qaeda's communications. Some fifty postal inspectors would begin the "enormous task" of "sorting through the outbound international mail" to look for possible clues to terrorist activity, according to an internal FBI report in Maryland prepared two weeks after the September 11 attacks but never made public. The FBI, through the grudging cooperation of library managers, would "mirror" ten computers in suburban Washington believed to have been used by two of the hijackers. And then there was this: "All fugitives of Arab descent," the FBI advised, "have been made a priority for capture, federally and locally."

These were the kinds of over-the-top tactics that troubled James Ziglar, the commissioner of the Immigration and Naturalization Service, as he sat at SIOC on 9/11 just hours after the attacks. With the government caught flat-footed by the attacks on the World Trade Center and the Pentagon, no one doubted the need to mobilize at breakneck speed against the next terrorist attack. But as Ziglar saw it, there was a right way to approach the problem and a wrong way. Ziglar considered himself a "Goldwater conservative"; he liked to quote the late Arizona senator's famous screeds in defense of individual rights, and he swore by his maxim that "freedom depends on effective restraints against the accumulation of power in a single authority." An affable Southerner, Ziglar had worn many hats in a long career in both the private and public sectors: Supreme Court clerk, Wall Street investment banker, white-collar lawyer, congressional aide, and Senate sergeant-at-arms. But as he sat in SIOC on 9/11, none cast a bigger shadow for him than his role as a young aide in Richard Nixon's Justice Department in the office with the Orwellian name of Internal Security. The post offered Ziglar a window into the abuses of the 1960s and 1970s, a time when the FBI monitored Vietnam protesters, kept secret dossiers on some fifty thousand American citizens, and harassed political activists like John Lennon and Martin Luther King Jr. under the guise of ferreting out spies and subversives.

As he sat at the executive conference table in SIOC and listened to the nation's top cops plan a crackdown of their own, Ziglar couldn't help but think of the practices that had become so pervasive three decades earlier. Hours after the attacks, Bush's senior law enforcement aides were talking about widespread sweeps in heavily Muslim neighborhoods like Dearborn, Michigan, essentially knocking door-to-door to look for information on the next plot without any real nexus to terrorism or wrongdoing. To Ziglar, the tactic smacked of ethnic-profiling of the worst kind, but his concerns went beyond mere abstract ideology. Not only would it hurt relations with American Muslims—the very people the FBI would need as informants in this new war on terror—but it would mean an enormous drain of resources at the already strapped INS, resources that he felt could be better spent plugging the kinds of holes that officials would learn had allowed two of 9/11 hijackers to enter the country under their real names without even being watch-listed by the CIA. If there was specific evidence suggesting someone had information about terrorism, he was all in favor of going after it and going after it hard. But neighborhood-by-neighborhood sweeps and arrests? That troubled him. As David Ayres, Ashcroft's longtime advisor and powerful chief of staff, was planning a course of action, Ziglar squirmed in his seat. Finally, he broke in.

"I know you're not a lawyer," Ziglar told Ayres bluntly, "but we do have this thing called the Constitution."

The table grew quiet, faces tightening around it, as Ziglar began a brief but passionate discourse on the history of American colonialism under British rule. "What you're suggesting is like the king executing general warrants on the population," he continued. "That's what the king would do to find the colonials in rebellion against the crown." The idea of wide-ranging sweeps to look for Muslim subversives and extremists, Ziglar said, "is a violation of the Constitution, and I'm not going to be part of it."

Ziglar paused. "The INS won't be involved," he finally concluded.

So there it was: the first shot across the bow in the administration's hours-old war on terror, and it had come not from one of the administration's traditional adversaries—the ACLU, the "liberal" media, or some militant Islamist firebrand—but from one of the artillery men in the fight. Ziglar's broadside won him few friends in the room. Eyes rolled, heads shook in amazement. A few senior FBI officials huddled afterward, out of earshot of Ziglar. They were chagrined by a performance that they saw as both condescending and ill-advised at the very moment when the country should be pulling together; even more remarkable, several felt, was that it had come from a man in the job only two months as head of a second-tier law enforcement agency that was widely viewed, with some justification, as dysfunctional and poorly equipped to protect the country's porous borders.

"Who does this asshole think he is?" one senior FBI official grumbled to a colleague minutes after Ziglar's solitary stand. "As if he's the only who cares about the Bill of Rights?"

The Constitution would be a constant frame of reference in the fight, a talisman of sorts that people on all sides of the simmering debate could grab on to. Which side of it were you on? Were you for upholding it, or tearing it down? Were you willing to use the broad commander-in-chief powers it granted the president under Article II of the Constitution to defend Americans from another horrific attack, or would you cling to the notions of individual liberties, due process, and prohibition of unreasonable search and seizure spelled out in the Bill of Rights? And what about the "coequal" branches of government: What role if any would Congress and the courts have as a check on the commander-in-chief? Most important, could all these tensions coexist? Was there a middle ground? For the architects of this new war, there was a constant drumbeat: the rule of law still had to be followed, they said, but just what those rules really meant was often malleable, subject to twisting, flexing, and reinterpreting so long as the tactics were justified to stop another attack. "Think outside the box, but not outside the Constitution," Ashcroft would often tell his senior aides. Some of his listeners took it literally; for others, the mantra came with more of a wink and a nod.

For the Bush war team leading the fight—men like Alberto Gonzales at the White House, Donald Rumsfeld at the Pentagon, Michael Hayden at NSA, Robert Mueller at the FBI, Ashcroft at the Justice Department, David Addington in the vice president's office, and of course Dick Cheney himself—this was not a time to stand on tired conventions. The threat was now all too real. They had seen the carnage up close and felt the burning rage of a nation attacked. They had heard the cold, calm fear in the final words of Barbara Olson, a conservative commentator who was a friend to many in the administration, as she made two cell phone calls to her husband, Solicitor General Ted Olson, from Flight 11 to tell him that her plane had been hijacked by men armed with knives and box cutters. They saw it in the fateful last steps of John O'Neill, a top terrorism official at the FBI who became head of security at the World Trade Center, only to die on his second day on the job racing back into the building to try to rescue survivors. They heard it in the hate-filled rhetoric of Osama bin Laden, who had declared in a religious fatwa issued three years before the 9/11 attacks that it was the "individual duty of every Muslim" to kill all Americans.

The images were powerful, and they gave rise to a wholesale and radical rethinking of how the government protected itself and the country from another attack. The rules of engagement were often unclear, but the agenda was not: "Don't ever let this happen again," Bush had implored. With the country awash in a unifying zeitgeist of shock and outrage, Bush captured the mood of the country—and saw his poll numbers soar—as he donned a firefighter's helmet at Ground Zero days after the attacks and climbed atop a wrecked fire truck to stand arm in arm with the rescue workers clearing the rubble. It was a poignant, powerful moment, with Bush doing what he did best: connecting with people on a personal, heartfelt, gut-check level. "I can hear you," Bush told the thronged workers so desperate for hope and inspiration. "The rest of the world hears you, and the people who knocked down these buildings will hear all of us soon."

The pledge from Bush and his top advisors to do everything in their power—and everything under the law—to stop another attack was a strong tonic for an American public anxious for redemption. It would spur the largest mobilization of law enforcement resources in the country's history, and it would lead Congress, just five weeks after the attacks, to pass a dense, 342-page package of sweeping counterterrorism measures known as the USA Patriot Act, a smorgasbord of a bill pushed so urgently by Ashcroft and the administration that few lawmakers who voted for it had time to read its fundamental reworking of the law, much less understand it.

With the shackles now off, agents at home and abroad would look for the faintest whiff of terrorism, in suspected sleeper cells from the jails of Los Angeles to the quarry fields of Oregon to the beaches of Miami, in an effort to stop the terrorists before they could hit again. Government informants, many with criminal histories of their own, would alert the FBI to any possible plotters and take credit for launching aggressive sting operations that bordered on entrapment. Portions of the Geneva Conventions governing the treatment of war prisoners would be deemed "quaint" and "obsolete," in the words of Alberto Gonzales. Hundreds of suspected Taliban sympathizers plucked from the battlefields of Afghanistan would be captured and jailed for years in the naval base at Guantánamo Bay, only to be returned to their home countries after being cleared of terrorist ties. CIA officers would kidnap suspects from the streets of Europe—some with real terrorist ties, others simply with the misfortune of having the wrong Arab-sounding names—and whisk them away on secret planes to face secret interrogations at the hands of foreign intelligence services. Those al Qaeda operatives who were kept in the CIA's own secret prisons faced "enhanced" interrogation measures approved at the highest levels of the Bush administration, things like water-boarding, a technique used by some of the most brutal regimes in history to make a prisoner fear he's drowning. Inside the United States, out-of-status immigrants with no known terrorist ties would be held for months in American facilities, often without access to lawyers or even any record of their confinement or the charges against them. And dozens of American citizens would be jailed for weeks or months as "material witnesses" to possible acts of terrorism after investigators were unable to present evidence they had actually committed a crime.

President Bush, meanwhile, would secretly authorize wiretappers at the National Security Agency, long banned from spying on Americans after the abuses of the Vietnam era, to eavesdrop without warrants on the international e-mails and phone calls of Americans suspected of ties to al Qaeda. Analysts at the CIA would quietly monitor their international bank transactions. Computer programmers would decipher algorithms filled to the brink with meta-data to "connect the dots" and seek to outwit the plotters before they could hit again. And military analysts and FBI agents would begin keeping files on peaceful protests against the war in Iraq to look for violent subversives who might be plotting to attack U.S. troops and bases. The brash initiatives often butted up against the limits of what law and policy allowed, or crossed them altogether. But in the view of the policymakers, the risks were too great to do anything less. They made no apologies.

For anyone who dared question the limits of the new strategy, Bush's attorney general had a jagged rejoinder: "We need honest, reasoned debate, and not fear-mongering," the square-jawed Ashcroft told members of the Senate Judiciary Committee at a hearing less than three months after the attacks. "To those who pit Americans against immigrants and citizens against non-citizens, to those who scare peace-loving people with phantoms of lost liberty, my message is this:

your tactics only aid terrorists, for they erode our national unity and diminish our resolve. They give ammunition to America's enemies, and pause to America's friends. They encourage people of goodwill to remain silent in the face of evil. Our efforts have been crafted carefully to avoid infringing on constitutional rights while saving American lives."

Ashcroft could have been speaking to his INS commissioner, Jim Ziglar, inside the emergency command center at the FBI. Instead, it was the politicians on the other side of the aisle—the Democrats on the panel—who recoiled at the clear message Bush's attorney general was sending: you're either with us in this war, or you're against it. The tone of the bombshell remarks—coming, perhaps appropriately, on the sixtieth anniversary of Pearl Harbor—was so spitfire that even some of Ashcroft's top aides blanched when reading them beforehand in the prepared text. Ashcroft shrugged at the thought of how civil libertarians in the audience might react to the broadside. "They don't help us. We're not here for the ACLU," he told one aide privately beforehand. The "phantoms of lost liberty" line would become one of the most oft-quoted ever uttered by an attorney general—always remembered bitterly, it seemed, by Ashcroft's critics, their faces contorting at what they saw as a challenge to their own patriotism. Senator Russell Feingold, the only Democrat to vote against the Patriot Act, wanted to know: Was Ashcroft accusing the Democrats of aiding bin Laden merely by holding a hearing and asking questions about the reach of the government's powers? Ashcroft demurred. But after the hearing, Senator Patrick Leahy—who had been instrumental just two months earlier in inserting some time limits on the Patriot Act's powers—was still bristling over the broadside. "This is not a question of whether you are for or against terrorists," Leahy said. "Everyone is against terrorists. This is about whether we are adequately protecting civil liberties."

In time, the courts, the Congress, and the public itself would begin to push back against the administration's clench-fisted grab for executive power. But that debate would have to wait. Even the term itself that Leahy summoned—civil liberties—seemed somehow abstract and trivial when measured against the long shadow of 9/11. For all the early agitation of the Jim Ziglars, the Russ Feingolds, and the Pat Leahys, most people—the policy-makers, the public, even the famously "liberal" media—were not quite ready, it seemed, to talk about how this war was to be waged, how effective it would be, and at what cost. The horror of 9/11 was too raw and too real.

WE IN THE MEDIA were no doubt swept up in that same national mood of fear and outrage. With New York as the media capital of the world, reporters and editors mourned alongside their readers. *The Wall Street Journal*'s own offices were shuttered. I was covering the Justice Department for the *Los Angeles Times* when the towers fell, and as I stood with a gaggle of other reporters outside the FBI headquarters in Washington on 9/11 in the hours after the attack, waiting all day for any scrap of information from the officials huddled inside the building at SIOC, black humor took hold. We knew the Pentagon had already been hit, a bomb was rumored to have gone off at the State Department, and United Flight 93 had crashed in a Pennsylvania field en route to either the White House or the Capitol. As we sat for hours on the concrete Jersey barriers surrounding the FBI building, we looked skyward; another reporter quipped that if al Qaeda was looking to strike again, we were sitting outside the next likely target, the next to go. And those concrete Jersey barriers along the building's perimeter sure as hell weren't going to protect us.

I passed the time waiting for a briefing outside the FBI headquarters by calling sources and possible witnesses to the attacks. I was able to get a phone number for a young Wall Street stockbroker I'd met in Southern California. He had escaped an upper floor of one of the Twin Towers just hours before. With his voice still quivering as we spoke, he described what he had seen. "People were screaming and things were flying everywhere," he told me. "There's blood, there's glass, there's everything. You get to the point that you're so scared you're not even scared. This is as close as I've ever gotten to a war." The quote, which ran the next day on the front page of the *Los Angeles Times*, summed up the trauma for me about as well as anything I'd heard.

Eight days later, after a chaotic week of three-a-day briefings at the Justice Department and constant deadlines on the status of the 9/11 investigation, I was speaking by telephone with a well-placed law enforcement source about the status of the FBI's investigation. I was trying to find out what was known about the hijackings, and what was still left to be answered. "There's something you'll want to see," the source said. "Stand by the fax machine."

Minutes later, as I pulled out the fax and glanced at it page by page, the words became more and more bone-chilling. It was an internal FBI report that recounted the frantic last few minutes of Flight 11's descent into the World Trade Center, told in the harrowing words of an American Airlines flight attendant named Amy Sweeney. Snippets of fateful final phone calls had come out publicly in the days since the September 11 attacks, but nothing like this. With remarkable calm, Sweeney had called in to her airline's operations center in Dallas to report the hijacking of her 747. She recounted the violent details—the hijackers had stabbed two crewmembers and slit the throat of a business-class traveler. Coolheaded, she managed to relay the seat numbers of some of the hijackers from the flight manifests. Even as she was speaking, she reported with eerie calm that the hijackers "had just gained access to the cockpit." Then, moments later, with the Hudson River below her and New York's famed skyline fast approaching, came her chilling final words: "I see water and buildings. Oh my God! Oh my God!"

Any reporter who has ever drawn the unenviable assignment of knocking on the door of a victim's family for an interview knows the fine line between telling a legitimate news story and trespassing on the privacy of a family in mourning. This was one of those moments for me, as I sat down at my keyboard to try to relate the dying moments of a thirty-five-year-old mother of two who had the presence of mind to try vainly to stop a catastrophe in the making. I let her words tell what happened. No one else had the story. The front-page scoop in our paper—and Sweeney's final words—were quickly read on the air by Ted Koppel on ABC's *Nightline* and reprinted in newspapers around the world. Rather than scorn, I received thanks from several friends and relatives of Sweeney, who were grateful in their time of mourning to have her story told publicly. It was a reminder of why reporters get into the news business in the first place. Sweeney's account proved critical, and three years later, the 9/11 Commission in its final report would credit Sweeney and a second flight attendant, Betty Ong, for providing the last-minute reports that "tell us most of what we know about how the hijacking happened."

Coverage of 9/11 and its aftermath consumed all else for reporters in Washington. Stories about important law enforcement issues that once would have gotten heavy treatment—drugs, gang violence, white-collar crime, civil rights—were often relegated to the back pages, or not written at all. A Washington reporter for another major newspaper drafted a story that was set to run on September 12, 2001, disclosing the unusual arrangements that the Secret Service had made allowing one of President Bush's underage daughters—Jenna Bush, then nineteen—to make a bar-hopping trip south of the border at popular watering holes like Ma Crosby's and the Corona Club in Ciudad Acuña. The timing of the south-of-the-border drinking jaunt was particularly rich because it came less than a week before Jenna Bush was to appear in court in Austin, Texas, on a charge of underage drinking; in Mexico, the drinking age was only eighteen. As drafted, the story detailed how American and Mexican government agents, working together in a remarkable diplomatic collaboration, managed to pull off the trip from a base at a Mexican Best Western, with the security and logistics for Jenna Bush and her friends arranged at high levels of each government.

A few years earlier, with Washington abuzz over presidential ethics and personal favors in the Clinton White House, a scoop about a president's daughter receiving special dispensation from the Secret Service and a foreign government to facilitate a bar-hopping trip with her friends was the stuff that would have energized the radio talk show airwaves for weeks. But times had changed, and there was less of an appetite for media distractions in the new climate. Nothing else seemed to matter anymore. The story never ran on September 12 or any time after. A photo of the jaunt and a small story about it appeared in a small Texas paper, but the tale behind the trip and the Secret Service's border maneuverings never became public.

Instead, the media's collective energies were sucked dry by the aftermath of 9/11. Every morsel of information about the FBI's hijacking investigation, and every tantalizing hint of future attacks, became grist for the front page. The FBI, long accused of shunning local cops and failing to share needed information with them, began sending out detailed intelligence bulletins to police stations around the country with the latest bit of analysis about possible threats. The alerts were considered "law enforcement sensitive" and "for official use only" and were not supposed to be disclosed to the media, partly because the information often amounted to uncorroborated and needlessly alarming tip sheets. But with some 16,000 recipients among federal, state, and local law enforcement agents, it's hard for even the FBI to keep a secret. The leaked intelligence bulletins would become the low-hanging fruit for reporters to pick for front-page stories about prospects for the next big attack. Crop dusters and hazmat trucks in the Midwest, scuba divers off the coast of Southern California, and tourist helicopters in New York were all considered possible modes of attack in the new climate of fear and angst. Many of us in the media felt obligated to report them all. The public, we figured, had a right to know what threats lurked, and to plan accordingly. And better yet, reporters knew that there was an enormous appetite for such stories on the front pages and the evening newscasts.

Typical was an FBI alert that a source provided me in 2002, which warned about the increased threat of a fresh round of attacks and quickly become a prominent part of a front-page story in the next day's *New York Times*, where I had gone to work that fall. "In selecting its next targets," the FBI alert said, "sources suggest Al Qaeda may favor spectacular attacks that meet several criteria: high symbolic value, mass casualties, severe damage to the American economy and maximum psychological trauma." Often, the leads proved maddeningly vague at best, flat-out wrong at worst. An all-points bulletin in late 2002 for five Muslim men whose photographs were published around the world—fueled by a personal appeal by President Bush himself, who said "we need to know why they have been smuggled into the country, what they're doing in the country"—turned out to be a hoax, apparently started by a jailed tipster who wanted to ingratiate himself with his jailers. The targets of the manhunt, it soon became apparent, had not even set foot inside the United States. But as one FBI official explained to me at the time: "In today's climate, if something had happened and we hadn't done anything, what would the public reaction have been?"

It was difficult to argue with the logic, and many of us in the media shared the sense that any shred of information had to be pushed out to the public. Just as the media would later be pilloried for its coverage of the pre-war buildup in Iraq over weapons of mass destruction in 2002 and early 2003, the same phenomenon was playing out at home in coverage of the war on terror. Reporters pride themselves on a healthy, often outsized dose of skepticism—seeing Talese's "warts on the world." After 9/11, it abandoned many of us when it came to matters of terrorism.

So it was for me when Attorney General Ashcroft returned to Capitol Hill one day in early 2003 for a hearing that promised to make news. The prepared testimony that government officials give to Congress is notoriously dry stuff, sometimes so monotonous that the statements are simply entered into the record without ever being read aloud. Most politicians use the text to repeat what they have said in a thousand different forums before. But Ashcroft was not like most politicians. He had a flare for public drama, political timing, and hardball tactics—whether it was interrupting his testimony before the 9/11 Commission to level sensational charges against one of the panel's own members; announcing the arrest of a "dirty bomber" live from Moscow amid an eerie orange glow to the annoyance of even the White House; or accusing his critics of needlessly inventing those "phantoms of lost liberty."

So, as other reporters and I sat at the press table awaiting Ashcroft's testimony before the Senate Judiciary Committee, we knew enough to expect the possibility of real news from Ashcroft. The mood was tense. Democrats were seething over the leak a few weeks earlier of an eighty-eight-page draft of a Justice Department proposal that appeared to be a "Patriot Act II" in the offing, aimed at expanding the already substantial counterterrorism powers that the executive branch had amassed weeks after the September 11 attacks. Pat Leahy suspected that a secret movement was afoot to harness still more power, and he accused the Justice Department of misleading him about its ambitions. But Ashcroft was in no mood to be put on the defensive by the liberal Vermont senator or anyone else.

"The United States is winning the war on terrorism with unrelenting focus and unrelenting cooperation," Ashcroft declared at the outset. Then, a few minutes into his prepared remarks, Ashcroft let fly. That very morning, the attorney general disclosed in somber tones, the department had unsealed terrorism charges against two Yemeni men, including a cleric named Mohammed Ali Hassan al-Moayad, accused of acting as bin Laden's "spiritual advisor" and personally delivering $20 million to him to help al Qaeda wage jihad. As if the image of a radical cleric hand-delivering $20 million to bin Laden was not powerful enough, Ashcroft drove it home with the stuff that reporters crave: the local angle. As part of al-Moayad's jihad fund-raising operation, Ashcroft told the senators, the cleric "said he received money for jihad from collections at the Al-Farooq mosque in Brooklyn."

I didn't wait for a break in the testimony before hurrying out the oversized wooden door of the hearing room to find a pay phone and call the news editor in the *Times'* Washington bureau. I knew the editors would be going into their noon meeting soon to begin planning out the next day's front page, and I figured they'd want to know about this bombshell to factor into their thinking. "This is big," I told the news editor on the other end. "Ashcroft says bin Laden was getting money from a mosque in Brooklyn." Sure enough, the story ran the next day at the top of the front page, under the headline: "Millions Raised for Qaeda in Brooklyn, U.S. Says." I had only been at the paper a few months, and getting the coveted lead spot in the paper—the day's most important story—was a bit of a coup for any new reporter.

But the splash was not as well received in Brooklyn, either by the Muslim community or by my new colleagues at the newspaper. I quickly got a phone call and several e-mails from Andy Newman, a talented writer in our Brooklyn bureau whom I had never met. He was upset because he felt that the paper had, in effect, bought into the administration's hype. He thought the coverage was, if not inaccurate, at least exaggerated. This wasn't about Washington politics, Andy told me. This was about real people at the mosque who, he felt, had now been tarred on the front page with an unfairly broad brush. The same mosque had already become suspect a decade earlier because of its brief association with the so-called Blind Sheikh, who helped orchestrate the 2003 bombing at the World Trade Center, and the latest allegations were sure to reignite those suspicions. Andy had read through the same indictment in the case that I had, and he thought the evidence was thin. The only specific reference in the court papers to an actual Brooklyn money trail, in fact, was the government's assertion that an associate of the radical cleric spoke at the mosque in 1999 and had hoped to raise $27,000 in the names of needy families. In a note to one of his editors in the Metro section, Andy took particular issue with the assertion—made by Ashcroft and echoed in my story—that "some" of the millions for al Qaeda were raised in Brooklyn. "From the sketchy evidence," Andy wrote in his e-mail, "the 'some' could have been as little as a few thousand dollars and as much as several hundred thousand dollars, but not more."

Andy went back and interviewed the people most affected by the coverage—the leaders and worshippers at the mosque itself—and he talked with Abderahman Mohamed, the imam, who seemed almost wanly bemused by the resurgent notoriety of his mosque. "Twenty million dollars," he told Andy, smiling as he repeated the figure now publicly associated with the mosque. "That is an imaginary number," he said, adding: "I'm sorry for the way these messages are being disseminated by newspapers and read by naive people who don't know what's going on and just believe what they hear."

No reporter likes to have the credibility of a story attacked, especially from inside his own newspaper. Talking to Andy, I was defensive, and perhaps a bit naive myself: the attorney general, at a public hearing using unsealed, sworn court documents, had laid out the case against the mosque as a fund-raising tool for al Qaeda. That wasn't enough to justify the prominent treatment we'd given the story? I never wrote another word about the case, as our reporters in New York picked up the story. After the initial splash, the story quickly faded to the inside pages. But as I followed our own coverage and read the court documents as they came out over the next several years, it became clear that Andy's initial suspicions were well-founded. The case, quite literally, was going up in flames. The government informant who told the government that al-Moayad had boasted of hand-delivering $20 million to bin Laden—a man with a sketchy past himself—became so disenchanted with his FBI handlers that he set himself on fire outside the White House. And his testimony became so suspect that he was called as a witness not by the Justice Department's prosecutors—who had once planned to build their case around him—but by the defense.

Al-Moayad was ultimately convicted and sentenced to seventy-five years in prison on terrorism charges, but the government's focus had changed markedly since Ashcroft's dramatic first salvo. The thrust of the government's case was now on the cleric's support for Hamas in Palestine, with his sporadic attempts to funnel money to al Qaeda now clearly secondary and far less sensational. Several jurors, in fact, said that the evidence tying the Yemeni cleric to al Qaeda was the weakest part of the case. And the suggestion of a link between the Brooklyn mosque and Osama bin Laden, that stunning allegation that helped generate headlines around the world? It had melted away to all but nothing.

CHAPTER TWO

Collateral Damage

THE NEIGHBORS at the Royal Oak Apartments always thought there was something a bit odd about the elderly Pakistani doctor up in apartment number eight. For one thing, Taj Bhatti just looked different. In the rural slice of Appalachia that was Marion, Virginia, his olive complexion drew notice from the neighbors in the building, a regal stone-and-brick structure that sat atop a historic old movie theater. On the second floor, old Mrs. Carroll, a caretaker of sorts for the building, wondered aloud whether Bhatti was "a Negro"; the landlord, G. C. Jennings, had to correct her. "He's from the Middle East or somewhere," the landlord said. Sure, Bhatti was friendly enough. With his soft, mischievous eyes and an almost flirtatious manner, the bespectacled doctor with the thick salt-and-pepper mustache always seemed to be cooking up a curry dish or lentil soup for one visitor or another. Still, "he was just a really strange fellow in a lot of ways," Jennings said. There was his odd schedule; he seemed to come and go at all hours of the day and night, sometimes disappearing for weeks or even months at a time. And all that clutter. His two-bedroom apartment, which doubled as an office where Dr. Bhatti would sometimes see his psychiatric patients, was littered with electronic gadgetry, books and journals, and a hodgepodge of computer parts, strewn alongside memorabilia from his keen interest in aviation. One neighbor even Googled the doctor's medical practice and gave the landlord a printout because she was so curious. Yet for all the hallway banter about the odd doctor in number eight, Jennings never for a minute

thought that his tenant might be some sort of terrorist, at least not
until that knock on the door one evening in June of 2002 at his home in
Marion just a mile or so from Bhatti's apartment building.

Jennings was watching TV on the couch when his wife nudged him.
It was the FBI. They wanted to talk to him about one of his tenants.
The FBI was conducting a terrorism investigation, Special Agent
Doug Fender told Jennings, and they were interested in this Bhatti
character. Taj Bhatti: that was a name Jennings didn't really want to
hear. The good doctor had been months' late on his rent—again—and
Jennings had to change the lock on the door. Finally, he'd had to move
all of Bhatti's furniture and books and belongings to a smaller apartment because Jennings had a new tenant who wanted the two-
bedroom place. "That SOB?" Jennings sneered. "What do you want to
know about him?" The landlord didn't know much. He hadn't seen
Bhatti around the place for months, in fact, and Jennings was still anxious to collect his back rent. "Can I go in his apartment?" the agent
asked. When he wasn't collecting rent, Jennings had been a criminal
lawyer for many years, and the question startled him. "Don't you have
to have a search warrant?" Well, Fender answered, if the place was
abandoned, then no. Jennings was still skeptical, but he figured the FBI
must know what it was doing. The Twin Towers had fallen just nine
months before, and Jennings, a former state legislator in Virginia as
blue-blooded as anyone, wasn't going to stand in the way of an FBI terrorism investigation. "I'll unlock it for you, but what you do is your
business," he finally told the agent.

Jennings drove over to the apartment building and, unlocking the
door, led Fender and a team of FBI agents and local sheriff's deputies
inside. Boxes were piled high, and medical books and psychiatric journals lined the walls. Hundreds of computer discs lay strewn about. The
agents confiscated them. They examined a couple of sporting rifles and
confiscated those too. A small combination safe sat on a desk. The
agents opened it from behind and found some of Bhatti's personal documents and a few hundred dollars in cash; they took that too. Jennings
joked that he could use the cash himself to help defray all the back rent
Bhatti owed him. Lots of foreign art, apparently from Pakistan, was
strewn about the place. The agents examined the paintings. Fender
asked Jennings about Bhatti's travels, about whether he'd noticed any
Islamic prayer rugs lying around. Jennings laughed. "I wouldn't know

a prayer rug if one hit me in the head," he said. Fender stopped to examine a postcard he'd found—with a photograph of a crop duster on it. That one really interested the FBI agent. They came across a music box; "Happy Birthday" began playing on it as the agent picked it up. "You better stand back," the agent told Jennings. "It could be a bomb."

Finally, the agents left with box-loads of stuff, promising Jennings that they would return it all when they were done examining it. As the agent handed the landlord a receipt for the items, Jennings became more and more uncomfortable with what he'd just witnessed. The lawyer in him was wishing that he'd demanded a search warrant from the FBI before he'd let them go through all his tenant's belongings like this. "What the hell's going on?" he finally asked as the agents were finishing up the search. The agent wouldn't reveal much, except to say: "We're investigating terrorism around the world." The September 11 hijackers, he added cryptically, "had connections, they had help." Jennings still wasn't convinced. He locked the door behind him as he led the agents out of the apartment. *The Constitution's gone out the damn window*, he thought to himself.

Days later, the FBI showed up again—this time with guns drawn at the log house of Bhatti's longtime girlfriend, sixty-two-year-old Nancy McNey. She was out on her front porch on a pleasant June evening when agent Fender and a team of agents came rushing up from the street. "FBI! Is Taj Bhatti here?" an agent demanded. Bhatti, it turned out, had been staying with McNey off and on for many months in her home in nearby Abingdon. He was in the bathroom when the agents arrived; they pounded on the door and told him to finish his business and come on out. He was under arrest, a warrant said, as a "material witness" in an investigation into terrorism and weapons of mass destruction. "You stay out here," a local police officer out on the porch told the still-trembling McNey. "What's happening?" she finally managed to ask. "It's nothing you have to worry about," the officer responded. Her mind was racing. "Is this because he's from Pakistan?" she asked. The officer wouldn't get into any details. About all he would say was that it had something to do with terrorism. Inside, agents sat Bhatti down on a couch in the living room and began asking him some questions as they searched through McNey's bedroom and her office. Finally, they led the doctor away in handcuffs down to the local Washington County jail, where he shared a cell with a handful of other men locked up on far more mundane charges. His jailers had run out of bunks, so Bhatti rested his slight sixty-five-year-old body on the floor to rest for the night. It would be a long night.

With the clanging of the county jail door behind him like a scene out of some grainy Hollywood film noir, Bhatti had earned temporary membership in an ignoble club—some 2,700 men locked up after 9/11 by American authorities, both on American soil and off, because of suspicions of terrorism. Add to the club's membership the tens of thousands of people in the United States flagged at airports and border checkpoints from terrorist watch lists, questioned, and sometimes briefly detained, and the ranks swelled considerably. Bhatti was also part of a sizable subset. They were the ones who, despite the noxious label of terror suspect, were never shown in the end to have any links to al Qaeda or terrorism at all. It was a diverse group, bonded mostly by Muslim-sounding names and foreign ethnicities: American citizens with high-paying jobs and impressive-sounding résumés, illegal immigrants rounded up in cities around the country, security workers at American airports, hazmat truck drivers in Pennsylvania, foreign nationals picked up by happenstance on the battlefields of Afghanistan and sent to Guantánamo for years without lawyers or formal charges.

There was Shanaz Mohammed, a thirty-nine-year-old from Trinidad, held on an immigration charge for eight months as a "special interest detainee" in Brooklyn under the most extreme conditions before finally being deported back home. And there was Maher Arar, a Canadian software engineer who was arrested by U.S. authorities in 2002 at JFK Airport in New York and sent to Syria to face what he said was months of torture and beatings with a metal cable, even after Canadian authorities told the United States they didn't think he was a terrorist. And Al-Bader Al-Hazmi, a radiologist in San Antonio born in Saudi Arabia, who spent thirteen days in U.S. custody as a material witness. Al-Hazmi seemed to speak for all his fellow detainees when he asked a reporter searchingly after his release from jail: "Who is this Kafka that people keep mentioning?" Like Taj Bhatti, the detainees were often nameless, faceless. Their stories and even their identities were often concealed from public view by the government, the evidence against them shrouded in mystery. All would have to live with the black mark of terror suspect. They were, in sum, the collateral damage of the war on terror.

THE GOVERNMENT'S POWER to lock up the accused is a unique and awesome responsibility. In 1940, Attorney General Robert Jackson admonished a conference of U.S. attorneys to wield that power judiciously. He warned that a "prosecutor has more control over life, liberty and reputation than any other person in America" and that "while the prosecutor at his best is one of the most beneficent forces in our society, when he acts from malice or other base motives, he is one of the worst." Jackson would go on to become a renowned Supreme Court justice, writing many oft-quoted opinions, but it was his words as attorney general that would stick in the minds of every young federal prosecutor facing difficult decisions about matters of life and liberty. Hand in hand with that responsibility came certain principles of jurisprudence grounded in centuries of court precedent, common law, international treaty, and, ultimately, the Constitution. These were notions of justice that had stood the country well: that those accused of a crime have a right to know the charges against them, to confront their accusers, and to see the evidence used to jail them; that they have a right to consult with legal counsel and to speak freely and confidentially with their lawyer; that they have a right to remain silent and be free from cruel, inhuman, or degrading treatment meant to coerce statements from them; that they have a right to petition a court for review of their jailing; and that, above all else, they assume a presumption of innocence in the face of even the most dire of accusations. Quickly, all these basic precepts would come under challenge in the war on terror, tested to the extreme by Bush's "new paradigm," as the administration moved to create, on its own authority, a new system of justice in waging war against al Qaeda.

In matters of guilt and innocence, there are few slam dunks. For every dangerous criminal that the authorities lock up to protect the common good, there is always the risk that the wrong man may find his life picked apart by government investigators, his reputation smeared, his freedom deprived, or even, as in the case of fourteen men ultimately exonerated through DNA evidence, sentenced to death row. There is no easy formula for weighing the risks against the rewards, and the balance struck by any given administration says much about its character and its priorities. For much of its history, the American justice system has placed a premium on ensuring that a society's zeal to rid its streets of the guilty does not trample the rights of the innocent in its path and, just as important, that the justice system includes enough checks and balances, enough safeguards, to know the difference. There have been, of course, the notable and in some ways predictable exceptions, especially in times of national fear and crisis. The Palmer Raids targeting some ten thousand suspected radicals, socialists, and anarchists in 1919 were one; the internment of some 120,000 Japanese-Americans during World War II was another; Senator Joseph McCarthy's Red Scare in the 1950s a third. More often, however, the justice system has tilted toward restraint over aggression.

Under President Bill Clinton, the administration had an attorney general in Janet Reno who was notoriously cautious by nature. Justice Department officials knew that the bar on pursuing a sensitive case was high—almost too high, some lawyers complained. Indeed, after 9/11, critics would accuse her of adopting too cautious a legal position to the detriment of pursuing Osama bin Laden. But to move on a case that was less than rock-solid, on shaky legal foundations—a Richard Jewell, briefly suspected in a bombing of the 1996 Olympics in Atlanta, or a Wen Ho Lee, accused of nuclear espionage—was to do so at one's own career peril. Reno was a stickler for issues of process, and was reluctant to authorize the use of classified, or secret, evidence and hidden sources to lock someone up. "It's very important," she said, "to have the right to confront your accuser."

In one case in early 1999 that never became public, a Latin-American man was locked up based on secret intelligence collected through the INS in connection with a drug case. But it soon turned out that the INS had the wrong man, someone guilty of nothing more than having a name similar to an actual suspect. Reno, never one known for outbursts of emotion, was visibly angry when she found out about the mishap. "How could this have happened?" she demanded of an aide. Quickly, she moved to restrict the use of secret evidence to try to ensure that there was never a repeat.

After 9/11, the calculus changed. It was a different time, a different threat, a different mindset. The "preemptive" approach to law enforcement adopted by the Bush administration in its counterterrorism crackdown fundamentally altered the nature of the government's mission and lowered the bar dramatically in determining what it took to become a suspect. Guilt and innocence became almost antiquated notions, because the intent was no longer to simply accumulate enough evidence to prove in court that someone had committed a crime. Now, the mission was to identify someone who might have the means and motive to be involved in terrorism before he could strike. Where once the American justice system had placed a premium on not locking up the wrong people, now the overriding priority was to avoid, at all costs, the chance of letting the right one get away. Al Qaeda agents were trained, after all, to disguise themselves by blending into the civilian population. To find them, the government was bound to have to lock up some of the wrong people along the way.

"In a war like this, where our enemies fight that way, I think the error rate is necessarily going to be higher than what it is in other kinds of conflicts," said Bradford Berenson, an aide to Gonzales in the White House counsel's office after 9/11 who helped design some of the key legal policies. "That's regrettable. It's also inevitable." Were the FBI and the CIA locking people up who they had good reason to think weren't really involved in terrorism? Even the most cynical Bush-bashers were loath to make such a salacious charge. But too often, it would become clear, there was something approaching a reckless indifference to whether or not the government had good reason to believe someone was actually a terrorist before moving against him. It was understandable, in a way, because the risk of missing the next Mohamed Atta was now considered simply unacceptable. The One Percent Doctrine, Cheney called it: if there were a one percent chance that a plot was real, it had to be treated as such. The question was: How many Taj Bhattis was the government now willing to risk jailing in the quest to get the next Mohamed Atta off the streets? Ten? A hundred? A thousand? How many was too many? And at what cost to the country's notion of justice? No one knew the answers to the difficult formula. The new math in the war on terror was often as murky as the threat itself.

These were the debates that would play out in the cavernous conference rooms and well-appointed government suites of official Washington, far removed from the Blue Ridge Mountain region of Virginia that Taj Bhatti called home. His small town of Marion shared the same state seal as all the new, high-tech homeland security sites that sprouted up like mushrooms in Northern Virginia outside the nation's capital some 320 miles away, but they were fellow Virginians in name only. A town of 6,200 on a good day, Marion was much closer in mindset and makeup to its neighbors down the road in Tennessee and North Carolina. It is an area where sheriffs double as Methodist ministers and judges are known to answer their own phones. Confederate soldiers had battled the Union army here to try to protect the nearby salt mills and lead mines, Mountain Dew soda was invented here, and the renowned writer Sherwood Anderson wrote some of his last novels from a home in the countryside here before he was laid to rest over at the Round Hill Cemetery under a tombstone shaped like a sail. "Life not death is the great adventure," the storyteller's epitaph reads.

For Taj Bhatti, the great adventure had taken him to the United States from his birthplace in the town of Punjab in what was then part of India, learning his lessons at his small schoolhouse under a tree on a small, handheld chalkboard. He came to Buffalo, New York, in his early twenties to do a medical residency, and he stayed. An American citizen for more than thirty years, he worked as a psychiatrist in a number of Veterans Affairs hospitals dotted around the country, volunteering as a pilot in the Air National Guard along the way. But like a lot of American success stories, his was muddied and imperfect, part inspiration and part soap opera. There was a messy divorce in South Dakota and the suspension of his medical license there amid evidence that he had sexual relations with several female patients. In Virginia, he faced allegations of improper medical treatment of other patients, along with another suspended license. The charges were unfair, Bhatti always insisted to anyone who would listen, but he muddled along and tried to piece his life back together.

Munir Bhatti had lived with the peaks and valleys of his father's life for many years, but he never would have predicted the call that was to come that Thursday night in June 2002 from a distraught Nancy McNey. His father had just been arrested as part of some sort of terrorism investigation, she told him in a panic. He was a "material witness," the FBI had told her. Munir, a management consultant who worked out of his apartment in Southern California, didn't even know what a material witness was. Nor, for that matter, did many people in Marion, Virginia. Terrorism investigations were rare in the Blue Ridge region even after 9/11, and material witness warrants were rarer still. Enacted in 1984, the material witness law gave federal authorities a mechanism to hold people indefinitely who were believed to be witnesses to a crime as a way of compelling their testimony. Traditionally, the law had been used to lock up reluctant witnesses linked to drug runners, illegal immigrant rings, mob figures, and the like who the authorities feared would flee before they could be brought before a grand jury to tell what they knew about a crime.

But in the immediate aftermath of 9/11, Bush administration officials would credit two of their most accomplished prosecutors—Michael Chertoff, head of the criminal division at the Justice Department, and Mary Jo White, the U.S. attorney in Manhattan and a holdover from the Clinton administration—with taking the old model and reconfiguring it to fit the changing times. To prosecutors, the material witness law was an important tool in temporarily detaining people in terrorism investigations when there wasn't enough evidence to bring criminal charges against them. It was, in essence, a place-holder. To human rights groups, it was a bald-faced abuse of the law's original intent, a dangerous end run around the system meant to protect the rights of the accused. "The material witness law has been twisted beyond recognition," Human Rights Watch and the ACLU declared in one 2005 report on the practice. "Procedures designed for the temporary detention of witnesses who might otherwise skip town," the report concluded, "have been misused to hold men who were in fact criminal suspects." The government refused to say how many people it had held as material witnesses, sealing court records on national security grounds and leaving the media and rights groups to guess based on anecdotal evidence. At least seventy, all but one of them Muslim men, was the figure that Human Rights Watch estimated as of early 2005. The true number may have been far higher; it was impossible to know for sure. Many of the jailed "witnesses" were never called before a grand jury to testify about anything they had witnessed, and most were never charged with any crime at all, much less with terrorism. Their lives, for a time, were simply on hold: not charged, but not free either. And Taj Bhatti was one of them.

Soon after his arrest at his girlfriend's home, Bhatti was brought to the local FBI office for questioning. No lawyer was present. The interrogators wanted to know about his international travels, his religious beliefs, his views on Israel, his interest in planes, his psychiatric work, even the phone number in his address book for someone in Pakistan who now worked for the nuclear commission there at a time when A. Q. Khan's rogue nuclear proliferation network was still up and running. The Pakistani contact was just an old college buddy he had known in the 1950s, Bhatti explained. He hadn't talked to him in probably twenty years. He tried to explain the rest too, but he didn't sense that he was making much headway with his interrogators. "The impression I got," Bhatti said, "was that they thought I was part of a sleeper cell."

Three thousand miles away, Munir Bhatti frantically began trying to find out what was happening to his father. He thought about getting on a plane to Virginia, but he wasn't allowed to see his father, and he figured he could save time and get more accomplished by working the phones from Southern California. One of his first calls was to the court-designated lawyer, Dennis Jones, who Munir learned was representing his father. In the homespun ways of Appalachia, Jones' expensive suits stood out, so Munir figured at least his father had a good, well-heeled lawyer on his side. Munir told Jones he wanted to try contacting the FBI directly. He thought maybe he could talk some sense into the bureau. It was an idealistic view of how law enforcement works, and Jones, like any good defense attorney, was dead set against it; he didn't want Bhatti's family talking to anyone, especially not the FBI.

Munir slept on it overnight, then made the call anyway. He reached Doug Fender, the FBI agent in Bristol who was leading the investigation. He pled his case. His father was a lot of things, he said, but he was no terrorist. The agent struck Munir as strangely sympathetic, suggesting that there wasn't much to the case but that his hands were tied. But the agent did have a few questions of his own for Munir. The FBI couldn't quite get a handle on his father's religious views. What was he exactly? Munir burst out laughing. He'd been trying to figure that one out most of his life. Although he was born a Muslim in Punjab, Bhatti hadn't set foot in a mosque in the United States in years. A bit of a hedonist by nature who loved a good glass of sherry, he'd tiptoed into all sorts of spiritual renderings over the years, but about the closest he'd come to organized religion of late was a turn as a Mormon, even sending Mormon proselytizers out to Munir's door in Pasadena a few years earlier. Now, Bhatti was probably more an atheist than anything, Munir said. The agent kept pressing. The FBI had found on Bhatti's computer an article that Bhatti had downloaded from *The New York Times* about weapons of mass destruction, the agent told Munir. *So what?* Munir thought to himself. *Who hasn't?* Fender asked about his father's interests in aviation and electronics. Munir tried to explain it all: his father's time as a pilot in the National Guard, how father and son would go to air shows together when Munir was a kid, all those hours his father would spend in the attic in their home in South Dakota back in the early 1980s assembling primitive computers from a mail-order kit. This can all be explained, Munir said as he hung up.

Then, Munir did something else that would ultimately help determine his father's fate. He drafted a press release, raw but impassioned. If the wheels of justice couldn't protect his father, he figured that the antiseptic of public sunlight just might. "US Citizen Detained Without Bail and Without Being Charged," he typed across the top. He faxed and e-mailed it off to anyone he could think of: his senators in California, the ACLU, a couple of lawyers he knew, and a handful of newspapers. Then, he waited. No one in the national media noticed. But in the newsroom of the *Bristol Herald Courier*, a small paper in southern Virginia with a circulation of around forty thousand in the Blue Ridge region, the city editor thought it might be worth checking out. She faxed Munir's urgent plea for help over to Chris Dumond, a twenty-three-year-old cub reporter barely a year out of college who served as the newspaper's one-man bureau in Washington County. Dumond was a bit skeptical. A local resident in custody in a terrorism case in the heart of Appalachia, a place with no real terrorist targets and so few Muslims that there wasn't even a mosque? And no one had heard anything about it before this? Dumond figured it was just another crazy tip, a dead end, but he dutifully checked it out. He contacted some of the regulars on his beat—the desk officer at the jail, a court clerk, the usual suspects for routine court information—to find out if this Bhatti character was even in custody. He got nowhere. Finally, a court clerk acknowledged that there was some paperwork on a guy named Bhatti, but it had been sealed under orders of the federal magistrate judge in Abingdon. Dumond asked to see the order sealing the documents. "The sealing order has been sealed. You can't see anything," the clerk told him.

Maybe the tip wasn't so crazy after all, he thought to himself as he walked away. Nothing motivates a reporter like the sound of a door

closing in his face. Dumond kept poking. Next, he tried to get ahold of
Bhatti's girlfriend, Nancy McNey. Reaching her by phone, she confirmed the arrest and read to him portions of the warrant that law
enforcement officials had used to nab Bhatti; it was supposed to be
sealed too, but the agents had apparently left a copy at her home by
mistake when they came with guns drawn to arrest her boyfriend. The
warrant talked menacingly of Bhatti—this mysterious, eccentric psychiatrist from Pakistan—as a witness to possible acts of terrorism
against the United States and the use of weapons of mass destruction.
This was serious stuff, Dumond realized. So serious, in fact, that his
editors at the newspaper weren't satisfied just hearing about the details
over the phone from Nancy McNey. They sent him out to her home in
Abingdon to look at the warrant himself.

As he arrived at her door, days after Bhatti's arrest, McNey still
seemed traumatized—wide-eyed, stammering, frantic about what
might happen to Bhatti behind bars. She showed Dumond the arrest
warrant. Even as he scanned the document, McNey wasn't sure
whether he was supposed to see it. He raced back to the spare bedroom
in his apartment that served as his office and wrote up a 482-word
piece for the next day's paper. That night, as he was preparing to put
the story to bed, the managing editor at the newspaper wanted to make
sure the young reporter knew what he was getting himself into in writing a piece that contained material from sealed documents and
unnamed sources. "Make sure you can hold up your end of the bar-
gain," the managing editor told him. Dumond was undeterred. He had
all the brashness of any ambitious twenty-three-year-old reporter; he
could still remember the first time he'd seen *All the President's Men* at
age fifteen and been mesmerized by the power of the press to spotlight
abuses and ferret out government secrets. "Let 'em come get me,"
Dumond answered with a laugh. He had no idea.

The story ran on the front page under the headline: "Retired Doctor Held Under Sealed Warrant." The story caused a stir in town, and
local residents were squaring off over why a local doctor was in custody
in a terrorism investigation and whether the newspaper should have
printed the leaked story at all. As much as reporters like to think of
themselves as flies on the wall, mere observers to events outside their
influence or control, the public scrutiny that the media generates has a
way of inevitably shaping and redirecting the events it covers. Just

what impact the public scrutiny in Bhatti's arrest had on the government's handling of the case is unclear. What is known, however, is that the very day after the story ran, U.S. Magistrate Pamela Meade Sargent, the same judge who had signed Bhatti's arrest warrant, ordered him released from custody following a hearing that she closed to the public and the press. He was freed under a protective order that temporarily prevented him from leaving western Virginia and required him to appear before a grand jury the next month. And there was another condition: the doctor could not talk to anyone, even his own family, about what happened to him. After a week in custody, Bhatti walked out of jail a free man, for now. Elated though he was, his son was left to wonder how much longer his father might have sat in a jail cell, a secret prisoner in the war on terror, had it not been for the rough press release that he dashed off. If Nancy McNey hadn't been there when the FBI came for his father, Munir reflected later, "I wouldn't have even known that he was arrested. It's pretty scary to think that we live in a country where that can happen."

Exactly what first attracted the FBI's attention to Dr. Bhatti remains unclear to this day. Some people in town were convinced that a neighbor had gone to the FBI with his suspicions about the odd doctor. Local reporters hypothesized that an aggrieved psychiatric patient may have had a grudge. Bhatti's frequent phone calls and e-mails to Pakistan and his travel there—he would go back once every year or so to visit a sister and a brother—might even have attracted the attention of the National Security Agency in its effort to trace terrorist communications from "dirty" numbers overseas. Whatever the trigger, FBI officials maintained they had good reason to investigate Bhatti. This was no fishing expedition, the bureau insisted; "there was probable cause," an FBI official assured me later, refusing to elaborate. That was a claim that would never be judged in the light of day, however, because the records in the case remained sealed by order of the judge six years after the case was effectively closed. The process worked, Judge Sargent said later. "This is why we have a system of checks and balances." But for the public, it was a claim that was impossible to judge. Six years after Bhatti walked free, the judge's order had barred even Bhatti's own lawyer from talking about the case. All Dennis Jones would say was this: "As far as an individual's liberty is concerned—especially for an American citizen with Dr. Bhatti's history and his service to the country—what the government was doing to him was probably the single most egregious constitutional violation of civil rights that I've experienced in thirty-four years of practicing law."

Even with Bhatti's release from custody that June day, the case wasn't over yet. A month later, Judge Sargent summoned Dumond, the *Herald Courier* reporter, to her court to answer a question no reporter wants to be asked: Who was your source? Who showed him what was supposed to be a sealed warrant on Bhatti's arrest? "That information was given to me in confidence," the reporter answered. He would not give up his source. Undeterred, Judge Sargent had an answer of her own: a contempt citation against Dumond that would land him in jail for up to thirty days or more unless he started talking. Long before *The New York Times'* Judith Miller would spend eighty-five days in jail in the Valerie Plame–CIA leak investigation for refusing to identify a source, Chris Dumond would find himself in the government's crosshairs over the uneasy balance between informing the public and protecting government secrets in this new, post-9/11 age. Another hearing was scheduled for two weeks later, and Dumond braced for the worst. If the judge did not back off from her order, he could go straight from the hearing to the county jail—the same one Bhatti had just recently vacated. The newspaper had already opened a line of credit at the local Bank of America to post bond—if the judge would even allow him to post bond.

Dumond threw a purple toothbrush in the breast pocket of his blazer, along with a pack of Marlboro Lights and a lighter. He figured he'd need the supplies once he got in lockdown. He'd been diagnosed with mononucleosis just a few weeks earlier, and he felt awful. As the hearing time neared, he sat anxiously with one of the newspaper's lawyers and a few other executives from the paper in an office across the street from the courthouse. It was a sweltering August day, and Dumond was sweating; from the heat, the nerves, or the mono, he wasn't certain. He tried to call Nancy McNey four or five times. He wanted her to know that she might get dragged back into the case. He couldn't reach her. Instead, the judge's office phoned for the paper's lawyer; Sargent wanted to see him and his client in her chambers before the hearing. They filed across the street, unsure what to expect. There inside the chambers, seated immediately to the judge's left at a round table, was Nancy McNey. Dumond was stunned to see her.

They hadn't spoken since the day she showed him the warrant. He tried to look stone-faced, as the judge began to recount how McNey had come to her chambers that day to disclose her role in the newspaper's story.

"We've had a conversation," the judge said, gesturing toward McNey, "and she believes she is the one who gave you the information and releases you from confidentiality." Dumond was dumbstruck. He wanted to hear it for himself. He asked if he and McNey could speak privately. The pair walked to a small courtroom across the hall, just the two of them; reporter and source. Dumond was young enough to be McNey's grandson, but he wanted to know if she realized what she was doing in coming forward. "Are you sure?" he asked her. "I can't tell you that nothing bad is going to happen to you because of this." McNey nodded, reaffirming what she had told the judge in her chambers. The hours and days after Bhatti's arrest were such a fog for McNey that she still wasn't certain what she had or hadn't done. "Was I the one who showed you that information?" she asked Dumond. Yes, he answered; she had. "Well," she said finally, "if I did it, I did it, and I'm responsible for it, so let's get it over with."

Dumond was on the witness stand for all of maybe two minutes. He testified that McNey had in fact shown him the arrest warrant. The judge released him from the possible contempt of court charge, but she made clear that the secrecy of the grand jury proceedings remained paramount in her mind. And what of the public's right to know about the jailing of a local citizen without charges? If the judge harbored any sympathies for the competing interests at play in her courtroom, she did not voice them. Some matters, it appeared, were best kept secret. "The only repercussions of this fall on Mr. Bhatti," the judge told the courtroom. "He is the one who has to live with this."

PUBLICLY, THE BUSH ADMINISTRATION presented a united front in its aggressive push to lock up any and all possible terrorist suspects in order to defeat al Qaeda and deter the next attack. The front was a facade. Although hidden at the time, schisms were rupturing the administration at its highest levels from the beginning over how to go after suspected terrorists and what do with them once they were caught. "What is the end game here?" one senior administration offi-

cial asked me rhetorically as policies were beginning to fracture. "I
don't think anyone really knows." Respected administration lawyers
like Ted Olson, the solicitor general and a victim of 9/11 himself
because of the death of his wife, and his deputy, Paul Clement, were
warning privately that the courts were all but certain to rein in the
administration's claims to virtually unchecked powers in detaining
foreign terror suspects at Guantánamo Bay; it was a question of when,
not if.

At the center of the tensions—serving sometimes as referee, more
often as enforcer for the White House's hard-line policies—was
Alberto Gonzales, or "Fredo," as President Bush liked to call his old
friend, confidant, and counsel from Humble, Texas. If Karl Rove was
Bush's brain, Gonzales was his consigliere, his protector. Long before
Gonzales became indelibly associated in the public mind with the
politicization of the Justice Department, he was the White House
counsel charged with giving legal imprimatur to the will of the White
House in its most aggressive and often audacious counterterrorism
policies. Often, the will of the White House meant sidestepping, or
smashing altogether, the legal conventions that had governed American justice for decades. That inevitably put Gonzales at odds with
Ashcroft and his Justice Department over charges of White House
encroachment. Early on, Gonzales put himself in the middle of one
particularly sensitive clash that never became public centering on the
prosecution of John Walker Lindh, the so-called American Taliban
captured alongside the Taliban in Afghanistan in a prison uprising near
Mazar-i-Sharif.

The question of what to do with Lindh was a subject of fierce
debate within the administration. Bush himself voiced some measure
of sympathy for the plight of the twenty-year-old from Northern California, who had converted to Islam in high school and donned traditional Muslim garb before heading to Afghanistan in a bizarre spiritual
quest. "We're just trying to learn the facts about this poor fellow,"
Bush told a television interviewer days after Lindh's capture. "Obviously he has, uh, been misled, it appears to me. He thought he was
going to fight for a great cause, and in fact, he was going to support a
government that was one of the most repressive governments in the
history of mankind." Ashcroft, as usual, took a harder public line, saying that Lindh had been led by Osama bin Laden himself. "He chose

to embrace fanatics, and his allegiance to those terrorists never faltered," Ashcroft said. "Terrorists did not compel John Walker Lindh to join them. John Walker Lindh chose terrorists."

The Justice Department fought hard within the administration to prosecute Lindh in the criminal courts, but it faced problems. An ethics lawyer in the Justice Department, Jesselyn Radack, had already signaled that the FBI may have violated the law by interrogating the imprisoned Lindh in custody—and eliciting incriminating statements from him—even after his family in Northern California had retained a prominent defense lawyer for him; Radack was quickly silenced after raising her concerns. As the case moved ahead in early 2002, Lindh's lawyers were agitating over the military's treatment of Lindh, who had been blindfolded, duct-taped naked to a stretcher, and held in a metal shipping container for two days, and they were seeking detailed documents from the government as part of the discovery process in court. Providing documents to the defense could produce embarrassing details about Lindh's custody, and the White House knew it.

Michael Chertoff, the Justice Department's criminal chief, got word through back channels that officials at the White House were meeting to talk about what to do about Lindh and the discovery issue. As would become more and more frequent, the Justice Department did not have a seat at the table; the discussion went on without them. A senior Justice Department official called Gonzales to find out what was going on—and why the department charged with handling criminal prosecutions was not even involved. In a heated phone conversation, Gonzales made clear that the White House was calling the shots and that he, as White House counsel, had decided not to turn anything over to Lindh's defense lawyers in the way of documents. "We're not going to provide discovery," Gonzales said.

The process of turning relevant discovery material over to the defense and the courts was a staple of the criminal justice system, and there were safeguards in place to protect classified material in doing so. Any prosecutor who openly defied a discovery order was in danger of a contempt proceeding. Ashcroft's people were already upset about the creeping influence of the Pentagon's lawyers in making what prosecutors thought should be criminal decisions about other terrorist suspects in custody. Now, Gonzales and the White House were signaling that they would not abide by the discovery process laid out in the courts. The Justice Department balked; the question of what would and would not be turned over in the legal process was a decision for John Ashcroft and his senior aides to make, not the White House, Gonzales was told angrily. Anything else, they said, would be a misuse of the criminal justice process. And no White House official—even the president's counsel—was going to dictate how the Justice Department proceeded with a seminal case.

Ultimately, the Justice Department turned over some material but sought to withhold other sensitive statements from prisoners at Guantánamo Bay before cutting a deal with Lindh that landed him a twenty-year prison sentence. Spurred partly by principle, partly by turf protection, the Justice Department was standing its ground against the White House. The sanctity of the criminal justice system had, at least in the eyes of the Justice Department, been preserved in the showdown. There were no threats of resignations from the Justice Department, not this time; those would come later, sparked by even more controversial national security decisions by the White House. But the fissures were emerging in the war on terror, and Gonzales was already at the center.

As White House counsel, Gonzales was discreet, affable, loyal to a fault, able to handle sensitive matters quietly without fear of leaks or political backlash. This was what Bush expected of Fredo, and this, for much of his presidency, was what he got. They had a long history. As governor in Texas, Bush had tapped Gonzales first as counsel to the governor. Bush had been impressed by Gonzales' Horatio Alger–like story of personal perseverance: the son of Mexican immigrants, living in poverty with seven siblings in a two-bedroom home without a phone or hot water, Gonzales had gone from serving in the Air Force to hawking sodas at Rice University football games to attending Harvard Law School before joining a blue-chip law firm in Houston. Always at the governor's side, Gonzales proved adept at providing political insulation for Bush. He helped get him out of jury service on a drunk-driving case that might have forced Bush to disclose his own DUI arrest years earlier, and he set in place a system for cursory reviews of difficult capital cases that the governor's critics would deride as a rubber stamp for death. Bush came to trust Gonzales more and more. He made him secretary of state in Texas, then a justice on the state Supreme Court, and finally, after Bush's disputed election in 2000, he brought him along to

Washington as his White House counsel, the president's own lawyer, in one of Bush's very first appointments. Gonzales had little grounding in either Washington politics or constitutional law, but Bush said: "I know first-hand I can trust Al's judgment." For his part, Gonzales saw his job as something of a White House ethics officer. "My charge is to make sure that we don't even approach the line of what some could consider unethical," he told an interviewer two months after taking office in the West Wing. "There will be some instances where something is very important to the president's agenda. My job is to try to find a way to do it in a way that's legal."

Find a way to do it in a way that's legal. With the benefit of hindsight, the words would look strikingly ambiguous, open to all sorts of interpretations about a lawyer's legal and ethical responsibilities. Did Gonzales see his job as taking legally questionable policies and changing them to give them a more solid foundation? Or was he merely giving his legal blessing and sanction to policies that remained ultimately untenable? With Gonzales, it was tough to tell. Even in the most critical of meetings, he was smiling and pleasant, but ultimately inscrutable. He had none of Bush's easy-to-read mannerisms. One senior official who worked closely with Gonzales compared him to Peter Sellers in *Being There*; it was impossible to know whether the blank stare and the terse curl of the lips covered up something, or nothing, even on the most critical of issues.

Gonzales was the point man for the White House beginning in 2003 in resisting efforts by the 9/11 Commission to get access to critical documents as part of their investigation, including the memo Bush had received on August 6, 2001, warning that bin Laden was "determined to strike in U.S." Gonzales' relations with the commission began on shaky ground. In a series of initial meetings, Gonzales found the commission's executive director, Philip Zelikow, to be overly aggressive in his approach and, from then on, he refused to meet with him. Co-chairmen Tom Kean and Lee Hamilton and other commission members began personally laying out for Gonzales their requests for the documents they were seeking and proposed ways to protect the sensitivity of the material and the White House's claims of executive privilege. The commissioners went into the meetings expecting a give-and-take with Gonzales, a dialogue with the most senior lawyer in the building. Instead, Gonzales sat silently much of the time, nodding his

head and saying little one way or the other as he listened to their proposals. What he did say often centered on the White House's concerns
about media leaks, but beyond that, he was leery of making any com-
mitments about the commission's access to documents, even when
faced with the threat of subpoenas. "I'll take that back to my client"
was all he would say as he adjourned one meeting. For Gonzales, the
client was paramount.

"He has the president's ear" was a phrase I would hear often in covering Gonzales. Was he channeling Bush and Cheney on critical matters of legal policy in the war on terror, a mere legal functionary, or was
he shaping the policy himself? With Gonzales, it was almost impossible to tell what ideas, if any, actually originated with him. When he was
nominated for attorney general in 2004, I traveled to the place where
he'd first made his name—Texas—and spent a week interviewing several dozen former colleagues, from law partners at his old firm of Vin-
son & Elkins, to fellow judges on the bench at the Texas Supreme
Court, to other senior Bush aides from the governor's office in Austin.
I wanted to get a better understanding of the symbiotic relationship
between Bush and Gonzales, between politician and lawyer. The plati-
tudes from Gonzales' old colleagues flowed freely: nice guy, friendly,
inspiring life story, solid co-worker, able lawyer, loyal aide, hard-nosed
racquetball player. The obvious follow-up questions—How did Gonzales distinguish himself? When did he shine? How did he earn Bush's
trust? What did he actually believe in?—elicited only blank stares.
Journalism is built on great anecdotes, but if there were moments in
his past that revealed the unvarnished Alberto Gonzales, I didn't find
many. His work was opaque.

It was a frustrating reporting assignment, akin to the experience
suffered a few months later by a colleague of mine at the *Times,* Todd
Purdum, when he was asked to profile another Bush loyalist from
Texas, Harriet Miers, the successor to Gonzales as White House counsel, during her short-lived nomination for the Supreme Court in 2005.
Purdum, an artful writer with a sharp eye for the subtleties of political
body language, interviewed officials throughout the White House to
try to get a better idea of what Miers was really like. Again came the
banalities from colleagues: intelligent, meticulous, selfless, insightful.
But again, when Miers' colleagues were pressed for details, for real-life
episodes, the questions elicited mainly the same searching faces I had
seen in Texas a few months earlier from Gonzales' colleagues. "She is a

very good bowler" was one of the few specifics that White House aide Josh Bolten could muster regarding Bush's nominee to the high court. Change the bowling to racquetball, and you seemed to have Alberto Gonzales.

Even before 9/11, Gonzales made clear that Bush would do things his own way when it came to matters of legal policy, unrestrained by tired tradition and convention. In one of Bush's first strategic plays to remake the federal judiciary in a more conservative mold, the White House ended the American Bar Association's half-century role in vetting and rating judicial candidates before they were nominated to the federal bench. The move scored Bush major points among Federalist Society members and other conservatives who had often derided the group as too liberal in its judicial ratings. Gonzales met personally with Bush several times on the bellwether issue before announcing the snub. "It would be particularly inappropriate, in our view, to grant a preferential, quasi-official role to a group such as the ABA that takes public positions on divisive political, legal and social issues that come before the courts," Gonzales wrote to the bar. The White House was showing the first signs of its independent streak, a go-it-alone approach that seemed to mute long-heard voices outside the inner circle. That streak would only become magnified in the face of the extraordinary legal choices the administration faced after 9/11.

Gonzales confronted one of his first major public tests just two months after the September 11 attacks, as Bush announced his surprise plan to set up so-called military tribunals for trying foreigners as terrorists. The plan, which promised secret trials and the denial of basic rights of appeal for anyone convicted in the tribunals, set in motion six years of sparring in the courts and in Congress over America's legal, international, and moral obligations to the prisoners it captured. William P. Barr, attorney general under Bush's father, first suggested the concept for the tribunals to a Gonzales aide, pointing as precedent to the capture of German saboteurs as enemy combatants in World War II. Gonzales ran with the idea. In the weeks after 9/11, the details of the plan were drafted under extraordinary secrecy through Gonzales' office, with heavy input as always from Cheney's top people. When it was finally announced, the plan drew stinging rebukes from both Republicans and Democrats over the charge that the White House was setting up what amounted to a kangaroo court system.

Two weeks after the announcement, Gonzales was the keynote

speaker at a luncheon of the American Bar Association in Washington. He was seated at the dais before his speech with Suzanne Spaulding, a former assistant general counsel at the CIA who was helping to host the event. As the two chatted over lunch, the talk turned inevitably to the White House's recent announcement about the military tribunals, and Gonzales told Spaulding how surprised he was by all the sudden notoriety the plan was generating. He seemed genuinely shocked by the criticism, as if to say: What's all the fuss about? Spaulding, with a strong resume herself on national security matters, smiled politely and held her tongue. She wasn't about to challenge the president's lawyer right before he gave a speech before her group. But she was struck by how unaware—almost oblivious, she thought—Gonzales appeared to be regarding the potential political and legal fallout of such a radical departure from long-standing legal practice. If the White House hadn't operated out of such a bunker, if it had sought out other opinions before dropping its bombshell, Spaulding thought to herself as she smiled at her lunch companion, maybe this wouldn't have come as such a shock.

For people outside the White House, the Bush administration's decisions on how it would treat those it suspected of terrorist ties appeared haphazard and inconsistent: a legal black hole. One reason for the confusion, those on the inside acknowledged privately, was that there was no clear system. Even the most seasoned prosecutor could not provide a coherent explanation for the differing standards. Often, the rules were made up on the fly on a case-by-case basis; a system of justice designed to establish clear process had instead become very much ad hoc, driven as much by timing, expedience, judicial pressure, and political will as by the sober administration of justice. Why, after all, was a John Walker Lindh prosecuted in the civilian courts to face a possible life sentence in prison, while a Yaser Hamdi, a Saudi college student with U.S. citizenship who was captured along with Lindh and the Taliban, was ultimately sent home to Saudi Arabia a free man after being jailed in a military brig for three years? Why was a Maher Arar whisked away from JFK to face interrogation and worse in Syria over his suspected al Qaeda links, while a David Hicks, a onetime kangaroo-skinner from Australia, was jailed for five years at Guantánamo before ultimately cutting a deal with a military commission that sent him home to serve out a few months in jail on a mostly suspended sentence? Why was a Jose Padilla, the so-called dirty bomber and former gang member from the streets of Chicago, jailed first as a "material witness" to terrorism, then held largely incommunicado for three and a half years in a military brig in South Carolina as an enemy combatant, then finally prosecuted on much less sensational charges in a criminal court in Florida?

The answers were all but impossible for the public to decipher because of the extraordinary secrecy surrounding the thousands of detentions. In an administration renowned for its tight-lipped ways, the veil of silence cast over the prisoners in the war on terror was perhaps the most troubling. Overseas, "high-value targets" with al Qaeda ties were kept in secret CIA "black sites"—secret prisons in Europe and Asia—for nearly five years, with no record or acknowledgment of their captivity. At Guantánamo Bay, the identities and circumstances of the hundreds in custody remained a mystery. On U.S. soil, authorities refused to release the identities of the "special interest" detainees arrested on immigration charges after 9/11. Human rights lawyers bristled at the secrecy. Frustrated, former Secretary of State Warren Christopher confronted a top Justice Department official at a judicial conference, saying that the secret detentions reminded him of what happened to Argentina's infamous "disappeareds," the political prisoners who simply vanished in the "dirty wars" of the 1970s. And judges around the country began pushing back.

"Difficult times such as these," U.S. District Judge Gladys Kessler wrote in 2002 in ordering the administration to release the names of 1,200 terrorism detainees, "have always tested our fidelity to the core democratic values of openness, government accountability and the rule of law." Citing a thirty-three-year-old court precedent, she said: "Secret arrests are 'a concept odious to a democratic society,' and profoundly antithetical to the bedrock values that characterize a free and open one such as ours." The Bush administration appealed her ruling; to make public the names and circumstances of those arrested and detained in terrorism investigations, the government argued, would be to give al Qaeda a road map to the investigations themselves. The national security argument won out: an appeals court reversed Judge Kessler's order for the names to be made public and, in 2004, the Supreme Court let that ruling stand. The veil of secrecy had held.

But one military lawyer considered the secrecy so odious that he took matters into his own hands. On his last day of duty assigned to Guantánamo Bay in 2005, Navy Lieutenant Commander Matthew M. Diaz printed out a military listing of the names and identifying information for 550 detainees held at Gitmo. The Center for Constitutional Rights, which had recently won a major victory in the Supreme Court over the detention of the Guantánamo prisoners, was suing to get hold of the names, and Diaz had seen a draft motion the military was preparing to oppose the release. He was upset. He thought the military was stonewalling. Diaz didn't go to higher-ups to protest the policy, a decision he would come to regret. Instead, he took the thirty-nine-page printout of the prisoners' names and identifying information from a military database and shrunk the pages in a photocopier into small pieces the size of index cards—small enough to fit inside a Valentine's Day card with a big heart and a Chihuahua on the outside. Then, he tucked the cut-up pieces inside the unsigned card, put the valentine inside a bright red envelope, and mailed it to a lawyer for the Center for Constitutional Rights.

The center got the names it had wanted, but not this way. It turned the surprise valentine over to a federal judge hearing its lawsuit, and the FBI traced the printout to Diaz. To the military, his actions were a disgrace, a dereliction of duty that jeopardized national security. To Diaz, his actions were a moral imperative. It was, his lawyer said at his court-martial in Norfolk, Virginia, a "crisis of conscience" that made him do it, a moral dilemma brought on by conflicting loyalties to the military and to his own sense of justice. It was dumb, his lawyer, Patrick McClain acknowledged. But, he said, "it was really Matt's patriotism, more than anything else, that drove this. He believes in the law." In the end, however, a different set of laws—the ones protecting the government's secrets from prying eyes—won out, and Diaz got six months in the brig.

With challenges to the administration's terror policies bubbling up in the courts in 2004, Alberto Gonzales and the White House were well aware of how badly the lack of transparency and the helter-skelter nature of the prisoner detentions were hurting their public credibility, both at home and among allies abroad. The criticism and mischaracterizations, Gonzales thought, were unfair. In February 2004, Gonzales and the White House decided to pull the curtain open a bit. So he went back before the administration's old sparring partner, the American Bar Association, hoping to lay out the rationale for determining who got locked up in the international struggle and why. The talk got little attention in the media except for a few write-ups in legal journals, but it provided an eye-opening moment—as telling for what Gonzales hadn't intended to convey as for what he did. In Gonzales' view, the different options for locking up al Qaeda suspects—once separate and distinct legal concepts—were now all part of the same mix. Jailing someone as a material witness to a crime, like a Taj Bhatti, prosecuting him criminally, like a John Walker Lindh, or jailing him in a military brig as an enemy combatant without a lawyer, like a Jose Padilla, were all now merely different tools in the same government tool belt. If holding someone as a material witness or prosecuting them criminally turned out to be "less-than-ideal options," Gonzales said, "we may initiate some type of informal process to present to the appropriate decision makers the question of whether an individual might qualify for designation as an enemy combatant."

As always, there were skeptics in the audience: one questioner wanted to know the rationale for denying Guantánamo prisoners access to lawyers during their interrogations; another wanted to know how many unlawful combatants the administration was actually holding in secret. To those who demanded that the Bush administration follow time-honored rules of jurisprudence, Gonzales had this to say: the country was on a wartime footing, and many of the old rules no longer applied. "The administration's detractors fundamentally misunderstand the nature of the threat this country is facing," he said. "To suggest that an al Qaeda member must be tried in civilian court because he happens to be an American citizen, or to suggest that hundreds of individuals captured in battle in Afghanistan should be extradited, given lawyers and tried in civilian courts, is to apply the wrong legal paradigm. The law applicable in this context is the law of war—those conventions and customs that govern armed conflicts." The right to a lawyer "is a fundamental part of our criminal justice system," Gonzales said, but, "it is undeniably foreign to the law of war."

Four months later, the Supreme Court spoke. Those jailed by the administration as enemy combatants, the court said in issuing a historic ruling in the case of Saudi-American Yaser Hamdi, cannot be detained indefinitely and must be given the chance to challenge the evidence against them and tell their side of the story before a judge or some other neutral party. The decision suggested that the fundamental misunderstanding of which Gonzales spoke had come not from the White House's detractors, but from the White House itself. "A state of war," Justice Sandra Day O'Connor wrote for the court majority in what would become a line for the ages, "is not a blank check for the president."

THE MANY HUNDREDS of men rounded up on America's streets after 9/11 had come from everywhere and from nowhere: from Pakistan, from Egypt, from India, from Trinidad. Some had snuck into America across porous borders or come with bogus papers; the majority had come here legally, on legitimate visas, as students, as workers, but had overstayed their legal welcome. In another age, the INS might not have thought twice about them. They worked at deli shops and gas stations, at airports and trucking companies, from Manhattan to Virginia to Kansas. Their histories were as far-flung as their birthplaces. But they had some things in common, troubling things: they were young, they were Muslim, they were apparently in the country illegally, and, after 9/11, someone thought they could be terrorists.

Be on guard, Bush, Gonzales, and Ashcroft had told the American people after the 9/11 attacks; report anything suspicious. And report they did: 96,000 tips in the first week alone after the attacks via phone and Web sites. An aware, alert public was essential to the fight, policymakers believed. That mindset would help stop another potential disaster just three months after 9/11, as an alert flight attendant noticed Richard Reid trying to light something in his shoe. And an anonymous, handwritten letter to the FBI's Buffalo office in 2001, prior to the 9/11 attacks, would help lead investigators the next year to what became known as the Lackawanna Six, a group of Muslim American men who had ventured to an al Qaeda training camp in Afghanistan before getting cold feet and coming home.

Emboldened, Bush and Ashcroft even proposed an ill-fated plan called Operation Tips to set up a network of a million domestic tipsters from the private and public sectors—from utility workers and telephone repairmen to postal carriers and the local cable guy—in order to ferret out information on possible terrorist activity inside Americans' homes and businesses. "Government-sanctioned Peeping Toms," civil rights advocates called the plan, which was ultimately scaled back in the face of protests. For every real tip given to the authorities, there were thousands of bogus ones, spewing forth from curious store clerks, well-meaning bystanders, aggrieved employees, or vindictive exes. The "jilted lover" tips, senior FBI officials began calling the leads privately. Still, the tips came. A clerk at a rental agency thought it odd that some Muslim men had returned a rental truck so soon. An assistant at the photo-developing shop noticed shots of New York City landmarks on a roll of film. Cops on a routine traffic stop spotted a magazine on the backseat with pictures of the World Trade Center. A landlord thought his tenant was acting strangely. Someone reported hearing an acquaintance making vague "anti-American comments."

As best they could, FBI agents scurried to investigate the targets of the tips. Every lead now had to be followed; discretion was a thing of the past. If the subject was an "out of status" immigrant, the authorities had a built-in strategy: lock him up indefinitely as a "special interest" detainee on an immigration violation that once would have gotten him a one-way ticket home or a "voluntary deportation" order. No longer. Of some 1,200 people detained in the weeks and months after 9/11, nearly 800 in all were picked up on immigration violations and sent to jails around the country—in Kansas, Louisiana, Florida, New York, and New Jersey.

The unluckiest of the lot—seven dozen men in all—were sent to a sprawling detention facility in Brooklyn. They arrived there in armed convoys, in chains, and guards hustled them into the prison through a sally port to be patted down and strip-searched. At the bottom of the ramp, they were lined up against a large block wall. The first sight that greeted them was a white T-shirt on the wall with a picture of the American flag blowing in the breeze. A guard had taped it there, makeshift, right at eye level, next to the regulation plastic sign reminding the guards to lock up their guns before going inside. "THESE COLORS DON'T RUN," read the T-shirt's large block letters underneath the fluttering red-white-and-blue. Before long, there were red blood spots on the shirt too. Those stains didn't run either. That was where the guards would shove the newly arrived prisoners' faces into the wall, so close to the flag, as one inmate recalled, that they were made to "kiss it." "Look straight ahead!" one guard ordered an inmate on videotape, pressing his torso against the wall so that the American stars and stripes gazing back at him from the wall were unmistakable.

Who were these men? Did they have links to terrorism? Were they part of the feared "second wave" of attacks? No one knew for sure. And the FBI, it seemed, was in no hurry to find out. What mattered now was that the men were locked up, off the streets, out of the way. For weeks at a time, many of the men were kept in the harshest of conditions, blocked out from the world. They couldn't talk to lawyers, couldn't talk with the diplomats from their home embassies trying to reach them, couldn't even contact family members whose husbands, sons, and fathers had now simply disappeared. Lawyers for men housed inside the facility in Brooklyn would show up and ask to see their clients, only to be told, wrongly, that they weren't there. The lawyers weren't the only ones kept in the dark; in the immediate aftermath of the attacks, the Justice Department was putting out daily updates on the hundreds of people it had detained as part of its terrorism investigation. Then, weeks later, officials in Washington discovered almost by fluke that, in violation of federal protocol, New York was holding another three hundred or so "special interest" detainees without telling immigration officials at headquarters; three hundred prisoners who, in the eyes of Washington, hadn't existed the day before. Washington put out new numbers; the total of 9/11 detainees practically doubled overnight. Finally, chagrined, officials at Main Justice stopped putting out the numbers altogether.

Hundreds of the 9/11 detainees were not even charged for weeks, and they were not released from custody for three, six, even nine months after being picked up in connection with the investigation into the September 11 attacks. Under INS policy, illegal immigrants brought into custody were supposed to be removed from the country within ninety days. For the "special interest" detainees picked up after the attacks, however, a new policy was established: "Hold until release," meaning that the INS—despite its legal misgivings—could not deport or release anyone in custody until the FBI offered formal assurance that they had no connection to terrorism. For the hundreds picked up, often on what would prove the flimsiest of leads, it was assumed they had a terrorist connection until the FBI could determine otherwise. It was a policy shift mandated by the highest levels— Ashcroft himself, possibly higher, Justice Department investigators later found. The policy was "not up for debate," said Stuart Levey, a point man in the effort at the Justice Department. The risk of doing otherwise, officials believed, was simply too great. "We have to hold these people until we find out what is going on," Michael Chertoff, head of the Justice Department's Criminal Division, told his deputy. "If we turn one person loose we shouldn't have," said David Laufman, chief of staff to the deputy attorney general, "there could be catastrophic consequences."

Any possibility that an illegal might be a terrorist had to be treated as grounds for keeping him locked up. Showing that the prisoner was not a terrorist threat, Ashcroft said, was like "proving a negative." Soon enough, however, it became clear to senior Justice Department officials that the bulk of the many hundreds of detainees had nothing to do with terrorism. Senior law enforcement officials were given assurances it would take the FBI a few days, perhaps a few weeks at most, to clear prisoners with no real terrorism ties. They were wrong. The CIA ran the names of the detainees through their terrorism watch lists quickly enough, almost always coming back with no matches. Yet even then, the detainees remained in lockdown, in legal limbo. At the FBI, investigators would find, there was little effort to distinguish between real terrorism suspects and those out-of-status immigrants caught up in the dragnet. In the end, only a handful of the more than seven hundred were shown to have any links to terrorism, and even those few links were sketchy at best.

For the Immigration and Naturalization Service, and its stable of lawyers, the no-release policy caused particular heartache. The FBI was calling the shots on terrorism detainees, not the INS, but the INS lawyers were the ones who had to go into immigration court and argue that the prisoners should be jailed without bond. Often, they had nothing beyond a boilerplate assertion about the 9/11 attacks to make their case. Immigration judges, growing anxious about the broad sweep of the new policy, began ordering detainees released from jail on bond pending further proceedings, or removed from custody and deported altogether to their home countries. The problem was that the Justice Department wouldn't honor the orders, and INS lawyers were caught in the middle. After a judge ordered one detainee freed on bond, his lawyer tried to make good on the order by posting bond. He was blocked. "Frankly," an INS lawyer in Newark wrote in an e-mail, "I do not know what to tell him because I cannot bring myself to say that the INS no longer feels compelled to obey the law."

Jim Ziglar, the head of the INS, considered the no-release policy a perversion of the immigration procedures established by the courts, and he struggled to roll it back. Ziglar reached his personal tipping point after a U.S. senator complained to him about an engineer in the Midwest being held on an immigration violation. The man had no possible ties to terrorism that Ziglar could determine, but the FBI was refusing to clear him for release on bond. Finally, Ziglar put in a personal call to a top official at the FBI. "He's going to be released at 5 p.m. today," Ziglar advised his counterpart, "with or without clearance from the FBI." The response was curt: "You can't do that," the FBI official said. "Oh, yes I can," the INS commissioner answered. By day's end, the INS had the approval from the FBI clearing the engineer to be released from lockup.

The scope of the legal and bureaucratic problems in the handling of the 9/11 detainees and the physical abuse at the hands of the Brooklyn guards were first exposed in an exhaustive, months-long investigation conducted by the office of Glenn Fine, the inspector general of the Justice Department. Fine, a boyish-looking lawyer with a reputation as a relentless watchdog over government abuse and mismanagement, had first earned national exposure a quarter-century earlier as a stand-out guard for the Harvard basketball team, ranking among the Ivy League leaders in assists before being drafted by the San Antonio Spurs. (He skipped training camp to become a Rhodes Scholar instead.) At the Justice Department, Ashcroft made sure to get the still agile Fine on his team whenever he joined him at the FBI court for a pickup basketball game. But off the court, Fine's stinging reports on Justice Department problems were a frequent source of heartburn for Ashcroft and the Bush administration. Fine's massive report on the 9/11 detainees landed on June 2, 2003, and it made immediate front-page news around the country. The *Times* put my story on the report at the top of the front page under a two-column headline. "U.S. Report Faults the Roundup of Illegal Immigrants After 9/11," it read. "Many with No Ties to Terror Languished in Jail." The morning my story appeared in the paper, I was walking past our news desk when I noticed Rick Berke, our deputy bureau chief, gesturing with annoyance toward the phone and trying to make eye contact with me. The handset was a good six inches from his ear, but the person on the other end could be heard yelling in loud, angry tones. I had seen that look before on Rick's face. It usually meant that Ashcroft's chief PR person,

Barbara Comstock, a former opposition researcher with the Republican National Committee, was on the phone complaining about a story of mine.

Comstock thought my story on Glenn Fine's report was unfair and inaccurate in several respects, and she was demanding a correction. She took particular issue with two phrases in the lead of my story: the Justice Department's "roundup" of hundreds of illegal immigrants, and the "unduly harsh conditions" in the jail in which investigators found that many had languished. Comstock thought we were taking unfair editorial license. Berke stood his ground. We pointed Comstock to page 187 of the report, which talked of the "prolonged confinement for many detainees, sometimes under extremely harsh conditions." But there was no supposed "roundup" of detainees by the Justice Department, Comstock angrily insisted. Indeed, the word itself did not appear in Fine's report, but the editors agreed with my assessment that, given the breadth of the findings, it was a fair and accurate characterization of what the investigation found. Alberto Gonzales himself, the son of immigrants and the president's right-hand man, would finally admit as much two years later in a candid assessment at a Senate hearing. Recalling the climate after 9/11, Gonzales said: "There was a great deal of concern that there may be a second wave of attacks. People didn't know. And so there were undocumented aliens that were rounded up."

Fine got a bit banged up himself over the report. On Capitol Hill, House GOP staffers began circulating a set of anonymous talking points to help beat back the criticism unleashed by the inspector general's report. "If the report's only achievement was to be a kick in the teeth to the Department of Justice employees whose dedicated work has prevented there from being another major terrorist attack in the U.S., it would be merely contemptible," the critique said. "However, the report will likely leave a deadlier legacy. It will have a chilling effect on aggressive immigration law enforcement." Despite the pushback, Ashcroft, to his credit, thanked Fine publicly for identifying bureaucratic issues that the department needed to address, and the Justice Department, at Fine's urging, began a series of reforms to try to ensure that the types of wholesale problems cited by his inspector general were not repeated. But when it came to the overall thrust of the administration's response to 9/11, Ashcroft was in no mood for reconciliation.

The policy of holding any and all illegal aliens indefinitely until they could be ruled out as terrorists, Ashcroft asserted, was the right one. Those arrested after 9/11 "were in the United States illegally. The policy of the department—for which we do not apologize—was that until individuals apprehended who are here illegally who have no, who don't have a right to bail or bond. . . before we could release them prior to their deportation we wanted to have them cleared. We believe that's the right policy in protecting the American people," he told the House Judiciary Committee a few days after Fine's report. (Months later, in fact, Ashcroft would continue to insist that hundreds of those deported after 9/11 had "links to the September 11th investigation.")

Ashcroft's spokeswoman, Comstock, was even blunter in her assessment: "We make no apologies," she said, "for finding every legal way possible to protect the American public from further terrorist attacks." Ashcroft's critics cringed. "Why Won't He Apologize?" asked one headline in the *Legal Times*. The words echoed the stance of another attorney general in an earlier time of crisis, one who had denied Fourth Amendment rights to aliens and justified the use of a sweeping dragnet in the name of protecting security. "I apologize for nothing that the Department of Justice has done in this matter; I glory in it," Attorney General A. Mitchell Palmer testified before Congress after the World War I–era raids that would bear his name in history, sweeping up thousands of suspected "radicals," anarchists, and other mostly blameless foreigners in response to a series of bombings against prominent Americans, including Palmer himself. If some federal agents "were a little rough or unkind, or short or curt, with these alien agitators whom they observed seeking to destroy their homes, their religion, and their country," said Palmer, a Pennsylvania Quaker, "I think it might well be overlooked." Eight decades later, as Ashcroft mounted his own no-apologies campaign, even some senior officials in the Bush administration were wishing privately that Bush's attorney general could be a bit less strident, a bit more yielding, in his defense of the government's own rough-edged tactics after Glenn Fine's report. "That's just John being John," said a senior administration official who counted himself as an admirer of the attorney general. "John gives no ground."

. . .

FOR ALL HIS FIERY ORATION, Ashcroft was the most unlikely of field generals in the Bush administration's war on terror. Devout in his faith and deft in his politics, Ashcroft never set out to make the battle against al Qaeda his historical legacy. In fact, he never set out to become attorney general at all. What Ashcroft wanted most of all when George W. Bush was campaigning for the White House was to return to the U.S. Senate, a place he had called home for six years as an iconoclastic archconservative best known for his brass-knuckle style of politics, his strong faith, and his baritone vocals as a member of the "Singing Senators" barbershop quartet. But unexpected career moves became habitual for Ashcroft. A man who seemed to shun expectations all his life, Ashcroft toggled between the devout and the secular, studying in the decidedly irreligious environs of Yale and recording an album on eight-track tape with a group of traveling gospel singers before throwing himself into elected politics in Missouri. In the fall of 2000, Ashcroft appeared headed back to the Senate after a short-lived bid for the presidency. But a plane crash—the first one to change the course of Ashcroft's public life—killed his opponent, Missouri governor Mel Carnahan, on a campaign trip. The sympathy generated by the disaster, in the view of many analysts, helped tilt the election in the late governor's favor, and Carnahan's widow filled his seat in Washington. Years later, Ashcroft would joke at a speech he gave that he was the only U.S. senator ever to lose to a dead man, but at the time, it was a painful defeat that left him without any obvious career path—at least until he received an unexpected phone call six weeks later from Andy Card, chief of staff to President-elect George W. Bush. Bush wanted to meet with Ashcroft the next day in Texas to talk about a job.

The two had never been particularly close, but privately, Bush was an admirer of the Missouri senator and respected both his strong religious faith and his sense of political loyalty. "I like Ashcroft a lot," Governor Bush confided in November 1998 to a friend and political advisor, Doug Wead, in one of a series of conversations that Wead was secretly tape-recording with the future president. "He is a competent man. He would be a good Supreme Court pick. He would be a good attorney general. He would be a good vice president." Bush didn't even mind the prospect of a two-man race against Ashcroft for the White House. "I want Ashcroft to stay in there, and I want him to be very strong," Bush said. "I would love it to be a Bush-Ashcroft race. Only because I respect him. He wouldn't say ugly things about me. And I damn sure wouldn't say ugly things about him."

In passing over more moderate candidates in favor of Ashcroft as his attorney general, Bush was sending at once a thank-you note to the religious base that helped elect him, and an eye-poke to the liberals who loathed Ashcroft's unabashedly moralistic views on abortion, the death penalty, and God's role in public policy. Bush liked a good fight, and with Ashcroft's nomination he got it: a bruising, six-week confirmation battle that laid bare allegations of racial and religious insensitivity by Ashcroft and produced the closest vote for the post in more than seventy-five years. Before his first day at the Justice Department, Ashcroft had already become, in his own words, "a marked man."

In style and substance, Ashcroft was the alpha male to Janet Reno's beta female, and the hard-to-miss differences between Bill Clinton's attorney general and George W. Bush's pick would reverberate in the halls of the Justice Department for years to come. "Ms. Reno," as she liked to be called, was a matronly, self-deprecating figure who wanted to know every detail of an issue and was famous, sometimes infamous, for holding meeting after meeting with senior advisors and low-ranking career lawyers before finally reaching a decision. On her very last night in office, in fact, she phoned an immigration lawyer at home to get his counsel on a point of legal minutiae before bidding the department goodbye. In contrast, "General Ashcroft"—her successor's preferred moniker—was nothing if not decisive. He commanded a room but could appear strikingly aloof during meetings and cloistered himself with a small group of powerful aides drawn from his days in the Senate, largely shutting out the career lawyers who had shaped policies under Reno. Ashcroft, aides said, saw many of the career lawyers at the Justice Department as not-so-closeted liberals out to undermine his agenda; the resistance of the U.S. Attorney's Office in San Francisco to the idea of even hanging photos in the office of their new bosses—Bush, Cheney, and Ashcroft—did not help matters.

Even before 9/11, Ashcroft saw himself as a change agent in the stodgy old culture of the Justice Department, a place that he believed was populated by lawyers trained to contest everything and to say "no" because it was the safer, easier option. Symptomatic of that culture, he thought, was what happened his first week at the Justice Department after he asked his support staff to water the congratulatory flowers he'd received. They refused. "We don't water flowers," the new attorney general was told. "I couldn't believe that attitude," he said later.

Long before Ashcroft began breaking down walls at the FBI after 9/11, the son of an Assemblies of God minister was breaking down walls of church and state that had kept religion out of the attorney general's office. Ashcroft, whose father anointed him with Crisco oil on the morning of his inauguration to the Senate, began holding 8 o'clock Bible study and prayer sessions each morning at the Justice Department in his office for anyone who wanted to "read, argue, memorize and pray." A front-page story in *The Washington Post* on the ritual caused a brief brouhaha in more secular circles, but Ashcroft was undeterred. Contrarian by nature, Ashcroft was used to public criticism over his strong policies and his even stronger faith; "Lightning rod" would become practically a permanent line in his job description as attorney general. For John Ashcroft, a public stoning was almost emboldening. He would quote Scripture passed on to him as a boy by his father: "Blessed are you when they revile you and persecute you, and say all kinds of evil against you falsely for My sake. Rejoice and be exceedingly glad, for great is your reward in heaven."

So different in temperament, Ashcroft and Reno met only once in the aftermath of Bush's contested election victory in 2000, with Ashcroft, as the new attorney general, inviting his predecessor to fly back up to Washington from Florida and visit with him at the department that she had run for eight years. The Missourian was a gracious host, sending a department car to the airport to pick up Reno, who had battled Parkinson's disease for years and was prone to shaking spells. Ashcroft waited on Pennsylvania Avenue to greet her himself, then led her to the attorney general's private dining room for lunch. That itself was a change in culture at the Justice Department. Reno, famously removed from the social niceties of Washington and not one for the trappings of power, hardly ever set foot in the AG's private dining room, but Ashcroft made frequent use of it, entertaining visiting dignitaries there or sitting around the long dining room table with his federal prosecutors to share bowls of ice cream after a pickup game of basketball at the FBI's underground court.

Ashcroft seemed to view the lunch with Reno more as a courtesy call than anything else. But amid the customary talk about the department's challenges and priorities, Reno surprised her successor by handing him a set of memos that spoke to what she saw as a grave threat in the department: the FBI's inability, in essence, to connect the dots. They were copies of memos Reno had written the year before to Louis Freeh, the FBI director, who reported to her. "Threats to US National Security Interests," one of the memos was titled. In it, Reno had taken the unusual step, in a high-level communiqué, of urging Freeh to "immediately develop the capacity" to search its own files, analyze security threats, and share information both internally and with other agencies—weaknesses that she believed were imperiling the FBI's ability to combat terrorism and espionage. "I think our national security requires that we get started immediately on this effort," Reno wrote. Reno and her senior aides had pushed the FBI for years, without much obvious success, to get off the dime in fixing its computer systems and bolstering its analytical capabilities. The failure was one of her great regrets in leaving office. Now, she said, it was up to Ashcroft. He took the memos and handed them to one of his aides. "Well," he told Reno, "I hadn't expected to get much of substance out of this meeting." The comment struck Reno as odd, even dismissive. She wondered whether Ashcroft realized just how serious a problem at the FBI he was inheriting.

What if anything Ashcroft did with Reno's warnings in his first months as attorney general is unclear. Within days of taking office, Ashcroft was distracted by another pressing national security priority at the FBI—the discovery of an FBI mole in the bureau's midst. But when it came to terrorism, senior officials at the FBI found him strikingly uninterested in his first months in office. That summer of 2001, the terrorism chatter in the intelligence community was "blinking red," as CIA director George Tenet would later say. The FBI was seeing an increase in chatter too; officials there figured al Qaeda was up to something big, but exactly who, where, or when was difficult to pin down. FBI officials weren't even sure whether the target was overseas or on U.S. soil. But there was enough chatter, enough buzz, that Tom Pickard, the acting FBI director after Louis Freeh's departure, held conference calls with the special agents in charge of each of his field offices that July and let them know about the increased nervousness at headquarters about possible attacks. But when Pickard briefed Ashcroft on the bureau's terrorism concerns, Pickard found him oddly unresponsive. After two such briefings about terrorist threat information, Pickard said Ashcroft told him that "he did not want to hear this information anymore."

Where Reno would make personal visits to the FBI to debrief agents about the details of secret wiretap applications they wanted her to sign in terrorism cases, Ashcroft seemed more bothered than anything by the task. Ashcroft complained that the bureaucrats were allowing the warrant requests to bottle up, then rushing to get his signature at all hours of the night as court deadlines neared for extending the ninety-day window on wiretaps. In fact, several wiretaps early in Ashcroft's tenure in 2001 had required hurried trips to the attorney general's ranch in Missouri—where he would often fly out from Washington to spend his weekends—so that underlings from the Justice Department and the FBI could get his signature. Several of the hastily scheduled visits did not go well. An annoyed Ashcroft would leave his visitors outside on the porch with barely a word, and notice soon filtered down to rank-and-file intelligence agents and lawyers that after-hours applications for wiretaps were frowned upon in Ashcroft's office except under the most dire of circumstances. Otherwise, they should follow a strict nine-to-five schedule if they wanted the attorney general's attention.

Ashcroft would hotly dispute Tom Pickard's account about the attorney general's purported lack of interest in terrorism before 9/11, insisting that he was constantly "pulsing" the FBI that summer for information on terrorism and was pushing the White House on ways to capture or kill bin Laden months beforehand. Terrorism, Ashcroft maintained, was a top priority of his long before the Twin Towers fell. Funding the fight, however, was a different matter. In May of 2001, Ashcroft's budget people began putting together their proposals for the next fiscal year. The preliminary listing of the department's top fiscal priorities made no mention of counterterrorism. Dale Watson, then the FBI's head of counterterrorism, said he "almost fell out of his chair" when he saw the budget guidance because of the stark omission. The counterterrorism budget was essentially flat. The FBI had asked for an extra $58 million for 149 new counterterrorism field agents, two hundred intelligence analysts, and fifty-four more translators—all critical areas in the fight against terrorism. Ashcroft's people at Main Justice nixed the increases in their budget plan. Pickard appealed directly to Ashcroft. These were critical areas that needed more money,

Pickard told Ashcroft pleadingly. The attorney general told him to put his appeal in writing. He did, but the answer came back the same: no go. Ashcroft's budget package went over to the White House, minus the requested increases sought by the FBI for tracking terrorism. The date was September 10, 2001.

By the next morning, there was no longer any dispute over where terrorism ranked as a Justice Department priority. Ashcroft was headed to Milwaukee with a few of his aides in a private plane. Reno and other attorneys general before her had usually flown commercial, but Ashcroft, in another break from tradition that grated at FBI officials, began insisting on borrowing the bureau's plane for his events. Just as President Bush was reading "The Pet Goat" to schoolchildren in Florida, Ashcroft was scheduled to read to schoolchildren in Wisconsin as part of a White House literacy campaign. As his plane was passing over Lake Michigan, word came that the Justice Department's command center needed to speak with the attorney general immediately. Ashcroft placed the call, and his ruddy face turned ashen. He began scribbling notes on the back of the remarks he was supposed to deliver that day. *Tower has been hit... Second tower has been hit.* He ordered the pilot to turn the plane around, as he told the handful of his aides aboard the plane what had happened. "Our world has changed forever," he told them.

Whatever apathy Ashcroft may have displayed toward terrorism issues before 9/11, the attacks on the World Trade Center changed him forever too. Before the attacks, some Justice Department aides had seen him as listless and adrift at the helm of the department following the bloodletting of his confirmation battle in the Senate. Now, he had a mission—"Don't ever let this happen again," Bush had told him—and he attacked it with abandon. Before, the FBI saw him as a distant and disinterested boss on terrorism matters. Now, Ashcroft was at the FBI every day, alongside Bob Mueller at the SIOC command center to monitor threat reports as they filtered in by the minute; he even claimed as his own a small office suite adjoining the FBI command center. Before, he had been a fist-pounding advocate of privacy rights and railed against Big Brother tactics by law enforcement. In one congressional hearing on privacy rights and computer encryption policy that he chaired as a senator in 1998, Ashcroft declared: "There has been an insistence that we turn over the keys to our individual pri-

vacy to the federal government, but there has been no talk about safeguards or privacy. Apparently, innocent citizens are expected to trust
the bureaucracy not to abuse them." The Founding Fathers, he said,
recognized the balance between personal privacy and the needs of law
enforcement. "In no way," he said, "did they favor the notion that a key
to every home, diary, bank account, medical record, business plan or
investment should be provided to the federal government for use without the individual's knowledge." Now, after 9/11, Ashcroft would
become, ironically enough, the engine in unleashing the power of the
FBI to comb through vast amounts of personal data in pursuit of the
next Mohamed Atta, literally sweeping up records from an entire city's
hotels if it meant stopping a possible attack—real or unlikely—on a
tourist target in Las Vegas or Boston. Things were different now,
Ashcroft reasoned. "The rules of engagement had changed," he said.

One Sunday a few weeks after the 9/11 attacks, senior leaders at the
Justice Department got an urgent call from the Justice Department
command center. Some of them were just leaving church when they
got word that Ashcroft was summoning them for a mandatory secret
meeting that evening at a secure, debugged conference room at the
Justice Department. A few officials had to scurry back to Washington
from out of town to make it in time. They figured something big was
up. Larry Thompson, the number two at the department, was there.
So were Bob Mueller from the FBI, Mike Chertoff from the Criminal
Division, Asa Hutchinson from the Drug Enforcement Administration, and Jim Ziglar from INS, along with all the other key lieutenants
in the new fight against terrorism. Ashcroft walked into the room last
and began talking in somber tones about the fragile state of the country at this moment in its history. "When a patient has a heart attack,"
he said, "you don't know if they'll survive or not." It was the immediate
after-care, he said, that often determined the patient's fate. "Well," he
continued, "America has had a heart attack, and whether we're going
to survive or not is in question." He was concerned that the department leaders would lose their focus, would take their eye off the ball,
would forget the horror of what had just happened all too quickly. This
was a time for unity and teamwork, he said, not for division. He was
particularly agitated about the threat of media leaks. If anyone was
thinking of going public with any concerns about how this war was to
be prosecuted, he cautioned, they should best save it for their memoirs.

At rapt attention, his listeners kept waiting for the punch line, the big announcement or policy shift or intelligence lead that had brought them to the secure conference room under such urgent circumstances. It never came. No one was quite certain what to make of the performance. It was a Rorschach ink-blot test of sorts, all dependent on one's view of Ashcroft. Some in the room saw the performance as inspiring, a rally-the-troops moment typical of a man who liked to lead his U.S. attorneys on personal walking tours of Washington's monuments to impress upon them the strong grip of history. Other listeners saw it as strangely anticlimactic, the urgent but scattershot musings of a man they worried might be on the verge of some sort of nervous breakdown from sheer exhaustion. Whatever the impact, the moment was classic Ashcroft, an outsized personality who savored the spotlight and now found himself at the forefront of a historic fight.

In the coming weeks and months, Ashcroft, his team of deputies, and senior national security officials at the White House would fine-tune their "preemptive" terrorism strategy in the effort to deter another attack. "Spitting on sidewalks," Ashcroft called the strategy. It was an obscure reference, borrowed from Bobby Kennedy four decades earlier when he paced the halls of the Justice Department as attorney general to his brother. Amid rising concerns about organized crime in the 1960s, RFK had vowed to nail the mobsters for "spitting on sidewalks"—arresting them on the most trivial of charges if that's what it took to get them behind bars. It was like jailing Al Capone for tax evasion. Now, Ashcroft vowed to use the same sledgehammer against a different enemy. "Let the terrorists among us be warned," Ashcroft declared in a speech to the U.S. Conference of Mayors six weeks after the attacks. "If you overstay your visa—even by one day—we will arrest you. If you violate a local law, you will be put in jail and kept in custody as long as possible. We will use every available statute. We will seek every prosecutorial advantage. We will use all our weapons within the law and under the Constitution to protect life and enhance security for America."

So it was, for instance, that a Muslim man working with one Saudi charity in Virginia who had suspected links to terrorist financing was arrested and ultimately deported. Abdullah Alnoshan's crime? When he filled out his immigration papers in 2002, he had asserted that he was coming to the United States to become the public relations representative and religious affairs director for the Muslim World League. In fact, he had become the actual director of the group, not just its PR representative, and that tiny misrepresentation, the government charged in an odd "gotcha" moment, amounted to immigration fraud. The authorities didn't have enough evidence to charge him with anything remotely connected to terrorism, but one more suspect was off the streets.

The strategy was provocative and powerful. After all, who wouldn't want terrorists off the streets on whatever charge the government could muster? But it ultimately rested on a shaky foundation; it assumed, almost as a matter of faith, that the terrorist suspects identified by the government were in fact involved in terrorism, and that they needed to be locked up on the smallest of infractions in order to protect the public. In fact, many of the hundreds of suspects swept up in terrorism investigations were not involved in terrorism at all. Most of the time, they were guilty of nothing more than spitting on Ashcroft's proverbial sidewalk—entering the wrong title on an immigration form, using a fake ID at an airport baggage job, overstaying a visa by a day or a week or a month. And for that, they were treated in the new justice system as possible terrorists.

For Ashcroft, immigration became the battering ram in his war on terror. Bush himself, who reached out to Hispanic voters in the 2000 election, would adopt a much softer tone when it came to the hot-button issue of immigration, but his attorney general was not one to pander. Among Ashcroft's base of conservative political supporters, the scourge of illegal immigration was red meat, and he and his senior aides knew it. Ashcroft would order "voluntary" interviews with five thousand Middle Easterners, despite the objections of law enforcement officials who considered it a waste of time. He would restructure the immigration courts to cut backlogs and speed deportations, pushing out liberal-leaning judges along the way. And, making good on a Bush campaign promise to minority voters, Ashcroft's Justice Department would issue new policy guidelines that banned racial profiling in routine police investigations—but that carved out a gaping exemption for singling out ethnic groups in national security investigations. Under the policy, minorities could not be singled out for traffic stops and the like simply because of their race; but Middle Easterners boarding a plane in California, for instance, could be subjected to increased scrutiny if the government had information suggesting that a plot was underway. To Ashcroft and his senior aides, the hard-line approach to immigration was the small cost of protecting America in the post-9/11 age, a commonsense approach to a historic crisis. To civil rights advocates, however, it smacked of racial profiling and xenophobia. "We have decided to trade off the liberty of immigrants—particularly Arabs and Muslims—for the purported security of the majority," said David Cole, an immigration rights advocate and noted legal scholar at Georgetown University.

Bush and Ashcroft were casting the struggle against terrorism as one of good versus evil, a global clash of cultures depicted in often starkly religious terms. Bush himself seemed startled by the backlash from Muslims he met around the world. "Do they really believe that we think all Muslims are terrorists?" a puzzled Bush asked his staff after meeting privately with a group of moderate Islamic leaders in Indonesia in 2003. The administration's rhetoric put the FBI in a particularly difficult spot, as the bureau was seeking to improve its frayed relations with American Muslims and develop better intelligence leads. Ashcroft did not help matters when he gave an interview in early 2002 to conservative columnist Cal Thomas. "Islam is a religion in which God requires you to send your son to die for him. Christianity is a faith in which God sends his son to die for you," Ashcroft was quoted as saying. Ashcroft's staff quickly moved to distance him from the incendiary remarks, but for many Muslim immigrants, the dustup only confirmed their worst fears about the us-versus-them theocracy that seemed to have taken hold in Washington. They were now considered the enemy.

The hard-edged approach to immigration caused deep divisions within the Justice Department as well, as immigration officials clashed often with Ashcroft's close circle of advisors. Bo Cooper, general counsel at the INS both before and after 9/11, thought the administration's approach amounted to a "scorched earth" policy. He and Kris Kobach, a senior aide to Ashcroft on immigration matters, would get into heated disagreements about just how far-flung the net for terrorists should reach. Cooper would argue that the INS was wasting resources and, more important, public credibility by using the hunt for terrorists as a pretext to round up Middle Eastern and Asian immigrants who might be in the country illegally. Kobach countered that the prospect of getting the one true terrorist suspect in the mix outweighed the costs. "If you can stop just one tower from coming down," he told INS lawyers in one particularly contentious discussion, "it will be worth it." Those like Cooper who questioned the policies on legal and operational grounds found themselves quickly ostracized, cut off from the debate. "You were either for national security, or you were against it," Cooper said later.

One particular flash point, unknown publicly at the time, came over the Bush administration's efforts to enlist and effectively "deputize" local cops and sheriff's deputies to act as immigration agents in detaining suspected illegal immigrants even on civil violations. Many local police chiefs were dead-set against the idea because they thought it would hurt local crime-fighting efforts by turning them into immigration cops in the eyes of immigrants, both legal and illegal, whom they relied on for help and cooperation. At the INS, lawyers saw a bigger problem: they believed that unless Congress specifically authorized the idea, the policy would be illegal based on a 1996 opinion on the issue from the Justice Department's own Office of Legal Counsel, the binding word on matters of legal interpretation throughout the executive branch. The Justice Department, anxious to move ahead with the idea, ordered up another legal opinion from the Office of Legal Council after 9/11. The draft version came back the same: the Justice Department couldn't deputize local police as immigration agents without congressional authorization. Ashcroft's advisors weren't happy. They signaled that OLC might review the issue yet again before finalizing the opinion. A new version landed on Bo Cooper's desk on a Friday. Cooper was astounded. It was a 180-degree reversal from the earlier draft opinion of just a few weeks earlier; it now concluded that the 1996 memo was mistaken and that local police could in fact act as immigration agents without the specific okay of Congress.

Cooper spent the weekend poring over the new OLC opinion and preparing a memo refuting a policy position that he thought was both shortsighted and legally impermissible. It was not the outcome that bothered him, so much as the end run process used to get there. Congress had put in place a specific and detailed process for setting up programs to allow local cops to act as immigration agents, including a checklist of safeguards requiring training, certification, and high-level supervision. Now, in the view of Cooper, Ashcroft's advisors wanted to bypass Congress and throw the door open to deputizing all local cops, almost willy-nilly, by ordering up a new legal opinion. Cooper dashed off his rebuttal and sent it to Main Justice. He never heard back from anyone. By Monday, the new legal opinion had become final, reversing the old one. It was now, for better or worse, the official legal position of the U.S. government.

Relations were also becoming even tenser between Ashcroft and his immigration chief, Jim Ziglar. Ziglar's impromptu speech reminding his Justice Department colleagues about "this thing called the Constitution" on the day of 9/11 had not ingratiated him with Ashcroft's people, and the standoff over the FBI's "hold until release" policy for 9/11 detainees set the stage for another series of heated run-ins over immigration policy. Ashcroft and his aides would attack the INS as increasingly dysfunctional under Ziglar's brief reign, and the agency suffered another very public embarrassment in March of 2002 when it was reported that a Florida flight training school had received routine visa extension notices for two of the September 11 hijackers, Mohamed Atta and Marwan al-Shehhi, six months after they killed themselves. Under siege, Ziglar acknowledged his agency's many shortcomings and its often conflicting missions, but he felt Ashcroft and the administration had made him and the INS the fall guys in the Atta visa mess for a communications breakdown by one of the INS's private contractors. He threatened to resign, agreeing only grudgingly to stay on.

All the while, Ashcroft and his senior aides were kicking around a controversial plan to require tens of thousands of foreign students, teachers, researchers, and others inside the country legally—mostly young Muslim men from countries in the Middle East and other regions that had suspected ties to terrorism—to register with the INS. Ziglar and his people opposed the as yet unannounced plan, warning that it would pose an enormous drain on the resources of an agency already struggling to seal the borders. Worse, Ziglar warned, it risked alienating the country's legal immigrants over a policy he thought would do little to find actual terrorists. "This is never gonna work," Ziglar said at one contentious meeting with Ashcroft's aides. "How many people you think who are really terrorists or criminals are actually going to show up?"

The debate dragged on until one day in June of 2002 when Barbara Comstock, Ashcroft's PR person, summoned Ziglar at the last minute to the Justice Department for a press event that was to involve immigration. Ziglar wasn't clear on what exactly the topic was supposed to be, and Comstock was cryptic, even evasive. He arrived at Ashcroft's fifth-floor office to find the attorney general wrapping up a meeting with his senior staff. Ashcroft walked out of his office and patted Ziglar on the back. "Jim, I'd like you to come up to the press conference with me," he said. Ziglar was still trying to figure out what was actually being announced in such a hurried fashion, and what he was doing there, but he got only blank stares. Ziglar went with Ashcroft and his aides to the waiting area outside the press room on the seventh floor. As the door to the press room opened, he was directed to follow Ashcroft inside. To his surprise, no one else followed. It was just him and the attorney general.

Ashcroft took to the podium and began speaking, cameras rolling. "Good afternoon. I want to thank INS Commissioner Jim Ziglar for not only being here today, but for his service to the United States of America." He then moved on to the big news of the day: the Justice Department and the INS were announcing a far-reaching plan to begin that fall to fingerprint, photograph, and register some 100,000 foreign visitors, the biggest and most aggressive foreign registration program in decades. The plan, Ashcroft said from the podium, "will expand substantially America's scrutiny of those foreign visitors who may pose a national security concern and enter our country, and it will provide a vital line of defense in the war against terrorism." Behind him on stage, Ziglar stood in stunned silence. Without even telling the INS of his intentions beforehand, the attorney general was announcing an immigration plan that the agency itself had actively opposed. And Ziglar was up there on stage as a prop. He stood almost motionless, staring at the floor. After Ashcroft finished rolling out the plan and taking a few questions, a reporter in the audience asked if Ziglar could address the question of how the INS planned to fund the ambitious plan. Ashcroft interjected. "I think I've answered it very clearly," the attorney general said.

Ziglar didn't say a word for the entire press conference. His agency had no plan on how this program was supposed to work, much less how it would be funded, and now he was being handed an albatross of an operation and told, on live television, to make it work. He was still fuming as he and Ashcroft left the stage together. Afterward, he confronted Ashcroft. "This was the worst drive-by shooting I've ever witnessed," he told the attorney general. That night, he went home and let his wife know that his long-sought "exit strategy" from the Bush administration had just been determined for him. There was no way he could stay, not after what had just happened. Two months later, he turned in his letter of resignation to the White House. Shunning protocol, he did not bother giving the letter in advance to Ashcroft, his boss, before putting out a press release. Following the public announcement that Ziglar was stepping down, Ashcroft put out a brief statement of his own. "Commissioner Ziglar has served the administration and the Department of Justice admirably during a very important time under extraordinarily difficult circumstances. We appreciate his commitment and service to the country," Ashcroft said. Ziglar went off to do a fellowship at Harvard focusing on the country's rich heritage of immigration and the civil liberties implications of 9/11.

The foreign registration program went on without him, sowing lawsuits, confusion, large-scale public protests by legal immigrants, and backed-up lines at INS offices. Even the basics of publicly posting government notices in advance of the registration proved a disaster; the Arabic version of the announcements was written backward—left to right, with both the words and letters in inverse order—so the instructions telling Middle Easterners when and where to report for photographing and fingerprinting were reduced to utter gibberish before anyone even noticed. The next year, after the Department of Homeland Security created by Bush and Congress had inherited the much ballyhooed foreigner registration program from the Justice Department, officials there suspended its major elements; they decided their resources could be better spent on other counterterrorism measures, and the 9/11 Commission would find little evidence to support the claim that the registration program turned up any actual terror suspects among the many thousands who registered. To Ashcroft, the rollback of the registration program was a dangerous mistake that made the country more vulnerable to "potential incursions of the enemy." To Ziglar, the move was small consolation, welcome but too long overdue. "Cooler heads prevailed," he said, "but the damage was already done. The program was a nightmare."

. . .

THE THOUSANDS OF MUSLIM men jailed by American authorities in the early months and years after 9/11 registered but a blip on the American psyche. They were someone else's problem. They were foreign-looking men with foreign-sounding names, out of sight and out of mind in immigration holding cells in Brooklyn, in an old county jail in Appalachia, in a military naval base in Cuba. They were not one of us. Then came Brandon Mayfield. He was one of them and, at the same time, one of us. Raised in a farmhouse in rural Kansas, the son of Irish-German parents, Mayfield went off to join the Army and served for eight years through 1995, becoming a lieutenant. It was at Fort Lewis in Washington State that he met Mona, an Egyptian-born immigrant who had come to the United States at the age of five with her family. They married, and so began his conversion to Islam.

Even in the Army, Mayfield had developed a certain affinity for the Muslim people. Stationed in Germany, he became the unofficial foster parent for a family of Muslim refugees from Bosnia who were living near the base, giving them flour and sugar and lining up donations from other servicemen. He never detected much hostility from the other soldiers over his newfound faith. If anything, it was an interesting curiosity, a conversation starter. When he first arrived to take over a maintenance platoon, one of the soldiers had called him "comrade" out of apparent respect. "Oh, how interesting that you're a Muslim," the soldier said to him. "We just had a Muslim who left as a platoon leader." The outgoing platoon leader, it turned out, was a man named James Yee, and he had left to become a chaplain. Yee was anonymous then, but years later, he too would be accused of aiding the terrorists before the case against him collapsed. This was the weird six degrees of al Qaeda suspects at work; one Muslim soldier replaced by another.

After leaving the Army, Mayfield was trying to figure out what to do with the rest of his life. A stern, quiet, serious-minded young man, he had read a book about the Constitution called *We Hold These Truths*, by philosopher Mortimer Adler, and it got him thinking about going to law school and becoming a lawyer. His mistrust of the government had begun to harden by then; efforts in Congress to strengthen antiterrorism laws in 1996 after the Oklahoma City bombings even prompted him to write a letter of concern to the local paper. He figured the politicians were just looking for a way to scare people and fan fears about Muslims and others. By the time 9/11 hit, Mayfield was, in many ways, living a typical American middle-class life, working as a lawyer in coastal Oregon, with his children going to good public schools and playing sports on leafy fields. But he was also an active member of the local mosque, attending most Fridays to worship, and that set him apart.

The Muslim community in Oregon was rocked in 2002 by the high-profile arrests of members of the so-called Portland Seven, a group ultimately convicted on terrorism-related charges for traveling to China and trying to aid the Taliban in Afghanistan. Mayfield had even represented one of the men, Jeffrey Battle, in a nasty child custody dispute. As a lawyer, Mayfield would get pulled aside by others in his mosque who wanted advice on what to do about the increasingly frequent inquiries they were getting from the FBI after 9/11. Some members of the mosque even suspected they were being followed. Valid or make-believe, there was a palpable sense among many in the mosque that they were all now under scrutiny.

Then, one afternoon in April of 2004, Mayfield was working on a case at his small, solo law office when he got a call from his wife, who had just gotten home with two of their three children and had trouble getting in the house. "Did you leave the door bolted?" she asked, annoyed. "No," he told her, "you must have bolted it." There was a pause. "No, I didn't," she said firmly. Another pause. "Well," he said finally, "how could it be bolted then?" He retraced his steps from that morning. He was the last one to leave the house, but he couldn't figure out what had happened. Mayfield didn't think much of it, not at first. Then, a week or so later, came another call to his office from his wife. This time, she sounded more alarmed than exasperated. "The door's bolted again," she told him. She must be imagining things, he told her. "I'm not crazy," she shot back. As proof, she put their fifteen-year-old son on the line for corroboration. "Here, Shane, tell your dad it's bolted."

Now Mayfield was alarmed too. "Listen, go in and look very carefully for anything out of place," he told her. "Look for anything that's moved or suspicious." Sure enough, they found what looked to be a few telltale clues. The blinds, open before, had now been drawn. The light on the VCR was blinking, as if the power had been turned off. And a large footprint was visible on a freshly vacuumed carpet upstairs, a strange sight in a Muslim home where everyone knew to take off their shoes at the door out of religious observance. Mayfield called the police. A dispatcher told him he'd have to come into the station in person to file a report. He didn't bother. He wasn't sure it was worth his time. Whatever had happened, he didn't figure it was a burglary. After all, nothing was missing that they could tell. No, this was something else, something different. Then he remembered a strange episode at his office a few days earlier, when his computer kept crashing on him. His son, the techie in the family, had looked it over. "Dad," Shane told him, "it looks like someone took the hard drive out and put it back wrong."

Mayfield began to think he was being followed too—by a van with a business logo on it, maybe, or an SUV. Driving to his office, he would abruptly pull into a driveway and turn around, or stop in a parking lot for a few minutes to see if someone was trailing him. Driving home, he would circle around the block a few times before slowly pulling into the driveway. Then, about a week after Shane had noticed the computer tampering, the boy was home sick from school when he wandered downstairs from his room at noontime to get something to eat. Outside, he noticed a man in his thirties in casual clothing walking up to the door. There was no knock, just a jiggling of the doorknob. Someone was trying to get inside the house. Shaken, the boy didn't stick around to see who it was. He scurried upstairs through the back of the house and made his way through a crawl space to the attic. He had taken the phone with him and, just then, his Aunt Naveen in Kansas called, looking for his mother. "Someone's breaking into the house right now!" Shane whispered from his alcove. "You need to call the police, call your mother," his aunt implored. Mona hurried home, then Brandon. Whoever had been there was gone. Mayfield called the utility companies. Had anyone been out to the house that day? No, came the response. "It's probably nothing, it could have been anybody," he told his wife and son that night, struggling to inject a father's calming reassurance to a household that was becoming more unhinged by the day. Even as he said it, he didn't believe it himself. Something was going on.

The next time, they knocked. "FBI," said the man on the other side of the door at Brandon Mayfield's law office at the end of the dark first-floor hallway. Mayfield opened the door a crack to see who it was—two agents, a man and a woman. They wanted to ask him some questions, they announced. Mayfield didn't know what to think, but his mind veered to a lecture he'd attended at Portland State University by Stanley Cohen, a flamboyant and controversial, ponytailed defense lawyer from New York, who advised local Muslims on how to respond to the FBI or any other law enforcement officials who might come around the mosque asking questions. "Just say no; they're not your friends" was the message Mayfield took away from the lecture. In a different climate, there may have been a chance for a dialogue. Not now.

In the eyes of many Muslims like Mayfield, the FBI was their adversary, the hunter and the hunted. A student at Harvard University would tell Bob Mueller as much to his face at a lecture a few years later, describing in plaintive terms for the FBI director the "virtual internment" of Muslim-looking people in America and the scrutiny they felt. Whatever trust may have existed in the immediate aftermath of 9/11 had now evaporated by the time the agents came knocking at Brandon Mayfield's door. Some FBI officials realized the relationship had turned poisonous and urged that the bureau do more outreach, mend fences—not just for the sake of PR, but as a matter of good law enforcement. Without the Muslim community as an ally willing to report the true bad apples, they realized, the bureau was hamstrung. But the effort to do outreach was killed for lack of funding; the FBI's unending computer problems, it seemed, were draining much of its extra cash. And so the relationship continued to languish, and the tensions continued to grow. When the FBI comes calling, attorney Cohen had urged his audience that night in Portland, don't answer their questions; get everything in writing. Mayfield had turned around and given the same advice to the worshippers at the local mosque when they would ask him for legal advice about FBI queries of their own. Now, as he peered through the crack in the door at the FBI, he took his own counsel.

"Any questions you have, give me them in writing and I'll get back to you," Mayfield said. The agents asked to come in. "I don't want you in my office. I have client files in here. I don't want to talk with you." He tried to close the door. The lead agent had his foot in the crack of the door to prop it open. The agents' marching orders were to try to talk to Mayfield, interview him and find out what he knew, maybe even get him to cooperate with them. Only if he balked were they to arrest him. Now, the agents clearly had an uncooperative witness blocking the office door. They pushed it open. "We have a warrant for your arrest," the lead agent announced. The next few moments were a blur for Mayfield, as the agents cuffed him, sat him down at a small desk in his entryway, and announced that they were taking him into custody and executing simultaneous search warrants on his office, his car, and his home. At the house, Mona was watching in disbelief as the agents combed through their lives. The agents knew their way around. Confirming the family's worst suspicions about the strange events of the last few weeks, they would learn that the FBI had executed several covert searches at the house, approved under a warrant from the Foreign Intelligence Surveillance (FISA) Court, which was created in 1978 to oversee secret spy and terrorism investigations. The FBI had secretly photographed dozens of items, "mirrored" computers for the contents, and taken samples of everything from nail clippings to a half-dozen cigarette butts as possible DNA evidence.

Meantime, Brandon's mother in Kansas called Mona at home, alarmed by the presence of FBI agents at her door asking questions about her son. "What do we do?" his mother asked. "Where's Brandon?" As Mona watched the FBI fill up six boxes of evidence—CDs, computers, checkbooks, a couple of guns; this time, all done in the open—another phone call came to the house for her. It was *Newsweek*'s Michael Isikoff, a dogged, well-sourced reporter who had uncovered the Monica Lewinsky scandal inside the Clinton White House six years before. He wanted to know about Mayfield's possible connection to a terrorism investigation. The word was out. At Mayfield's office, meanwhile, the agents placed a copy of the arrest warrant on the desk in front of the young lawyer for him to read. On a wall nearby hung two copies of the Bill of Rights, Amendments One through Five, and next to it Six through Ten. Mayfield had recently had the two printouts enlarged to poster size at a local copy shop and framed them.

As he sat at the desk, an old shoulder injury agitated by the tight handcuffs, he tried to maneuver the pages of the arrest warrant in front of him with his cuffed hands so he could read them. The words were a blur. The lead agent read aloud from the search warrant, listing the items the FBI was authorized to seek. In a daze, the words sounded almost incoherent to Mayfield, like some foreign film desperately in search of subtitles, but a few snippets jumped out at him: the FBI was looking for any detonators and blasting caps hidden in the office. Detonators and blasting caps? Mayfield stared at the agent. What the hell is going on here?

This is all a mistake, Mayfield thought to himself as the agents led him away to an unmarked black SUV, with a few neighbors in the office complex parking lot peering through the stained windows in wonder. He figured he would be back at the office by afternoon to finish up his work. He even knew the judge who was to handle his initial appearance in court. But once in federal lockdown, irons around his ankles, he finally read through the arrest warrant for the first time with a clear head. It was only then that he began to realize just why he was there: the Justice Department had somehow matched his fingerprint to one taken from a plastic bag at the scene of the massive railway bombings two months earlier in Madrid, a horrific attack that ranked as the worst terrorist attack in Europe since World War II. The coordinated blasts had killed 191 people and injured some two thousand. And the FBI thought Mayfield was in on it. No way am I making it back to the office this afternoon, Mayfield thought to himself. I could be here a long, long time.

Newsweek broke the story that day on its Web site. By the next day, Mayfield's name was prominent in more than 125 news reports around the world, reaching tens of millions of people from Oregon to China. "U.S. Lawyer's Prints Found on Bag Linked to Madrid Bombings," read the headline on a dispatch from France's main news service, Agence France-Presse. I wrote the *Times*' story on the arrest with help from a reporter in Portland and, like just about everyone else, we ran the news prominently on the front page. I was well aware of the Justice Department's growing fondness for using material witness arrest warrants to hold people on what often proved to be negligible suspicions, but this case, at first glance, seemed like a pretty good one. The FBI had managed to bungle lots of things over the years—translations, computer programs, bullet-lead tracing analysis, DNA—but fingerprint matching was about as basic and foolproof as it got. And officials at the FBI were telling me that they had found this guy's fingerprints right there on a mysterious bag loaded with detonators in Madrid near the scene of the crime. That was tough to refute.

There was only one problem. The print didn't actually belong to Mayfield. Spanish authorities, we would learn only later, had warned the FBI's lab people in Quantico, Virginia, for weeks prior to Mayfield's arrest that they had the wrong match, that the print lifted from a blue bag containing seven copper detonators inside a van near the bombings did not belong to their Oregon suspect. Besides, the Spaniards were looking at a bunch of Moroccans in connection with the bombings; it seemed "so out of character," Spanish authorities said, for an American to somehow be involved with that group. The FBI wasn't swayed. Working off a questionable copy of the latent print from the blue bag, the FBI's forensics people were convinced that they had a "100 percent" match; a computer search of millions of fingerprints in an FBI database had produced twenty possible matches, or "candidates," and an FBI forensics examiner, eyeing them side by side, had matched Mayfield's print conclusively with latent fingerprint number 17 taken from the blue bag. But what about the odd pattern in the upper left corner of LFP 17? It didn't seem to match with Mayfield's. The examiners explained it away: it must have been the overlap from someone else's print on top of Mayfield's. An FBI forensics team even flew to Madrid from Virginia to convince the skeptical Spanish scientists that they were the ones who had it wrong. When the Spaniards countered with the negative forensic tests of their own to try to debunk the Mayfield match, the FBI wouldn't take no for an answer. "They had a justification for everything," Pedro Luis Mélida Lledó, the head of the Spanish fingerprint unit, said after meeting with the FBI officials.

Spanish officials weren't the only ones with doubts. FBI investigators out in the field thought they had plenty of circumstantial evidence to raise suspicions: Mayfield attended the same mosque as several men from the Portland Seven convicted in the plot to aid the Taliban, he had represented Jeffrey Battle in the custody dispute, and his law practice was listed in a Muslim yellow pages. An FBI affidavit would even mention that the yellow pages were published by someone with a purported connection to Osama bin Laden. Again, the six degrees of al Qaeda at work. There was a lot of smoke. Still, there was nothing linking Mayfield directly to the Madrid bombings. In fact, there was no record to suggest that he had traveled abroad recently; he didn't even have a current passport. The links to the actual bombings were so tenuous—and the FBI's six-week, round-the-clock surveillance of Mayfield so unrevealing—that some FBI investigators were beginning to suspect that Mayfield, if he had any involvement at all, might have somehow touched the blue bag by happenstance in Oregon before someone else at his mosque took it to Spain. Even with the purported fingerprint match, "the problem is there is not enough evidence to arrest him on a criminal charge," Beth Anne Steele, an official in the FBI's Portland office, admitted in an e-mail to a colleague the day before Mayfield was taken into custody. But the FBI was nervous that word was leaking out about their Portland suspect; a reporter for the *Los Angeles Times* in Paris had already begun calling around to European officials about a supposed American fingerprint match. If word got out, FBI officials feared, Mayfield might start destroying evidence, or flee altogether. "There is a plan to arrest him as a material witness if and when he gets outed by the media," Steele advised her colleague.

There were other complications for the FBI even before the arrest: Mayfield seemed to be on to them. His FBI trailers had noticed his odd driving habits of late, the U-turns and cruises around the block, as if he were trying to avoid surveillance, and they had noticed Mona with a pair of binoculars in the parking lot of her husband's office, as if she was trying to spot someone off in the distance. Worried the case could be blown, the FBI sped up its timetable and moved in on Mayfield for the arrest at his office, putting the cuffs on him. Their suspect was off the streets, with no risk of his fleeing, and now the feds could worry about building a case against him. As he sat in solitary confinement in a county jail cell, Brandon Mayfield knew nothing of the contretemps within the FBI over his arrest or of the lab's tense dispute with Spanish counterparts. What he knew was that fingerprint evidence was tough to disprove and, if he were to be charged criminally in the Madrid bombings and convicted for the crime—even though he had nothing to do with it—he would face the death penalty. Short of that dire scenario, he knew too that if he refused to testify before the grand jury as a material witness, he would be looking at jail time; and if he *did* agree to talk to the grand jury but said something misleading that the FBI could seize on to accuse him of making a false statement, he could be prosecuted and go to prison for that too.

The grim choices, and the pitfalls growing out of them, were dizzying. He mulled them all over as he waited in a holding area on May 20, exactly two weeks after his arrest. None of the options looked good. Another hearing was scheduled that day, and he had to decide what he was going to do. He anguished over the impact of all this on his children. School officials at Shane's high school were keeping a close eye on the boy because they worried about threats against him from the other kids. At home, when Mayfield would appear on TV on the local news, his twelve-year-old daughter would tearfully touch his face on the television screen as she saw images of him segued with the horrific scenes from the Madrid bombings. How much longer could he stay away from his children? Mayfield didn't know what he was going to do. He wanted to talk to Mona before going into the courtroom, to go over their legal options and figure out what was best for him and his family. He'd asked to see his wife in the holding area before the hearing, but she was nowhere to be found.

Instead, his public defender, Steve Wax, walked in excitedly. He had news, big news: the Spaniards had identified an Algerian man as a match to the mysterious fingerprint on the blue bag. The FBI and the Justice Department were backing down; grudgingly, they had come to realize that the notorious latent fingerprint number 17 did not belong to Mayfield at all, and an assistant U.S. attorney had just relayed the news to Wax. Hours later, a judge freed Mayfield from custody after a closed hearing. Changing from his jail-issued uniform into a pair of khaki pants and a blue dress shirt, Mayfield emerged from the courthouse to a crush of cameras. He spoke in English and Arabic, clutching the Koran and a purple Muslim prayer rug. Even if he was convinced that being a Muslim man in America was what landed him in jail in the first place, he wasn't going to run from his faith now. He said a prayer in Arabic. "I want to thank my family and friends who were supporting me through this, what I would call a harrowing ordeal. I just want to say: God is great, there is no God but God."

The FBI apologized—three times, in fact. More than two years after his arrest, the government made good on its apology with a huge financial settlement: $2 million to Mayfield and his family for the pain and embarrassment of his infamy. At least it should cover the legal bills and get the kids through college, Mayfield figured. Investigators at the Justice Department inspector general's office would scrub every facet of the case, trying to determine what had gone so wrong on an investigation so important. In essence, it came down to this: led down a wrong path by the most improbable of false hits on the fingerprint from the blue bag, the FBI wanted to believe it had the right man, and they wanted to believe it too badly. Mayfield's Muslim faith was not a factor in first identifying him as a suspect, the Justice Department investigators concluded; the original examiner did not even know anything about Mayfield's background as he mistakenly matched the print. But, officials acknowledged, Mayfield's religion and his curious connections to known extremists may have helped to irreparably color the rest of the investigation. "I think the fact that he was a Muslim convert," said Karin Immergut, the U.S. attorney in Portland, "couldn't be ignored." Long after Mayfield was freed, FBI officials continued to defend their handling of the investigation. "I think it was exceptional with one exception, and that is the missed fingerprint identification at the laboratory," Gary Bald, head of counterterrorism at the FBI, said in a court deposition. "I think everybody did a great job." The decision to jail Mayfield was the right one "because it was based on the facts that were at hand," Bald said. "Which, unfortunately, turned out not be true."

Except for that fingerprint match. Almost three years to the day after his arrest, I met with Mayfield for a late lunch at a nondescript, half-empty Lebanese restaurant just down Canyon Road from his law office. He'd kept the same small office, but he and his family had recently moved to a new suburban home. Too many memories in the old one, he said. I asked him about the FBI's deeply held contention that, except for the missed fingerprint match, this was a good case, just the kind of painstaking investigative work the bureau needed to be doing after 9/11. Mayfield mulled over the question for a moment or two. "Except . . . for . . . the . . . fingerprint match," he said slowly, punctuating the words as a slight smile crossed his lips. "Except for that fingerprint match . . ." he repeated, his voice trailing off. He started to finish the thought but decided the better of it. Enough had already been said in the last three years. He just shook his head and took a last bite of his chicken kabob. He had to go pick up his son.

CHAPTER THREE

"Don't Embarrass the Bureau"

BASSEM YOUSSEF was sitting in on a Bible study class at a church in suburban Virginia one Wednesday evening when the pastor struck up a conversation with the newcomer about his life and his faith. A born-again Christian, Youssef had been doing a lot of soul-searching of late. Not long before, his career as an FBI agent seemed to be cresting: prestigious awards, "exceptional" performance reviews, the top job in the FBI's Saudi Arabia office in the late 1990s, undercover assignments infiltrating suspected terrorist groups under an Islamic alias and debriefing Middle Eastern suspects. It was all heady stuff for an immigrant who came to Los Angeles from Egypt with his family at age thirteen and whose father had pushed him to become an accountant, not a cop. To add to the pedigree, Youssef was one of the few agents at the FBI fluent in Arabic. Youssef didn't need a translator to listen to the government's secret spy tapes; he could do it himself.

When the September 11 attacks hit, Youssef waited for the phone call—the one he thought was sure to come, the one telling him to suit up for duty on the biggest investigation in bureau history. It never came. He volunteered to supervisors in counterterrorism. No response. Hat in hand, he offered to send managers his "638," the FBI résumé that attested to his bona fides in investigating terrorism. Still, nothing. Eventually, months after the attacks, he was tasked to help run a new, off-the-radar FBI unit called Document Exploitation, or "DocEx," operating what might have been the world's biggest police evidence locker. The FBI wanted agents to be able to sort through the large volumes of material and leads culled from the battlefields of Afghanistan. To Youssef, it was pedestrian work that he figured could be handled by a glorified clerk or a green agent straight out of the academy at Quantico; strictly a "tag and bag" job. He couldn't figure it out. Some of his bosses, he knew, saw him as a bit too eager, a bit too pushy, a bit too much of a self-promoter in the button-down culture of the FBI; he was known to some agents as an "FOL," a "Friend of Louie," a smug nod to the former FBI director, Louis Freeh, who had come to admire Youssef's work in Saudi Arabia. Still, to Youssef, the aftermath of 9/11 seemed like a time to put aside petty internal rivalries. The country was at war, and here he was working the mess hall miles from the front line.

It was a trying time, and as he sat at a small table in the Baptist church at the Wednesday night Bible study in the spring of 2002, he was desperate for a sympathetic ear. He and his wife were first-timers at the Bible class, and the pastor sat down next to them to get acquainted. They talked about both the divine and the secular, and the pastor asked Youssef what he did for a living. Youssef told him he worked at the FBI. The pastor was impressed. "Wow, you must be in demand," he said. "Well," Youssef answered haltingly, "actually, I'm not doing much of anything these days. I'm kind of on the outs with my bosses." The more of Youssef's story he heard, the more flummoxed the pastor became. "You have to let your congressman know," the pastor urged. It was an interesting suggestion, something Youssef hadn't even considered. Except that he didn't even know who his congressman was. Someone named Wolf, he learned. "This is crazy. You really have to go to your congressman," the pastor repeated. Youssef wasn't sure what to do. He asked the pastor to pray for him.

Then, the next morning, he called Wolf's office. Congressmen get hundreds of constituent letters and phone calls every month, the bulk answered in due time by interns or administrative assistants. But Youssef's call got immediate, high-level attention: a senior staff aide to Wolf got on the line and asked him to put together a memo laying out his case. Youssef started to write something out. "I believe that what I have to say relates directly to our country's ability to detect and prevent future terrorist attacks," Youssef wrote in the letter. Now he really had their attention: the congressman wanted to see him personally.

Better yet, Wolf wasn't just any congressman. Youssef didn't realize it until he Googled him, but Frank Wolf was the powerful Republican chairman of a House appropriations panel that oversaw law enforcement, and with the purse strings in his hand, he had instant gravitas with any agency chief come budget time. Wolf liked Bob Mueller personally and respected the job he was doing as FBI director in trying to remake the place. But, like many others, he was still uncertain whether the bureau itself could be fixed, and whether the public was getting much of a return on the massive infusion of new funds it was pouring into the FBI rat hole. As congressional paymaster, Wolf was one vote that would count heavily in that debate.

For nearly two hours, Youssef talked with Wolf in the congressman's Capitol Hill office about his recent frustrations. Wolf couldn't get enough of the story. Youssef laid out his experience in counterterrorism, from investigations into Islamic militants in St. Louis and Los Angeles to liaison work with the Saudi royal family in Riyadh. He talked of how few agents the FBI had who could speak Arabic or understand the culture. "And you're not doing counterterrorism?" Wolf asked, incredulous. "No, sir" came the response. The congressman was incensed. What he did next surprised even Youssef: the congressman wanted a sit-down with Mueller, a face-to-face, to ask him about the bureau's staffing and management decisions. Did the FBI know what it was doing? The seriousness of what Youssef was doing, and the potential impact on his own already stalled career at the FBI, were just now sinking in. "This is bad," he said to his wife that night in their home in Northern Virginia as he recounted the meeting to her.

Yet a few weeks later, on June 28, 2002, there he was back in the waiting room outside Wolf's office, summoned for a 10 a.m. meeting. He got there early. Into the foyer walked Mueller with two aides. Youssef and Mueller had never met, and the agent went to introduce himself to his boss. Mueller looked perplexed, as if he wasn't sure what was going on. He knew Wolf wanted to see him, but the congressman hadn't made clear exactly what was on the agenda. He was soon to find out. Wolf emerged from his office and beckoned the men inside. The congressman showed Mueller to a low-sitting couch in the office. Youssef was seated in a formal chair, looking down at the lanky director perched awkwardly on the low-sitting sofa a few feet away. What have I done? Youssef thought to himself as he squirmed in his seat. Loyalty was an elixir at the FBI going back to the days of J. Edgar Hoover; "Don't embarrass the bureau" was a famous maxim at headquarters, so pervasive a tenet that an ex-FBI-agent-turned-writer made it the title of a novel set in the Hoover era. Long after Hoover was dead, there was still a lingering perception, as Senators Chuck Grassley and Pat Leahy said in a letter to Mueller in another workplace case, that "the F.B.I. will not tolerate criticism from within its ranks." Yet here was a rank-and-file agent about to confront the FBI director in front of a powerful congressman over how the newly christened war on terrorism was being waged and who was being tapped to wage it. Lesser hubris had killed bigger careers.

But with the congressman's prodding, Youssef laid out his case and his concerns—how he was fluent in Arabic, how he had helped infiltrate an Islamist group in Los Angeles, how he had worked on the 1993 World Trade Center bombing investigation and the 1996 Khobar Towers bombings, how he had done nothing of substance connected to terrorism for months after the attacks of September 11, and how he now felt marginalized, inexplicably, at a time when the bureau most needed agents like him. Mueller, respectful if clearly a bit uncomfortable, listened attentively and promised the congressman that he would look into the case. "I assure you there'll be no retaliation against you," Mueller closed by telling his agent. Retaliation? Youssef thought to himself. Who said anything about retaliation?

The meeting ended civilly enough. But privately, "the director was truly appalled," not over the complaint itself, but over the agent's decision to confront Mueller with it in front of a member of Congress, recalled John Lewis, a senior aide to Mueller. The director and his aides felt sandbagged, blindsided by one of their own men. Lewis himself, who ran the section that included Youssef's small unit, was still bristling some three years later as he recounted the episode in a sworn deposition, sitting face-to-face with Youssef in the tony Georgetown office of the labor lawyer the agent had now retained to sue the bureau. "To put the director of the FBI in that position, to show him that lack of courtesy, to surprise him with a member of Congress in my judgment is absolutely outrageous. It shows a tremendous disloyalty to the director. It shows me that at least at that time he was far more interested in Bassem Youssef than he was serving this government or the FBI," Lewis said. "I've never heard of such a thing to put the director of the FBI in that kind of ambush with a member of Congress, and a powerful one at that. I'm still shocked." Nor was Lewis happy about all the time that Youssef was taking from work as leave to deal with hours-long depositions in his discrimination lawsuit—at the expense, Lewis believed, of the war on terror. "The same feelings that we had on the morning of September 12th are prevalent today, only worse, in my view. There are some very, very dangerous people out there who are working feverishly to visit 9/11 upon us again, and we have to stop that," Lewis said. To "stave off another 9/11," he said, "we really have to have all hands on deck." The message was clear: Youssef wasn't helping the team.

What Youssef didn't know as he sat in Congressman Wolf's office was that the FBI's international terrorism section had already been planning to move him to their section to do real counterterrorism work, and Mueller had signed off on the move just two days before the heated Capitol Hill meeting. Mueller himself apparently didn't remember the new assignment, and he didn't bring it up with Wolf. It was the kind of posting that might have allowed Youssef to put his cultural, investigative, and language skills to use. But the transfer, mysteriously, was never completed, and Youssef found out about his planned reassignment only after it was abruptly canceled. Just what happened to derail the promotion was never explained by the bureau, but the Justice Department's Office of Professional Responsibility, which investigates employee complaints, reached its own conclusion: the cancellation was Youssef's punishment for daring to speak out. OPR investigators found that, given Youssef's "considerable" expertise and "remarkable skills" in terrorism, the agent was within his legal rights under FBI whistle-blower regulations to go to the director with his claims of workplace discrimination and that he had a "reasonable belief" that "the FBI harmed its mission in combating terrorism by failing to use his expertise." Even more important, the Justice Department investigation found that the FBI's abrupt change of course in failing to move Youssef over to the approved terrorism slot so soon after the tense Capitol Hill meeting was likely a "reprisal" for his actions. The move, investigators found, appeared to be "retaliatory."

Neither the investigators nor Youssef ever got a clear indication of why he was so poorly utilized after 9/11. One possible explanation might have seemed like a bad, politically incorrect joke had it not come from an FBI official as part of a formal investigation: some FBI supervisors apparently mistook Youssef for another Egyptian FBI agent who had fallen out of favor with his bosses. The *other* Middle Eastern agent, this one a Muslim, had come under a cloud within the FBI for allegedly refusing on religious grounds to wear a wire to monitor fellow Muslims in undercover investigations, and he was the subject of an internal investigation over possible insubordination; Youssef, the Coptic Christian Egyptian, was not. The irony was almost comic: the FBI, now responsible for separating out the small numbers of militant, radical Islamists in the United States from the larger universe of law-abiding ones, couldn't tell its own Middle Eastern agents apart.

At one level, Youssef was no different from the million other aggrieved employees upset with their bosses; another Norma Rae, this one with a gun and a badge. But as an FBI agent fluent in the culture and history of terrorism, he was also uniquely positioned as both witness and watchdog to something much bigger. He was perched on a fault line at the FBI at a time when the very mission of the country's most storied agency was undergoing a seismic shift. Could the FBI remake itself? Did its people have the training, the expertise, the intelligence know-how to avoid repeating the cataclysmic failures of the past? Unwittingly, Youssef had pried open a window into a cultural clash within the bureau over these critical questions. His complaints, private at first and then awkwardly public, revealed the deep schisms within the bureau, schisms over what it took to fight terrorism and whether the FBI was up to the job.

Years later, the dearth of able linguists and agents at the FBI and the paucity of training in Islamic cultural issues would become front-page news, even fodder for John Kerry's failed presidential run in 2004. Youssef was asking these same questions—agitating over them, in fact, and making enemies within the bureau because of it—within months of the September 11 attacks. The FBI was throwing all its energies at terrorism, vacuuming up massive amounts of information to try to detect the next attack. But did it know what it was looking for?

Youssef's lawsuit against the FBI, claiming he was discriminated against because of his Egyptian heritage, forced Mueller and his top aides to give sworn depositions that produced raw and sometimes embarrassing moments for the bureau and its senior leadership. "Do you know who Osama bin Laden's spiritual leader was?" Bassem's lawyer, Steven Kohn, asked Dale Watson, the veteran head of counterterrorism at the FBI before and after the 9/11 attacks. "Can't recall," Watson answered in the videotaped deposition. Watson sat with his arms crossed tightly, his irritation evident. Kohn pressed on. "And do you know the differences in the religion between Sh'ia and Sunni Muslims?" Kohn asked, Youssef at his side. "Not technically, no," Watson answered. The depositions became the stuff of parody for late-night TV comedians. Never one to shy away from skewering the Bush administration, Jon Stewart of Comedy Central's *The Daily Show* aired excerpts from the Watson videotape and, with his trademark smirk, deadpanned: "Okay, let's try multiple choice: Hummus is (a) a terrorist organization or (b) a delicious chickpea dish." The depositions would continue, but after the Watson embarrassment reduced the bureau to a merciless punch line, Youssef and his lawyer were no longer allowed to videotape them. Jon Stewart would have to get his material elsewhere.

FOR MUELLER AND HIS CIRCLE of senior aides, the public skepticism and occasional ridicule were a constant nemesis in their efforts to remake the FBI after the failures of 9/11. Mueller had taken over the bureau just a week before the September 11 attacks. He was in a near-impossible position. "Baptism by fire," Congressman Wolf called the director's first few months on the job. Senator Arlen Specter, a senior member of the judiciary committee and one of the FBI's most unrelenting critics, was left to wonder aloud in one hearing with Mueller "whether any director can handle this job."

A former rifle platoon leader in Vietnam and winner of the Bronze Star, Mueller brought a military man's sense of mission and discipline to the job. As a longtime prosecutor before joining the bureau, he was famed in law enforcement circles for his razorlike precision in mapping out legal strategy and paring down complex cases on organized crime, racketeering, economic espionage, and the like. Over the years, the Justice Department relied on him to parachute into trouble spots—like the flailing U.S. Attorney's Office in San Francisco—to do triage. He'd done stints in private practice, but the Justice Department seemed his natural fit. In the mid-1990s, he'd earned many admirers, and more than a few raised eyebrows, when he gave up a $400,000 job at a Boston law firm to return to the Justice Department as a lowly line-level prosecutor—far below his previous rank as head of the entire Criminal Division nationwide. "I want you to do me a favor," Mueller told Eric H. Holder Jr., then the U.S. attorney in Washington, in a phone call pitching the idea. "I'd like to come work for the U.S. Attorney's Office and prosecute homicide cases. I just want to be a line guy." The self-demotion was so startling that Holder wasn't sure if he'd heard him right.

After Bush's election in 2000, Mueller served as Ashcroft's top deputy during the transition period, and Ashcroft became his biggest booster, lobbying for his appointment as FBI director. At the FBI, Mueller was inheriting an agency that was under siege even before the September 11 attacks. At the close of Louis Freeh's eight-year tenure as director, the FBI had badly bungled the legal paperwork in the government's prosecution of Oklahoma City bomber Timothy McVeigh, failing to turn over thousands of pages of relevant documents and forcing a frustrated Ashcroft to delay McVeigh's execution. Worse yet, the FBI had uncovered a spy in its own ranks—Robert Hanssen—whose spying for the Russians had gone undetected for three decades. The national security damage was massive: Hanssen had outed a dozen American moles, sold the Russians the plans to the U.S. continuity-of-government operations, and even disclosed the existence of a secret tunnel under the Soviet embassy. The FBI was still struggling to suture the wounds from the Hanssen and McVeigh debacles when 9/11 hit, triggering many months of fierce second-guessing over the FBI's failure to pick up on the missed signals preceding the attacks.

Mueller was there at Camp David with President Bush and his war team just days after the attacks, delivering a somewhat rambling presentation on the hijacking investigation after Bush surprised him with a request for a status report. And he was there at the White House with Bush and the National Security Council, talking about the need to properly preserve evidence in the 9/11 investigation to avoid tainting any prosecutions that would grow out of it. Ashcroft interrupted him. "Prosecution cannot be our top priority," Ashcroft said. "If we lose the ability to prosecute, that's fine, but we have to prevent the next attack. Prevention has to be our top priority." Bush nodded in agreement. Mueller had spent a lifetime as a prosecutor working within the system, following the rule of law as set out by the courts, but now the mindset had changed overnight. He had a new mandate, and his job and the future of the FBI rested on carrying it out and stopping another attack.

For the team of counterterrorism officials not just in the FBI but throughout the executive branch, the mandate was a thankless one. The quixotic nature of the task was perhaps best captured in a tongue-in-cheek note that Major General Bruce Lawlor, a senior official at the Department of Homeland Security, sent to a colleague, Asa Hutchinson, during one 2003 terrorist scare. Hutchinson, a former congressman who helped lead the Bill Clinton impeachment proceedings, was now asked to lead the effort to protect the nation's transportation system from all possible terrorist threats. That meant ensuring that no bomb, no radiological device, no hardwired shoes, and no box cutters could make their way onto cargo containers, passenger airplanes, ships, trains, or any other manner of daily transport across the borders. "Dear Asa," Lawlor wrote in a note to Hutchinson, "1.8 billion transactions a year. How do you like your odds? Sincerely, Bruce." But at least homeland security officials like Hutchinson and Lawlor—in charge of laying the bricks and mortar for the new national defense system—could point publicly to what seemed like tangible results: hardened cockpit doors in aircraft, enormous new luggage X-ray machines clogging the lobbies of airports, newly federalized screeners directing passengers to take off their shoes as they waved their magic wand across their bodies. The actual results in making the country safer were open to wide interpretation, and not infrequent ridicule, but a public anxious for reassurance could see that their government was at least trying to do *something* to make them safer.

For Mueller and the FBI, suddenly cast as intelligence agents, the signs of progress were far less tangible and far more ephemeral. The FBI was now in the intelligence collection business, and success there would be a much tougher thing to measure. What progress the bureau might achieve would normally fall under the category of "not for public dissemination." Indeed, with the FBI now recast as an intelligence agency, Mueller faced the kind of dilemma that John F. Kennedy had foreshadowed in addressing the CIA after the agency's Bay of Pigs debacle in 1961. "It's not always easy," Kennedy said of the intelligence business. "Your successes are unheralded; your failures are trumpeted."

The FBI had become, in effect, the cop of last resort. Each agency in the national security field now had its own particular assignment: the Pentagon was there to engage the enemy on the battlefield overseas, taking out suspected al Qaeda operatives with predator drones many hundreds of miles from the fighting if necessary; the CIA was there to interrogate overseas suspects in secret black sites, steal the enemy's secrets, spirit suspects away to other countries, and conduct paramilitary operations; the National Security Agency was there to run the spy hardware and listen in on suspicious phone calls; the Department of Homeland Security was there to seal the borders, to stop the terrorists from getting on a plane with a dirty bomb or a detonator strapped to their belts. The FBI was the backstop, the kid with the beat-up baseball mitt waiting by the fence if the ball sails past everyone else. If the next Mohamed Atta penetrated all those defenses and made it into the country—and few doubted he could—it was up to the FBI to find out about it beforehand and stop it. Their agents were the last line of defense, and they were reminded of it every day. "Counterterrorism: Prevent, Disrupt, Defeat" blared the motto in foot-high letters that greeted agents in the lobby of the FBI building. For anyone who missed the message, a display across the street outside the Justice Department's Great Hall declared the department's new number one priority: "Prevent Terrorism and Promote the Nation's Security."

The pressure on FBI agents and managers was acute. At the Justice Department, Ashcroft emboldened the FBI to go places from which it had once been banned, rewriting the FBI's guidelines in 2002 to allow agents to visit mosques, Web sites, libraries, and other public sites in search of leads on possible terrorist activity. The aim, Mueller said, was to "help remove unnecessary bureaucratic obstacles to the effective investigation of terrorist cases." With the new powers came clear expectations for the FBI's agents: Don't let 9/11 happen again. Agents and supervisors were now manning the command center at SIOC twenty-four hours a day, chasing any lead that might signal the next big attack. The FBI was flooded with tips and leads from the public about possible terrorists. The vast majority led nowhere. But they all had to be checked out. And by late 2002, the FBI's mission had expanded to include collecting U.S.-based intelligence on Iraq in advance of a possible war there.

For agents like Brad Doucette, a veteran of nearly twenty years at the FBI, the demands were unending. Doucette was pulling double duty at FBI headquarters beginning in late 2002, leading Iranian Hezbollah terror investigations and overseeing FBI interviews with Iraqi-Americans at the start of the war in Baghdad the next year. The Iraqi interviews were particularly frustrating; "We're spinning our wheels," he would tell his wife, Suzanne, a former FBI agent herself. He couldn't understand why the FBI wasn't doing a better job of targeting its leads, picking its spots, rather than casting a huge net that brought an enormous volume of negligible intelligence. But the work had to be done. Beginning early every morning, he and the agents assigned to him would pore over stacks of leads, not wanting to miss anything that might prove relevant to the war on terror.

Phone calls from his agents or from Mueller's top aides would come late into the night and early in the morning. Not infrequently, it was a senior FBI official needing information for the Presidential Daily Brief to be delivered to Bush at daybreak the next morning. The PDBs, as they were known, had become the prime intelligence vehicle to keep Bush and the White House informed about anything and everything related to possible terrorism. Getting them right had become particularly critical after the embarrassment caused by the revelation in the course of the 9/11 investigation about the PDB that Bush received at his Texas ranch on August 6, 2001, titled "Bin Laden Determined to Strike in U.S."

For intelligence agents like Doucette, the stress of avoiding a repeat—of making sure that everyone from the president on down knew of every shred of terrorist intelligence—was palpable. Doucette lost 30 pounds, his five-foot-eleven frame dropping to 150 pounds. The color washed from his face. He was feeling light-headed, and his wife urged him to go to the doctor; medical tests showed him suffering from exhaustion. His usual outlets, Washington Huskies football and amateur astronomy, held little interest for him anymore. Then, one April morning in 2003, another middle-of-the-night phone call from an agent woke up Doucette in his home in suburban Washington. It was a call from SIOC. Then came another call from an agent in New York. Suzanne Doucette, stirred from her own sleep, could tell there was some sort of trouble with a case, as her husband became more and more agitated and began yelling into the phone. Whatever it was about, she didn't want to know. She went to sleep in a guest room. At dawn, a loud bang startled her. In the bedroom, she found her husband lying dead on the bed, a tiny spot of blood behind his right ear from the FBI-issue, 9mm pistol he had put to his head. She reached for the phone to call 911 but couldn't get a dial tone; he had yanked the line out of the wall before pulling the trigger.

The coroner ruled the death a suicide. Mueller came to Suzanne Doucette's home three times afterward, delivering personal letters from Bush and Ashcroft. The gesture touched Suzanne, but she had one plea for Mueller, and it was an intensely personal one: "When people get home, let them sleep. Stop the phone calls," she told him. "You can't destroy your own people to get a piece of information to give the president." Those phone calls. Long after she'd buried her husband, Suzanne could still imagine the phone ringing at 3 a.m., waking Brad from a restless sleep. "That's what killed him," she said later. "He just didn't want anything to happen on his watch." Friends and family saw Doucette as another fatality of 9/11. "He was not one to complain at all," said Doucette's stepdaughter, Kelli Shope, "but you knew the work was incredibly hard. He knew people's lives were on the line."

Lives were on the line: it became a familiar and haunting refrain at the FBI. No agent or supervisor wanted to be the one who failed to connect the critical dots, the one who missed the next attack. The words of an FBI agent in New York, written in a memo just days before 9/11 that warned of bureaucratic snares that were slowing their terrorism investigations, echoed in the halls of the J. Edgar Hoover Building: "Someone will die," the memo said, and "the public will not understand why we were not more effective and throwing every resource we had at certain 'problems.' " Each big lead, it seemed, now took on life-and-death urgency, as supervisors were asked to make quick analyses of thorny legal and investigative issues that might have once dragged on for weeks or months. Now, the FBI would be on the line with the Justice Department for near-instant decisions aimed at forestalling another tragedy; the "bloody shirt calls," senior officials began calling them.

The sweat-inducing middle-of-the-night phone calls now became routine not just for agents like Doucette, but for national security lawyers at Main Justice like David Kris, a career Justice Department lawyer who was at the heart of the new preemptive strategy after the

September 11 attacks. A registered Democrat who rose up the ranks in Janet Reno's department, Kris nonetheless managed to win the trust of the new Ashcroft administration. He was revered throughout the building for his mastery of the most arcane legal intelligence issues, and he became the resident expert on federal intelligence law before leaving the department in 2003 from near exhaustion. When a predusk emergency threat required immediate action at the FBI's SIOC, Kris was often the man who got the call for legal guidance and approval as to how the FBI could proceed within agreed-upon legal guidelines.

In what he called an "amalgamation" of several real-life scenes, Kris described the dire mood that colored the early months and years after the 9/11 attacks. As Kris told it, the panicked call would come in at 2 a.m. on the STU-3 at his home—the secure phone line that allowed him to discuss the most sensitive terrorism and intelligence investigations in the dead of night, with his wife and children asleep. "There's an assistant director of the FBI on the other line," Kris recounts, and the FBI has a suspect under surveillance who is now walking on the streets of Manhattan toward the Iraqi permanent mission with a duffel bag in his hand and a suspicious-looking device inside his coat pocket. The FBI suspects the worst, and it wants authority from the Justice Department to pick him up, or take him down. Kris is still wiping the sleep from his eyes as he tries to assess the latest national security emergency. "I'm sorry, who is this again?" Kris asks. "Mr. Kris, he's now five blocks away. Can we put hands on?" Kris tries to probe for more details on what the FBI has—the basis for its suspicions, the history on the suspect, the nature of the surveillance—as the assistant director presses him for a decision. "Mr. Kris, he's now four blocks away," the AD says. The clock is ticking, and the target is nearing. Kris isn't sure what to advise. "Sir, he's three blocks away." Finally, Kris relents. "Okay, okay, if he gets within a block, tackle him, take him down, whatever. Just don't let him in the building with the W-88 warhead."

For all the urgency pulsing through the FBI after 9/11, officials at headquarters still sensed a damning complacency in some quarters of their own agency. Headquarters wanted more agents devoted to terrorism, more leads developed, more information funneled back to them. The motive was not only to avoid another attack, but to avoid the embarrassment of being caught flat-footed and unawares. But the cookie-cutter approach to creating a national terrorism agenda had a clear downside, rankling agents and supervisors in far-flung field offices around the country. For years, FBI field offices had operated largely as fiefdoms, empowered to shape their own law enforcement agendas based on crime problems particular to their regions. Fears about militant Islamists had percolated for many years before 9/11 in heavily Middle Eastern areas like Dearborn, Michigan, but the issue wasn't on agents' radar in the Topeka FBI office or in many others. Now, terrorism was everyone's number one priority.

Still, even as Mueller and his aides set about remaking the bureau after 9/11, stories came in to Washington about agents who were assigned to chase terrorism instead idling their time watching CNN because they weren't certain what they were supposed to be doing. Or worse yet, supervisors were still assigning large numbers of agents to nonterrorism cases like bank robberies and white-collar crime, because those were the cases that generated results. Agents wanted to make cases, lock up bad guys, and score prosecutions. Many older agents who came up in the 1970s were still guided by the remnants of the Hoover era, when success was tallied by reporting to Congress on the number of stolen cars the FBI had impounded; "Fines, recoveries, and convictions" was the mindset. In the view of some local field offices even after 9/11, that meant pursuing the hot, pressing crimes that produced actual arrests and that often differed from locale to locale: the rising scourge of methamphetamine in Iowa, or violent street gangs in Washington, D.C., or white-collar crime in Houston, or child porn in the San Fernando Valley. These were real crimes, demanding real investigation, some agents would say; not some "connect the dots" motif of vague intelligence leads that might not amount to anything.

Even when FBI field offices were going after terrorist suspects, they weren't always letting headquarters know what they were doing. One day in late 2002, Mueller and his deputy director, Bruce Gebhardt, were meeting with Ashcroft when one of the attorney general's top aides asked about some search warrants in an overseas terrorism investigation. It was the FBI's own investigation, but Mueller knew nothing about it. Gebhardt, handpicked by Mueller a few months earlier as the number two at the bureau after the pair had worked together in San Francisco, was furious at being kept in the dark, and he was tired of what he saw as weak excuses from FBI supervisors for the ongoing foul-ups. Just a few days earlier, he had been stunned to hear about a debate in an FBI field office over whether the bureau should try to get approval from the secret FISA Court for a wiretap on a terrorism suspect. Live wiretaps are labor-intensive operations, often requiring round-the-clock coverage, and the local supervisor felt that he didn't have the staffing for what appeared to be a marginal case.

Gebhardt was incredulous. More than a year after the 9/11 attacks, and some of key people in the field still didn't get it. He had a favorite saying for such moments, an expression he'd first heard two decades earlier from an instructor at the FBI training academy, and he summoned it now as he reflected on the lax attitude: "I'm amazed and astounded and at a loss to understand." Gebhardt fired off a blistering memo to all his special agents in charge, or SACs, who ran the FBI field offices across the country, a call to arms to the FBI's top lieutenants to do more: open more terrorism investigations, seek more wiretaps, make more cases, interview more suspects, give headquarters more information about anything and everything they were doing in the way of terrorism. Gebhardt's frustration, from the top ranks of the FBI, flew off the page:

> *This morning I am sitting in on a briefing for the Attorney General and one of his attorneys starts talking about search warrants on a case between the FBI and another agency. The case involves countries that are known for terrorist activities, plus some of those searched were from Yemen and other areas of interest. Found in the search were some really interesting items. The Attorney General is being briefed on this and the Director of the FBI is sitting right next to him. Were we aware? NO!*
>
> *"I'm amazed and astounded and at a loss to understand."*
>
> *I am asking all of you to get involved. Ask your Counterterrorism Squads for a weekly briefing in writing so you know what is going on. Ask questions. Ask the squads if they have a FISA on this guy and when they say, "No," ask why not? You need to instill a sense of urgency. They need to get out on the street and develop sources. You need to demand that information is being sent to FBIHQ. You are the leaders of the FBI. You cannot fail at this mission. Too many people are depending on us.*
>
> *I guarantee you that the Director and I are not going to call you to*

discuss your bank robbery solution rate. We will be calling you, how-
ever, to ask you (in detail) about your terrorism cases. In some cases, we
will invite you back to FBIHQ to personally explain: why you do not
have any FISAs; why you do not have any sources; why you are not
uploading everything.

Lately guys, "I'm amazed and astounded and at a loss to under-
stand."

The memo was as close to an ass-whooping from headquarters as
many of the SACs had ever received, and it caused an immediate stir in
field offices around the country. It left little doubt that careers were in
jeopardy for anyone who simply paid lip service to the new mandate of
fighting terrorism and opening case files. But how to go about it? As
Gebhardt well knew from more than a decade in counterterrorism and
counterintelligence, these cases didn't materialize by fiat, with a simple
snap of the fingers; it could take months or years to cultivate the
sources needed to bring a good case or to convince a judge there was
enough evidence to approve a FISA wiretap. The bar had clearly been
lowered in going after possible terror suspects, but how low? Was
headquarters now suggesting that the slightest whiff of suspicion was
grounds for a wiretap or a preliminary investigation into American citizens?

A few weeks after Gebhardt's private memo landed on desks around
the country, I was speaking with an FBI source about the remaking of
the bureau. The source alluded to the internal tumult and the Gebhardt memo, which had not become public. After a bit of coaxing, I
was able to get a copy of the memo, and it provided the framework for
a front-page story in the *Times*. The story began: "Senior F.B.I. officials have grown frustrated with the bureau's performance in the war
on terrorism, and they are demanding that agents nationwide become
more aggressive and single-minded in hunting terrorists, internal
memorandums and interviews show." Besides Gebhardt's broadside,
the story also included another internal memo that I'd obtained, this
one written days earlier by Mueller. In it, the director told FBI staffers
that he no longer wanted to see field offices establish their own distinct
law enforcement priorities. Localized crime problems, he wrote, "will
no longer be a basis for regional priority setting. While every office
will have different crime problems that will require varying levels of

resources, the F.B.I. has just one set of priorities," he said, and those begin with deterring another terror attack.

The story brought an unusual rejoinder from Mueller himself. In a letter to the editor published in the *Times* a few days later, Mueller wrote: "Senior officials of the Federal Bureau of Investigation have not 'grown frustrated with the bureau's performance in the war on terrorism,' as suggested by a front-page article." A transformation of the type the FBI was undergoing would mean regular communication with employees about the "inevitable bumps," Mueller said. "This does not—and should not—suggest any slippage in the pursuit of that mission, but rather an expected part of leadership during such a transformation. I believe that the American people expect nothing less."

Eight days later, Mueller put out another internal memo to his staff, warning how much was at stake in the fight. The FBI's ability to adapt to its new mandate "is now being tested in the extreme," he wrote to his staff. "Change will be needed in many areas and needed quickly. Bureaucratic intransigence cannot be an impediment or excuse." Again, I was able to get a copy of the memo, again the editors played the story on the front page, and again I heard quickly from the bureau about the leak. Mueller had a notoriously prickly reputation with the press going back to his days as a U.S. attorney. My dealings with him had been civil enough up to that point—he had liked a profile I wrote on him the year before at the time of his nomination and made a point of complimenting me on it privately at a Justice Department event—but a senior official quickly let me know that the director was not happy with the latest round of stories in my paper on the dustup within the bureau and the way it was portrayed. Mueller felt that he needed to be able to communicate with his agents freely, and privately, "without it ending up on the front page of *The New York Times*," the aide explained. I understood the sentiment, but I still found his reaction surprising. If anything, Mueller's internal memos and my latest story—which ran under the headline "FBI, Under Outside Pressure, Gets Internal Push"—cast Mueller as an aggressive and demanding leader at a time when many Capitol Hill critics thought the bureau was too slow and sluggish to shake its old ways. But in this case, whatever political mileage might have been generated for Mueller seemed to be outweighed by that old FBI adage: "Don't Embarrass the Bureau."

By all indications, Mueller and Gebhardt got what they wanted in rallying their troops to push harder, to stay more focused on terrorism as the bureau's overriding priority. The number of FISA applications— the surveillance warrants that Gebhardt urged his field offices to seek— doubled from 2001 to 2003. With it surged the number of national security letters that field offices were now allowed to use. NSLs, as the letters were known, allowed the FBI to demand all sorts of critical business records from private companies in the course of investigations— telephone records, e-mail patterns, financial statements, credit scores, credit card statements. NSLs were once regarded as intrusive, invasive forms of record collection that could be authorized only by a select few senior officials at headquarters or the biggest field offices in Washington, New York, and Los Angeles. Before 9/11, it could take six months or a year to get one approved. The Patriot Act changed all that, now giving dozens of field office chiefs the power to authorize the records demands in hours or days.

And authorize them they did. With little in the way of formal training on their use, the letters demanding records were "given out like candy" in the aftermath of 9/11, said a veteran FBI agent who saw the bureau's dramatic transformation up close. For agents now handed a powerful new tool to look at phone numbers, e-mails, and financial connections, there was a sense of both amazement and glee at the ease with which they could now gather evidence. Once, FBI officials would have had to go before a court or a grand jury to justify why they needed the records and seek a formal subpoena. Now, there was an attitude, the senior agent said, that "you mean I can just do that on my own? No one wanted to be a nattering nabob of negativism in 2002. The feeling was 'don't just stand there, do something.' "

The national security letters, generating access to myriad details from someone's personal life, were often a way to determine whether the subject of an investigation had contact with other people of interest and to establish patterns. "You're trying to find out if people know each other and they talk to each other," the agent continued. "So-and-so goes to the mosque and so-and-so says their wives know each other, and we want to see if he really knows them, so that if he denies it when we talk to them, we can say, 'Well, okay, then why were you talking to him?' " Or, the agent explained, a person of interest in a terror investigation "goes to a meeting of the Iranian student association in Kansas City, and he's holed up in a hotel. We take a picture of every license plate in the parking lot. Did these guys deserve to have their license plates run? Well, yeah, I don't have a problem with that. There's no expectation of privacy in a parking lot." A judge might be loath to approve the use of records demands, surveillance techniques, or other investigative tools in such cases with tenuous links to actual evidence of wrongdoing, the agent acknowledged, but "a judge is thinking about the Bill of Rights." The FBI, on the other hand, was thinking about stopping the next attack, and it now had the broadened power to get such records without having to go through a judge. The rules had changed.

Was the FBI in danger of overreaching? From the outset, some senior officials worried that it was. Michael Woods was among them. A national security lawyer at the FBI, Woods had become one of the bureau's go-to experts on intelligence and wiretap law during Louis Freeh's tenure. The legal procedure he set out in a memo for building a court-approved wiretapping became so embedded in FBI culture just prior to 9/11 that it earned him a legacy among lawyers and judges: the Woods Procedures, they were called. Woods had seen firsthand the pushback from the secret FISA court in the late 1990s over the judges' concerns about due process and the FBI's sloppiness in seeking wiretaps, and he saw the dramatic change in the legal and institutional mindset at the FBI after the September 11 attacks. He was there at SIOC on 9/11 as the FBI received the urgent Teletypes telling them that a plane was headed for the White House, and he was there hours later in an FBI car, racing along the shoulder of the freeway, as armed escorts took him and other senior officials to a secret, Cold War–era bunker in case everyone at headquarters was killed. When the Patriot Act gave the FBI its broad new power to demand records on terror suspects, Woods was the one called on to analyze the legal impact, but he was also the one to warn about possible misuse and abuse.

"NSLs are powerful investigative tools, in that they can compel the production of substantial amounts of relevant information," he wrote in a memo that was approved by Mueller and sent out to all the FBI field offices just ten weeks after the attacks. "However, they must be used judiciously. The USA Patriot Act greatly broadened the FBI's authority to gather this information." But if used improperly, the memo warned, there was the danger that Congress would scale back the power. Executive Order 12333, the Bible of intelligence protocol signed by President Ronald Reagan two decades earlier, still required that the FBI conduct its intelligence investigations through the "least intrusive" means possible, Woods noted. "Supervisors should keep this in mind when deciding whether or not a particular use of NSL authority is appropriate. The greater availability of NSLs does not mean that they should be used in every case."

Woods' warnings went unheeded. The NSLs were used in practically every type of case—a building block, the FBI said, not only for identifying real suspects but, more often, for eliminating bogus ones by prying into their personal records. As he reflected back several years later in an interview, Woods said the path was the frustrating if inevitable result of the climate after 9/11 inside the FBI. "All of a sudden, every lead needed to be looked at. The atmosphere was such that you didn't want to be the guy who overlooked the next Moussaoui. . . . If you're telling the FBI people over and over you need to be preemptive, you need to get out there before something happens, you're pushing people toward a fishing expedition. We heard over and over again, connect the dots, and we were pushing the envelope and doing things that, in the old days, would have seemed beyond the pale."

National security letters and the catchall they had become were the FBI's dirty little secret for years after the 9/11 attack. The broadened authority given to the FBI under the Patriot Act to use the letters in demanding business records with little in the way of court approval went largely unnoticed by the media, the public, even the lawmakers who had approved the legislation in October 2001. This was not by accident: the FBI's authority included a somewhat draconian provision that banned anyone who received a letter from publicly disclosing it, under the threat of criminal prosecution. It was unclear whether a recipient could even contact a lawyer before turning over the records. So even if someone had wanted to risk the wrath of the FBI by drawing public attention to the issue, he couldn't. The letters were invisible, unnoticed. If they were challenged—which was rare—the forum was not the foreign intelligence, or FISA, court, but the local district court in the area where it was served. The process, said Judge Royce Lamberth, head of the foreign intelligence court at the time of 9/11, meant almost certain approval. "You've got seven hundred district judges around the country who have never even heard of a national security letter probably, certainly will have never litigated one and won't know much about it," Lamberth said. "And the temptation there is to rubber-stamp them."

A pebble in the pond came in the summer of 2005, when the FBI used a national security letter to get records for library users in Connecticut as part of a terrorism investigation. The FBI's access to library records had been a hot issue in the debate over the Patriot Act, and for the librarians in Connecticut served with the NSL, the idea of giving the government its user records was anathema to their mission of intellectual freedom. They bristled, ultimately challenging the letter through the ACLU under a cloak of anonymity because they could not publicly identify themselves for fear of prosecution. I did a modest story on the development, although even the identity of the institution served with the letter was a closely guarded secret. But public court filings had left telling, sometimes blatant, clues as to the identity of the target and, a few months later, Alison Leigh Cowan, our Hartford reporter, was able to crack the mystery: the FBI wanted Internet records from a Connecticut consortium called the Library Connection, a nonprofit organization that serves twenty-six libraries in the Hartford area, including one that the FBI suspected was used to send a suspicious e-mail tip to the government about terrorism. The secret was out, yet the Justice Department pressed for nearly a year to keep the identity of the library consortium secret anyway and ban the group from discussing it, arguing that disclosure could somehow compromise national security.

The government finally gave up the fight, concluding that whatever implied threat was contained in the e-mail had no merit, but the episode—and the vindication that the librarians claimed in vanquishing the Patriot Act—left a bitter taste in the mouths of government lawyers. "What are you celebrating?" Kevin O'Connor, the United States attorney for Connecticut, asked of the librarians and their advocates. "You're celebrating the fact that you prevented the government from investigating a potential terrorist threat."

A few months after the Connecticut library consortium was first identified, *The Washington Post*'s Bart Gellman did a lengthy front-page piece focusing on the Connecticut case in the broader context of the FBI's heightened use of national security letters. It included one jaw-dropping figure: the FBI, the article said, was using some thirty thousand national security letters a year outside the court system. There was already a clear sense in Washington among people who followed the issue that the FBI was using the records demands much more frequently than ever before, but the volume cited by the *Post*—a one-hundred-fold increase since 9/11—was startling. If it was true, of course. Justice Department and FBI officials quickly disputed the accuracy of the report, suggesting to me and other reporters who asked that the number was off the mark, even wildly exaggerated. The Justice Department, worried about securing reauthorization of the Patriot Act, adopted a shoot-the-messenger approach, with a senior official telling lawmakers in response to the *Post* story: "We urge the Congress not to let a distorted and misleading portrayal of the FBI's use of this vital investigative tool skew the debate over how best to ensure our national security." The Justice Department offered Congress a much more modest figure for the number of FBI records demands: nine thousand.

In fact, the actual number, or the closest real approximation, would come out two years later in a blistering report from Glenn Fine, the inspector general: the number of records requested by the FBI had reached as high as 47,000 in 2004 and totaled 143,000 over a three-year period. The real number might have been significantly higher, investigators found, but the system for tracking and auditing such requests was so haphazard that it was tough to tell. The FBI wasn't following its own rules, and it had used the powers granted to it after 9/11 in the Patriot Act to sweep up reams of personal records in what looked, to all but the truest believers, like just the kind of fishing expedition that the FBI's Michael Woods had warned about five years earlier.

The inspector general's report, finding pervasive problems and potential illegality in the use of the letters, led to a remarkable mea culpa by Mueller himself at a live, televised news conference. He acknowledged that the FBI had failed to put a system in place to guard against abuses, to police itself in using its newfound powers. "The question should and must be asked: How could this happen?" a somber Mueller said. "Who is to be held accountable? And the answer to that is: I am to be held accountable." As important as the FBI's records demands were in stopping terrorism, he said, "it is equally important that as we exercise these authorities we do it consistent with the privacy protections and civil liberties that we in the FBI are sworn to uphold."

MUELLER HIMSELF had found out about the systematic problems in the FBI's records demands a few months earlier, he said, as the inspector general's investigation was moving toward an end. But at lower levels, problems had been welling up for at least two years. As it turned out, one of the agents who helped sound the alarm on possible abuses was none other than Bassem Youssef, precariously positioned once again on the edge of another firestorm three years after his awkward sit-down with Mueller in Congressman Wolf's office. Like a lot of good agents, Youssef had a knack for finding himself in the thick of things.

There's a saying among Justice Department prosecutors and FBI agents that speaks to whether or not they are willing to take on risky assignments: big cases, big problems; little cases, little problems; no cases, no problems. Youssef liked big cases. In 1989, at the start of his career, he was working a terrorism investigation involving a Palestinian man in St. Louis with suspected ties to Hamas. He was listening to a tape of a wiretap recorded days earlier at the target's home; he wanted to try to pick up any Arabic nuances or dialects that the translator might have missed. As he listened, a chilling scene unfolded. The target of the wiretap, Zein Isa, and his wife were angrily confronting their sixteen-year-old daughter about her lifestyle—her job at Wendy's, her friends, her new boyfriend, who was black. Youssef heard the father start screaming at the daughter, mostly in Arabic. "Did you know that this is your last day? That you are going to die tonight?" After a struggle, the father was heard shouting: "Die! Die quickly! Die, my daughter, die!," as he fatally stabbed her at least a half-dozen times. It was self-defense, the father told police. The killing had been covered in the local media, but Youssef hadn't paid much attention—until he realized that the killer was his own FBI target and that he had a tape recording of the killing. A stunned Youssef, holding secret evidence in what was now a criminal and very public investigation, reported the existence of the tape to his bosses in the Justice Department's intelligence section in Washington, and it became Exhibit A in the court case against Zein Isa and his wife, who were both convicted of murdering their daughter.

A decade later, with Youssef now based in Riyadh as the FBI's legislative attaché in Saudi Arabia, he again found himself in an unexpected spot. As part of his liaison work, Youssef was visiting with a member of the Saudi royal family at a wildlife refuge when the prince introduced him to a tall, regal-looking man who was also a guest at the refuge that day. His name was Sa'ad bin Laden. The prince felt obligated to tell Sa'ad that Youssef was with the FBI, but the two men kept talking anyway. Youssef asked him about his half-brother, already implicated in the 1998 East Africa bombings and on the lam in Afghanistan. Sa'ad mentioned, almost in passing, that Osama's mother still kept in touch with him in Afghanistan. Just how mother and son communicated was not made clear, since Osama had stopped using his satellite phone the year before, but Youssef wrote up the intriguing tidbit in an FBI EC—an electronic communication—and sent it on for dissemination to the intelligence community. He figured it might be of some use. It didn't win him many friends, however, among some of the FBI people assigned to monitor bin Laden; they suspected that, once again, Youssef was operating outside his lane.

So it was that Youssef stumbled into controversy once again in early 2005 in the FBI's frenzied use of national security letters. By then, Youssef was officially an FBI whistle-blower over his complaints about his treatment at the bureau, and he considered himself persona non grata in many corners of the building. He even had difficulty getting someone to give him the commemorative 9/11 pin that Mueller wanted his agents at headquarters to wear. His discrimination lawsuit was continuing to generate potentially damaging acknowledgments from FBI officials about the dearth of counterterrorism experience among the upper echelons. One particularly eye-opening deposition came from Gary Bald, who had taken over as head of counterterrorism at the FBI in 2005 after working mostly organized crime and drug cases throughout his career. Wouldn't it be essential, asked Youssef's lawyer, Steven Kohn, for an FBI counterterrorism official to have a background in international terrorism? "I disagree," Bald answered. "The reason is because you need leadership. You don't need subject matter expertise. The subject matter expertise is helpful, but it isn't a prerequisite." What about an understanding of Middle Eastern culture or history? Was that important? Again, Bald demurred. "I think it's helpful, not required. I wouldn't say it's important, although I wish I had it. It would be nice," said Bald, who left the bureau not long after to head up security at an international cruise line.

It would be nice. The sentiment grated on Youssef, and on other current and former FBI officials as well. The idea that an FBI counterterrorism official doesn't need "subject matter" experience "is absolutely ridiculous, it's asinine," said Edward Curran, a longtime FBI terrorism and espionage supervisor who left the bureau in 2000. That attitude, he suspected, was one reason why the World Trade Center was hit not once, but twice. "You'd think after the first bombing [in 1993] we would have solved the problem rather than waiting for the second one. The problem right now, we have people that don't know what they're supposed to be doing."

Youssef was still struggling to understand the FBI's counterterrorism priorities in January of 2005 when he was transferred from DocEx, the evidence locker, to another low-profile office called the Communications Analysis unit. DocEx's office had been off-site; this one was at headquarters, and he figured his bosses wanted to keep a closer eye on him to keep him from stirring up further trouble. If that was the actual agenda, it backfired. The communications unit was responsible for processing and analyzing telecommunications records for counterterrorism investigators, and part of Youssef's job was to work as a liaison to the phone companies in getting the agents the records they wanted. Soon after his arrival in the new post, a contact at one of the phone companies asked Youssef about getting follow-up letters that had been promised him by Youssef's predecessor in the unit. Youssef wasn't sure what he was talking about, but he was able to piece together that the unit had been using something called "exigent letters" to get phone and e-mails records on an emergency basis, without the normal paperwork to back it up. The concept had originated in the New York FBI office in the chaotic weeks after the 9/11 attacks, but when the oversight of the 9/11 investigation was moved to Washington headquarters, the model for the exigent letters migrated with it and was soon broadened to a range of counterterrorism investigations.

The initial "emergency" had become, in effect, the permanent state of play for getting records. The FBI, after getting the records on an emergency basis, had been promising the phone companies that they would come back to them with a subpoena or a formal national security letter to establish that the records demand was justified, but they

rarely did. Once the investigators had the records, as a senior FBI official later acknowledged, there was little incentive to produce the
paperwork to justify the demand. The problem was that Youssef now
had a phone company representative who wanted to know who was
going to give him the paperwork that he'd been promised. The telecom contact had even kept a spreadsheet showing all the emergency
information demanded by the FBI, and all the promised paperwork
that never materialized: they totaled more than a hundred. Youssef was
concerned and raised the issue with supervisors in the FBI's national
security law office to try to figure out how the process had broken
down. The real "emergency" requests used by the FBI to justify the
records grabs were "few and far between," he told a lawyer there in a
remark that she memorialized in an e-mail. "This is gonna kill us,"
Youssef said.

Unknown to him, lawyers there had already been made aware of
similar problems a year earlier, and now Youssef added his voice to
those rising concerns based on what he had witnessed in the communications unit. Officials promised to look into the problem, but the complaints went nowhere. It was not until more than a year later, as Glenn
Fine was nearing the end of his own investigation at the inspector general's office in early 2007, that Mueller moved to shut down the use of
the emergency letters altogether. The FBI had issued more than seven
hundred of these supposed emergency records demands, investigators
found, under a legal authority that it never really had.

THE WIDE DRIFT NET cast by the FBI and the Bush administration
rested on two critical assumptions: that there were other sleeper cells
on U.S. soil poised and ready to strike; and that if the intelligence community had enough data—enough leads, enough phone numbers and
e-mail addresses, enough banking records, enough surveillance
tapes—it could identify them and stop them before they struck. In
other words, it could connect the dots that it had once missed. This
was the new "preemptive" mindset at the FBI and the intelligence
community, a page lifted from the futuristic aura of Hollywood's
Minority Report, in which Tom Cruise played a cop tasked with stopping crimes before they could occur. It was a radical rethinking of the
traditional law enforcement mindset, but would it work? There were

naysayers even within the government who were skeptical about the assumptions on which the new strategy rested. No doubt there were extremists who wanted to do the United States harm, but did they have the background, the connections, the training, the financial backing to actually carry out a plot? A secret thirty-two-page report, prepared by the FBI and the CIA in 2005 and first disclosed by ABC News, appeared to confirm what some within the government had quietly come to suspect. "We have not identified any true 'sleeper' agents in the U.S.," the report said flatly. The report indicated that while there was no doubt that al Qaeda wanted to hit the United States again, its ability to actually do so was unclear. And if al Qaeda did marshal the people and resources to plot another attack on American soil, what then? Would the FBI have the wherewithal to detect it? Would it be able to sift through the massive amounts of chaff it was accumulating to get to the wheat?

Among the skeptics were a number of key members of the 9/11 Commission, the ten-member bipartisan panel that probed the intelligence failings behind the attacks and recommended structural changes to deter another attack. Although it wasn't known at the time, the FBI came dangerously close to losing its authority for fighting terrorism altogether. When the commission began its work, there was close to consensus among most of the commissioners and senior staff that they would at least have to consider the creation of a separate domestic intelligence agency, modeled after Britain's famed MI5, to take over antiterrorism operations within the United States. The commission even brought in the head of MI5 to brief them on the possibilities for a reworked system. The FBI's pre-9/11 failures were too great, its cultural flaws too glaring, not to consider the option, some members felt. "You can't teach an old dog new tricks" became a favorite saying of commission staffers as their discussions inevitably veered to the question of what to do about the FBI. The more commission members knew about the inner workings of the agency, the less confidence they seemed to have.

When Mueller sat down to talk with the commission in 2004 in an effort, in effect, to keep the status quo, the odds were stacked against him, and his aides knew it. If a vote were taken that day, one senior person with the commission said privately later, the panel might well have voted for an MI5 to replace the FBI in its intelligence role. But

Mueller made a passionate plea: he came across as earnest, focused, sincere, realistic about the FBI's flaws and the need for reform. "He really got it," one person at the meeting said later. Commissioners came away from the meeting convinced that maybe Mueller could lead the FBI out of the morass. There were strong reasons not to go the MI5 route: the logistical nightmare of standing up a wholly new agency would inevitably mean lost time and opportunity in deterring terrorism; and there was a feeling that for all its faults, the FBI at least understood the boundaries on the rule of law in a way a classic intelligence agency like the CIA did not.

In the end, the commission's 2004 final report opted against recommending an MI5, but with clear caveats. "Our recommendations to leave counterterrorism intelligence collection in the United States with the FBI still depends on an assessment that the FBI—if it makes an all-out effort to institutionalize change—can do the job." The bureau had made "significant progress" under Mueller, the commission said. But, it went on: "We want to ensure that the Bureau's shift to a preventive counterterrorism posture is more fully institutionalized so that it survives beyond Director Mueller's tenure. We have found that in the past the Bureau has announced its willingness to reform and restructure itself to address transnational security threats, but has fallen short—failing to effect the necessary institutional and cultural changes organization-wide. We want to ensure that this does not happen again. Despite having found acceptance of the Director's clear message that counterterrorism is now the FBI's top priority, two years after 9/11 we also found gaps between some of the announced reforms and the reality in the field."

The FBI realized it had work to do, particularly in its analytical side. For many years, analysts had always been held in low repute in the FBI hierarchy, stepchildren just a notch or two above typists and translators in the eyes of some of the old-school FBI agents. Many agents lived by the traditional mindset, the belief that old-fashioned gumshoe detective work could solve any crime. Give an agent a gun, a notepad, and a pen, and he'd have a suspect in his sights by nightfall. This was a predominant view in the bureau. This was the vaunted agency, after all, that had brought down the notorious bank robber John Dillinger and nabbed the Lindbergh baby-kidnapper; the framed Hollywood posters from movies like *The FBI Story* with Jimmy Stewart, lining the executive hallways of the J. Edgar Hoover Building, were testimony to the bureau's unmatched reputation for solving tough cases. Agents, by and large, had little use for analysts who brought high-concept analytical tradecraft.

Compounding the problems were the FBI's dilapidated computers. Congress had devoted hundreds of millions of dollars prior to 9/11 to upgrading the system, but in what many inside the building took as a reflection of Louis Freeh's apathy toward computers—he didn't use one much himself—the project stagnated. For years after the explosion of the Internet, agents couldn't e-mail one another. The FBI's software system made it next to impossible to transmit photos as attachments, so when 9/11 hit, a Florida field office had to overnight photos of the suspected hijackers to Washington. Nor did the system allow agents to do keyword searches to see what relevant information might be sitting in an FBI file somewhere; trying to do a search of links between "al Qaeda" and "crop dusters," for instance, was all but futile. After 9/11, Congress poured more money into the newly revitalized computer upgrades, but parts of that plan collapsed as well, for reasons technical, logistical, and personal. It didn't help that managers overseeing critical aspects of the computer upgrades seemed to be in a perpetual state of turnover, with key personnel coming and going as the project lurched on. In one unpublicized episode that was apparently captured on tape, an FBI official who was deeply involved in the computer project was spotted in a bureau parking garage in flagrante delicto with a female employee. He left the bureau. In 2006, the FBI was finally forced to scrap its ill-fated attempt to create a "paperless" case file system and start from scratch. Changing course, the bureau put the contract out anew and went with a vendor that was promising off-the-shelf software instead. As of 2007, the latest version of the project was expected to cost $425 million.

Whether the fault lay with the FBI's computer or its inbred culture, senior bureau officials realized that the FBI's system for analyzing intelligence was badly broken. So it was that when a veteran FBI agent in Phoenix wrote a prophetic memo to headquarters two months before the September 11 attacks warning about suspicious activity swirling around Middle Eastern flight students, it got virtually no attention in Washington. Or that when the FBI in Minneapolis began poking around in the summer of 2001 into the odd flight training of

Zacarias Moussaoui, it was the CIA, not the FBI, that prepared an internal intelligence briefing under the headline: "Islamic Extremist Learns to Fly." The FBI could see every burr and every branch on a tree of interest, but the forest was another story. But with the new mantra of "connecting the dots" after 9/11, the FBI's expanding cadre of analysts became, at least in theory, essential players in the mix. Their primary task was not to open investigations or develop sources, as the agents did, but to pore through the available information in the files, look for patterns that might point to another attack, and get their analytical reports to everyone in the FBI and the outside intelligence community who might need to know about their conclusions. Mueller put in place new training programs and career tracks for analysts, he beefed up their numbers by the hundreds, he assigned them to work in field offices where they'd never set foot before, and he brought in intelligence executives from other agencies like the NSA to oversee the redoubled effort.

Still, the old ways lingered, and long after 9/11 was to have jump-started the new mindset, analysts complained that they were doing menial office work. Analysts were still being asked at times to pull duty answering phones, escorting visitors through the FBI building, and collecting office trash in the building for incineration. Those problems would ease, but progress in bringing the intelligence side up to speed remained "slow and uneven," auditors found in 2007. Even with the influx of hundreds of new analysts hired through a nationwide search, the staffing level of more than 2,100 intelligence analysts as of 2006 fell more than four hundred slots below what the FBI acknowledged it needed. And the perception that analysts were still seen as second-class citizens in the FBI caste system—the "professional divide," the inspector general called it—still festered. Merging the old and the new at the FBI, the divergent cultures of old-fashioned gumshoe agent and twenty-first-century analyst, was a critical task that many FBI officials dreaded.

The intelligence side of the bureau was under "tremendous stress, tremendous pressure," Wayne Murphy, who was imported from the NSA to lead the FBI's intelligence directorate, told a small grouping of reporters at one briefing I attended. To illustrate the point, Murphy launched into an abstract discussion of the management difficulties posed by merging different cultures in an organization as large and tradition-bound as the FBI. We'd all heard the theme before; Ashcroft himself was sometimes known to pop into a media briefing unannounced and start drawing concentric circles on a chalkboard showing how the "consumers" of the new intelligence system should be sharing information.

As reporters' eyes started glazing over at the latest telling of the oft-heard theme, Murphy must have sensed that he was at risk of losing his audience, so he switched to an analogy we could all appreciate to illustrate the tough road the FBI faced. Imagine you're a seasoned investigative reporter, he told us, and you've been working for months on a sensitive story. You've developed confidential sources who are giving you dynamite material, and you think you've got a great prize-winning story in the making. Then, your editors abruptly change course on you. They decide they can't afford to sit and wait for you to write the big story, so they assign twenty cub reporters to comb through your files, identify your confidential sources, compare your files with other reporters' raw notes, and look for anything and everything that could be published in the newspaper, as soon as possible. This, Murphy said, was what the awkward marriage of the FBI's analysts and its agents was like in the post-9/11 era. Heads nodded around the table as we considered the uncomfortable scenario he'd laid out. We finally got it. The FBI had a tough sell on its hands.

MIKE GERMAN got the message too. A veteran FBI undercover agent based in Atlanta, he had heard the mantra over and over again since 9/11: no lead was too obscure, no threat too remote. The FBI could no longer afford to take chances. So when an FBI colleague in Florida called German in early 2002 for advice on an investigation that involved a disturbing meeting between white supremacists and an American Muslim fundamentalist from the Middle East, he was anxious to help out. The Middle Eastern man, who had suspected ties to Hamas, the terrorist group, had picked up neighborhood leaflets distributed by the white supremacist group in the Orlando area—their version of a "help wanted" poster—and invited them to a meeting to talk about areas of mutual interest. A confidential informant working with the FBI to infiltrate the supremacist group was at the meeting and got the whole thing on tape.

The FBI in Orlando was looking for help in launching a possible undercover operation as a result of the meeting, and the assignment seemed tailor-made for German. He had been working undercover cases for more than a decade before 9/11. His target was homegrown terrorist suspects—not the Islamic variety, but the neo-Nazi type. With blond hair, blue eyes, and just a hint of a Southern accent from his North Carolina upbringing, German was a natural to infiltrate members of the white supremacist movement who were looking to fan racial flames and promote "a cleansing war" in the streets of America. Timothy McVeigh had shown the results of such extremist thinking in 1995, using the racist *Turner Diaries* as a loose basis for his bombing of the federal courthouse in Oklahoma City.

In the early 1990s, German had infiltrated a gang of Fourth Reich skinheads in Los Angeles intent on storming a landmark black church with pipe bombs and machine guns. A few years later, he wormed his way into a militia in Washington State that the FBI suspected was plotting to attack government buildings. His fellow militia members knew the young recruit as "Rock." As the plot moved forward, German, aka Rock, helped stage a militia training exercise to prep for all eventualities; he got his cohorts to don handcuffs in order to test whether they could pick the locks if they were nabbed by police. With the plotters cuffed, he told them he was hungry and went to get something to eat. For the FBI agents listening in on a wire, that was their cue. With Rock headed for a back door, the FBI came in the front to find the suspects already manacled and awaiting arrest.

Even after 9/11, the FBI hadn't devoted a lot of attention to what might happen if Islamic jihadists were to join forces with disaffected white supremacist types. But German was forced to consider that prospect as he read the transcript of the uncomfortable conversation taped by the FBI's informant. The Muslim man, explaining why he had sought out the white supremacists' group, began the meeting by acknowledging their different agendas. "But I also conclude," he said, "that the enemy of my enemy is my friend." The supremacist signaled his agreement. "Anybody that's willing to shoot a Jew or hit a Jew is my friend. Automatically." The Muslim man likened the United States to Germany before the rise of Hitler. "Everyone thinks Hitler is a, is a criminal, a sick individual," he said. "The man was a genius." The supremacist chimed in: "He was a hero to our people."

To get rid of the Jews, the supremacist said, "the only solution that we have is to replace the current government with a new government that's operating in the best interests of the American people." The FBI informant, listening quietly for the most part but apparently realizing his FBI handlers would be listening to the conversation, quickly broke in. "Man, we're not talking about anything, uh, you know, radical or off the wall." Not another Oklahoma City, he said, but simply opening the "hearts and minds" of Americans. But the Muslim man was dubious such a benign strategy could work. "Wars really change the minds of the American people," he said. Next came talk of suicide bombers. "Some people call that a criminal enterprise; I call it patriotism," the supremacist offered. Today, George Washington would be considered a terrorist. "I believe there's gonna be another civil war in this country," he said.

"We have to stick together," the Muslim man told his new ally. The answer to the Jews' "power grip," the supremacist opined, was to foster financial ties to the Middle East with businesspeople from Palestine, Egypt, and Saudi Arabia. He alluded to his involvement in American businesses that used ex-military personnel for overseas operations, and he asked for help in expanding those ties. "Hook us up with other influential people from the Middle East," he implored. The idea struck a chord. "I just wanted to come today," the supremacist said, "and extend an olive branch and say, hey, look, we're your buddies. And if there's any way we can help, we're there."

As German finished reading the transcript, he wasn't sure whether to be excited or disgusted. The FBI was anxious for any and all leads on possible terror plots, and here it had one handed to them. The meeting might not have included clear evidence of a crime, he thought, but it suggested to him enough of a predicate for further investigation. He figured the case was ripe for an undercover operative to infiltrate the group, develop intelligence, and see where if anywhere the "olive branch" might extend. After all, the FBI had launched undercover terrorism stings and prosecutions after 9/11 with seemingly thinner evidence than this.

In San Diego, two Pakistani men took part in what they thought was an al Qaeda plot to trade drugs for Stinger missiles, only to find out the al Qaeda plotters were FBI agents. In Albany, two leaders of a mosque with suspected links to Iraq were charged in a made-up plot to acquire a shoulder-fired missile for an attack. In Miami, a group of Haitian-Americans working with an informant talked of toppling the Sears Tower in Chicago in a bizarre plot that the FBI acknowledged was "more aspirational than operational." In Manhattan, in Newark, in Houston, in Ohio, the FBI had gone undercover and brought cases. Almost every time, the defense cried entrapment, and almost every time, the Justice Department won out in court and claimed another success in the war on terror. "The risk of waiting is just too great now," Michael T. Shelby, the United States attorney in Houston at the time of one of the stings there, told me in an interview. "Once we see that a threat is plausible, that it's real, and that a person has the intent to carry it out and takes some steps to show it's not just idle talk, that's enough for us to move."

But in the Orlando case, there was a problem, as German was to find out. The investigation was riddled with procedural missteps: meetings had not been properly documented per FBI protocol, paperwork was missing, and the informant had left the notorious "olive branch" meeting to use the bathroom while leaving behind his recorder taping the other men—a violation of federal law on "consensual," in-person monitoring. Mishandling of informants was not a new phenomenon at the FBI, unfortunately; one investigation in 2005 by the Justice Department inspector general found violations of FBI policies on confidential informants in nearly nine out of every ten cases, with drug dealers, gang members, and other informants sometimes allowed to commit crimes without the needed preapproval from the FBI as part of their undercover work. A pair of FBI counterespionage agents, it turned out, were even having long-term affairs, unknown to each other, with a Chinese-American informant they were "handling."

On her way out of the Justice Department, Janet Reno had tried to rein in the FBI's use of informants through tightened guidelines after the scandal created by the violent and incestuous ties between Boston mobster "Whitey" Bulger and his FBI helpers. But after 9/11, Ashcroft had relaxed the informant standards in 2002 as part of a broader effort to get FBI agents to respond more quickly to terrorism leads, and the problems had mounted. Too often, it seemed, FBI supervisors just couldn't tell what the rules were anymore in deciding what a well-paid informant could do to further an investigation and how long a leash to give him. Sometimes, the procedural screwups that resulted in an investigation could be fixed, patched over. But as Mike German pushed FBI officials in Orlando to pursue a case in response to the "olive branch" meeting, he worried that the FBI's bungling might have already sabotaged the investigation.

Months went by, and still there was no approval to go undercover. There was no case to pursue, some agents began to assert; the terrorism nexis, they said, was largely a fiction, created by the informant and fueled by German himself. After all, in the climate after 9/11, why wouldn't the FBI jump on a possible terrorist plot if there was any hint of credibility to it? German weighed the question himself a thousand times in his own mind, and he had an explanation for the slow-walk: the case had become too tainted to touch. With so many investigative missteps and possible violations of the law, he said, the FBI realized that the case was in jeopardy of being thrown out of court—and embarrassing the bureau—if it were pursued. German went to supervisors to complain about the missteps and the inertia.

Finally, German went to Mueller himself, sending him an e-mail in 2003 to complain about the way the case was being handled. The subject header on the e-mail—"National Security Matter"—was sure to get Mueller's attention. "I believe this matter requires your personal attention, inasmuch as it involves a significant national security threat, which is not being addressed, and serious misconduct by Bureau officials," German wrote. The complaint led to an internal review ordered by Washington, focusing not on German's charges of misconduct, but on the investigation as a whole. German's protestations didn't put the case back on track, but they did have an apparent impact. An agent on the case backdated some of the investigative reports in the file to make it appear as if they were prepared months before they actually were, and someone—it is still unclear who—used Wite-Out fluid to backdate the wiretapping form that the informant signed, indicating he understood that he had to be present at all times during the bugging operation. Someone, it appeared, was trying to cover his tracks.

The FBI had "mishandled and mismanaged" the German investigation, the inspector general found in a review. But the FBI continued to insist that the Florida investigation was never about terrorism, a view that was even endorsed by the inspector general in its wide-ranging report. Senator Chuck Grassley, who had championed German's case as part of what he saw as a pattern of stifling dissent at the

FBI, wasn't convinced. His aides pressed to get hold of the original case materials, including the transcripts from the notorious "olive branch" meeting between the supremacists and the suspected Hamas associate. When the senator read the excerpts—talk of Hitler, suicide bombings, revolution, and the killings of Jews—he was aghast. "If the FBI can't recognize the importance of information like this," he told Mueller, "I don't see how it can serve as an effective domestic intelligence agency."

The more vocal German became within the FBI, the more his own career suffered. Agents in Florida were told not to have any contact with him, German said, and agents working another undercover case in Portland, Oregon, distanced themselves from him as well. The head of the FBI's undercover unit made clear his attitude toward German and his complaints when he was overheard telling another agent that German would "never work another undercover case." German had been a regular instructor and evaluator at the FBI's undercover training program, a plum assignment. But the undercover chief, Jorge Martinez, was so vexed by German's internal criticism that he blocked him from any future teaching assignments. "As long as I am unit chief," Martinez told another agent, "Mike German will never come to another undercover school."

German's exclusion from the undercover training assignments amounted, under federal labor law, to "discrimination that could have a chilling effect on whistle-blowing," the inspector general's investigation found. The inspector general had a word for what German's supervisor did to him: retaliation. It was a word that dogged the FBI, a word that kept coming up again and again in FBI whistle-blower cases. *Retaliation*. Whistle-blowers were not a popular bunch in the FBI culture; the term itself elicited teeth-gnashing from the old-timers. When a news article about a purported whistle-blower was mentioned at a meeting at FBI headquarters in 2007, a supervisor let his feelings on the topic be known with two choice words: "Hang him." Mueller had repeatedly urged FBI employees and whistle-blowers to come forward with any allegations of wrongdoing, and a few became minor celebrities for it; Coleen Rowley, an FBI agent in Minneapolis, even landed on the cover of *Time* magazine after lodging complaints about the mishandling of the investigation into Zacarias Moussaoui's odd flight training in the summer of 2001. But FBI employees came forward at their own peril.

There was always the worry about the consequences, the worry about—that word again—retaliation. Mueller had assured Bassem Youssef that he wouldn't face it for speaking out about his concerns on counterterrorism staffing, yet Justice Department investigators had found he was soon subjected to it. Sibel Edmonds, a former translator for the FBI after 9/11, had confronted it after she complained about management problems and slipshod translation; she was fired in large part because of the internal accusations she lodged, investigators found. Even FBI whistle-blowers speaking out about the perils of whistle-blowing risked the wrath of their bosses. One longtime FBI agent in internal affairs named John Roberts went on *60 Minutes* in late 2002—with the prior approval of his bosses at the bureau—and told of the widespread perception of a double standard in how the FBI disciplined rank-and-file agents while it often overlooked wrongdoing by senior officials; when higher-ups were accused of wrongdoing, he said, the allegations often "just disappeared, just vaporized." Soon after the appearance, Roberts' boss, Robert Jordan—the man who, ironically, was in charge of internal disciplining at the FBI—read Roberts the riot act for his intemperate public comments. Angered, Jordan humiliated Roberts in front of his colleagues, investigators later found, and he passed him over for a promotion in favor of someone else. Jordan drew a reprimand from Mueller, and the inspector general ultimately concluded that his actions "left the appearance of retaliation against Roberts for his statements on '60 minutes.' "

Mike German knew the hazards of speaking out. He figured his sixteen-year career at the FBI had effectively ended the moment he began complaining to senior FBI officials about the bungled Orlando investigation. He had become, in his own words, "a pariah." As deadweight as he was at the FBI, he might as well have handcuffed himself along with the other white supremacists he'd rounded up back in Seattle in his former life. So, quietly, German left the bureau altogether in June of 2004. He had no job lined up, and he wasn't sure what he was going to do. A few months later, I heard over lunch with a source of mine who helped with FBI training that there was an agent who had recently left the bureau in an apparent rift over a terrorism-related investigation. His name was Mike German. I had never heard of German, and a search of media databases showed that nothing had been written publicly about his case or his departure. I had covered a number of FBI whistle-blower cases and the contretemps they had created, and the little that I knew about his situation sounded promising. I began pressing to try to interview the former agent.

Not long after, the labor lawyer whom German had retained agreed to set up a meeting. German—soft-spoken, clean shaven, and neatly dressed, looking nothing like a bearded, hard-scrabble militia member named Rock—arrived at his lawyer's office for our meeting clutching a copy of the recently published *9/11 Commission Report*, and he leafed through the dog-eared copy as we spoke across a long wooden conference table. "What's so frustrating for me," he said, gesturing toward the 9/11 report, "is that what I hear the FBI saying every day on TV when I get home, about how it's remaking itself to fight terrorism, is not the reality of what I saw every day in the field." German was maddeningly circumspect in discussing the Florida investigation itself; the details remained confidential and he would not discuss anything of substance surrounding the case, so I had to go elsewhere to get the details on it. But he was passionate and unflinching in discussing the impact the case had on his life at the FBI. "My entire career has been ruined, all because I thought I was doing the right thing," he said. A few days later, I wrote the first story to appear publicly on German's case, under the headline: "Another FBI Employee Blows Whistle on Agency." Mike German had joined the club.

Two years later, German did something that, for a former FBI agent, was almost unthinkable: he went to work for the American Civil Liberties Union. A lawyer, he would be working on national security issues for the FBI's longtime nemesis. German had always seen himself as a lifer at the FBI, but he figured if he couldn't affect the war on terror from the inside, he might as well do it from the outside. As he reflected back on the abrupt end of his FBI career, German was reminded of the old bureau saying that he'd heard at the training academy at Quantico: *Don't embarrass the bureau.* "That was the first commandment. That was drilled into my head in training. What I always thought it meant was: Don't do anything improper to embarrass the bureau. What I found it actually meant," he said, "was: Don't uncover anything that would embarrass the bureau. That was the ultimate sin."

CHAPTER FOUR

Threats, Pronouncements, and the Media Wars

I T WAS A ROUTINE REQUEST. At least it was supposed to be. The security people at USNORTHCOM, the newly minted military command in Colorado put in charge of protecting American bases after 9/11, had begun noticing some trouble at a few military recruiting events in 2005. As public opposition to the two-year-old war in Iraq was rising, so too was the stridence of some of the protesters. Spasms of actual violence and disruption were still rare, amounting to maybe a dozen episodes or so in the prior two years, but the anger was hard to ignore: an occasional cracked window at a recruiting station; an antiwar slogan spray-painted on a wall; a vial of fake blood or manure splattered against a door; a recruiting event cut short by threats and taunts from protesters, all generated by opposition to George Bush's war in Iraq. Some military officials even worried that opponents had their recruitment events under surveillance.

Military officials were concerned enough that they turned to an obscure but increasingly influential branch of the Pentagon: the CounterIntelligence Field Activity unit, or CIFA as it was known in the alphabet soup of the federal government. CIFA didn't exist three years earlier. It was a small but significant part of the vision that Defense Secretary Donald Rumsfeld, Deputy Secretary Paul Wolfowitz, and their senior Pentagon advisors had laid out in the wake of 9/11 for a more muscular, more aggressive, and more streamlined approach to gathering intelligence, less restrained by the traditional limitations placed on military spying and surveillance in generations past.

Rumsfeld saw the reengineering effort, built around the creation of a new undersecretary for all Pentagon intelligence, as a way to speed the flow of information. Rumsfeld "didn't want to have to noodle his way through three or four levels of bureaucracy to figure out what was being done," said one Pentagon official who worked closely with Rumsfeld on the plan. The idea of centralizing counterintelligence information under CIFA, a concept devised in the late 1990s, was a key cog in the intelligence overhaul. At Wolfowitz's direction in 2003, the Pentagon started a database known as Talon that was designed to be the military's clearinghouse for raw, unverified leads related to possible acts of terrorism, a potentially powerful tool to learn what violence and mayhem lurked outside the base gates. The federal government fell in love with databases after 9/11, and the Pentagon was its most amorous suitor, sometimes too amorous. A Pentagon program with the Orwellian name of Total Information Awareness, a data-mining project led by former Iran-contra figure John Poindexter, was shut down by Congress in 2003 after its logo—an eerie eye scanning the globe—became a symbol of Big Brother run amok. *Scientia est potentia* ("Knowledge is power"), the logo read.

Despite the congressional ban, the key remnants of the data-mining program were simply renamed and parceled out to different agencies. Some military officers were even convinced that an earlier Pentagon data-mining program known as Able Danger had managed to identify Mohamed Atta as a terrorist in Brooklyn two years before he hijacked American Airlines Flight 11. The claim was ultimately debunked, but the mindset lived on: with enough bits of information pulsing through the system, the thinking went, the U.S. government could identify almost any threat. So it was that the military officials at NORTHCOM asked their counterparts at CIFA to ping their powerful new database—do a broader study and find out how many episodes of violence and disruption were actually imperiling their recruiters as they built tomorrow's armies.

"Is there an organization? Is there a pattern?" military officials wanted to know, according to one Pentagon official involved in the effort. CIFA analysts started plugging keywords into their database, looking for episodes involving "recruiters," for instance, or "recruitment." What they found set off alarms, but not for the reasons they had predicted. Out from the system spat dozens and dozens of disparate leads and files that had nothing to do with violent attacks or disruption against military installations, or anything else that might conceivably fall under the wide umbrella of terrorist threats. A "Stop the War Now" rally in Ohio. A "Church Service for Peace" in New York. A protest against war-profiteering held outside the Houston headquarters of Halliburton, Dick Cheney's old firm. An antiwar rally at Hollywood and Vine in Los Angeles featuring a cutout of President Bush burned in effigy. A "Students for Peace and Justice" rally at the University of California at Santa Cruz. All were considered by the military to represent possible terrorist threats. The data included not just the names of the protest groups, but often what individuals were there, where they had met, and what they were so upset about.

There among the troublemakers was a tiny antiwar group in southern Florida called the Truth Project that would meet at a small Quaker meeting house in a suburban neighborhood of Lake Worth. The nonprofit group was made up mostly of graying, middle-aged opponents of the Iraq war like Rich Hersh, a retired, wheelchair-bound English professor who could still remember the German shepherds nipping at his heels at war protests he attended four decades earlier during Vietnam. Hersh's concerns about Iraq had ratcheted up not long after the war started in 2003, when his daughter, a high school senior, came home one day talking excitedly about how a military recruiter at school pitched her on the idea of becoming a Marine fighter-jet pilot. There was another, less glamorous side to the military that Hersh figured the kids weren't hearing, so he began organizing efforts to go into the schools and present a counterpoint—in effect, an anti-recruitment drive. His Truth Project group wanted to set up informational tables side by side with the military recruiters in the school cafeterias and offer kids the other side of the story.

It was his group's foray into the south Florida schools that dominated the discussion that November night in 2004 at the Quaker meeting house. The organizational meeting drew a decent crowd: forty people or so. There were a few unfamiliar faces, but there always seemed to be a few of those at these antiwar events. A lot of the onetime hippies just figured they must be on a government watch list somewhere, maybe even under surveillance by the interlopers. At past protests, Hersh and his cohorts would joke about that blond, clean-shaven young stranger sitting quietly in the back; he was wearing shiny black shoes, just like the ones Tom Wolfe wrote about undercover FBI agents wearing in San Francisco in the 1960s. At one of the group's events, a sign-in sheet with everyone's names, e-mail addresses, and phone numbers somehow went missing. Was someone really interested in their tiny little band of antiwar protesters? It seemed far-fetched. It wasn't until a year later that Hersh and his group got confirmation of sorts: there, listed in a thick catalogue of "suspicious" activities compiled by the Pentagon, was their November 13, 2004, planning meeting at the old Quaker meeting house. The event was never under actual surveillance, military officials insisted, but a "concerned citizen" had sent an e-mail reporting the antiwar event to the authorities and, just like that, the Truth Project wound up as a "credible" threat report on the military's database of suspicious terrorist activity.

Hersh had good company. By the time analysts at CIFA had finished sorting through the Talon database, they had found data collected in the military's files on more than 180 antiwar groups and events in all, culled from rallies at libraries, churches, college campuses, and anywhere else people gathered to protest the war, and a later review would put the number at 263 reports in all on protests and demonstrations. "Why do we have this stuff in here?" a senior official in Washington demanded of his analysts when he first saw a summary of the NORTHCOM findings. "Why are we talking about protest activities?" Without anyone noticing, the Pentagon had built its own secret dossier of mostly peaceful antiwar protesters, a 1960s-era throwback brought into the computer age at breakneck speed.

Officials at CIFA had some inkling even before the NORTHCOM search that material far afield from their mandate was making its way into their database. Months earlier, officials at CIFA were startled to see their terrorist database cluttered up with a file from one of the branch military police units on a homeless man at a library computer who had been spotted looking at a Defense Department Web site. This wasn't the kind of "suspicious" report that they were supposed to be collecting, the military MPs were reminded. Now, Pentagon officials realized they were looking at a much bigger problem: dozens and dozens of files on peaceful antiwar protests. Something had gone terribly wrong, they realized as they examined what the database had wrought. The antiwar file had not become public, not yet, but military officials knew it would cause a furor if and when it did. What was designed to be a Neighborhood Watch–type tip sheet for helping identify the next Mohamed Atta was instead now fingering the next Thomas Paine.

How had this happened? Military officials blamed overeager intelligence officers and MPs in the military services for compiling and forwarding threat information that never should have made its way into the terrorist database in the first place. "I don't want it, we shouldn't have had it, not interested in it," Daniel Baur, a senior official at CIFA, said after learning of the data collection and moving to purge the system of several thousand outdated, irrelevant, or questionable leads. "I don't want to deal with it." The collection of much of the information itself was not illegal, a report from the Pentagon inspector general ultimately concluded, but maintaining the records in the database for more than ninety days, it said, was a clear violation of policy.

The rules had changed after 9/11, and the lines prescribing what was and was not allowed had gotten fuzzier, almost by design. There was virtually no training on how this powerful new Pentagon database was to be compiled. "People were using technology that was way too big for them," said one military official who faulted the lack of formal training for the lapses. Suddenly, every morsel of information could be collected, stored, downloaded, analyzed, parceled out, and disseminated with the click of a mouse. At the Defense Department, there was a new mantra as it expanded its intelligence-gathering on U.S. soil: "force protection." Under Rumsfeld's expanded vision, the Pentagon was going places on American soil where it had rarely dared to tread before for fear of colliding with the doctrine of posse comitatus, which limited the military's role in domestic law enforcement operations. Threats within U.S. borders had long been the FBI's turf. But under the guise of "force protection," military intelligence officers—to the annoyance of the FBI—were now going straight to local police and sheriff's departments around the country with uncorroborated and often baseless leads for help in deterring what they saw as possible threats to their military bases. Everyone remembered the death and damage inflicted on the USS *Cole* by a couple of al Qaeda operatives on that tiny dinghy, and no one wanted to see anything like that happen again.

In increasing numbers, military officials were using secret records demands from private companies—their own version of the FBI's infamous national security letters—to pull financial data on Americans, both military personnel and civilians, who might pose a security risk. The Pentagon and the CIA had tried to get formal authority from Congress after 9/11 to issue the records demands, but congressional leaders had rebuffed them. Instead, lawyers at the Pentagon let their surprised counterparts at the Justice Department know that under their reading of the Patriot Act, they now had the expanded authority to get hold of American business records on possible security threats. Sometimes there was a legitimate military interest; other times, the links were tenuous at best. Security officials in the military branches, officials at the FBI complained, were reading their mandate so broadly as to sweep in almost anything or anyone who might be considered a threat to the military mission. In the connect-the-dots climate after 9/11, it was tough to blame them. No one ever ordered them, at least not directly, to cross a line, to disregard the civil and military constraints in place for a generation. But the competing message was clear and overriding: if there's a possibility that a threat to U.S. interests is real, go after it, and go after it hard. And if the stop-the-war protesters outside the Army gate might pose a threat, someone had to be alerted.

The message came from on high, from Bush himself, and it bled down from the top levels of the executive branch, through rank-and-file Pentagon analysts, FBI agents, and Homeland Security Department investigators, and down on to state troopers and local beat cops assigned to the FBI's local Joint Terrorism Task Forces, which sprouted by the dozens after 9/11 as a way of coordinating terror investigations. In Alabama, the state's homeland security Web site publicly listed antiwar activists, gay rights protesters, animal rights activists, and supporters of other causes as potential "single issue terrorists." In Milwaukee, two dozen members of a group called Peace Action Wisconsin, including a priest, a nun, and a bunch of high school students, missed an antiwar teach-in held in Washington because some of their names mysteriously showed up on a No Fly List as they were detained at the airport. In Northern California, members of a group called Peace Fresno were startled to learn from a photo accompanying a newspaper obituary that the quiet young man they knew at their antiwar meetings as Aaron Stokes was actually an undercover sheriff's deputy named Aaron Kilner. Teams of New York Police Department undercover officers, posing as protesters, traveled around the country for a year prior to the Republican National Convention in 2004 to gather covert intelligence on people planning to protest at the GOP convention to be held in the city. In Iowa, Justice Department prosecutors subpoenaed membership lists from sponsors of an antiwar rally at Drake University, only to drop the demand after a community outcry; an editorial in the Dubuque paper said the government's demand "has the smell of McCarthyism and the flavor of Vietnam-era espionage." In Missouri, the Justice Department subpoenaed three young men to testify before a grand jury because of unexplained suspicions that they were plotting anarchist-inspired violence at the 2004 political conventions, and the FBI sent agents knocking on the doors of dozens of other protesters around the country to find out what they knew about possible disruptions in the offing. "The message I took from it," said Sarah Bardwell, a twenty-one-year-old intern at a Quaker antiwar group in Denver who was visited by six investigators from the FBI's local Joint Terrorism Task Force at the door of her group house in the summer of 2004, "was that they were trying to intimidate us into not going to any protests and to let us know that 'Hey, we're watching you.' "

As PENTAGON OFFICIALS had feared, the story of their database dossiers on war protesters broke publicly, in December of 2005. Bill Arkin, a military analyst for NBC News and a longtime gadfly to the Pentagon, got ahold of a four-hundred-page Pentagon document indexing all the files on peaceful antiwar protests culled from the military's internal database. NBC News ran with the powerful exposé on its evening newscast and, soon enough, the targets of the Pentagon's interest became instant rock stars in the antiwar arena, their notoriety seen as a badge of honor that might have made John Lennon proud. One antiwar group at the University of California at Santa Cruz even had T-shirts made up to memorialize the moment: "Credible Threat," the T-shirts read mockingly.

A little over a year after what was supposed to be an uneventful planning meeting at the Quaker meeting house, Rich Hersh found himself a minor celebrity as a featured witness at an unofficial hearing that House Democrats held into domestic surveillance in January 2006. (House Republicans, then still in power, blocked any official hearing, forcing the Democrats to set up makeshift witness tables in the basement of the Rayburn Office Building, just down the hall from a noisy furnace room.) Hersh decried the "disruption of peaceful groups by agents of the Bush administration" and talked of his suspicions that the government had rummaged through his garbage, hacked into his e-mail, and listened in on his phone calls. Once, he might have been written off as nothing more than a paranoid kook. Now, with his group listed prominently in a secret Pentagon database and the public learning more by the day about the government's secret counterterrorism tactics, it was hard for anyone to dismiss his claims quite so cavalierly anymore.

"Is the Pentagon Spying on Americans?" asked the headline on the online version of NBC's initial report on the military database. I cringed as I read the story at my computer terminal at the office that Tuesday evening. It was a scoop I wished I'd had myself. Over the past two years, I'd broken a number of stories on the government's growing interest in antiwar demonstrations, and I'd gotten beaten up badly by the Bush administration for our aggressive coverage of the issue, even losing my press pass over it. That was what made the NBC story doubly frustrating; for all the heartburn the coverage had caused my newspaper and my editors, I figured the story of the Pentagon's secret antiwar files was one that we should have broken first. As I had come to learn through my own run-ins, there were few issues that roiled Bush administration officials so much as the suggestion that its spymasters might somehow be returning to the "bad old days" of the 1960s and early 1970s. The rampant political spying in the Vietnam era was a black mark on the American government, particularly for the FBI, and Mueller had worked to assure the public that the bureau would not revisit that era under his watch. "The FBI will be measured not only by our ability to protect the nation from terrorism," Mueller said. "We will also be measured—as we should be—by our commitment to protecting the rights and freedoms we enjoy as Americans. If we accomplish the first goal, but fail in the second, it will indeed be a Pyrrhic victory."

These were the bitter lessons passed down from earlier generations, from men like William "Crazy Bill" Sullivan, a longtime FBI official in the Hoover era. Sullivan, whose hair-trigger temper earned him his nickname, was a friend and ally of Hoover's who helped put in place some of the bureau's most notorious surveillance programs, like COINTELPRO and the infiltration of "black extremists" and the New Left in the 1960s. But by 1971, the bombastic New Englander was on the outs with Hoover over personality and policy clashes, and Sullivan was forced to resign after more than thirty years at the bureau. True to his nickname, he left in a blaze, banging out a blistering, typo-filled farewell letter on his typewriter and delivering it to his estranged mentor. In it, he lamented to Hoover the moral deterioration of an agency that he once saw as "the epitome of purity" when he joined as a rookie FBI agent more than three decades earlier. He railed against Hoover's "entirely unwarranted" fanning of communist fears in the 1950s. And he warned—years before the Church and Pike committees in the mid-1970s began to lay bare the rampant abuses of the era—that the excesses were continuing even then.

"I think we have been conducting far too many investigations called security which are actually political," he wrote. "This is our policy and it should be changed at once. What I mean is investigations mainly of students, professors, intellectuals and their organizations concerned with peace, anti-war, etc. We have no business doing this. Now, if there are definitely subversives (a word that always bothered me, hard to define) among them seeking to violate our laws, all well and good, investigate them as individuals with great care so as not [to] smear the organization they are with. Just think of the time and money we have wasted on nothing but political investigations. Is it any wonder so many students and professors detest the FBI. I am not the only one who thinks this. Many, many field agents think the same and some have resigned and commented about it."

Sullivan was long gone by the time Coleen Rowley joined the FBI in 1981, and a whole new set of laws and regulations was in place to guard against the types of political abuses that Sullivan had warned about. But as both a lawyer and an agent at the bureau who was at the center of one of the FBI's most vexing investigations before 9/11, the one into Zacarias Moussaoui, Rowley was well aware how times of national crisis could test the bureau's mettle and lead it back to places it had long ago deserted. That was why she was so troubled when she read an internal memo that analysts at FBI headquarters put out in

October of 2003. With major antiwar protests looming in Washington and San Francisco, Intelligence Bulletin 89 warned law enforcement officials around the country about the potential for disruption at the protests and urged local police to report anything suspicious to their local Joint Terrorism Task Force. "Tactics Used During Protests and Demonstrations," the memo was called.

In her FBI field office in Minneapolis, Rowley read the memo with a furrowed brow. The memo talked about how violent protesters might use homemade bombs or fake IDs to further their ends. That was good information to have. But the analysis also talked, in surprising depth, about tactics that were unquestionably legal—how protesters had used the Internet to raise money for protests, had set up "training camps" to rehearse their demonstrations, and had hired lawyers to represent anyone arrested in acts of civil disobedience. The FBI's interest in ferreting out violence at protests seemed understandable enough to Rowley, but the dual focus on what seemed to be clear, protected First Amendment activities struck her as odd, even reckless. What was the FBI doing examining the way antiwar protesters organized themselves?

Rowley set aside the memo on a corner of her desk, not sure what if anything to do with it. It lay there, untouched, for a few weeks. Then came a second memo from FBI headquarters, this one in advance of another set of protests over a free trade meeting in Miami. Again, the memo examined and analyzed legal tactics side by side with illegal ones based on intelligence that the FBI had gathered from a variety of sources, public and private, about recent protests. This time, Rowley was so bothered by the pattern that she decided to do something about it.

By now, Rowley had become a squeaky wheel in the normally staid halls of the FBI. Less than a year before, she had appeared on the cover of *Time* magazine as one of three whistle-blowers named as "Persons of the Year" after she reported to Congress on the FBI's failure to move against Zacarias Moussaoui as a terrorist threat. But as her profile rose, some fellow agents thought Rowley had gotten too self-important for her own good, or that of the FBI. She had violated the old maxim: Don't embarrass the bureau. She became particularly outspoken in her concerns about the looming war in Iraq, and she alienated many colleagues by going public with a note she wrote to Mueller eight months earlier, in March of 2003, warning that the coming war was a distraction from the country's real focus on terrorism and would "bring an exponential increase in the terrorist threat to the U.S., both at home and abroad." Again, she questioned the FBI's counterterrorism capabilities—an unusual public airing that the head of the FBI Agents Association fumed "can be seen as providing aid and comfort to our al Qaeda enemies." Rowley's estrangement from her colleagues became such a festering sore that she asked to be reassigned from her post as the chief FBI lawyer in the Minneapolis field office. But the notoriety didn't silence her.

Troubled by the FBI memos she read about the tactics at the upcoming antiwar protests, Rowley filed a formal internal ethics complaint in Washington, charging that the intelligence bulletins improperly blurred the line between actual crimes and lawful free speech and could have a chilling effect on peaceful political protests. Even Mueller himself was said to be concerned about the loose wording—and possible misinterpretation—of the FBI's nationwide bulletins. FBI officials in Washington didn't think the memos caused any real "chill," but Coleen Rowley, *Time* magazine cover girl, was not someone who could be ignored any longer. So officials kicked the complaint over to the Justice Department's Office of Legal Counsel for review. It found the FBI standing squarely on the right side of the bright line. "Given the limited nature of such public monitoring," the legal opinion concluded, "any possible 'chilling' effect caused by the bulletins would be quite minimal and substantially outweighed by the public interest in maintaining safety and order during large-scale demonstrations."

Not that there wasn't a genuine danger of crossing that line. FBI agents around the country complained that they were confused about just what was and was not allowed anymore under the eased guidelines Ashcroft had put out encouraging them to visit public rallies, peruse Web sites, and go anywhere the public was allowed to go. Did that mean agents should begin poking around into the activities of a group that angrily accused Bush of being a dangerous war criminal, or Cheney of being a war-profiteering criminal? When did First Amendment speech cross over into an actual threat? Many agents weren't so sure anymore. The confusion prompted FBI headquarters to put out new guidance in March of 2004. The FBI could go undercover at a rally if it had reason to believe a crime might occur, headquarters advised, but "agents may not conduct surveillance of individuals or groups solely for monitoring the exercise of rights protected by the First Amendment."

In Boston, agents were afraid of crossing that sometimes blurry line as they braced for protests and possible "terrorism threats" at the Democratic National Convention in the summer of 2004. The Boston field office went so far as to compile a list of protesters who had been arrested for crimes at past protests that had turned violent, and it examined whether anyone on the list was planning to attend the Boston convention. An analysis found no indication that violence was planned at the Democratic convention, but some FBI officials wanted to go ahead anyway that summer and start interviewing everyone on the list who had a history of violence at demonstrations. A supervisor in Boston nixed the idea. To start interviewing demonstrators so close to the convention, the supervisor decided, "might have a chilling effect on First Amendment rights." The many leads that the FBI did follow that summer, the inspector general ultimately concluded, "were conducted for legitimate law enforcement purposes," not to stifle anyone's free speech.

This was the kind of delicate debate playing out quietly in law enforcement, military, and intelligence circles as protests over the war in Iraq grew more virulent. There was little in the way of public information, much less debate, about the tactics the FBI and other intelligence agencies were employing, at least not until a source provided me with a copy of the intelligence bulletins on the antiwar protests circulated at the FBI in the fall of 2003. The memos, the same ones that had so troubled Coleen Rowley, were not meant for public dissemination. These were for cops' eyes only. The bulletins pointed up the FBI's concerns about vague hints of violence at the antiwar protests. As I read through them, I was struck by the FBI's commingling of bomb-throwing anarchists and peaceful protesters in the same breath, along with its decision to route all the intelligence culled from the protests through its Joint Terrorism Task Forces. The FBI seemed oblivious to the mixed message it was sending.

As I began drafting a story, the editors and I realized this would be a potentially explosive piece, closely scrutinized by both the left and the right. We were careful to balance the top of the piece with a strong emphasis on why the FBI was doing what it was doing. I quoted FBI officials stressing that the effort to analyze demonstrators' tactics was aimed solely at rooting out violent anarchists, not monitoring political speech, and we noted high up in the story that "the initiative has won the support of some local police, who view it as a critical way to maintain order at large-scale demonstrations." It was a balanced piece, sober in tone, and it ran above the fold on the front page of the Sunday newspaper. "F.B.I. Scrutinizes Antiwar Rallies," read the headline, then, the subhead: "Officials Say Effort Aims at 'Extremist Elements.' "

The story got picked up nationally, and officials at the FBI and the Justice Department were soon seething. That day, I began getting calls from fellow reporters letting me know that the FBI was pillorying me and my story. The facts were not in dispute, but the FBI thought the supposed "angle" and the "slant" were unfair. Then, the officials began calling my editors to complain in what would become a weeks-long campaign by the Justice Department.

By now, I had grown accustomed to the complaints. When I first moved from the *Los Angeles Times* to *The New York Times* a year earlier, in the fall of 2002, I had a decent relationship with Ashcroft and the Justice Department. Several of his senior aides even cheered my hiring following two years of what they thought was unfair coverage from the "gray old lady" of *The New York Times*. I could never quite figure out their upbeat reaction to my arrival, since I had written any number of stories that were sharply critical of the Bush Justice Department, just as I had with the Clinton Justice Department. As best I could tell, some of Ashcroft's aides were enamored with a lengthy front-page piece I had done at the *L.A. Times* four months into Ashcroft's administration, long before 9/11, suggesting that all the high-octane predictions during his confirmation about Ashcroft rolling back a quarter-century of civil rights gains may have been a bit overblown. ("A strange thing happened on the way to Armageddon," I wrote in the piece. "So far at least, Ashcroft has led the Justice Department on a path that, to the surprise of many, is not altogether different on civil rights matters than that of his Democratic predecessor." Civil rights leaders on the left chided me for my analysis, saying it was much too early to judge the damage that Ashcroft was capable of doing. "Just you wait," one warned me. In hindsight, he may have had a point.)

So as I began covering the Justice Department for *The New York*

Times in the fall of 2002, I had regular access to Ashcroft and his people and, despite a "no reporters allowed" rule for the attorney general's
pickup basketball games at the FBI, I was invited to join him one night.
Guarding the attorney general, I nicked him on the nose while trying
to block a 1950s-style set shot that he made. "Don't send me to Guantánamo," I joked, gesturing over to the FBI security detail standing
stone-faced on the sidelines. "Don't worry," he said. "I've given a lot
more than I've gotten from you tonight with the fouls." As far as
metaphors go, this one would become an apt one for my relationship
with the attorney general and his Justice Department. I was always
conscious about not letting whatever access I had gained to Ashcroft's
inner circle influence the tone or substance of my coverage. In fact, my
coverage of the Justice Department grew sharper-edged the more we
learned about the administration's problems and policies on terrorism,
the Patriot Act, gun enforcement, and a range of other hot-button topics. The collapse of the Jose Padilla "dirty bomber" case was one turning point in the coverage for me, and Inspector General Glenn Fine's
scathing report on the 9/11 detainees was another.

Now, when Ashcroft announced a purported al Qaeda link to some
mosque in Brooklyn, I was no longer quite so quick to run to the news
desk to pitch a potential front-page story. To Ashcroft and his aides,
my critical coverage amounted to a reporter's bias; to me, it reflected a
growing and healthy skepticism in the face of facts from the administration that often just didn't add up. Ashcroft stopped speaking to me,
I was "disinvited" from some press events, and the press shop issued
more than a dozen edicts to staffers instructing them not to talk to me.

While the *Times'* national prominence made it a convenient target,
I was far from the only reporter to tangle with Ashcroft's press
machine. When the dean of the Justice Department beat reporters,
ABC's Beverley Lumpkin, posted a short item on her Internet blog in
2002 about the department's decision to buy $8,000 worth of blue
drapes to cover up a twelve-foot-high, half-nude female statue that had
often stood in the background of Ashcroft's media shots, she quickly
found herself ostracized. The image of the famously religious Ashcroft
covering up the nude statue became fodder for Jay Leno and company
for years to come. Ashcroft simply stopped calling on Lumpkin at
press conferences, leaving her to wave her hand in vain from the front
row. When Lumpkin volunteered to cover a new beat at the Depart-

ment of Homeland Security, a Justice Department official even took credit for pushing her out. "Those blue drapes, they never forgave me for it," Lumpkin said. By 2003, press relations had become so polarized at the Justice Department that nearly two dozen reporters representing virtually every major newspaper, wire service, and magazine in the national media sent Ashcroft a letter that I helped draft bemoaning our inability to get "timely, useable and accurate information" from the Justice Department.

There was a brief thaw for beat reporters, but tensions over my own coverage of the department only grew worse in June of 2003 when I wrote a story raising questions about the role Mike Chertoff, the criminal division chief and a judicial nominee, might have played in the decision not to give John Walker Lindh access to a lawyer in Afghanistan. Justice Department officials, worried about the impact on Chertoff's pending nomination to a federal appeals court, blasted the story. Then, an official passed on to Senator Orrin Hatch a titillating if ultimately meaningless tidbit: I had worked on stories at the newspaper with Jayson Blair, the serial fabricator who set off a scandal that was then reaching a boil. (I had worked with Blair on three stories about the D.C. sniper case the year before. None of those published stories was found to have relied on any fabricated or plagiarized material by Blair, and an internal review at the paper found that several reporters, myself included, had actually brought our concerns about Blair's reporting to our editors long before the scandal broke.)

Hatch, then the chairman of the Senate Judiciary Committee, was gaveling a committee meeting on Chertoff's nomination the day my story appeared. Normally a genteel man to the point of being saccharine, Hatch lit into the story. He was outraged that the *Times* had published a story on the eve of his committee's vote on Chertoff's nomination in what he said was an effort to "impugn" a good nominee. Then he noted with dramatic effect that the author of the story on Chertoff had "shared bylines with the infamous Mr. Blair." The remark was a stunner. Several reporters at the press table could be heard hissing at Hatch's blindside attack. Senator Leahy, the ranking Democrat, fired back, likening the guilt-by-association linkage to "McCarthyism." Luckily, I wasn't at the hearing to witness the scene, but I began getting calls about it within minutes from fellow reporters and congressional aides who were there. My simmering disputes with the Justice Department had now gone public, with a senior Republican senator drawn in for good measure.

Days later, I got a call at the office—from Hatch himself. His tone was very different, the fist-pounding oratory from the hearing now gone. "I, um, just called to apologize," the senator said. He explained that he had reviewed his remarks at the hearing and realized he had gone too far. I thanked him for the call, but his mea culpa wasn't complete. A few weeks later, I ran into Hatch in the hallway at the Dirksen Office Building after another Judiciary Committee hearing, and he came up to me to apologize again—in person. A Mormon, Hatch began quoting a biblical verse about forgiveness, and then, in a final gesture of contrition, put both arms around me and gave me a big bear hug. Over Hatch's shoulder, I could see a couple of other reporters snickering at the odd sight of the apologetic senator and the aggrieved reporter in a clench. I knew I wouldn't live this one down for a while.

For all the bad blood, nothing quite prepared me for the reaction to my front-page story about the FBI's interest in antiwar demonstrations. Iraq was the third-rail issue for the administration, and Justice Department officials were infuriated by the charge from civil rights advocates that they were somehow trying to silence antiwar voices. A few weeks after my story on the internal FBI bulletins ran in the paper, a fellow reporter in the Washington bureau and I were scheduled to interview an antitrust official at the Justice Department for a story we were doing on a price-fixing investigation. The Justice Department let it be known that I was no longer welcome at the interview. Phil Taubman, our Washington bureau chief, got on the phone with Mark Corallo, who had taken over as head of public affairs. The conversation was civil enough, but Corallo made it clear that the Justice Department did not appreciate what it considered my overly critical coverage and my overly abrasive style of interviewing. Taubman heard him out, and they ended the conversation with an understanding that I would be allowed to attend the interview as scheduled.

The next day, I showed up at the Justice Department for the interview with my colleague and scanned my department-issued press pass through the security gate. A red light came on. I let a security guard behind the glass partition know that my press pass wasn't working. She ran it through her own scanner. "It's been canceled," she said. "On whose orders?" I asked. She glanced back at her computer screen.

"Mark Corallo, director of public affairs," she answered. I was finally able to get a personal escort to take me upstairs to the scheduled interview, but Taubman was furious when he found out what had happened. He felt double-crossed, and he called Corallo to tell him so. The Justice Department was now in the business of canceling a reporter's press pass because they didn't like his stories? This conversation, unlike their first one, got quite heated. "You realize," Phil told him, "that this is basically a declaration of war on *The New York Times.*" Corallo ripped into both my coverage and the newspaper as a whole, angrily suggesting that our top editor, Bill Keller, was biased against the administration because of opinion pieces he'd written as a columnist and thus shouldn't be running the newspaper.

For all the shouting, Corallo quickly backed down and my press pass was restored within a few days, but across the street at the FBI, Cassandra Chandler, the FBI's assistant director for public affairs, was still upset about my story on the antiwar protests. She put out an internal memo to the special agents in charge of the FBI's fifty-six field offices ripping my story, my ethics, and my "slanted and biased" reporting. "In the meantime," she wrote, "we encourage each of you to please avoid providing information to this reporter." Already persona non grata at the Justice Department, I'd now been blacklisted by the FBI too. Upset about my coverage of a free speech issue, the FBI and the Justice Department had responded by trying to take away the tools essential to a free press—my press pass and my access to FBI officials. The unintended irony only underscored a main reason we had written the story about the antiwar protests in the first place.

Chandler set up her own meeting with Phil Taubman and, over breakfast at the Hay-Adams Hotel near the White House, tore into my coverage. What she didn't know was that a source, upset by my blacklisting, had already provided me with a copy of the e-mail she'd sent out about me, and I'd shown it to Phil in advance of their meeting. He heard her out, defended my reporting as fair and accurate, then threw in a curveball. Whatever the FBI's gripes, he told Chandler, the newspaper didn't appreciate the FBI sending around internal e-mails making unfounded personal attacks on one of its reporters and discouraging people from talking to him. Chandler was blindsided. She was still incensed when she returned to the FBI office. "How the hell did they get that memo?" she demanded.

Not long after, the FBI was organizing an in-house seminar for some of its communications people from field offices around the country on how to deal with the press. The bureau had invited a number of prominent national reporters to take part in a panel discussion on how they went about covering the FBI. Not surprisingly, I wasn't on the list. Not that I wasn't considered. It turned out there had been some discussion at the FBI about broadening the list of media invitees to include a wider sampling of disparate voices, even those perceived inside headquarters as being overly critical of the bureau; maybe a D.C. reporter from Al Jazeera, the Arab-based network that had become the landing spot for al Qaeda tapes, someone suggested, or maybe Lichtblau from *The New York Times*. An FBI official with whom I was on fairly good terms (there were still a few left in the bureau) told me later about the exchange. "Great, so now I'm being lumped with Al Jazeera?" I asked in mock astonishment. "Trust me," the FBI official responded. "Al Jazeera would have gotten a seat at the table before you."

Stripped of my press pass, blacklisted by the FBI, and now lumped with Al Jazeera. So, this was what it was like to be a big-league reporter.

THERE'S A MOMENT in time when a fuse is lit, a passion born. The moment is powerful and pungent, and it carries with it the sight and sound and feel of possibilities both real and imagined: the "swish" of a ball hitting net for the first time as a clapping, bounding five-year-old dreams of becoming the next Michael Jordan; the red haze of a sunset bleeding into the greens of a forest range on an aspiring artist's debut canvas; the sound of rolling laughter and hands slapping knees as a nervous amateur comedian first connects with his audience on open-mic night. The instant I first knew I wanted to be a reporter, the moment carried with it the acrid smell of smoke, the flash of sirens, and the halting sobs of a woman left homeless. It was after 3 a.m. one morning more than two decades ago, when sirens rattled the dilapidated newsroom of *The Cornell Daily Sun*, sending me and a few other late-night stragglers to the window to check out the commotion on the street below as fire trucks wailed.

Just another run-of-the-mill fire in downtown Ithaca, a short sprint from the pedestrian mall that the *Daily Sun* called home. It was the kind of story my college newspaper would typically ignore: it didn't sound terribly serious, and it held no consequence at all for the college students who would be scanning the headlines the next morning over granola bars at the Willard Straight Hall cafeteria. Besides, the newspaper's 3:30 a.m. deadline was fast approaching. No matter. "Let's go," my colleague-in-arms, Marc Lacey, as raw and eager as I was, said excitedly as we grabbed our notepads, our pens, and our press passes and raced the few blocks to the scene.

The flames were still smoldering when we arrived. The house was gutted. No other reporters were there yet. Sitting on the curb behind the yellow police line was a distraught middle-aged woman. In tears, she used her shirt as a makeshift handkerchief. A firefighter emerging from the building told how the flames "just sort of jumped out at us" from a second-floor bedroom. Then we approached the woman herself, as she described her escape from the fire and her fear that she'd lost everything. It wasn't a remarkable story by any measure, and our reporting was, in truth, somewhat shoddy, perhaps even libelous: the tearful woman charged that her estranged husband had set the blaze as revenge. "He told me he's going to ruin the house if I didn't get back together with him," she sobbed. "I know for a fact he did it." For all we knew, the husband was nowhere near the scene when the fire started, but we went with the wife's sensational charge anyway, even making it the lead of the story. Racing back to the newsroom minutes before deadline, we got the story in the next day's paper—on the front page, no less. An inauspicious beginning, to be sure, but this was our story, and we were there on the scene to tell it, managing to beat the professional paper in town, *The Ithaca Journal.* Even as college students, the competitive juices of journalism drove us. Clipping out our article for my thin scrapbook, I scrawled in the margin: "Journal didn't cover husband-wife angle until 3 days later—Police have determined arson responsible." I had my first scoop.

To a wide-eyed cub reporter, this was what journalism was all about: getting there first to chronicle the living, breathing sagas that people might want to read about the next morning. The task became a daily dare, a constant challenge for the insatiably curious: Hey, tell me something I didn't know. A year or so later, on a college road trip to New York City, Marc and I stopped at a local landmark on West 43rd

Street and posed for a photo; the two of us shook hands underneath an understated sign in Gothic lettering that announced the storied occupant: *The New York Times*. Someday, we said, we'd be back there for real, not as gawking tourists but as reporters. It was the sort of by-the-campfire blood oath that two teenagers might make to memorialize a secret, preposterous pledge. But somehow, we did both manage to make our way back to 43rd Street. We'd go on to cover race riots and presidential scandals, tsunamis, earthquakes, wildfires, and genocide. But whenever Marc and I would get together over the years, the story that always demanded another retelling was "the fire." That was when the fuse was first lit.

Like many reporters, I've always seen journalism as a noble public service, as much a calling as a career. But as the media's standing in the public eye has sunk in recent years, we as journalists have been forced to question our own self-perceptions. We are, our legions of critics tell us constantly, in pursuit not of the truth, but of something more perverse, something more self-serving. The media industry has no doubt brought on some of the flagellation through its own glaring missteps: the scandals of Jayson Blair at the *Times* and Jack Kelley at *USA Today*, the pursuit of tawdry, sensational stories, the rush to get it first without knowing all the facts. But the kerosene on the fire of mistrust was furnished by an administration in Washington that cast the media as destructive or, worse, irrelevant. George Bush himself seemed to set the tone even before his election in 2000 in an aside he made to his running mate, Dick Cheney, at a campaign stop in Illinois, all caught on a live mic that Bush didn't realize was on. "There's Adam Clymer, major league asshole from *The New York Times*," the candidate said of a veteran political reporter who had written stories about Bush's record in Texas that the candidate thought were unfair. "Oh yeah, he is, bigtime," Cheney answered back.

The attitude went beyond any single reporter or newspaper. Journalists "don't represent the public any more than other people do," Bush's longtime chief of staff, Andy Card, told one interviewer in a comment that seemed aimed at rebutting the Fourth Estate's longheld, constitutionally grounded role in a free society. "I don't believe [journalists] have a check-and-balance function," Card said. Bush bragged about not reading the newspapers much (even though he did), and Cheney and other hard-liners close to the president pushed a strategy that prized secrecy over public scrutiny, confrontation with the press over conciliation. Cheney even banned the *New York Times'* reporters from his plane for a time. Not since Nixon's darkest days in Watergate had the White House and the press suffered from such a bitter and adversarial relationship. Cooler heads would come to question the administration's hard-line media strategy. Indeed, when Robert Gates replaced Donald Rumsfeld as Secretary of Defense in 2007, he seemed to be speaking as much to his fellow officials in the executive branch as to the graduating cadets at the Naval Academy when he said: "The press is not the enemy, and to treat it as such is self-defeating."

The administration's penchant for secrecy was driven by Cheney and his top aides. Cheney believed the executive branch's business was best conducted in private, and he even went so far as to try to abolish the executive branch agency that sought unsuccessfully for four years to monitor his office's use of classified material. Cheney detested leaks. Three months after 9/11, he and his staff were outraged by an apparent leak to *The New York Times* about a government investigation into two Islamic charities with suspected ties to terrorist financing. When the Justice Department was given the job of leading a multiagency task force that year to look at the problem of leaks, Cheney's people saw the chance for a crackdown, and they pushed for far tougher criminal penalties on those government officials who disclosed unauthorized information. The steps they sought, officials familiar with the heated but hidden internal debate said, were more in line with Britain's broad Official Secrets Act than with the American system's premium on a free and open press. Aides to Ashcroft balked. Ashcroft himself had rolled back the Freedom of Information Act soon after 9/11 by giving agencies much more discretion to keep material secret on national security grounds. Where the policy under Reno established a "presumption of disclosure," Ashcroft tilted the balance toward secrecy. But the proposals from the vice president's office went too far even for the Justice Department's liking.

Senior Justice Department officials considered the ideas being advocated by David Addington, Cheney's powerful counselor, to be "draconian." While they thought leaks were a problem, they also believed the current laws on the books went far enough in deterring them. Their resistance to new criminal penalties for leaks led to several tense private conversations with Addington. The leaking, Addington told the Justice Department, had to stop. "We need the criminal penalties," he demanded in one meeting. Addington had a domineering reputation as the smartest lawyer in any room—and one who wasn't afraid to let the others know it. He was "someone who spoke for and acted with the full backing of the powerful Vice President," Justice Department lawyer and frequent rival Jack Goldsmith wrote, "and someone who crushed bureaucratic opponents." This time, though, the Justice Department held its ground, refusing to take the more severe steps on media leaks that Addington was advancing. He and Cheney lost out, but the message left by the tense, closed-door episode was unmistakable: this was a White House that liked its business kept confidential, and the prying eyes of the press and the public were not helping the fight against terror.

If Dick Cheney was the vise-grip intent on ensuring the administration's tight-lipped ways, Alberto Gonzales was, as always, the enabler, drawing up new legal interpretations as White House counsel in Bush's first term to keep information from the press and the public whenever expedient. It was a role he had played before. As lawyer to Governor Bush in Texas, Gonzales cleared the way for Bush to house his state papers in his father's presidential library for a time in a move that shielded the records from public view. At the White House, the pattern continued. Gonzales helped to craft a new executive order signed by Bush in 2001 that allowed the sitting president to determine whether records for past presidents—including, not coincidentally, Bush's father—should be kept secret even after a twelve-year waiting period. The presidential records, in the view of Gonzales and the Bush White House, belonged not to the American public, but to the president himself. It was a view that harked back to Nixon's fight over who owned the secret White House audiotapes. "We thought it would be more appropriate," Gonzales told reporters, "to really give the primary responsibility regarding presidential records to the former president whose records they belong to, and to have the incumbent president sort of be the backstop in making decisions about whether or not those documents should in fact be released."

Always mindful of his client, Gonzales took the concept of executive privilege to its furthest reaches. He withheld from the public and the press the names of energy industry executives whom Cheney had met with in developing the administration's energy policies. He tried, unsuccessfully, to block the 9/11 Commission from getting access to key documents and from hearing testimony from key figures like national security advisor Condoleezza Rice. Gonzales, a 2004 report from the the Reporters Committee for Freedom of the Press charged, "has been an active defender of what is best described as quasi–executive privilege, invoked repeatedly by the Bush administration in attempts to keep government information from public scrutiny."

The Bush administration's war on terror quickly became, in many critical respects, a war of information as well, aimed both at collecting information on suspected terrorists and at keeping information from the American public. The First Amendment was both a bludgeon and a shield. It gave administration officials a bullhorn that they could use to rally the faithful and attack the skeptics. But it also provided a net-tlesome platform to trumpet views that, in the administration's view, could threaten national security.

Information in the wrong hands, administration officials believed, could only help al Qaeda. Soon after 9/11, librarians at public universities that stored government material were ordered to destroy CD-ROMs in their collections on national reservoirs and dams because government officials told them the information could aid the enemy; a librarian at Syracuse University, repulsed by the directive, cut the CD into tiny shards and threw them away. Government Web sites on hazardous waste sites and nuclear material were taken down. The administration's classification of government documents ballooned, and American spy agencies began reclassifying tens of thousands of pages of documents that had been already publicly available for many years, like the number of American spies in business in 1946. Material that reporters once could walk into a government press office to peruse at their leisure, like the travel arrangements of cabinet secretaries, now had to be sought under the Freedom of Information Act, often to be turned down under Ashcroft's new guidelines. The Justice Department invoked the rarely used "state secrets" privilege to bottle up arcane bits of information like the specific languages translated by an FBI whistle-blower. Government photographs showing the coffins of dead soldiers brought back from Iraq were released only in error when a military clerk mistakenly approved a Freedom of Information Act request. And page after page of procedures used to compile the government's error-filled No Fly Lists were blacked out in their public release, earning the government a tongue-lashing from a federal judge over its "frivolous claims" to secrecy.

By 2004, the culture of secrecy that had infected the Bush administration was generating a rash of discomfort that went well beyond just the ACLU and those usually concerned with government overreaching. Judges were becoming fed up, and presidential historians were beginning to describe the Bush administration as the most secretive in the country's history. One open government group catalogued all the documents the government was now classifying—from the truly sensitive covert operations to the more dubious ones like the World War II spy files—and found a 60 percent surge just since 2001.

I called up a White House official I knew and asked him: Why so secretive? "We are in a wartime environment," the official explained. In its wartime footing, that meant the government was collecting more intelligence, the official said, and with it came more secrets. (The official, appropriately enough, insisted on being quoted anonymously for the story I was writing on the administration's penchant for secrecy. Old habits die hard.) Even if the identity of the unnamed White House source was obscured, the message from the White House was clear: in the post–9/11 age, the government had more secrets than ever before that the public just didn't need to know. And we were about to stumble onto one of the biggest.

CHAPTER FIVE

Sworn to Secrecy

TWENTY-THREE DAYS after the Twin Towers fell, President Bush signed off on a secret eavesdropping operation so sensitive that even many of the country's senior national security officials, men and women with the highest security clearances in his administration, knew nothing about it. Within twelve hours of its inception, however, the program's cover was blown.

It happened at the FBI, as intelligence officials there were chasing the latest in a torrent of overseas terrorism leads that swept through the bureau after 9/11. By accident, technicians stumbled on to something odd. Someone on U.S. soil was being wiretapped, they realized, but the FBI wasn't involved, at least not directly. This was an NSA operation. More troubling still, there was no court order to be found. "What the hell's going on here?" one FBI official asked when he first learned of the apparent breach. The National Security Agency—the powerful spy agency so secretive that the joke for many years was that its initials stood for "No Such Agency"—was supposed to be in the *foreign* intelligence business. What was it doing targeting and wiretapping Americans? By custom and by law, that just didn't happen, at least not since the dark days of Watergate, when the NSA was caught spying on political activists, war opponents, and hostile reporters under the guise of national security. Whatever was going on, this was serious.

An FBI official ran the issue immediately up to Dale Watson, the head of counterterrorism at the FBI. The NSA is up to something, Watson was told. Watson looked shocked to be asked about the issue so quickly, as if he knew something but couldn't say. "What's going on here? Is this legal?" Watson was asked. "You better go talk to the deputy," Watson responded. The deputy was Tom Pickard, a veteran G-man who had been the acting director of the bureau until just a month earlier. Pickard knew nothing about the program. The NSA was targeting people on U.S. soil? "What the fuck are you talking about?" the deputy director asked. So Pickard went to Bob Mueller. Up and up the FBI's dumbwaiter went the NSA hot potato, landing finally at the desk of the FBI director, a veteran, by-the-book prosecutor who had been running the bureau for all of four weeks. It's okay, Director Mueller told Pickard. The NSA operation had been approved at the highest levels; everything was in order. Still, Pickard seemed troubled. "If I could find out," he told colleagues wryly after the exchange, "anyone could."

Within days, the White House began slowly expanding the small universe of intelligence officials allowed to know about the wiretapping program. It was a move made out of grudging necessity; the intense questions at the very start of the program about its legality were already causing too much skittishness among U.S. intelligence and counterterrorism officials—not just at the FBI, but at the highest levels of the NSA and the Justice Department as well. The brushfire had to be contained. "If you're going to keep a secret," one intelligence official told his boss after learning of the program, "you've got to tell the people who are going to stumble on to it."

Secrecy was both the Bush administration's rhapsody and its ruin. Nowhere was that more obvious than in the NSA program, and nowhere was the zeal for secrecy ultimately more damaging to its national security operations. Intelligence officials who needed to know what the NSA was doing and how the United States was gathering its terrorism intelligence weren't allowed to find out. Government lawyers who came to suspect that the White House and the NSA were operating outside the lines of their legal authority were shut out, often by design. The vice president's office blocked even lawyers for the NSA from seeing the legal opinions at the Justice Department justifying the operation at their own agency. Most members of the full congressional intelligence committees, mandated by law to be briefed on all intelligence programs as a check on executive branch abuses, were never told about this one. Whatever was going on, they didn't need to know. And those who did know were bound by a secret handshake.

The secrecy, inevitably, bred suspicion. The NSA's wiretapping program would not break into a full-blown internal crisis inside the Bush administration for almost two and a half years, and it would not erupt into a very public scandal for almost another two years after that. But from its earliest days—indeed, its earliest hours—unease was roiling the administration over the program, burning everyone it touched and sparking intense nervousness over the same question that officials at the FBI had whispered: *What the hell's going on here?*

At the Homeland Security Department, even Tom Ridge, a senior member of Bush's own cabinet entrusted by the president with the task of protecting the country from another attack, knew not to ask what was going on. NSA officers would show up at his office with foreign intelligence leads that seemed to point to people in the United States; the origins of the leads were never clear. "There was always this notion that something was going on, but you didn't know what," Ridge said. Some of the leads seemed legitimate; many others seemed to lead to nothing and simply faded away. Suspicious, Ridge began to ask the NSA staffers assigned to his office where all this stuff was coming from. "We got it," the NSA aides would tell him. "That's all you need to know."

At an AT&T facility in San Francisco, a technician named Mark Klein answered the door of his office complex one day in the summer of 2002 to find an NSA representative who was there on an undisclosed assignment. Not long after, Klein learned of a secret room being built on the sixth floor of another AT&T facility on Folsom Street. The room, off-limits to almost all employees, housed powerful computer equipment capable of sifting through vast amounts of Internet traffic as it passed through the facility's fiber-optic lines. Room 641A was so tightly controlled, in fact, that when employees noticed an air conditioner leaking fluid down to the fifth-floor room below, no one could get inside to fix it; the only technician with the proper clearance was out of town. Working an Internet room one day, Klein came across three documents that detailed how all the sophisticated routing equipment inside the secret room was linked up in a way that appeared to give the NSA access to vast streams of data pulsing throughout the United States. Then he heard from other AT&T technicians about similar mystery rooms in other cities across the country. As Klein pieced together all the strange things he'd seen, the first thing he thought about was George Orwell's *1984.*

At the nation's secret intelligence court in Washington, responsible for reviewing applications under the Foreign Intelligence Surveillance Act, or FISA as the law is known, court and government personnel knew to route all wiretap applications growing out of a certain "special access" program only to a single judge and to bypass the other ten judges on the court. On the most secretive court in the land, this was a program too secret even for them to handle.

At the FBI command center one day in late 2001, a senior intelligence official started discussing a wiretap issue with Michael Woods, one of the bureau's in-house experts on the dos and don'ts of eavesdropping law. The official was being unusually cryptic. "Are you read into the program?" the official asked, his voice hesitant. "Do you know what I'm talking about?" Woods' blank expression gave the answer. He had no clue. The conversation ended there.

And at the Justice Department, just days after the NSA program started, James Baker walked into the fourth-floor office of Deputy Attorney General Larry Thompson with a stack of wiretap applications for Thompson to review—fourteen or fifteen in all. The warrants required Thompson's signature so they could be sent to the Foreign Intelligence Surveillance Court for a judge's review and approval. Baker's office, known as the Office of Intelligence Policy and Review, or OIPR, was the gateway to the court in the wiretapping process. Anyone who wanted to get a FISA wiretap warrant had to go through Baker's office first. Ashcroft and Thompson, his number two, were the only ones allowed to sign them before they went on to the court. Thompson eyed the latest pile of applications, most of them a quarter-inch thick and totaling forty or fifty pages or more. The stack, unfortunately, was nothing new. In the bleary-eyed days and weeks after 9/11, with lawyers in Baker's shop working six-day weeks, a crush of wiretaps had become the norm. Each wiretap warrant, each intelligence lead, now carried both the promise of a foiled plot and the fear of another missed opportunity.

As they plowed through the batch of the latest wiretaps, Thompson and Baker went through what had become a routine if hurried checklist—determining the source of the intelligence, what U.S. residents were involved, how the government had met its burden of establishing probable cause to eavesdrop on someone suspected of being connected to a foreign agent or power. This was all now routine stuff, the protocol necessary for Thompson to give his sign-off for the wire-taps. Then Thompson got to an application that looked like all the others—except that on this one, there was no indication of just how the Justice Department had gotten on to the terrorism lead in the first place or why the suspect was being targeted; the source was a mystery. Where had the information come from? "What's the connection?" Thompson wanted to know. Baker stopped him. I can't tell you, he said. Thompson was stunned.

It was an extraordinary moment, reflective of the Alice in Wonderland quality of the new order of post-9/11 intelligence. Thompson was the second-ranking law enforcement official in the country, a widely respected former prosecutor held in such high regard by Bush himself that he was often discussed as a Supreme Court nominee. Baker was a career government lawyer; diligent, hardworking, widely respected himself, but notches below Thompson on the Justice Department flow chart. And here he was in the awkward position of telling the number two official at the Justice Department: *You don't need to know.*

In what would amount to a silent protest, Thompson refused to sign off on the wiretap. It seemed clear that whatever he was being asked to approve was no anomaly; wherever these top secret wiretaps were coming from, there seemed sure to be more waiting in the pipeline. If Baker wanted these ultrasecret taps approved, he'd have to go straight to the attorney general himself. Thompson would tell associates he was piqued about the whole episode—and understandably so. His first concern was for the integrity of the process in place for this secret operation, or lack of it, and his duties as an officer of the court. Thompson asked one of his top deputies, David Kris, to write him a memo analyzing the troubling question of whether he should sign this new breed of warrant that Baker had brought to him. It was the blind leading the blind, since neither Thompson nor Kris knew what the secret program even was. Kris was regarded as a hard-liner on matters of legal process and procedure, and when Thompson asked him for his legal opinion on signing these mysterious new warrants, his answer was firm: Don't do it. "You don't know what it is," Kris told Thompson, "so how can you in good faith sign it?"

Soon afterward, Thompson went to Ashcroft himself. Ashcroft and Thompson shared Missouri roots and a close relationship built on mutual trust, and Thompson played a vital if sometimes awkward role as the Justice Department's unofficial liaison to the White House in some of Ashcroft's more dysfunctional moments with Bush's White House staff. The lessons of 9/11's failings were all about building up communications and tearing down walls, but this time, another wall went up again. Thompson related to Ashcroft the strange goings-on with these mysterious wiretaps. What was this about? Where were these new wiretaps coming from? Ashcroft went silent. He looked uncomfortable. "I'm sworn to secrecy by the president and the vice president," Ashcroft said. Thompson let it lie. He wouldn't bring the topic up with Ashcroft again. Nor would he ever approve any of the mystery wiretaps that Baker brought to him. Soon enough, Baker and his staff in the intelligence shop would know better than to even bother asking Thompson. Whatever was going on would go on without his signature.

IT ALL BEGAN in Afghanistan. That had been bin Laden's safe haven for five years, that was where most of the 9/11 hijackers had received their training in suicide missions at al Qaeda terror camps, and that, Bush's senior intelligence advisors believed, was where the NSA had to set its powerful sights if it had any hope of foiling the next 9/11. America couldn't afford another blunder. There was, in the official determination of the intelligence community, "a serious and continuing threat to the homeland." That was bureaucratic parlance for saying that a second wave of attacks was surely coming. To counter that threat would require unbridled executive power, Bush and Cheney believed. Within hours and days of the attacks, the NSA began ratcheting up its unmatched spyware, with the help of the U.S. telecom giants, to pore through vast amounts of communications flowing into and out of Afghanistan—tracing, analyzing, monitoring, and often reading and listening to anything that looked like it might have a connection to a known al Qaeda haven.

Once, the agency's efforts would have essentially stopped at the American borders. If an American was involved in phone calls or e-mails deemed suspicious, that was the FBI's terrain, and the government would have to go to the secret FISA court to provide good reason why it wanted to target that particular person, phone number, or e-mail address. "Individualized suspicion," the lawyers called it. There wasn't time for that anymore, not after 9/11. To find the needle in the haystack, the NSA had to be involved at all ends of the operation, and it had to be able to cast aside the notion of establishing why any particular person was suspected of having terrorist links. In the new wartime footing, the hundreds of billions of minutes of international calls into and out of the United States each year were now potential "signals intelligence," ripe for mining to understand the enemy's plans.

Existing laws were just "not up to the job," argued John Yoo, a mid-ranking lawyer in the Justice Department on 9/11 who would go on to write many of the crucial legal opinions justifying the White House's use of broad wartime authority. "Under existing laws like FISA, you have to have the name of somebody, have to already suspect that someone's a terrorist before you can get a warrant. You have to have a name to put in the warrant to tap their phone calls, and so it doesn't allow you as a government to use judgment based on probability to say: 'Well, 1 percent probability of the calls from, or maybe 50 percent of the calls, are coming out of this one city in Afghanistan, and there's a high probability that some of those calls are terrorist communications. But we don't know the names of the people making those calls.' You want to get at those phone calls, those e-mails, but under FISA you can't do that. . . . The conditions after 9/11—we'd just been attacked; we're at war; the attackers came from Afghanistan—I think the president has the constitutional authority to intercept those calls to prevent a second attack. I definitely think so."

The FISA court demanded evidence that an American might be linked to a terrorist organization or foreign power before the court would take the intrusive steps of listening to his every conversation; that was a burden that NSA officials knew they would rarely be able to meet, as they relied on complicated "link analysis" of communication patterns, algorithms, and data-mining tools to predict who might fit the profile of a terrorist. What judge was going to approve that? This was a new science that many judges on the court just didn't seem to understand, intelligence lawyers complained; even before 9/11, intelligence officials would complain that the technical briefings they prepared for FISA judges, explaining how government wiretappers could follow "chains" of communications or use endless strings of ones and zeros to pinpoint the target of their intercepts, would elicit mainly blank stares and befuddlement from the judges. An intelligence lawyer tried to explain to a judge in one closed briefing how they could gather up large volumes of communications data—on phone calls, e-mails, and the like—and simply lop off the stuff they didn't end up needing. "Where does the rest of it go?" the judge asked, concerned about the privacy of innocent people whose communication had been swept up. "Nowhere," the intelligence official answered. "Well, it has to go somewhere." "No, it doesn't."

To intelligence officials and their legal advocates, this was all essential stuff, a new mindset for a new threat, unencumbered by the traditional burdens of the court system. "Blindly following FISA's framework," Yoo wrote, will "hamper efforts to take advantage of what is known as 'data mining.' " The aim, he said, was to "see patterns of activity that reveal the al Qaeda network before it can attack." David Addington, the chief counsel to Dick Cheney, was less diplomatic in telling colleagues what he thought of the FISA system of judicial oversight: "We're one bomb away," he said, "from getting rid of that obnoxious court."

Many critical questions remain unanswered today about the actual operations, particularly in its early months, of what was known in intelligence circles simply as "the program." At this writing, the White House has succeeded in keeping many of the key legal and operational documents on the program from the prying eyes of Congress, the press, and the public, even in the face of congressional subpoenas and litigation. In years to come, it may become clear that the scope of "the program" went well beyond what is now understood.

What is clear, however, is that the NSA operation was, from the very first wiretap, Dick Cheney's brainchild. It was Cheney who inspired it, Cheney who set the moving parts in motion, Cheney who pushed to expand it, Cheney who personally conducted the critical briefings on it in his office for a select few congressional leaders, and Cheney who imposed the extraordinary lid of secrecy on it.

The operation dovetailed with the vice president's vision for restoring the power of the presidency, a power that he believed had been badly undercut by the reforms spurred by the abuses of the Vietnam and Watergate eras. Cheney admired "strong" presidents—an FDR, a Teddy Roosevelt, maybe a Woodrow Wilson at his peak. Wilson had ordered the interception of all telegraphs, cables, and phone calls into and out of the United States during World War I. Franklin Roosevelt had authorized his spymasters to grab everything going into and out of the country the day after Pearl Harbor. Abraham Lincoln had approved the interception of telegraphs to try to track Confederate troop movements during the Civil War and suspended habeas corpus. George Washington, long before the telegraph was even invented, had begun intercepting mail between the British and Americans. These were men who led the way in times of crisis, without needless meddling by Congress or the courts. What lawmakers saw as essential checks and balances, Cheney saw as handcuffs.

As the young chief of staff to President Gerald Ford, Cheney was part of a White House that initially chafed at the idea of allowing Congress to impose rules and laws on the government's eavesdropping. Those decisions, fellow aides to President Ford like Don Rumsfeld and George H. W. Bush believed, were an integral part of the president's inherent constitutional authority as commander-in-chief. The War Powers Act of 1973, Cheney asserted, was a dangerous "infringement" of the president's constitutional authority because it required Congress to give its blessing to a president's declaration of war. And a 1974 law that gave Congress more authority to decide how the federal budget was actually spent, he felt, was an undue erosion of the president's fiscal authority.

His views were not always widely shared. Indeed, when the Iran-contra scandal blew up a decade later and led to criminal indictments against aides to President Reagan, Cheney found himself in the minority in authoring a congressional report—with the help of his young aide and protégé, David Addington—that concluded it was Congress, not the White House, that had overstepped its authority in legislating what the president could and couldn't do on matters of foreign policy in Nicaragua. By cutting off money to the Nicaraguan contras, Congress had engaged in what Cheney saw as "legislative hostage-taking." On matters of national security, the power of the president was supreme.

As vice president, Cheney found a platform from which to declare his expansive view of the presidency, and 9/11 was his bullhorn. Cheney was evacuated that morning to a secure bunker beneath the east wing of the White House, watching the horrific events unfold on CNN with his wife, Lynne, and a handful of senior White House aides, including National Security Advisor Condoleezza Rice, her deputy, Stephen Hadley, and Cheney chief-of-staff Scooter Libby. As they watched the South Tower of the World Trade Center crumble to nothing, the aides beside him groaned in collective horror. From Cheney, there came only silence, as he closed his eyes for but a brief moment. Within minutes, after a phone conversation with the president that no other government witnesses were able to corroborate, Cheney would be ordering U.S. warplanes to shoot down any threatening airliners from the sky. This was a day Cheney could not have imagined when Bush talked him into becoming his White House running mate fourteen months earlier.

America was now at war, and for Cheney, that demanded a commander-in-chief with the unrestrained authority to defend it. This would become the defining philosophy and framework of Bush's presidency, both at home in warding off another attack and abroad in opening up a new and ultimately disastrous battlefield in Iraq. It was this view that would allow the CIA to use an unmanned predator drone to fire a Hellfire antitank missile in 2002 at a car in a remote part of Yemen, far from the Afghan battlefield, killing six suspected al Qaeda operatives. It was this view that guided the administration's strategy of capturing suspected terrorists and locking them up for years, outside the court system, at CIA black sites around the world and in Guantánamo Bay. It was this view that President Bush believed empowered him to effectively ignore hundreds of provisions approved by Congress—from the Patriot Act to a congressional ban on torture—as he issued presidential signing statements under the "unitary executive" theory of government. And it was this view that led to the creation of the NSA eavesdropping program.

The program was Cheney at his most expansive. In overseeing the NSA as former Pentagon secretary under Bush's father, Cheney knew better than almost anyone the agency's wide reach. Technologically, the agency was perfectly positioned to begin hunting for the next al Qaeda plotter. Legally, it was all but banned—a result of the same Watergate-era reforms that Cheney believed had so badly damaged the power of the presidency. He aimed to change that—on his own terms. "The president of the United States needs to have his constitutional powers unimpaired, if you will, in terms of the conduct of national security policy. That's my personal view," Cheney would say later in defending the wiretapping program. "I believe in a strong, robust executive authority. And I think the world we live in demands it."

The NSA operation sprouted, as did many of the central counterterrorism initiatives in the Bush White House, from a seed planted by Cheney. Just weeks after the September 11 attacks, Cheney posed a question to George Tenet, the CIA director: What more can the NSA do? Cheney, despite his Napoleonic public reputation, often delegated not so much by giving direct marching orders as by posing questions. But coming from Cheney, from a man widely considered the most powerful vice president in American history, the impact was the same, whether it was cast as an order or a query. *Could* the NSA be doing more was a clear signal that the vice president *wanted* the NSA to be doing more. Tenet phoned Michael Hayden, the Air Force general who ran the NSA. "Is there anything more you can do?" Tenet asked him. Tenet already knew that his critics would try to pin 9/11 on the CIA's intelligence failings, and his question had an air of pleading desperation to it. "Not with my current authorities," Hayden answered.

That was an Air Force general's way of saying *not under the law*. The NSA was covered by a potpourri of different laws, regulations, and policies that governed its activities. The three most important were Executive Order 12333, the bible of intelligence work enacted by President Reagan; U.S. Signals Intelligence Directive 18, a catalog of NSA rules and regulations that governed the intersection of intelligence-gathering and Americans' privacy rights; and the Foreign Intelligence Surveillance Act, the 1978 law that created the secret intelligence court as the "exclusive" means for eavesdropping on Americans in intelligence investigations and set criminal penalties for anyone who violated it. These were dense, hidebound regulations that took even the most agile intelligence lawyers years to master, but in the NSA culture, their essence was this: the NSA did not spy on Americans. That was a lesson drilled into NSA technicians, analysts, and code-breakers from their first day in training at the sprawling, 350-acre complex in Fort Meade, Maryland. "We don't get involved in intercepting the communications of Americans. It's a violation of the law," said Connie Vilhauer, a linguist and intelligence analyst in counterterrorism at NSA for nearly twenty years through 2002.

Even accidental interceptions of Americans by the NSA's giant "ear in the sky" technology were considered verboten, with strict protocols on how the ill-gotten information was to be reported and destroyed. The precept was so sacrosanct that, in the 1990s, tripwires put in place at the NSA made it physically impossible for technicians to follow some types of intercepts onto U.S. soil, according to one intelligence official. For anyone still unsure of the rules, large yellow signs around the complex with bold black lettering spelled out the privacy rights of "U.S. persons"—a group defined broadly enough to include not only American citizens and permanent residents, but tourists, corporations, and even illegal aliens. For the NSA to target an American, the agency's own Web site declared long after the wiretapping program had started, "Court Order Required in the United States."

The NSA's role on American soil was limited largely to doing counterintelligence surveillance and wiretaps at foreign embassies and missions, the kind of eavesdropping that was standard fare in the spy business. Even that was legally problematic under restrictions imposed by the Vienna Conventions, a 1963 treaty that governed diplomatic relations, but a years-old legal opinion from the Justice Department gave the practice its legal blessing under the notion that an international gentleman's agreement made spying at embassies standard practice, according to a national security lawyer with knowledge of the still-classified opinion. But as far as collecting intelligence on Americans and others inside the country, that was clearly the FBI's job, not the NSA's. If Osama bin Laden himself had wandered over to the U.S. side of the border in Niagara Falls, Hayden remarked in 2000, the NSA wouldn't have been able to listen in on his conversations. That's what the law dictated, and the NSA, with its own tortured history of civil liberties abuses, was always careful to operate well south of the legal line, as Hayden liked to say.

This was the climate at the NSA on 9/11, and it was a climate that Hayden himself had worked hard to foster. Soon after taking over the NSA in 1999, Hayden made the carefully calculated decision to move his agency out of the shadows, to demonstrate to the American public that the NSA's code-breakers were working to protect them, not to spy on them. It was a public relations strategy built of necessity. News reports about Echelon, an NSA operation sweeping up huge volumes of communications traffic overseas, were riling European allies. Then there was the notorious *Enemy of the State*, the 1998 box-office hit that cast Will Smith as a Washington lawyer hounded by murderous thugs at the NSA who were using their spy hardware to go through everyone's phone calls, e-mails, bank accounts, and computer files.

This wasn't the kind of publicity the NSA needed. At an agency averse to public scrutiny, Hayden began making speeches, giving interviews, and even inviting reporters to his home, all in an effort to debunk the NSA conspiracy theorists. "I made the judgment that we couldn't survive with the popular impression of this agency being formed by the last Will Smith movie," Hayden told CNN in March of 2001, as he allowed the network to film inside the spy complex and peek behind its curtain. The American public was naturally distrustful of the NSA's vast power and secrecy, Hayden acknowledged. "That's a challenge for us, and that's why, frankly, we're trying to explain what it is we do for America, how it is we follow the law. Could there be abuses? Of course. Would there be? I am looking you and the American people in the eye and saying: there are not."

But Hayden had bigger problems than just PR at the agency he inherited. Budget cutbacks had forced the NSA to trim its staff by about a third in the 1990s, technological problems led to a system overload that left the agency's computers dark for an alarming three and a half days in early 2000, and members of Congress investigating all the technical problems were accusing the spy agency of "going deaf" and losing the ability to listen in on America's enemies. Many feared that the fiber-optics revolution in the communications industry had passed the NSA by. Where the spy agency was once able to vacuum up vast amounts of overseas satellite phone traffic on its own, the huge strides in fiber-optic technology in the 1980s and 1990s meant communications that once traveled through the air were now being routed by land and undersea cables—less accessible than before to the NSA's powerful interception equipment. That forced the agency to rely more than ever on the telecom companies for their cooperation.

Even before Bush took office in January of 2001, NSA officials had prepared a briefing document as part of the transition advising the incoming administration that the agency must become a "powerful, permanent presence" on the commercial communications network, despite the obvious legal and privacy concerns. Within weeks of Bush's inauguration, General Hayden and other NSA officials were meeting with American telecom executives to begin discussing ways that they could do just that—obstensibly as a way to make it easier for the agency to grab overseas phone calls and e-mails. But even that tentative early foray raised concerns: at least one company—Qwest, which served phone customers in the western United States—balked at the idea of letting the NSA install its own surveillance equipment inside the company's calling stations, with access to Americans' calls and e-mails as well as those overseas. Qwest's executives thought the idea was illegal.

For all the talk about the NSA "going deaf," the agency's hearing wasn't its biggest problem. More troubling was the fact that the spy agency, even when it did have the means to intercept communications, often didn't know what it had heard, where to go with the information once it had it, and which stuff was really important and what was just noise. So it was that on September 10, 2001, the NSA's hardware picked up two snippets of conversation captured from pay phones in Afghanistan linked to al Qaeda. "Tomorrow is zero hour," one caller said. "The match begins tomorrow," said the other. Neither remark was translated until two days later, on September 12, 2001. By then, it was too late.

Two days after the September 11 attacks, Hayden addressed his staff at the NSA. It was perhaps the grimmest time in the agency's half-century history. That Tuesday morning as al Qaeda struck, nonessential employees had been evacuated from the headquarters. Some employees in higher floors who had to remain behind were relocated to low-rises for their own safety. Black curtains were tacked up to the windows. Hayden himself called his wife to find out about his children, then got back to the task of trying to figure out whether more attacks were on the way. As he faced his shell-shocked staff that Thursday at Fort Meade in person and by a video hookup to NSA offices around the world, he told them that, right now, a quarter-billion people in the United States would love to have their current assignment: "Being able to go after the enemy." The NSA would go after al Qaeda hard, he told them, but it would do so, as always, by planting its flag on the right side of liberty. "We are going to keep America free," Hayden said, "by making Americans feel safe again."

Even as he spoke, however, Hayden was already beginning to move the agency quietly beyond its traditional mission. He wouldn't break the mold yet—that wouldn't come for another few weeks, with the president's blessing—but he was already remaking it. With Afghanistan as the focus, the NSA began a significant loosening of its own standards for tracking international communications that involved

323.4 C456s

342.73 D389t 2006

344.73 F654r

people inside the United States. So-called minimization procedures at the agency had, before 9/11, set a high bar for the NSA to report to other intelligence agencies even so much as the name or identifying information for someone in the United States who might be connected to an overseas wiretap. In the 1990s, the NSA was so protective of its sigint material—spy-speak for the communications, or the signals intelligence, it intercepted—that it was unwilling to share relevant material with the CIA. Now, Hayden began to bust open the spigot, relaxing the NSA internal procedures to produce a flood of thousands of leads for the FBI to chase on people in the United States who might have had some connection, even several times removed, to suspicious e-mails, phone numbers, or locales in Afghanistan.

The NSA was widening its reach by the day. In the immediate aftermath of the worst terrorist attack in U.S. history, those preliminary moves appeared, in many ways, both understandable and essential. What troubled some of the very few lawmakers who knew about the operation, however, was the unilateral way in which the executive branch was now moving to stretch and bend rules that had been in place for decades. Why not go to Congress for more authority, many officials would ask privately. Hayden was well aware of how dicey the agency's relations with Congress had been in recent years, and he wanted to make sure that congressional leaders knew, at least to some extent, the far-reaching steps that his agency was now taking. In a classified, closed-door briefing on October 1, less than a month after the attacks, he laid out his "expansive view" of his authorities after 9/11 and how they changed his reading of what the NSA could and couldn't do under foreign intelligence law.

In Washington, briefings take on the air of art form, and Hayden, balding, bespectacled, and bookish, was a master: polished, earnest, armed with PowerPoint presentations and scientific data, plainspoken and persuasive without seeming patronizing. His crisp blue military uniform gave him an instant air of authority and wonkish credibility, as he would speak about "actionable intelligence" or "value-added" reorganizations. At the briefing, Hayden seemed to invite a debate, encouraging lawmakers to raise any concerns they had with him about his new ideas for the NSA. Nancy Pelosi, the ranking Democrat on the House Intelligence Committee, took him up on it. She was frustrated by what she saw as a lack of detailed information about what the NSA was really doing, and the administration had stonewalled her staff when they tried to follow up afterward, citing classified material. Had the intelligence committees really been told all the bold new steps that the NSA was taking, or was this just a gesture, a classic attempt at Washington-style CYA oversight?

Ten days after the briefing, with her efforts to get clearer answers leading nowhere, Pelosi voiced her unease directly to General Hayden in a personal letter stamped Top Secret. "I am concerned whether, and to what extent, the National Security Agency has received specific presidential authorization for the operations you are conducting," Pelosi wrote. "Until I understand better the legal analysis regarding the sufficiency of the authority which underlies your decision on the appropriate way to proceed on this matter, I will continue to be concerned." As if to underscore her misgivings, she included a handwritten note at the bottom: *General Hayden—Thank you for your attention to my request. Nancy.* A week later, word came back from Hayden. "In my briefing," he said in a curt response, "I was attempting to emphasize that I had used my authorities to adjust NSA's collection and reporting." In other words, there had been no presidential directive. The NSA was acting on its own authority.

What Pelosi didn't know when she wrote to Hayden on October 11 was that, exactly one week earlier, Bush had authorized a much broader expansion of the NSA's authority to troll on domestic soil, one that went well beyond what Hayden had outlined for lawmakers earlier and that would test the limits of presidential power in the extreme. The Afghanistan effort had only been a pilot project. Cheney's pointed query to Tenet—*What more can the NSA do?*—had set in motion a series of intense discussions among Bush's senior national security advisors. When Hayden told Tenet there was nothing more he could do under his current authorities—that, in effect, he had already stretched the NSA's mandate as far as it could go—the general and the CIA director went to see Cheney personally. As Tenet recounted that critical meeting, Hayden laid out for the vice president "what could be done that would be feasible, prudent and effective." The question of what would be legal would come later.

For now, Bush's senior national security advisors were intent on using the NSA to leverage what they saw as America's built-in, if accidental, "home field advantage": the explosion of digital communications passing through American soil. Billions of e-mails and phone calls were now pulsing through giant U.S. "switches" or gateways as they caromed around the world. Because of the U.S. dominance in the telecommunications industry, a call from Kuala Lumpur to Riyadh might happen to pass through a switch on a fiber-optic line on Governors Island or elsewhere on U.S. soil for a fleeting nanosecond, giving NSA computers the chance to analyze it—with the cooperation of telecom giants like AT&T.

Indeed, after 9/11, U.S. intelligence officials began quietly encouraging the telecom industry to route more international traffic through U.S. switches in order to exploit their home field advantage even more fully. For all the technological prowess of the NSA, American intelligence officials needed the help of the private companies that actually carried the communications traffic. Despite the public misperception of the NSA pointing its eavesdropping devices into the sky to grab communications, or FBI technicians planting alligator clips on a telephone wire to listen in on a call, the reality is that intelligence agencies often rely on the telecommunications providers themselves to let them in the front door and furnish direct access to what they need. It is quicker, easier, more focused, and less labor-intensive than scouring through the data themselves. For the NSA, the information was there for the taking.

With the cooperation of the telecom companies, intelligence officials asserted that the agency could now give "hot pursuit" to suspected al Qaeda communications by tracing and monitoring the flood of e-mails and phone calls routed to and from the United States, as well as foreign communications. If a suspected al Qaeda operative in Dubai was calling Detroit, the NSA's pitch went, the agency could grab that call much more quickly without the courts slowing it down. (In fact, despite the public focus on phone calls, most of the NSA's intercepts—75 percent by one estimate—were e-mails.) This was a task made to order for the NSA; its Cray supercomputers, data-mining abilities, "packet sniffers," voice and word recognition software, and other technological wizardry were designed, at least in theory, to pinpoint e-mails and phone calls considered "suspicious" from amid the massive volumes of innocuous traffic it picked up. The FBI, in comparison, was reading smoke signals. "That's what the NSA does. They vacuum up the information," a senior intelligence official said.

"There's not a computer inside the FBI that has that kind of capability or volume."

But why stop at international calls and e-mails? Details of these pivotal early discussions remain murky, but Cheney, by all indications, sought almost from the outset to empower the NSA to also trace and monitor calls and e-mails in which both ends of the communications were entirely within U.S. borders. If that suspect in Detroit was talking to someone in San Diego or Lackawanna, Cheney wanted to know that too, and he saw no reason for the courts to have to be involved. NSA officials were hesitant; they could justify, they believed, the interception of *international* calls and e-mails without a court warrant, but communications entirely on U.S. soil? That was more problematic at an agency whose mission was so deeply rooted, by law and tradition, in the collection of foreign intelligence.

By the account of Alberto Gonzales, who soon became deeply involved in the secret discussions that September about the NSA's risky new mission, it was Bush himself—"the decider," as he once famously called himself—who refereed the high-stakes debate. The president, Gonzales said, realized the intense concerns that eavesdropping on purely domestic calls and e-mails would provoke, and he was the one who decided to draw the line at international calls. Requiring one end of the call to be on foreign soil, the president felt, struck "the right balance" between protecting the country and protecting its basic principles. "I made the decision," Bush himself said, "to listen to phone calls of al Qaeda or suspected al Qaeda from outside the country coming in, or inside the country going out because the people, our operators, told me this is one of the best ways to protect the American people." The president also agreed to impose what amounted to limited self-checks on the tremendous power he was claiming: the Justice Department would have to continually review and recertify the legality of the program, and Bush himself would have to renew his executive order every forty-five days or so. It was a check that he would come to regret.

How much did Bush really know about the NSA program before he signed off on it? Bush was not, as many aides acknowledged privately, a details-oriented president. He did not have the boundless appetite for policy minutiae of a Bill Clinton, or the intelligence background and know-how of his father, who headed the CIA before becoming president. For Bush 43, the thick, written briefing packets on intelligence matters favored by previous presidents quickly gave way to shorter, oral presentations delivered to him each day. Bush worked in snapshots and overviews, à la Ronald Reagan, and he often sought to lead by will and inspiration.

It is unclear how many briefings Bush got on the NSA program before signing off on it, or the exact nature and timing of those briefings. Whether he ever demanded to know the granular details of the NSA program's operations, its scope and its legality on an issue that would help define his presidency, remains unknown. But the decision to authorize the NSA program, Bush insisted, "wasn't an easy decision to make." He realized the legally murky terrain he was entering. Bush asked his aides, he said, why the NSA couldn't work within the seventy-two-hour emergency procedures set up at the wiretapping court. "I said, 'How come we can't use the procedures which you just described?' And they said, 'It won't work. It doesn't fit in with what Mike Hayden described as hot pursuit.' " That was a claim that many national security officials in his own administration would come to question, but for Bush, the assurance itself was enough.

There was no serious discussion about going to Congress to change the wiretapping law to specifically authorize the NSA's new role, or to challenge the law's constitutionality in court. The go-it-alone approach was a decision that some of Bush's senior aides would question deeply. Just as the White House was secretly moving ahead with the NSA program in late September and early October, Congress was rushing separately, in the dark, to approve a range of counterterrorism and wiretapping measures in the Patriot Act, measures that had lain dormant since the 1990s for lack of political support. There is little doubt that, in the climate immediately after 9/11, Congress would have approved at least a modest expansion, if not a wholesale reworking, of the NSA's lawful powers. FISA itself was amended more than a half-dozen times after 9/11, lowering the standards needed to get a court eavesdropping warrant. But that was not the way the Bush White House operated. Cheney and Addington were deeply suspicious of leaks by members of the intelligence committees and others in Congress after several embarrassing public disclosures, and the White House rationalized that to go to Congress for approval of what Bush was about to do would risk publicly disclosing the existence of the program itself.

Besides, in the view of Cheney, Gonzales, and the president's senior legal aides, Bush already had the power, and it was rooted firmly in the Constitution. "The President shall be Commander in Chief of the Army and Navy of the United States," Section 2 of Article II begins. Addington, referred to derisively by some rival government lawyers as "President Addington" because of his broad influence on national security policies, carried a tattered copy of the Constitution in his pocket; photocopies taped to the back contained extra statutes detailing presidential succession in times of national emergency. At times of internal debate, he would pull out his tattered copy and read from it with reverence. To hear Addington talk in private White House meetings, officials said, the president's wartime power was nearly absolute, with no room for accommodations with Congress or anyone else. "We're going to push and push and push until some larger force makes us stop," he said once.

For Cheney, Addington and other like-minded members of Bush's inner circle who pushed for a "robust" wartime president, Article II was the mother lode of a strong executive branch. In the view of the Justice Department's John Yoo, the Yale-educated lawyer enlisted by officials at the White House to work on the secret legal analysis of the NSA operation, the case for the NSA program was about as close to open-and-shut as the Constitution allowed. Neither the FISA law nor the Fourth Amendment's ban on unreasonable searches prevented the president from carrying out his wartime authority to listen in on "enemy" conversations, Yoo maintained, even if those conversations took place on American soil. In wartime, Yoo said, "we don't require a warrant, we don't require reasonable searches and seizures when the Army, the military's out on the battlefield, attacking, killing members of the enemy." Any invasion of Americans' privacy was, in Yoo's view, minimal. "Is there really an invasion of privacy," he asked, "for example, if computers are initially searching through communications first and only bringing correlations to the attention of a human, to a security officer when there's a certain level of confidence that they might involve terrorism?" As for the FISA law making it a crime for the president to order wiretaps without a warrant, Yoo had this to say: "There's a law greater than FISA, which is the Constitution, and part of the Constitution is the president's commander-in-chief power. Congress can't take away the president's powers in running war. They are given to him by the Constitution, in the same way that Congress couldn't pass laws saying you can't invade Normandy. . . . There are some decisions the Constitution gives the president, and even if Congress passes a law, they can't seize that from him."

Yoo had his many critics even within the Justice Department. While Yoo always insisted he was working within the system at the Justice Department, his rivals accused him of creating a back door for himself to Cheney, Addington, Gonzales, and Pentagon general counsel William Haynes in providing a legal fig leaf for what some Justice Department officials saw as a dangerously broad reading of the president's wartime authorities. "It will take fifty years," said a senior Justice Department lawyer who was critical of Yoo's work, "to undo the damage that he did to the place." After leaving the Justice Department, Yoo's name became synonymous with the administration's broad and far-reaching view of the president's wartime powers, and he was greeted back to the law school at Berkeley with calls for his resignation and black armbands worn by student protesters.

Despite his critics, Yoo's expansive views about surveillance law were not without some precedent. After FISA was passed in 1978, it was widely assumed among lawmakers, Justice Department lawyers, and legal scholars that the legislation was the last word on wiretapping law and that it meant exactly what it said it meant—that the secret court it set up was the "exclusive" means for the executive branch to spy on its citizenry for reasons of national security. The legislation included a window for emergency, retroactive wiretaps, as well as a fifteen-day grace period after a declaration of war for the president to eavesdrop without a warrant, but after that, most lawyers believed, he had to go back to the court for approval. Privately, however, legal advisors to presidents before Bush, along with several court opinions, had asserted principles in line with those of John Yoo—that the president had inherent authority to gather intelligence for national security and that no act of Congress could extinguish that power. The difference is that there is no record of any president ever daring to act on that controversial notion. At least not until October 4, 2001, when Bush signed off for the first time on his secret executive order giving the NSA presidential authority to go places it had once been expressly banned.

Now General Hayden had a presidential order in hand. That alone, the NSA director said, gave an "air of sufficiency" to the radical pivot that his agency was about to make. Still, Hayden said, he wanted more. He knew the legal gravity of what the administration was doing and the concerns it was sure to provoke if and when it became public, as he realized it almost certainly would. He went separately to three top lawyers at the NSA to tell them what was going on. "I need to know what you think," he recounted telling them. There was no pressure on them to give their blessing, he insisted. They discussed the president's broad wartime authorities under Article II of the Constitution. Nothing was put in writing. But the answer from all three NSA lawyers, according to Hayden, came back the same: the president was within his powers to authorize the program. The message that Hayden took away from his own lawyers: the NSA was "good to go."

Days later, Hayden gathered his operational team in a conference room and explained what the president had authorized and why. He realized the historic sensitivities at the NSA to just this type of operation on American soil, and he wanted to explain it personally. Cheney, as Hayden knew, had already been pushing to expand the NSA's reach still further. Hayden wanted to make clear to his people: they would take on this program "and not go one step further." They were already in uncharted territory.

On a brisk, overcast day in Buffalo in April of 2004, President Bush flew into town on Air Force One and visited a local symphony hall to talk about terrorism and the rule of law. "A conversation about the USA Patriot Act," the White House called his appearance. Outside the hall, hundreds of protesters donning Bush masks and waving homemade stop-the-war signs booed lustily as the presidential caravan drove by the fenced-in crowd on the way from the airport. But inside the hall, the invitation-only audience was all smiles and cheers. Hundreds of uniformed police officers, firefighters, and emergency responders erupted in applause, as if on cue, as they heard Bush defend his decision to invade Iraq a year earlier and vow that the nation would never "have our will shaken by thugs and terrorists."

The president's agenda was twofold: key provisions of the Patriot Act were set to expire at the end of the year in the face of a crescendo of public attacks, and Bush himself was holding a slim lead in the polls against John Kerry in a presidential campaign that Bush was looking to frame around national security. Buffalo offered the chance to trumpet both causes at once. The president sat on a high-backed stool, his legs dangling, his customary American flag pinned to the lapel of his char-coal gray suit. He played the part of the breezy talk show host as he traded folksy banter about the Buffalo Bills with his law enforcement hosts and quizzed them about al Qaeda.

To his right sat Michael Battle, the U.S. attorney in Buffalo. Three years later, following his promotion to a senior Justice Department job in Washington, Battle would become embroiled in scandal over the politicization of the department after he personally called several U.S. attorneys to tell them they were fired. But for the moment, Battle was the public face of the administration's success in fighting terrorism for the convictions his office had secured against the Lackawanna Six. "I appreciate you, Mike," Bush said. "Good job."

Then Bush moved on to the topic at hand: the Patriot Act. Not only did the counterterrorism law need to be renewed, Bush said; it needed to be strengthened and expanded as well. With an aw-shucks apology, Bush began explaining in decidedly layman's terms what the Patriot Act allowed the government to do in catching al Qaeda. "I'm not a lawyer," Bush said, "so it's kind of hard for me to kind of get bogged down in the law." The legislation, Bush explained, allowed government officials to share intelligence information more easily with one another, and it allowed the government to use things like roving wiretaps to eavesdrop on the terrorists more easily when they were talking to each other.

"Now, by the way," Bush paused, "anytime you hear the United States government talking about wiretap, it requires, a wiretap requires a court order. Nothing has changed, by the way. When we're talking about chasing down terrorists, we're talking about getting a court order before we do so." Bush chopped the air with his left hand to punch home the words: "We're talking about getting"—*chop*—"a court order"—*chop*. "It's important for our fellow citizens to under-stand, when you think Patriot Act," he said, placing his fingers to his temple in thought, "constitutional guarantees are in place when it comes to doing what is necessary to protect our homeland, because we value the Constitution."

A wiretap requires a court order. The notion was so deeply ingrained in the legal landscape that no one in the audience would have thought to doubt the premise. Bush would insist later, once the NSA program was publicly disclosed, that he was only talking about wiretaps autho-rized under the Patriot Act. *Those* were the kind, he said, that always required a warrant. There was no intent to mislead anyone, he said. But the warrantless wiretapping program he had authorized at the NSA could not have been far from his mind that overcast day in Buffalo. Less than six weeks earlier, his own Justice Department had staged a quiet but remarkable revolt over the program, with all the top leadership threatening to resign over an operation that the department's top lawyers now said they considered possibly illegal.

Over the past two and a half years, a team of NSA technicians, analysts, and translators working round-the-clock out of cubicles at an open office the size of a small newsroom at Fort Meade had eavesdropped without warrants on the phone calls and e-mails of several thousand people in the United States suspected of ties to terrorists. An Islamic charity in Oregon had apparently been monitored. So had a woman in Baltimore whose sister was suspected of being an al Qaeda "facilitator," an imam at a mosque in Albany with suspected ties to militants in Iraq, and a truck driver in Cleveland who talked of taking a blow torch to the Brooklyn Bridge. Then there was an Iranian-American doctor in Kentucky who came under suspicion by the NSA because his specialty—nephrology—apparently made intelligence officials suspect that he might be helping Osama bin Laden with his reported kidney problems.

The confiscation of al Qaeda computer discs in Afghanistan and the capture of leaders like Abu Zubayda beginning in 2002 opened up rich new veins of suspected dirty phone numbers and e-mail addresses for the NSA to trace and analyze, all producing fertile leads for the NSA to monitor. But for every real lead with a plausible terror connection, there were many others that washed out, the trail gone dead, the connection uncertain. NSA officials saw their surveillance and data-mining work as vital to stopping another attack, but at the FBI, officials complained privately that they were forced to chase many hundreds of NSA-generated leads that inevitably arrived at dead ends. The "Pizza Hut leads," FBI officials began calling them derisively, because in the six-degrees-of-separation world of tracing who had called whom and whom *that* person had called and whom *those* people had called, the NSA leads often seemed to wind up with the pizza delivery man. Even as Bush spoke that day in Buffalo, NSA officials were busy rejiggering the program to put in more internal controls in determining who could be wiretapped so they could pass legal muster with the pesky lawyers at the Justice Department who were threatening to shut it down. There was no talk of any of that at the symphony hall in Buffalo, of course. Bush's secret was safe for now.

For the White House, the NSA program demanded not only intense secrecy, but also, at pivotal times like the 2004 debate over the Patriot Act, active concealment and deception. Disinformation has been a staple of effective American spy-craft from the Revolutionary War down through the Cold War, and the administration was willing to do whatever it took to keep the NSA program under wraps. The intent, Bush and his aides insisted, was to keep Osama bin Laden in the dark about what U.S. spy agencies were really doing. The effect was to mislead the American public as well. Bush led the way, but he had help. When General Hayden appeared before a joint Senate and House panel in October of 2002, he talked about the lessons of the NSA's abuses from the 1970s and the privacy rules and regulations that are "drilled into NSA employees." There was no mention that those rules had been dramatically changed in secret just a year earlier. There was no mention of wiretapping without warrants. Just the opposite.

Hayden talked once again about the NSA not being able to track bin Laden's communications without court approval if he stepped over the Canadian border, and he talked about the privacy laws that protected people inside the United States from surveillance. "You can see the challenge," Hayden said, "of trying to cover people inside U.S. borders, even if they will mean us harm." What was needed, he said, was a public debate. "What I really need you to do," he said, "is to talk to your constituents and find out where the American people want that line between security and liberty to be." That was a difficult conversation to have, however, since most of the lawmakers listening to him that day—not to mention their constituents listening on C-SPAN— knew nothing about what the NSA was really doing.

In the early months and years after 9/11, several members of Congress who were unaware of the NSA program were practically begging Hayden and the Bush administration to let them change the law, to give the NSA the legal authority to operate more freely on U.S. soil. Congress makes the laws, Senator Michael DeWine of Ohio told Hayden at one hearing, and if the current law was too rigid or was being interpreted too tightly to allow the NSA to listen in on al Qaeda, Congress needed to know that. "I think you have an obligation, candidly," DeWine told Hayden, "to come back to us and to say, Senator . . . do you understand what we are not doing? Do you understand who we can't target? Do you understand what information we can't get? And I think that you have an obligation to do that as often as you can." Hayden didn't take him up on the offer, perhaps because he realized that the NSA was already doing exactly the type of surveillance that DeWine assumed they were barred by law from conducting.

Even as Hayden was urging a national dialogue on the NSA's powers, several proposals were coursing through Congress to try to make it easier—under the law—for the executive branch to get a court order for wiretapping suspected terrorists on U.S. soil. The Patriot Act had already lowered the bar and, in the conga line of legislative measures that followed 9/11, some lawmakers were pushing to lower the standard of proof even further. In the summer of 2002, Senator DeWine authored a proposal that would have eased the standard that the government had to meet in going to the FISA court for a warrant on a non-U.S. person, lowering it from "probable cause" to believe someone was an agent of a foreign power to simply a "reasonable suspicion." Congress didn't know it, but in the legal netherworld that Bush and the NSA had set up for wiretapping terror suspects, this new standard was essentially what shift managers at the NSA had already been using in secret for the last year to decide, on their own authority, whom to target.

After the NSA program was disclosed, Hayden and the Bush White House would cite as a main justification for the program the idea that the court process was not nimble or agile enough to move quickly against suspects. Now, unsolicited, a senior Republican senator was offering the administration a chance to change the system, to lower the bar even more. But remarkably, the administration actually opposed DeWine's idea. Thanks, but no thanks, administration officials said. Lowering the standard needed to get a wiretapping warrant, the Justice Department's James Baker told Congress in July of 2002, "raises both significant legal and practical issues." It might not pass constitutional muster under the Fourth Amendment, he maintained, and it could thus imperil terrorism prosecutions as a result. The current court system, he maintained, was working, and there was "perhaps much to lose" by changing it. Left unsaid, by Baker or anyone else, was the fact that Bush had already claimed the authority to operate outside the courts altogether.

Baker himself was tap-dancing in minefields. As the Justice Department's point man to the FISA court, Baker was in a more perilous spot than perhaps anyone else associated with the off-the-books wiretapping program. He was in the middle of a powerful cross-current: caught between a White House secretly asserting unilateral surveillance powers and a judicial-based system at the Justice Department and the FISA court, which placed a premium on due process and checks and balances, not unbridled presidential power. Baker was the boy with his finger in the dyke, struggling mightily to hold the system together even as the aftermath of 9/11 threatened to pull it apart.

Bearded and professorial-looking, the understated Baker had risen from the ranks in the Justice Department's intelligence shop. He demonstrated none of the bald political ambition of his predecessor, Frances Fragos Townsend. A savvy lawyer, Townsend had been a trusted and loyal aide to Attorney General Reno; she developed such a direct pipeline to Reno in the late 1990s, in fact, that rival Justice Department lawyers in the deputy's office worked out a secret system to have one of Reno's secretaries alert them whenever Townsend was popping in on the attorney general for a private, unannounced meeting so that they could make sure to be there too.

That wasn't Baker's style. He started as a lowly line attorney in the intelligence office in the mid-1990s in a shop of just a half-dozen or so lawyers reviewing wiretap applications and then, after Townsend's removal, went on to become head of the office as its numbers swelled to more than ninety lawyers in the years after 9/11. For all the David Addingtons and John Yoos in the Bush administration pushing for a new mindset on surveillance law, Baker was one man sounding a lonely and unpopular theme: *The old one works.* "In my opinion," Baker said in a rare interview he gave to PBS's *Frontline*, "FISA works. It worked in the twentieth century; it works today."

The law had been updated dozens of times since 1978 to reflect technological changes. Baker's bosses at the White House would talk of how slow and inflexible the court system could be, what a dinosaur it was, and how they harbored hopes of seeing it made extinct by that next attack. But the reality was that the Justice Department had gotten wiretaps in mere minutes when it was essential to a fast-moving terrorism investigation. In a matter of hours after the fluke arrest in 1999 of a man found with bomb-making material in the trunk of his rental car at the Canadian border, Justice Department lawyers had gotten a wiretap for a phone number found on a scrap of paper in the man's wallet, and they had traced the suspected al Qaeda terror cell from Seattle to New York to Montreal. And, just as important to Baker, the Justice Department's lawyers had always managed to do their spy work with the imprimatur of a judge signing off on the wiretap. To him, that mattered.

More often than not, that judge was Royce Lamberth, a jowly Texan appointed to the federal bench by President Reagan. To understand the Bush administration's decision to bypass the FISA court altogether at enormous political and legal risk, it helps to understand the feuding and distrust that infected the government's relations with the secret court in the years leading up to 9/11. Judge Lamberth, an outsized personality who favored cowboy boots and country music over wing-tip shoes and operas at the Kennedy Center, was a Shakespearian figure in the long-running drama. He became an icon to conservatives in the 1990s by going after the Clinton administration's transgressions, but he was a libertarian at heart, deeply distrustful of excess government power wielded by either Democrats or Republicans. He headed the FISA court as its chief judge beginning in 1995, and he insisted on handling many of the emergency wiretaps himself, a workaholic who reveled in the cloak-and-dagger aspects of the job atop the country's most clandestine court. "Every deepest, darkest secret our country has, this is where we do them," he said of the FISA court, housed for years in a nondescript, windowless chamber on the top floor of the Justice Department. Lamberth loved to amuse guests at cocktail parties with his oft-told story about signing emergency FBI wiretaps on the front stoop at his home in suburban Washington, his cocker spaniel at his side, while he made his wife go upstairs because she didn't have the proper security clearance.

But not far beneath the grandfatherly affability was a biting judicial temperament that made life equally miserable for D.C. drug dealers, corrupt politicians, or sloppy government lawyers who came before him. Lamberth could be so blunt-spoken and acerbic in his judicial opinions that an appellate court removed him from a major class-action case brought by Native Americans against the Interior Department for exhibiting alleged bias toward the government, which he suggested was guilty of racism. Justice Department lawyers knew the penalties for ending up in Lamberth's doghouse beside his famed cocker spaniel.

In the months and years before 9/11, Lamberth lashed the Justice Department and the FBI for bringing the court dozens of sworn wiretap applications that contained faulty or misleading information about the circumstances behind their investigations. Lamberth worried that, too often, the FBI and the Justice Department were doing end runs around court procedures by failing to tell the court that they had already opened a criminal file on someone they wanted to wiretap as part of a separate intelligence probe. He saw no "evil intent," Lamberth said, but he grew so incensed over the sloppy work that, in 2000, he banned one FBI supervisor, Michael Resnick, from ever appearing before the court again. Louis Freeh, then the FBI director, begged him to reconsider the banishment, but Lamberth refused. "We sent a message to the FBI: You gotta tell the truth," Lamberth said.

He blamed not only the bureau, but Fran Fragos Townsend at the Justice Department's intelligence shop for the comedy of errors that came before his court. When Ashcroft took over at the Justice Department as attorney general in 2001, Lamberth told the new attorney general: "You've gotta get rid of her," according to two officials with knowledge of the conversation. "Lamberth had lost confidence in her," one former official said, and the judge pushed Ashcroft to have Baker replace her. Soon enough, Townsend was exiled to the Coast Guard, only to revive her career later as Bush's top homeland security advisor at the White House. Baker took over for Townsend as head of the intelligence shop, but the fallout with the court left some lingering wounds in the months leading up to 9/11. Some intelligence lawyers and FBI agents even groused privately that Lamberth's tight leash had left everyone skittish, creating a "chill" and a play-it-safe mentality that made the FBI too hesitant to aggressively go after legitimate terrorism suspects like Zacarias Moussaoui. In a different climate, some officials asked, could they have used wiretaps more swiftly to get on to 9/11 beforehand?

Lamberth made no apologies for taking the Justice Department to task for its repeated missteps. The courts, he long believed, had an essential role to play as a constitutional check, a backstop, against government overreaching and abuse by the executive branch, and he was going to make damn sure that the government told the truth when it wanted to wiretap someone. "What we found in the history of our country is you can't trust these people," Lamberth once said. "There's nothing wrong with letting the judges take a peek. And we are only taking a peek. We're making sure that there's not some political shenanigans going on, or some improper form of surveillance, and there really is some valid purpose to it." The aim, he said, was for a neutral, detached judge to make sure "we weren't out wiretapping Martin Luther King."

When al Qaeda struck on 9/11, Lamberth was stranded on the freeway en route to the D.C. courthouse after a dentist appointment; from his car, he could see the smoke billowing from the Pentagon nearby. By the time the FBI had ushered him into the Justice Department's command center, he had signed off on five emergency FISA warrants from the car via his cell phone. Approving a wiretap by cell phone once would have been unthinkable, but times had changed in an instant, and Lamberth knew it. The very day after the attacks, the court moved to loosen up some of its procedures to give the Bush administration more speed and flexibility to confront an obvious national emergency. Still, Lamberth clung to a deep-seated belief that there had to be *some* judicial checks and that the executive branch shouldn't be allowed to use national security wiretaps as an end run around due process altogether. "You can fight the war and lose everything if you have no civil liberties left," Lamberth said. He would try to rein in what he saw as the legal excesses and potential civil liberties abuses of the Patriot Act, only to be overruled by the FISA appeals court in the one and only ruling it had been asked to give in its twenty-five-year history. (The appeals court, Lamberth growled loudly, was wrong.)

But there was little talk of checks and balances when Lamberth was summoned to Ashcroft's ornate, wood-paneled suite at the Justice Department in the wake of 9/11 to talk about some new, secret intelligence program. The locale for the meeting was significant. What Lamberth was about to learn about was very much an *executive branch* program, and it would be discussed on the administration's home turf, in the confines of the attorney general's office, not at the FISA court or the judge's chambers. This was not a judicial matter. Some officials in the administration were reticent about briefing Lamberth at all on this new program, but Jim Baker, according to the accounts of several officials, pushed for it; the risks of not telling the chief judge of the FISA court what the NSA was doing—and jeopardizing criminal and intelligence matters that still had to go before Lamberth's court—were too great to operate in complete silence. Ashcroft led off the meeting, then quickly turned it over to General Hayden to lay out what the president had approved: a major expansion of the NSA's capability to intercept communications that it believed were linked to al Qaeda. John Yoo expanded on the legal rationale for the program and the president's inherent powers as commander-in-chief under the Constitution.

Lamberth asked a few questions at the nearly hour-long briefing, but for the most part, he said little. If he had any visceral reaction in opposition to the president's decision, he did not show it. Years later, after the NSA program became public, Lamberth would denounce it as a bad idea. Now, however, a judge famous for his sharp tongue sat mostly in silence. And that was exactly the way the administration wanted it. Lamberth was there to be informed of the program, not to weigh in on it himself. Bush had the power to do what he was doing, with or without the say-so of the chief judge of the nation's intelligence court. Lamberth "wasn't being asked to *do* anything," one participant in the meeting said pointedly afterward. "It was clear no one was asking him to approve it. That was absolutely clear."

IN 2003, a Democratic senator from West Virginia with a powerful family name took over a key congressional seat with a familiar promise to pursue tough oversight of U.S. intelligence operations. A few blocks down Constitution Avenue at the U.S. District Courthouse, a federal judge who worked for many years as the lawyer for a mental hospital was just beginning her even more challenging stint as head of the foreign intelligence court after Judge Lamberth ended his memorable run the year before. Less than a mile down Pennsylvania Avenue at the Justice Department, a conservative legal scholar from the University of Chicago took over the powerful fifth-floor office that determined what was and was not legal for the president to do. And one floor down at the Justice Department, an Irish cop's grandson with a stubborn independent streak was made the number two official at the department under John Ashcroft.

The personnel moves at the three different branches of government were unrelated and unremarkable, barely noticed by anyone outside the capital, and even by many inside it. But taken together, they would ultimately have a profound impact on the NSA's still secret wiretapping program. The concerns about the spy program voiced by the four officials were sometimes unknown even to one another because of the high wall that the Bush White House had erected around it. But a program that had continued largely of its own momentum for two years would now face critical questioning like never before from the disparate voices among this new guard. All would come to ask, usually in more polite terms, the same essential question that had bedeviled officials at the FBI when they first stumbled onto the NSA's spying operation two years earlier: *What the hell's going on here?*

By the time West Virginia senator Jay Rockefeller took over as the ranking Democrat on the Senate Intelligence Committee at the beginning of 2003, his predecessors on the panel and other members of the so-called Gang of Eight in Congress had been privy to a half-dozen briefings by Cheney and General Hayden at the White House. The White House had insisted on limiting the number of people—lawmakers, judges, administration lawyers—who could know about the program. The more people who knew about the program, administration officials believed, the more chance there was for trouble. The secrecy, a report from the nonpartisan Congressional Research Service would ultimately find, appeared to violate a 1947 law that required *all* the members of the intelligence committees—not just a few leaders tapped by the White House—to be "fully and currently informed" of all noncovert intelligence programs like this one. The law also required that there be written records of such briefings, but that too was ignored in the oral briefings that select members were given.

Law or no law, the White House was adamant about keeping knowledge of the program to a tight circle. "Because the tools are so valuable," Alberto Gonzales said, only select members of Congress could be briefed. General Hayden realized just how sensitive those briefings would be and just how vulnerable his agency was to charges that it was overreaching. Hayden liked to talk in sports metaphors, and he believed that the NSA's history of problems going back to the 1960s had put it in a permanent defensive stance. Hitting with a count of one ball and two strikes, it couldn't afford to take any more close pitches. The Gang of Eight briefings had to be "in your face," he told his staffers as he prepped for them. "I don't want anyone coming out of this one, two, or even five years later to say 'Oh, I got some sort of briefing, but I had no idea.' "

In fact, that's exactly what happened. There were "omissions of consequence" in the secret briefings, insisted Tom Daschle, the South Dakota senator who was told about the program in secret by virtue of his position as Senate minority leader. Lawmakers weren't allowed to take notes at the briefings, leaving no historical record of what exactly they were or were not told. They couldn't tell their own staff members what they had heard. California Congresswoman Jane Harman joked that she was itching to tell her husband what was going on, but she knew she couldn't. Members of the Gang of Eight were even nervous about talking to each other about the secret program for fear of violating the White House's carefully prescribed ground rules. Few members asked questions and, in a program so densely technical, they admitted they often didn't know exactly what to ask anyway. Even by the Bush White House's high standards, this was secrecy at its zenith.

No one dared to press the White House too hard on what it was doing. No one, that is, until Jay Rockefeller learned about the NSA program in 2003. Rockefeller was taking the spot on the intelligence committee that had been filled by Senator Bob Graham as the ranking Democrat. Graham, briefed in the earliest days of the program, was methodical and mild-mannered to the point of nerdiness, notorious for carrying around color-coded journals to chronicle everything he did, from his chocolate Slim-Fasts for breakfast to his congressional briefings after lunch. But on matters of terrorism, he had stripped away his Clark Kent disguise to become something of a zealot even by post-9/11 standards; he talked of Armageddon and warned on the Senate floor in 2002 that if his colleagues ignored the rising threat of terrorism, "then frankly, my friends, to use a blunt term, blood is going to be on your hands." So dire were Graham's pronouncements that *The Washington Post* questioned whether the normally placid Democrat had now turned, improbably, into "a screaming-banshee Chicken Little" just in time for a possible presidential run in 2004.

Senator Graham was briefed five times on the NSA program in its first year of existence, but there is no indication that he ever raised concerns about it. It wasn't even clear to him until much later that the NSA was actually eavesdropping on American citizens without a court order. What was made clear in the briefings was that this was a program that the White House considered vital to stopping another attack, and who was the Florida senator to stand in the way? His successor on the intelligence panel, however, was much more troubled by what he was hearing—and not hearing—from Cheney and Hayden. Senator Rockefeller, a close friend of Graham, received his first White House briefing on the program in January of 2003. After another briefing from General Hayden and George Tenet on the program that July, he decided he would no longer sit quietly. The program described to him sounded all too similar to the Pentagon's dreaded Total Information Awareness concept, which Congress had explicitly banned a few months earlier. So Rockefeller, hours after the latest briefing, composed a letter to Dick Cheney so secret that his own copy had to be locked away at a secure government site. His frustration was evident.

July 17, 2003:
Dear Mr. Vice President,

 I am writing to reiterate my concerns regarding the sensitive intelligence issues we discussed today with the DCI, DIRNSA, chairman Roberts and our House Intelligence Committee counterparts.

 Clearly, the issues we discussed raise profound oversight issues. As you know, I am neither a technician nor an attorney. Given the security restrictions associated with this information, and my inability to consult my staff or counsel on my own, I feel unable to evaluate, much less endorse these activities.

 As I reflected on the meeting today, and the future we face, John Poindexter's TIA project sprung to mind, exacerbating my concern regarding the direction the administration is moving with regard to security, technology and surveillance. Without more information and the ability to draw on any independent legal or technical expertise, I simply cannot satisfy lingering concerns raised by the briefing we received.

 I am retaining a copy of this letter in a sealed envelope in the secure spaces of the Senate Intelligence Committee to ensure that I have a record of this communication.

 I appreciate your consideration of my views.
 Most respectfully,
   Jay Rockefeller

Rockefeller's concerns, he complained, were never answered—by the vice president or anyone else. At Cheney's direction, the program continued on. But the White House was now on notice: at least one member of the Gang of Eight was clearly troubled by the NSA's spying operation and all the unanswered questions it raised, and White House officials were getting increasingly nervous about what else Rockefeller might do. The walls they had worked so meticulously to erect around the NSA program were showing the first real signs of cracking.

At the Justice Department, nerves were beginning to fray as well, and Jim Baker's intelligence shop found itself, as always, in the middle of the ruckus. From the beginning, Baker had struggled to develop a system to ensure that the NSA's wiretaps did not improperly "taint" the several thousand traditional wiretaps his office was getting approved each year by the intelligence court. It was a system created in part at the urging of Judge Lamberth. After the judge's initial silence about the NSA operation when Ashcroft, Hayden, and Yoo had first told him about it, Lamberth became increasingly uncomfortable about the program's impact on his court. Bush could claim whatever executive power he wanted, but once the government came to his court for a wiretap, Lamberth was in charge. While there is no sign that Lamberth sought to end the NSA program, he did work with Baker to create an ad hoc firewall that, at least in theory, would protect the integrity of the process inside his court.

Not infrequently, the Justice Department would seek a court wiretapping order for an American target who had already been wiretapped by the NSA without a warrant; by one official's estimate, some 10 to 20 percent of all court warrants fell into this area of "double coverage." With each one came the risk that information obtained by the NSA through its warrantless wiretapping program might be used, wittingly or not, to get a wiretap order from the court; this was what lawyers called "the fruit of the poisonous tree" problem, and it could kill a case. So, Baker and Lamberth set up a system in which Baker's office had to flag any wiretap applications to the court involving NSA targets, and Lamberth was the only one who could review those applications.

His aim, the judge said, was to make sure that the warrants his court was approving could stand on their own and that the Justice Department was not improperly using information culled from NSA wiretaps to apply for warrants. "If anything was presented to the FISA court that came from that program, the FISA court had to be told about it," Lamberth insisted. Lawyers in Baker's shop knew that every phone number or e-mail address they wanted to target had to be run past the NSA first to determine if their sister agency was already tapping it—and any "hits" would have to be put, in effect, in a black box, segregated from the others for fear that they might be corrupted otherwise. The flagged applications could only be signed by Ashcroft himself (Thompson, his deputy, had refused because he didn't know where the leads were originating); and they could only be reviewed by Judge Lamberth, since none of the other ten judges on the court was even allowed to know about the program.

It was an odd, impractical, and in some ways unworkable arrangement for everyone involved, and Baker seemed to recognize the inevitable discomfort. He told lawyers in his office, in fact, that anyone who was uncomfortable with the arrangement could "opt out" and simply not take part in reviewing and routing this new breed of wiretap applications to the chief judge; several lawyers took him up on the offer.

In mid-2002, Lamberth left the FISA court. If it were up to him, he would have stayed on, but his seven-year term was up, and a fellow judge from the D.C. courthouse, Colleen Kollar-Kotelly, was named to replace him. Kollar-Kotelly, the longtime general counsel for St. Elizabeths mental hospital, famous as the home to would-be Reagan assassin John Hinckley, was a Clinton appointee who was best known until then for hearing the landmark Microsoft antitrust case. Low-key and meticulous to a fault, Kollar-Kotelly couldn't match Lamberth's boisterous, larger-than-life personality around the courthouse. But she did share his belief that the judicial process and the rule of law had to be considered sacrosanct in her court. "Predictability, continuity and stability are an integral part of the administration of justice," she wrote when named to the bench.

Along with all the middle-of-the-night emergency wiretap applications on the FISA court, Kollar-Kotelly also inherited from Lamberth the Chinese firewall that he and Jim Baker had set up to govern the NSA program. But soon enough, problems began creeping up. By 2003, Baker's shop began seeing signs that information culled from NSA wiretaps was improperly bleeding into the wiretap applications it was forwarding to Kollar-Kotelly's court. The firewall was in danger of being breached. The judge was furious when she found out about the lapses, and by early 2004, after several apparent breaches, the system was in danger of total collapse. As with Lamberth, there is no indication that Kollar-Kotelly ever moved to challenge the legality of the NSA program itself or tried to shut it down, but she did demand greater accountability over how it might bleed into her court system.

She was so infuriated by the lapses that she went directly to Ashcroft to demand changes in the system, insisting that senior officials certify the truthfulness of what they were telling the court and threatening to pursue perjury charges against anyone at the Justice Department who failed to disclose information that had originally come from the NSA program. The Justice Department was forced to shut down its end of the NSA operation for a period of weeks early that year to figure out how to build the wall back up and protect some semblance of due process. "There was an ongoing concern," one senior official said, "that the FISA applications had to be absolutely accurate." The message was clear: if there was another screw-up, if another "tainted," warrantless wiretap from the Justice Department's friends at Fort Meade were allowed to infect the court system, the game was up.

BUT A LONE JUDGE wasn't the biggest problem confronting Ashcroft and the White House over the NSA program. The administration was also facing mounting questions from its own senior lawyers about whether the program as a whole was illegal. Kollar-Kotelly's concerns skirted around the edges of the program; now, the questions would drill down to its core.

It started with Jack Goldsmith, a widely admired young law professor from the University of Chicago Law School who took over as head of the Justice Department's Office of Legal Counsel in October 2003. Goldsmith replaced Jay Bybee, who was confirmed as a federal appeals judge that March, two years before he would become publicly identified as the official who signed the infamous "torture memo" authorizing the CIA to use extreme measures in interrogating terror suspects. Goldsmith wasn't anyone's first pick for the job. John Yoo had made no secret of his interest in being promoted to the top legal slot after drafting so many crucial war-powers opinions as an OLC deputy, including the so-called torture memo, and Gonzales and the White House wanted Yoo, their man, for the job. But Ashcroft and his senior aides balked; they had grown weary of what they saw as Yoo's end runs to the

White House, and they wanted one of their own lawyers—someone like Adam Ciongoli, a counselor to Ashcroft—in the critical post.

Neither side budged, and Goldsmith was the compromise selection. Schooled at Oxford and Yale, he brought solid conservative credentials to the job: he worked at the Pentagon general counsel's office after 9/11, he had advocated against undue restraints posed on the United States by international laws and treaties, and he had a broad view of the president's wartime powers. (In the footnote to one law review article that he co-wrote, Goldsmith would even assert that, under limited circumstances, the Authorization for Use of Military Force against al Qaeda approved by Congress days after 9/11, clearing the way for the U.S. invasion of Afghanistan, "might authorize the President to target and kill persons covered by the AUMF found in the United States.") By his résumé, at least, Goldsmith believed just as strongly in the president's wartime authorities as any of the other "loyal Bushies" directing the war on terror.

But if Gonzales and the White House were expecting a rubber stamp from the new head of the administration's legal brain trust at OLC, Goldsmith would prove a bitter disappointment. He did not provide the kind of legal certitude that the White House had come to expect from John Yoo. Not long after Goldsmith took over, he and other Justice Department lawyers began reviewing some of the critical legal opinions that the office had generated in the first two years of the administration's war on terror. They were troubled by what they found. The two most important issues—and ultimately the most controversial—were the legal opinions on the NSA program and the ones on torture and interrogation policies. Both issues represented critical legal prongs in the Bush White House's war on terror, but both areas were ultimately found to rest on shaky legal foundations. Too often, Goldsmith believed, the legal opinions used to justify critical programs were sloppy, flimsy, ill-advised, and "deeply flawed." Often, it wasn't so much what the legal opinions justified, as how they got there. Sure, Goldsmith and his allies believed, the CIA might be justified in using harsh interrogation tactics on al Qaeda detainees—but declaring that anything short of death or pain equivalent to organ failure was legal? That went too far.

Much of that earlier work had been done by John Yoo. On the NSA program, in fact, Yoo's boss—Jay Bybee—had not even been briefed on the program; on matters of law involving the most sensitive program in the government, Yoo was clearly the court of first and last resort for the White House. Yoo had many admirers at the White House. Some of his colleagues and successors at the Justice Department, however, considered Yoo brilliant yet erratic, as sloppy as he was prolific. The paper trail showing how legal opinions had been reached was sometimes incomplete or nonexistent, Justice Department lawyers complained in reviewing his handiwork. When Justice Department lawyers would go to their counterparts at the Pentagon and the intelligence agencies to find out how certain legal decisions had been validated, one senior lawyer recounted, the answer they sometimes got was: "John said we could do it." The joke at the Justice Department was that legal positions about the war on terror in its early days seemed, at times, to have been formulated on the squash court between Yoo and his counterparts in the intelligence community.

After Goldsmith and the Justice Department began moving to withdraw some of the extreme interrogation tactics endorsed in earlier opinions, they were met with anger and derision from White House officials like David Addington, known for his biting sarcasm and sharp temper. "Since you've withdrawn so many legal opinions that the president and others have been relying on," Addington told Goldsmith in one heated confrontation, an index card gripped in his hand, "we need you to go through all of OLC's opinions and let us know which ones you still stand by."

When Goldsmith and other Justice Department lawyers dusted off the early legal opinions on the NSA program, they were shocked to find that Yoo had not even factored into his legal analysis a seminal Supreme Court precedent on presidential power: the Youngstown steel case, which found that President Harry Truman did not have the power to seize steel mills shut down during a labor strike in order to supply munitions for troops in the Korean War. In a famous concurring opinion in the case, Justice Robert Jackson offered a three-part test for presidential power, saying that the president acted at the "zenith" of his power when his actions were in concert with Congress, but at his "lowest ebb" in going against the express wishes of Congress. In the case of wiretapping, Congress had clearly spoken in 1978: the president needed a warrant for national security wiretaps. It was one thing for Yoo to assert, with some validity, that the Constitution gave the president broad powers as commander-in-chief after 9/11 to order wiretaps to protect the country from another attack. But it struck his successors as slipshod, even cavalier, to do so without even acknowledging that there was a Supreme Court precedent that spoke to the very question of how far the president's powers reached and what happens when a conflicting law like FISA is already on the books. (Yoo, writing in his memoir, cited earlier OLC opinions in arguing that the Youngstown case "had no application to the President's conduct of foreign affairs and national security.")

In November of 2003, Goldsmith sent Ashcroft a draft memorandum entitled "Review of Legality of the [NSA] Program." The memo remains classified, and its findings remain unknown. What is known is that Goldsmith saw it as his mission—"by far the hardest challenge I faced in government"—to put the NSA program on solid legal footing without destroying it altogether. A month after sending Ashcroft his memo on the legality of the program, Goldsmith would gain a powerful ally when James Comey moved into the fourth floor of the Justice Department as the deputy attorney general. Comey, a towering, six-foot-eight prosecutor with a quick, self-deprecating wit and movie-star charisma, had been the U.S. attorney in Manhattan for only two years when he became Ashcroft's number two, but his star was clearly on the rise in the Bush administration. He had first made a name for himself prosecuting gun crimes in the U.S. Attorney's Office in Richmond, Virginia, in the late 1990s, and he was elevated in 2001 to one of the most important prosecutors' jobs in the country: head of New York's Southern District, or the "Sovereign District," as it was nicknamed in deference to its famed autonomy and arrogance. Ashcroft's people liked Comey so much that they toyed with the idea of making him the head of the entire Criminal Division at Main Justice in the spring of 2003, but they decided he was too valuable where he was in Manhattan. When Larry Thompson departed as deputy attorney general a few months later, however, Comey was an obvious pick for the number-two job in charge of day-to-day operations.

In New York, Comey had gone after terrorism cases with zeal, and the Bush administration's critics on the left saw little reason to expect any major shifts in post-9/11 legal philosophies from the new man in Washington. "Nothing about Mr. Comey's tenure in New York," one civil liberties advocate said when Comey was tapped as deputy, "suggests he will be a friend of the Constitution when he joins John Ashcroft in Washington." What critics failed to take into account was Comey's well-honed reputation as an honest broker who was unafraid to make politically unpopular decisions and who shunned the hype and histrionics of official Washington.

Comey's famous call-'em-like-I-see-'em approach won him credibility with both his fellow prosecutors and with the media. "This is not the case of the century," Comey told reporters in Washington at one press conference announcing the indictment of a pair of Muslim men charged with terrorism in an FBI sting. "I don't want it misread by the media or anyone else as some sort of breathless announcement of a disrupting of a terrorist plot." Heads turned in the press gallery as we reporters tried to make sure we had heard the deputy attorney general correctly. Tamping down a terrorism case wasn't something we heard very often from the Justice Department podium.

Comey's early days as deputy attorney general beginning in December 2003 were consumed by the political firestorm over the leak of CIA agent Valerie Plame's name to columnist Robert Novak. In a move that would win him no friends at the White House, Comey named one of his closest friends and colleagues—Patrick Fitzgerald, the tough-minded federal prosecutor in Chicago—to investigate allegations that Plame was the victim of a White House smear campaign growing out of her husband's criticism of the Iraq war. Just as Fitzgerald was starting to bring White House witnesses before a grand jury in the leak investigation, Comey was quietly confronting an even more explosive issue that would again put him at odds with the White House—with even higher stakes. This one was the NSA program. Comey did not even know about the operation in his early days as deputy attorney general. Like Larry Thompson before him, he was excluded as a result of the high walls the White House had built up around the program. By the accounts of several officials, however, the concerns of a Justice Department lawyer named Patrick Philbin who became an aide to Comey on national security matters proved instrumental in changing that.

Philbin, like Goldsmith and Comey, was no shrinking violet on matters of national security. He had clerked for a conservative legal icon, Judge Laurence Silberman, and he was a strong believer in the president's wartime powers, drafting key legal opinions arguing that the U.S. courts had no jurisdiction over terror suspects at Guantánamo Bay and that the president had the inherent authority to create military commissions. But the NSA program proved troubling even for him. Philbin had learned of the operation as a deputy in OLC. Concerned that the operation was not getting the kind of oversight and legal scrutiny it demanded, he angled to get Comey directly involved in it after his arrival.

That proved a fateful maneuver. Comey, officials said, was stunned to learn that the administration had been bypassing the FISA court and was allowing the NSA to conduct wiretaps on Americans without warrants. The more he and his aides learned about the program, the more concerned they became. What the NSA was casting as a carefully targeted surveillance operation struck some officials at the Justice Department as a vast data-mining operation run amok, with the NSA combing through vast volumes of "meta-data" to trace and analyze phone and e-mail traffic across the United States. Virtually all the leads, officials at the FBI complained, were a waste of time. And the legal foundations of some aspects of the operation appeared suspect at best to lawyers like Jack Goldsmith.

By March of 2004, the Justice Department's concerns had grown so severe that senior officials there were considering refusing to recertify the program under the process Bush had set up in first authorizing it. The Justice Department's official sign-off, largely a perfunctory matter for the last two years, was due on March 11. A week before, Comey sat down with Ashcroft for an hour to air his concerns about the program. It was a private meeting, just the two of them. For the first two years of the program, there is no indication that Ashcroft voiced any concerns about the program or its legality. This, after all, was not his operation. Just the opposite. Ashcroft told associates that the White House, in seeking his sign-off at the very outset of the program in 2001, had "just shoved it in front of me and told me to sign it," according to one official with knowledge of the conversation. In fact, at the outset of the program, Ashcroft had sought a formal legal opinion from OLC validating the program only at the urging of Mueller and other advisors. Without that piece of paper, that legal justification, his aides worried, Ashcroft would be left dangerously exposed if the program blew up.

Even with the legal opinion in hand, some senior FBI officials were left to worry about their own potential liability growing out of their role as the "consumer" of the NSA's warrantless wiretaps. Everyone at the bureau knew of the convictions in 1980 of two senior FBI officials, including Mark Felt, better known in later years as Watergate's "Deep Throat," for authorizing "black bag" searches of the homes of radicals and terrorist suspects in the early 1970s. "We all saw agents prosecuted for things they thought were legal and proper," one FBI official said. Some senior people at the bureau would grow increasingly uncomfortable with their peripheral role in the NSA program and the potential legal peril it bought, and rightly or wrongly, they saw Ashcroft as the man advocating for the program from across the street at Main Justice. "Ashcroft kept pushing us in these different areas. He thought we weren't aggressive enough, but we didn't want to get out in front of the law," the official said. "The thought was: We're doing this today, but five years from now, where's Ashcroft going to be?"

For more than two years of the program's operation, Ashcroft had never blanched. Now, as he sat with Comey in his office that day in early March of 2004, he was hearing his top deputy spell out his concerns—and the concerns of his own Office of Legal Counsel—about why aspects of President Bush's signature antiterror program might be illegal. Comey explained what he thought the department had to do to put the program back on solid legal footing—the safeguards that he and his aides felt were needed, the checks they believed were now missing at the NSA, the operational changes they felt were necessary to make it legal. Ashcroft agreed to move ahead on his ideas. The attorney general and his deputy had a plan. But just hours later, that plan got sidetracked. Scheduled to appear at a press conference announcing guilty verdicts in a Virginia terrorism case, Ashcroft began having stomach pains so severe that he had to cancel his appearance. Ashcroft figured it was just a stomach flu. But a White House doctor had him rushed to George Washington University Hospital with what turned out to be a bout of severe pancreatitis. He had to have his gallbladder removed five days later, and he was so pumped up with antibiotics and painkillers that, as he was the first to admit, he was in "no position to exercise judgment or make decisions on behalf of the United States government."

With Ashcroft laid up in the hospital, Comey was now the acting attorney general. That meant he could, in theory, sign off on the program in Ashcroft's absence. The White House was waiting anxiously for his signature. On Tuesday, March 10—the very day of Ashcroft's gallbladder surgery—Comey met with Cheney, Gonzales, Addington, Card, and other senior officials to give them his startling decision: he would not sign off on the legality of the surveillance program. White House officials were furious. Cheney disagreed strongly. So did Addington, Gonzales, and Card. Without the Justice Department's sign-off, Bush would potentially be in violation of the procedures he had set up for the NSA operation if he allowed the program to continue. The White House now had a full-blown crisis on its hands, and something had to be done.

The Gang of Eight—the only members of Congress briefed on the program—were called to the White House Situation Room the next day for an emergency meeting. Gonzales and other White House officials let the lawmakers know what had happened; Comey wasn't going along with the program. Ashcroft and the Justice Department had signed off on these same activities for two years, but now Comey was saying no. What happened at that briefing remains in some dispute. Some lawmakers said they were given only snippets of the emerging crisis, with key details left out. Gonzales insisted that the "consensus in the room" was that critical intelligence operations should continue for now—with or without Comey's sign-off. There was even talk of getting Congress, more than two years after the program's inception, to approve some sort of emergency legislation to finally ratify what Bush was doing. But that idea was apparently scuttled because debate in Congress would risk exposing the nature of the program itself. That left only one immediate option: going to the bedridden Ashcroft to get him to overrule his independent-minded deputy.

That night, Comey was just leaving the Justice Department at about 8 o'clock to have his FBI security detail drive him home to Northern Virginia when he got a call from David Ayres, Ashcroft's chief of staff. Ashcroft was so ill that all visitors were banned from his hospital suite, but Ayres told Comey that Mrs. Ashcroft had just gotten a call—apparently from the president himself—announcing that two visitors were on their way to the hospital. Alberto Gonzales and Andy Card wanted to see the attorney general personally on behalf of the president.

As a longtime prosecutor, Comey had gone up against violent street gangs, mob figures, and terrorists. But he was about to begin what he would call the toughest night of his professional life. He knew this couldn't end well. The White House, he worried, was about to try to blindside a man in intensive care to get him to overrule the acting attorney general's decision. He hung up the phone and called one of his aides: Get as many people to the hospital as you can right now, he demanded. Then he called Bob Mueller at the FBI, who had been deliberating with Comey over the last week about how to handle the growing concerns about the NSA program, and he filled him in quickly on what was going on. "I'll meet you at the hospital right now," Mueller told him. Comey ordered his security detail to get him to George Washington University Hospital as soon as possible; they turned on the emergency lights and hit the gas.

Once they arrived, Comey didn't wait for an elevator. He ran up the stairs, his security detail in tow chasing behind the acting attorney general. As they arrived at Ashcroft's darkened hospital room, Janet Ashcroft was standing over her husband at his bed. Gonzales and Card hadn't made it yet; Comey had won the foot race. "How are you, General?" Comey asked him. "Not well," Ashcroft answered. Ashcroft seemed out of it. Comey went into the hallway to call Mueller, who was also en route to the hospital. Comey told the FBI director that he wanted to make sure he would be able to stay in the room whenever Gonzales and Card arrived. Comey handed the phone to his FBI security detail for Mueller to relay orders to them. Under no circumstances, Mueller told them, was Comey to be removed from the room. Soon, Jack Goldsmith and Pat Philbin arrived; they'd beaten the White House team too. Comey sat down in an armchair at the head of Ashcroft's bed to his left, with Goldsmith and Philbin standing behind him. Janet Ashcroft stood with them, clutching her husband's arm. Together, they waited for Ashcroft's visiting delegation.

It wasn't a long wait. Just a few minutes later, Gonzales and Card walked in. Gonzales was carrying an envelope. Everyone knew what was inside: the official certification with the line at the bottom for the attorney general's signature, the one that was needed to continue operations of a program that at least three lawyers in the room now thought might be illegal. Gonzales and Card walked over to Ashcroft's bedside and greeted him. Pointedly, they did not acknowledge Comey seated next to him. Then Gonzales told Ashcroft why they were there: they needed his sign-off for the program. Gonzales thought Ashcroft should hear for himself what had happened at the White House Situation Room that day and what congressional leaders were expecting.

The suggestion was clear: this wasn't just the White House asking; it was the will of Congress as well. His hope, Gonzales said later, was that Ashcroft was well enough to temporarily reclaim the mantle of attorney general that he had handed to Comey and could sign off on the program. Gonzales wasn't even sure if Ashcroft knew the strong stance that Comey had taken in defying the White House.

Ashcroft, weakened and drugged up, lifted his head from the pillow. In language that both Comey and Gonzales regarded as remarkably lucid, he outlined his concerns about the legality of the surveillance program, paralleling many of the same issues Comey had briefed him on the week before. He made clear that he shared those concerns. "I've been told it would be improvident for me to sign," he told Gonzales. "But that doesn't matter," he said, "because I'm not the attorney general." Gesturing to Comey next to him, he said: "There is the attorney general." Ashcroft put his head back down on the pillow. He looked so ill that Goldsmith figured he was going to die right there on the spot; it was, Goldsmith said later, "the most amazing scene I've ever witnessed."

The discussion was over. Ashcroft had stood by his deputy. The White House wouldn't get the Justice Department's standard sign-off, not this time. "Be well," Card told Ashcroft. Then, he and Gonzales turned on their heels and headed for the door, the envelope still in Gonzales' hand. There would be no long goodbyes. As Gonzales and Card left, Ashcroft's wife—who had watched the whole scene unfold—had one final gesture to cap off the night: she stuck her tongue out at Bush's two senior aides as they walked out the door.

Soon after their departure, Mueller arrived, and Comey filled him in on the remarkable scene. As they were talking, an FBI agent interrupted to tell Comey that he had an urgent call at the makeshift command center set up in the hospital suite for Ashcroft. It was Andy Card. He was upset, and he insisted that Comey come to the White House—immediately. "After the conduct I just witnessed," Comey told Bush's chief of staff on the phone, "I will not meet with you without a witness present." "What conduct?" Card demanded. "We were just there to wish him well." Comey wasn't buying it. "After what I just witnessed," he repeated, "I will not meet with you without a witness, and I intend that witness to be the solicitor general of the United States." That was Ted Olson.

Comey had the Justice Department command center track Olson down at a dinner party. But they didn't go straight to the White House. First, Comey had Olson and other senior aides meet him back at the Justice Department, where he related to them what had just taken place. Jaws dropped. There was talk of resignations—starting with Comey himself. If this kind of bullying from the White House was allowed to stand, he and his aides agreed, there was no way they could stay on in this administration. Then, Comey and Olson drove over to the White House for their appointed meeting with Andy Card in the West Wing. It was now eleven o'clock at night.

Card asked Olson to wait in a sitting area outside his office. Grudgingly, Comey went in by himself. Tempers had cooled a bit, and their conversation was markedly more civil than the one they had on the phone just a few hours before. Card was clearly concerned about where all this was heading. He had gotten word that there might be mass resignations at the Justice Department. With the start of Bush's full-fledged presidential campaign against John Kerry just a few months away, a revolt at the Justice Department wouldn't fit into the White House's vision for a campaign of keeping America safer. Comey held firm. There were elements of the program, he told Card, that gave the Justice Department serious legal pause.

The next day, the White House went ahead with the program anyway—without the Justice Department's certification. The line for the attorney general's signature remained blank. The White House was now operating a program that its own lawyers at the Justice Department had advised might not be legal. Comey prepared his letter of resignation. If the White House was going ahead with the program after all that had happened, there was no way he could stay on. He planned to turn in his letter of resignation the next day, that Friday, with at least a dozen other top officials or more—including Mueller— lining up behind the Justice Department's rangy pied piper. A few lawyers had already drafted their letters of resignation, just waiting for Comey's cue to make it official. Don't do it yet, Ayres urged him; wait until Monday. Wait until Ashcroft was well enough to resign with him. Now, there was talk of the administration losing not just the deputy attorney general, but the attorney general himself. Comey agreed to hold off. Friday, he told Ayres, would be his last day.

The next day, Comey went to the White House for the usual terrorism briefing with Bush and Cheney. But this morning was anything but usual. For one thing, three trains in Madrid had just been bombed the day before, killing nearly two hundred people in an attack that would tilt the outcome of Spain's elections. For another, Comey had just led what amounted to the biggest revolt at the Justice Department since the infamous Saturday Night Massacre at the height of the Watergate scandal three decades earlier. At the close of the White House terror briefing, Bush asked Comey to stay behind. He took him in his private study, and they talked one-on-one for about fifteen minutes. Comey laid out why he had done what he had done the day before. "You've been poorly served by your advisors, and I'm prepared to resign," he told Bush, according to the account of another official who was briefed on the conversation. Comey urged the president to meet with Mueller as well, who was waiting downstairs. He did. Mueller laid out for the president what the Justice Department believed needed to be done to put the program back on a proper legal footing. "Do what the department thinks is right," Bush told him. Comey took that as his mandate, and the Justice Department moved to put tight new controls on the NSA program.

A detailed checklist containing some twenty items would be developed to determine how exactly the NSA went about determining who was a suspected member of al Qaeda when it started eavesdropping. An audit of past wiretaps would be conducted, with the Justice Department's active involvement. The legal opinions validating the program would be reworked, stressing Congress's authorization to use military force against al Qaeda—rather than simply the president's inherent constitutional authority—as justification for the warrantless wiretapping. (Ironically, this new legal tack ultimately met with even more skepticism from Congress than the original legal justification.) And most critically, several specific aspects of the program would be shut down altogether. What exactly the NSA shut down in order to keep the program alive remains unclear even today, but according to intelligence officials, it appears to involve several distinct and technical aspects of the operations that relied on the use of data-mining to trace communications patterns across U.S. borders, elements that officials at the Justice Department thought were particularly problematic in a program already rife with legal complications. "Imagine you're doing ten things one day, and the next day you're only doing eight of them," one official said. "That's basically what happened here."

With an understanding in hand, the two sides—the White House and the Justice Department—put down their weapons. The program, in an altered form, was allowed to continue. There would be no resignations, no public revolt. An uneasy truce was in place, but the episode would not soon be forgotten by anyone in either the West Wing or Main Justice. Months later, when the Justice Department pushed for Comey's aide Pat Philbin to be named to the coveted spot of deputy solicitor general, Cheney pushed back, blocking the move. This, Justice Department officials believed, was the White House's payback for the Wednesday Night Massacre. Philbin was too closely associated with the Justice Department's rebellion, and he would ultimately leave for the private sector.

Goldsmith went off to Harvard to be greeted by student protesters who, ironically, blamed him for the administration's extreme views on presidential power. Comey stayed on for another fifteen months; after Gonzales was made attorney general in 2005, he would serve as the top deputy for six months to the man who had shunned him in the hospital room at Ashcroft's bedside. When Comey finally left for a lucrative job as top lawyer for an aerospace contractor, he bade farewell at the Justice Department's Great Hall and delivered the usual appreciations about his career in public service and the men and women with whom he had served. Speaking almost in code, he thanked the "people who came to my office, or my home, or called my cell phone late at night, to quietly tell me when I was about to make a mistake; they were the people committed to getting it right—and to doing the right thing— whatever the price. These people," Comey said, "know who they are. Some of them did pay a price for their commitment to right, but they wouldn't have it any other way."

The people Comey was talking to that day did know who they were, even if no else listening in the Great Hall did. What had happened at Ashcroft's hospital bedside was still known only to a few people at the upper ranks of the Bush administration, and it was talked about only in whispers even by them. The White House's secret program was still safe, if only for a while longer.

CHAPTER SIX

Blood on Our Hands

Y OU'VE GOTTA KEEP PUSHING on this Patriot Act stuff," the
source said, cryptic as always. "There's more there."

I had just written what seemed like my hundredth story on
the euphemistically named antiterrorism law when the plea came. It
was the spring of 2004, and by the time George Bush and his Democratic rivals for the presidency started debating the USA Patriot Act as
a second-tier issue in the presidential campaign, I'd written so many
stories on the 342-page legislative grab bag that even my editors
seemed bored. Not that I could blame them. I could almost anticipate
the roll of their eyes as I would walk haltingly up to the news desk to
pitch another story on some arcane matter of surveillance law and its
esoteric public policy implications. I'd written about technical, almost
indecipherable "fixes" in the act, about communities around the country joining in opposition to its Big Brother overtones, about a judge
ruling parts of it unconstitutional, and about the Bush White House
pushing vigorously for its renewal. I'd followed Ashcroft down to
Georgia and North Carolina as part of a nationwide barnstorming
tour he made to rally support for the Patriot Act; after I tried to pierce
Ashcroft's gaggle of press aides to ask him a few questions at one of his
carefully staged appearances, a sympathetic reporter for a local weekly
paper cast me in his article as a rumpled Washington "attack dog"
hounding the attorney general.

Occasionally, a story would poke through the denseness and political hype that surrounded the Patriot Act, like a long, analytical piece
I did in the fall of 2003, explaining how the Patriot Act had become,

for better or worse, a powerful catch-all for prosecuting money-launderers, drug-dealers, and even lovesick teenagers who had little or no connection to terrorism. The story found its way onto the top of the front page of the Sunday paper and caused a minor stir in law enforcement and intelligence circles for a day or two. But far more often, the daily trope on the Patriot Act would be relegated, deservedly so, to the back pages of the A section, lost among the obituaries and brassiere ads.

So I was not terribly hopeful when I spoke with an occasional source in 2004 who, after seeing my latest submission on the topic, was urging me to do more reporting on the Bush administration's antiterrorism operations. "There's more there," the source repeated. There's more there? What did that mean? The source, a government official, was unwilling to say. The tip, if it could even be called that, was beguilingly vague. This was one of the lesser known by-products of the *All the President's Men* phenomenon. Just as Bob Woodward and Carl Bernstein had inspired a generation of young journalists like myself to become government watchdog sleuths, they had also given rise to armies of self-styled Deep Throats. Sources who had seen Hal Holbrook utter "Follow the money" a few too many times now felt emboldened, with a simple but maddeningly vague command, to send reporters on their way in search of scandal and journalistic riches.

Round and round we went. The source had come to me blindly at the outset—what the CIA would call a "walk-in." Walk-ins pose a risk, be they government whistle-blowers or Russian double agents. Some may have an agenda, an axe to grind. Others may lack credibility. Some may not even be who they claim to be. This one had checked out on all counts. He wouldn't even give me his real name at first, and initially, I would have to make contact through an intermediary to arrange meetings, usually at a bookstore or a coffee shop in the shadows of Washington's power corridors. A few times, he didn't show. Soon enough, his credibility and his bona fides became clear, and his angst appeared sincere. He was agitated about something going on in the government's intelligence community, but just what was not clear. Was it even worth my time?

"There's talk of indictments over at the Justice Department," the source said in one conversation. This in itself was not news. The Justice Department issues indictments all the time. But that's not what the source was talking about; he was hinting not at people at the Justice

Department *filing* indictments, but *being* indicted. "Whatever's going on," the source said, "there's even talk that Ashcroft could be indicted."

It was just a rumor, but I had become known, rightly or wrongly, as one of Ashcroft's chief critics in the press corps, and here was a government source suggesting that whatever was going on in the Bush administration had cast a cloud of potential criminality over the nation's most senior law enforcement official. That was surely news. (There is no evidence, it should be noted, that Ashcroft or anyone else was ever under criminal investigation over the NSA's wiretapping program. In fact, Ashcroft would emerge as a white knight of sorts after James Comey's dramatic testimony about the visit to Ashcroft's hospital room by Gonzales and Card in March of 2004. But the rumors flying within the government at that time about possible criminality at the highest levels in what was then still a secret program spoke to the intense anxiety surrounding it.)

I spoke with a number of sources, and it soon became clear that the nervousness that the source alluded to was roiling the executive branch. As best I could tell, whatever was going on somehow involved counterterrorism operations, federal wiretapping law, and the FISA court. But the links were maddeningly tenuous. The original source, like all the others I contacted, would not discuss anything that could even be construed as classified; he saw himself as a compass, pointing me in the right direction without drawing a roadmap on how to get there. The best I could piece together, from conversations with a number of other people, was that there was anxiety within the administration over suspicions that the law was being stretched to accommodate some new counterterrorism operation. And it seemed that the FISA court, the linchpin of all intelligence wiretapping operations, might somehow have been subverted in the process. Whatever this new operation was, it was off-limits even to senior counterterrorism people normally in the know and appeared to be causing nervousness within the FISA court. My task now was to understand the source of that heartburn. A nice idea, to be sure, but a bit like asking a corner pickpocket to break into Fort Knox.

In an executive branch built to keep secrets, the FISA court was the gold standard. It did virtually nothing in public. Nothing ever leaked out of the place. It operated in the sealed-off confines of the top floor of the Justice Department, so cloistered that the Justice Department's public elevators do not even go there. The court functioned as a sort of modern-day Star Chamber with only one side—the Justice Department—offering secret evidence as to why an American should be wiretapped. Not only were the targets not represented in the hearing, but they would almost never even know they had been targeted. The court had issued a total of two public rulings in its history, and the sum total of its activities was made public one time each year in a filing by the Justice Department to Congress, revealing the total number of times the prior year that the court had been asked to approve warrants, and how often it had denied them. (The answer: almost never.)

So now here I was asked to examine the inner workings of the country's most secretive court. It was, at best, a part-time sidelight. I was busy writing daily stories through much of mid-2004, from the mundane (a run-of-the-mill drug bust breaking up a Canadian-American ecstasy ring) to the titillating (the resignation of Clinton advisor Sandy Berger from John Kerry's campaign for sneaking classified documents on terrorism out of a government reading room) to the provocative (the FBI's renewed interest in antiwar demonstrations). In between, I kept poking, never really sure what I was looking for, but never quite able to put out of my mind that intriguing lead about the Patriot Act and vague implications about possible criminality.

In the course of reporting on other big stories on my beat in mid-2004, I would drop in an occasional question to a few trusted officials about FISA and the Patriot Act. Were there some changes going on we didn't know about? Were there some new procedures that were causing concern, or abuses that were being covered up? I would get blank stares. I poked around in the intelligence community. Whatever was going on in the way of domestic surveillance, I figured, would have to be carried out by the FBI; no one else was authorized to operate in that arena, or so I thought. Again, the well was dry. I went back to my original sources. I needed more, I told them. They wouldn't, or couldn't, help me. Either they didn't know more, or they simply weren't willing to share it. I knew enough to suspect that there was some sensitive operation that was raising concerns within the government about the possible subversion of the court wiretapping process, but that wasn't nearly enough for a story. It was, at best, half of a lead desperately in search of two thousand words or so to follow it.

I had hit a dead end. Luckily, I sat three feet away from a reporter who had made his mark uncovering government secrets.

Jim Risen and I had both worked at the *Los Angeles Times* for many years before each moving to *The New York Times*, but our work there didn't overlap, and we didn't know each other before I joined the paper in 2002. I knew of Jim mainly by reputation—and it was an impressive one. "Jim has the best sources in Washington," another veteran *New York Times* reporter, David Johnston, no slouch himself when it came to developing sources, told me when I got to the bureau. Jim also had a reputation, as I was soon to learn, of being a bit challenging to work with. My first day in the bureau, Rick Berke, then the deputy bureau chief, escorted me to my new desk. "Now, you'll be sitting next to Jim Risen. He can be, um, a little difficult sometimes," Berke said gingerly. "Is that going to be okay?"

Jim reveled in his prickly reputation. He was an old-school reporter who never bothered to learn the *Times'* newfangled computer system and would proudly quote his version of the rules of journalism taken from Homer Bigart, the legendary World War II reporter. Among them: Don't ever read your own stories in the paper the next day (you'll only be disappointed); and don't eat lunch at your desk (go take out sources instead). Jim has a supreme confidence, born out of a knack for often being right in picking up intelligence trends long before other people. (In the buildup to the Iraq war, he would mumble to me across our crowded cubicle, or to anyone else who would listen, that the administration's rhetoric about Saddam Hussein's weapons of mass destruction was "all bullshit.") Jim would often spar with editors over stories, but he flashed his contrarian image like a bumper sticker. "Kick your editor, not your dog," he'd declare after each bruising encounter.

Somehow, for all the notoriety that preceded him, Jim and I clicked, bonded by a nagging skepticism that we weren't getting the full story about the administration's war on terror. Just as the people I covered at the Justice Department and the FBI saw my coverage as overly critical and skeptical, so too did the people in the intelligence community view Jim's work on the CIA. Jim covered mainly intelligence; I covered mainly law enforcement and the justice system. It was a marriage of complementary parts that had led us to break important stories together long before there was any talk of illegal government wiretapping, on everything from Chinese spy scandals to 9/11 intelligence failures.

Jim and I have very different styles of interviewing. Even when we worked on stories together, we would usually interview people separately, each with our own sets of sources, but our contrasting approaches would come into stark relief whenever we had to do interviews together. Jim likes to chat up a source, get them talking about anything and everything besides what he was actually interested in hearing. I'm more direct in my interviewing, trying to look for an opening to come back at a critical question again and again in hopes there might be a more satisfying answer the next time I ask it. Invariably, Jim and I would leave a joint interview sniping at each other over our competing techniques; Felix Unger and Oscar Madison in reporters' garb. Jim would accuse me of something short of waterboarding in my interrogation techniques. "Jesus, leave the poor guy alone," he snapped at me as we were leaving the office of one official after an interview. Equally annoyed, I would suggest to Jim that it might help us get more usable information—something we could actually put in the newspaper—if we asked our sources about something other than last night's Redskins game and why Joe Gibbs didn't finally bench quarterback Mark Brunell.

Somehow, both interviewing styles seemed to work. Sitting next to one another by a window at the *Times'* bureau that looked out to nowhere, we would share tips and tidbits that we had picked up in our beat reporting. Even as I was struggling to understand what was causing such nervousness about the Patriot Act and wiretapping law in mid-2004, Jim was pushing on a lead of his own, something involving an overseas intelligence operation. I knew he was working on something sensitive, but he didn't share the details with me at the time, which was unusual. That alone suggested it was something particularly sensitive. I had shared parcels of my reporting with him, looking for any advice, but like him, I was hesitant about saying too much even to a trusted colleague. It would be many weeks before we realized that we had been tugging on different strands of the same ball of yarn. Whatever I was pursuing seemed to be causing agitation focused at least in part on the FISA court; what Jim was chasing was an intelligence program that appeared to be focused overseas. The twain, at first blush, did not meet.

Jim, to his credit, put more of the puzzle together than I had, realizing that the a key piece I'd been missing led to Fort Meade, Maryland, the home of the National Security Agency. I had been looking down Pennsylvania Avenue, at the FBI, when I should have been looking up the Baltimore-Washington Parkway to the NSA. From what Jim was hearing, it seemed that the NSA had somehow claimed authority to conduct its own wiretapping operation of terrorism suspects on American soil—a shadow operation that worked outside the established confines of the court system. As remarkable as what the administration was doing was who was doing it, because the NSA had a clear history for the last three decades of not spying on Americans. But many pieces to the puzzle were still missing. Who was being wiretapped? Was the NSA doing this on its own authority? Had Bush approved it? What about the courts? And Congress? Was this legal? Was it effective? The questions filled a notepad.

Armed with the additional information that Jim had been able to gather, I began widening the very small circle of sources I had initially contacted about the story. I now had a better sense of what questions to ask. While my early inquiries had been circumspect, now they became more direct. The NSA was the key component. It became clear that a number of senior people were not read in to the program or given the security clearance to be briefed on it, but they had heard enough to know that something was afoot, something involving the NSA that tested the limits of executive power in a way rarely seen before. "This was a closed program," one source told me when I asked about the NSA's expanded role. Even senior government officials who normally had access to the most highly classified operations in the executive branch were shut out. And the ramifications for domestic policy, it became clear, were equally dramatic. The idea that the NSA was running the operation was a seismic shift in how domestic surveillance was carried out. "This is really a sea change," a former official who had heard whispers about the program told me early on. "It's almost a mainstay of this country that the NSA only does foreign searches."

I contacted another official I knew who was well versed in national security and counterterrorism law, and I arranged to sit down with him. I brought Jim along. We began to lay out what we knew, and what we suspected, about the NSA program. We were trying to get a better understanding of how its activities comported with standing law and policy. Did the president have the authority to do what he was doing, or was this against the law? We suspected, I told him, that the NSA had essentially gained access to the biggest telecom "switches" in the country, using the agency's data-mining technology to comb the huge trunks carrying massive volumes of traffic, in order to zero in on suspected dirty numbers and eavesdrop on them without warrants. The source cut me off in mid-sentence. "Stop," he said, standing up from his desk, clearly agitated by the thought that he was hearing what was probably classified information about a government program that strayed far outside standard legal norms. "I don't want to know anymore. I think I'm going to throw up." In hindsight, water-boarding him might have been more merciful.

As the outlines of the story became clearer, Jim decided to reach out directly to the NSA late in the summer of 2004. He told a press aide to General Hayden that he needed to speak to the director about a sensitive matter. He didn't get into the details. I was at my desk sitting next to Jim when he finally got Hayden on the phone and asked him about an NSA program to eavesdrop on Americans without a warrant. He read to Hayden the top paragraph of a draft of the story. The usually unflappable Hayden was clearly jolted, and a bit flustered. An Air Force general, accustomed to carefully scripted briefings on classified material in bug-free, secure facilities, was now being asked on an open phone line about perhaps the most classified program in the government. Whatever the NSA was doing, Hayden told Jim, was "intensely operational." And, he added quickly, it was "legal, appropriate, and effective." Jim tried to ask him a few more questions. Hayden refused to say anything more. But he didn't deny anything either.

The conversation ended there. Jim walked over to the office of Phil Taubman, our bureau chief in Washington, to tell him what he had learned. Soon, Phil had another contact on the subject—from Hayden himself. So began a series of conversations that would ultimately reach to the highest levels of the White House and *The New York Times*. With Hayden at the point, the administration's plea was simple yet impassioned: *Don't run this story.*

The *Times* had been through many contretemps in its long history over whether or not to publish newsworthy stories involving sensitive national security information and, despite the vitriolic charges from its critics, it was never a decision the paper made with reckless abandon. In more than a few cases, the newspaper has decided not to publish anything at all. "Nothing gave us more trouble during my years on the *Times*," James "Scotty" Reston, the elder statesman of the *Times*' Washington bureau for some three decades, wrote in his memoirs, "than the conflict with the government over what should and should not be published during periods of war or threats of war." The most famous clash, of course, centered on the Pentagon Papers in 1971, when the Nixon White House tried unsuccessfully to block the paper from publishing the secret history of the Vietnam War. The most regrettable decision, perhaps, had come a decade before that when the newspaper pared down a story detailing widely discussed plans for the Bay of Pigs invasion of Cuba; President Kennedy himself came to lament the decision, saying that if the *Times* had made a bigger deal of the story, he might not have made such a "stupid mistake" in ordering the invasion.

But for all the dustups in its history, the *Times* had rarely faced the kind of full-throated plea to kill a story that it would confront over the NSA program. By the time it was over, Bush and ten senior advisors in the White House and the intelligence community would make personal pleas not to run the story in a series of meetings spanning fourteen months, beginning in October of 2004 weeks before the presidential election. "I've never had a case where the government raised such strident alarms, at such a high level, as the NSA eavesdropping program," Bill Keller, the top editor at the *Times*, remarked to me later. "This was, at least in recent times, an unprecedented show of official alarm."

At first, Bush's advisors spoke in hypotheticals in lobbying us to kill the story: if a program as we described really existed, they said, its disclosure would do serious and perhaps irreparable harm to national security. Once this hypothetical charade ended, the administration officials started getting into real-life details, revealing far more to us in the way of classified information about the NSA program than we'd ever learned from any actual sources. Bush's advisors had become, in effect, our best sources, telling us myriad new things about the program and filling in critical gaps in our understanding. Under the ground rules established for the meetings, we couldn't use any of the information we were learning in the newspaper, but the disclosures were eye-opening even so.

The administration's message was remarkably focused and remarkably insistent: If we published what we knew, we would be handing al Qaeda an advantage that it would exploit to attack the United States again, and *The New York Times*—by disclosing the program in the country's most prominent newspaper—would bear responsibility for the consequences. Wrapped in their pleas were a few morsels of technical information that might conceivably tell al Qaeda something that wasn't already widely and publicly known about detailed aspects of intelligence collection, and the paper has never published those particular details. Nor will I do so here. But I found the administration's overarching argument unpersuasive. To me, it was never clear what Osama bin Laden and his henchmen would gain from learning—confirming, really—that the United States spy services were listening to them. Bush and his senior advisors had declared time and again, in the context of the Patriot Act and beyond, that they were using every means in their arsenal to track and monitor al Qaeda's phone and e-mail communications in order to listen in on the enemy and head off another attack.

That the government was making good on its pledge was hardly a tip-off to anyone. What was news, however, was that the president had decided to circumvent the court system to do it and, despite what Bush and his aides had very publicly led everyone to believe, was not getting court orders to approve the targets of its eavesdropping. It wasn't clear to me why, if the program were disclosed, Osama bin Laden or Ayman al-Zawahiri would care whether or not the government was getting a FISA warrant before listening in on their conversations. But there were certainly many people in the United States who would. This wasn't to say that the program was right or wrong, legal or illegal, effective or ineffective; but it certainly raised important issues about a topic of tremendous public interest, which is a newspaper's overriding priority.

In our meetings, we pressed the administration on many of the legal and public policy concerns surrounding the program. On nearly every central point, Bush's advisors bolstered their case with assertions that, ultimately, proved misleading or simply untrue: There was never any serious legal debate within the administration about the legality of the program, Bush's advisors insisted. The Justice Department had always signed off on its legality, as required by the president. Those few lawmakers who were briefed on the program never voiced any concerns. From the beginning, there were tight controls in place to guard against abuse. The program would be rendered so ineffective if it were disclosed that it would have to be shut down immediately. At one point, Bush's advisors even suggested to the editors that the NSA was not actually listening to the content of the phone calls themselves or reading the e-mails, but only tracing who had contacted whom through the use of wide-ranging data-mining techniques (a law enforcement technique known as a "trap-and-trace" or a pen-register, methods that were once also widely thought to require a warrant).

On each of these points, we had reason to suspect that the White House was actively misleading us and that its impassioned pleas might have less to do with concern over national security harm than with the legal and political fallout that the story might trigger. But to prove that—and to put it all in some publishable form in a story that, by necessity, would rely almost exclusively on anonymous sources—was a tough task. The small group of us at the newspaper who were involved in the story all realized that. And just as administration lawyers were split over the question of the NSA program's legality, just as intelligence officials were split over the question of its effectiveness, we at the newspaper were split over the question of whether or not to disclose its existence.

Jim and I thought the story should run. That alone should surprise no one. On sensitive stories, the reporters are the ones invariably pushing to publish but, unlike bloggers and other instant journalists in the new Internet age, we as reporters don't have the ability to simply publish something of our own accord. Which is the way it should be. The "mainstream media," as the bloggers like to call us, have a built-in backstop, a check and balance, and it's called the editor. Editors are the ones who ultimately decide what goes in the paper and what prominence it should be given. Editors and reporters do not march in lockstep. In the case of the NSA story, Rebecca Corbett, the investigative editor in the Washington story who shepherded the piece, also felt the story could be published without any obvious threat to national security, and she pushed for its publication. Bill Keller and Phil Taubman weren't so certain.

A week before the election in November 2004, we had a draft of a story in hand that laid out the NSA program and the legal and operational concerns about it. The editors debated whether to run it—and, if so, when. The *Times* had just run an explosive story about the Bush administration's failure to guard munitions in Baghdad, a story that critics on the right had lambasted as a last-minute ploy to hurt Bush. In fact, the timing of the Baghdad story had nothing to do with the election, and Keller made clear to us that if the NSA story was ready to go before the election, it would run before the election too. The election would not be an inducement to run the story, but nor would it be an impediment. The problem was that he didn't think the story was ready. He had questions, including the central one: whether, as the administration so urgently insisted, the story would harm national security if it were published.

Keller, a Pulitzer Prize–winning reporter in Moscow, had taken over as the paper's editor the year before in the aftermath of the Jayson Blair fiasco, and he was widely credited inside the newsroom for steadying the newspaper through one of the darkest periods in its history. Keller believed strongly that a newspaper's default position should be to publish sensitive stories and that it should not abdicate that fundamental role and hand it to the president or anyone else. The starting question in such occasional debates, as Keller liked to say, was not "Why would we publish this?" but "Why would we *not* publish this?" The White House answered the "why not" question with ferocity. It was a hard sell pitched by an administration that had not yet suffered the kind of crippling body blows to its credibility that it would just a year later. When top White House officials insisted that disclosure of a program would risk American lives, any responsible editor was bound to take notice. If the NSA was in a position to intercept the next call from an al Qaeda operative in Kabul to a sleeper cell in San Diego, was *The New York Times* really going to compromise that ability? By publishing, would we simply be outing a valuable intelligence program that, according to the White House's claims, everyone believed was on sound legal footing? These were the kinds of difficult questions that the editors had to ponder.

The decision was made to hold the story before the election, but within days of Bush's reelection, we began a new round of meetings— both inside the paper and, again, with the administration. This time, the administration sought to flesh out its case for the legal underpinnings of the program, pointing to the authorization that Congress had given Bush days after the 9/11 attacks to use "military force" against al Qaeda. The program was on solid legal ground, officials insisted, and it always had been. If the program was both vital *and* legal, the argument went, why disclose it? By mid-December of 2004, the editors had made a decision. It was a close call, they felt, but the concerns about the national security threat posed by public disclosure of the program held sway. The story would not run. As disappointed as I was at the time, I'm not sure in hindsight that there are any editors in the country who would have come to a different decision just three years after the 9/11 attacks.

The story was dead, at least for now. And now, *The New York Times* and the White House shared a closely held secret. For me, the decision was made all the more difficult by the fact that I was left to cover the never-ending debate over the Patriot Act, a debate that was raging publicly in Congress even while the eight-hundred-pound gorilla that was the NSA program was prompting bigger and bigger questions inside the government. The NSA program went to the heart of what Congress was debating so publicly: the tools the government needed to track terrorism and the balance between national security and civil liberties. The debate had devolved into a political war of dueling slogans and jingoism. "The Patriot Act is expected to expire, but the terrorist threats will not expire," Mr. Bush would declare with fist-pounding earnestness, as he assured listeners that the government always got court warrants for its wiretaps. "Safe AND Free" came the frequent retort from the American Civil Liberties Union, which had rallied everyone from librarians to town council members in opposition to the law. Knowing about the NSA program, I found it increasingly awkward to write about all the back-and-forth haranguing with a straight face.

Publicly, administration lawyers and politicians were arguing such legal minutiae as whether the government should have to establish that the business records it demanded were "relevant to" a terror investigation or, instead, sought "in connection with" a suspect. These were the kinds of legal distinctions so nuanced that perhaps a half-dozen national security lawyers in Washington really understood what they meant. When the Patriot Act was first approved in October 2001, President Bush had declared: "This new law that I sign today will allow surveillance of all communications used by terrorists, including e-mails, the Internet, and cell phones." Yet all the while, Bush and the NSA appeared to be operating outside the judicial system altogether. After getting back to the office from one congressional hearing that I covered on the Patriot Act that spring of 2005, I walked straight over to Rebecca Corbett's desk in frustration to suggest that maybe someone else should cover the whole debate in Congress; in light of what we knew, I told her, I no longer felt comfortable covering what seemed a bit like a Washington game of three-card monte. "Can't you get someone else to cover this crap?" I pleaded. Unfailingly upbeat, Rebecca was the kind of editor who could somehow make even the grimmest assignment seem palatable, and she talked me out of the idea; I was stuck on the story.

COVERING ONE HEARING at the Capitol on the reauthorization of the law, I listened from the back row as Jane Harman, then the ranking Democrat on the House Intelligence Committee, one of the few members of Congress to be briefed on the NSA program, delivered an impassioned call to include tougher restrictions in the Patriot Act. She spoke of the need to balance the government's legitimate need for strong counterterrorism measures with stronger civil liberties safeguards—and more checks and balances—to prevent against abuses. "Mend it, don't end it," was her mantra on how to fix the problems she felt were endemic to the current law. As Harman left the hearing room with aides in tow, I followed her out to the hallway. Jim and I hadn't done any reporting on the NSA program for months; Jim was now on sabbatical to write a long-planned book on intelligence in the Bush administration, and I was writing other stories. I'd tried to put the NSA program behind me, but I was taken aback by what I'd heard inside the hearing room. I approached Harman with notepad in hand and told her that I'd been involved in our reporting the year before on the NSA eavesdropping program. "I'm trying to square what I heard in there," I said, "with what we know about that program." Harman's golden California tan turned a brighter shade of red. She knew exactly what I was talking about. Shooing away her aides, she grabbed me by the arm and drew me a few feet away to a more remote section of the Capitol corridor.

"You should *not* be talking about that here," she scolded me in a whisper. "*They* don't even know about that," she said, gesturing to her aides, who were now looking on at the conversation away with obvious befuddlement. "The *Times* did the right thing by not publishing that story," she continued. I wanted to understand her position. What intelligence capabilities would be lost by informing the public about something the terrorists already knew—namely, that the government was listening to them? I asked her. Harman wouldn't bite. "This is a valuable program, and it would be compromised," she said. I tried to get into some of the details of the program and get a better under-standing of why the administration asserted that it couldn't be oper-ated within the confines of the courts. Harman wouldn't go there either. "This is a valuable program," she repeated. This was clearly as far as she was willing to take the conversation, and we didn't speak again until months later, after the NSA story had already run. By then, Harman's position had undergone a dramatic transformation. When the story broke publicly, she was among the first in line on Capitol Hill to denounce the administration's handling of the wiretapping pro-gram, declaring that what the NSA was doing could have been done under the existing FISA law. She even offered up legislation—the "Lis-ten Act," it was called—that would have effectively banned the NSA program.

But all that would wait for another day. For now, there was no pub-lic debate, no statement of official outrage, no legislation that would make it expressly illegal for the president to wiretap Americans with-out a warrant. Because there was no story. As the months wore on, I became convinced that one of our competitors in the media would surely stumble onto the story; it seemed too hot to hold forever. Each tidbit that came out in the context of the Patriot Act, FISA, or govern-ment eavesdropping set off fears in my mind, real and imagined, that the story would break publicly somewhere else, and my own paper would get beat.

At Alberto Gonzales' confirmation hearing for attorney general in January of 2005, I sat nervously in the press gallery as Senator Russ Feingold—a staunch defender of civil liberties and the only senator to vote against the Patriot Act four years earlier—quizzed the would-be attorney general on just how far the president's wartime powers stretched. Could the president, in asserting his broad powers as commander-in-chief to set his own interrogation policies on the defin-ition of torture, also order wiretaps on Americans without a warrant in violation of existing laws? Gonzales knew just how close the adminis-tration had come to having the NSA program revealed two months earlier. Now, he squirmed. The question, Gonzales said, raised a "hypothetical situation" that was impossible to answer. Feingold pressed him. Could the president violate the law as commander-in-chief? Gonzales said he would have to consider "the national interest." Laws were assumed to be constitutional, he said, "and to the extent that there is a decision made to ignore a statute, I consider that a very significant decision and one that I would personally be involved with, I commit to you on that, and one we would take with a great deal of care and seriousness." Feingold was unimpressed by the nominee's Louis Armstrong–like scat. "Well," he told Gonzales finally, "that sounds to me like the president still remains above the law." It was a remarkable exchange that tiptoed right up to the edge of the NSA program.

Not long after the hearing was over, I called a Feingold aide I knew. I tried not to reveal too much. Was the senator asking about warrantless wiretaps out of academic curiosity, I asked, or was he poking around about something in particular? Just curiosity, came the response from the aide. (I could almost hear him wondering on the other end of the line: Why are *you* asking? Just curious, or poking around on something specific yourself?) Relieved, I hung up the phone. The secret—ours and the administration's—was still safe.

Jim and I talked often while he was off writing his book, meeting for lunch or to play basketball at the gym. But I could tell from Jim's tone that basketball wasn't on his mind when he called me at work one day toward the end of his book leave in the spring of 2005 with a different sort of invitation. "Why don't you swing by the house tonight," he said. "I wanted to talk to you about something." He'd become more and more nervous that our own phone lines might be tapped, and he insisted on talking in person when the subject involved anything sensitive. I could only guess what he wanted to talk about as I made the long drive up Interstate 270 to Jim's home in rural Maryland. I was well aware of Jim's frustration over the NSA story, and I knew he felt strongly that the story was one that needed to be told, somehow. I wondered if he had come up with a way.

Jim skipped the small talk and sat me down at the computer in his home office. On the wall hung a framed prize for his last book, *The Main Enemy*, a collaboration with Milt Bearden that recounted the CIA's Cold War espionage battles with the Soviets and the KGB. Now, Jim was finishing a follow-up he was writing on modern-day intelligence battles. "I'm thinking of putting this in the book," he said, gesturing toward the computer screen. "Take a look." Jim likes to write in type so big that only a few words fit on the line of his computer screen; I would razz him endlessly at the office about the early onset of old age and the need for him to pick up some reading glasses. As I sat down now, the words jumped off the computer screen at me—not so much because of the thirty-two-point type, but because of what they revealed. Under the working chapter title of "The Program," he had laid out the culture and history of the NSA and the restrictions put in place after the abuses of the Vietnam era. After a few thousand words, he cut to the chase: the NSA, he wrote, was once again spying on Americans, without the involvement of the judges who were charged by law with preventing Watergate-type abuses.

I reached the end of the rough draft and sat in silence for a moment, staring at the terminal. I couldn't resist razzing him one more time. "You kind of bury the lead, don't you?" I asked, laughing. Jim rolled his eyes. "Oh, gimme a freakin' break. I know how to write a goddamn book," he said, gesturing toward the award up on his wall. My needling aside, we both realized the gravity of what he was considering. The newspaper had decided months earlier, after a long and intense debate, that the NSA story was too sensitive to publish, and now Jim, on his own, was toying with the heretical idea of making it public in his book. The decision, if he actually moved on it, was potentially a career-ender at the *Times*, and he knew it. "You sure you know what you're doing?" I asked. He shrugged. He hadn't reached any decisions, and he wasn't looking for my blessing or sanction; his narrower aim was to make sure I was comfortable with my name being mentioned in the chapter in connection with what unnamed senior officials had told me about "the program." I told him I was fine with that. I figured that if the story was going to get out there publicly, I might as well at least have some limited part in it. "Just spell my name right," I told him. Then, on a more serious note, I said: "Do what you think is right." I wouldn't try to stop him, and I don't think he would have listened to me even if I did.

Jim agonized for many weeks over what, if anything, he should do with the story. Finally, in the fall of 2005, after a few conversations with the editors, he let them know that he was thinking of including the chapter in his book, and he urged them anew to put the story in the newspaper. So began another round of internal discussions over the

NSA's program and what to do with it. This was a complicated scenario laden with pitfalls for everyone involved, and Jim and the editors began hashing out the possibilities in one meeting in the Washington bureau that September. The rest of us were at a brown-bag lunch in a downstairs conference room when Jim broke out of his meeting with the editors and rushed over to me excitedly in the back of the room, almost knocking over a flower pot along the wall. He grabbed me by the shoulders so forcefully that a couple of other reporters were looking over to see what all the commotion was about. "The story's back on!" Jim whispered. "We may run it."

Jim's book, as the newspaper acknowledged, was one trigger for reconsidering the story, but we realized we weren't in the newspaper yet. What we had was an understanding for the editors to revisit the issue, but the burden was clearly on me and Jim to change the editors' thinking since the decision to hold the story almost a year earlier. With or without Jim's book, I knew that the story would never make it into the paper unless we persuaded the editors, this time around, that the reasons to run it clearly outweighed the reasons to keep it secret.

We went back to old sources and tried new ones, redoubling our efforts. My reporting brought into even sharper focus what had already started to become apparent a year earlier: the concerns about the program—in both its legal underpinnings and its operations—reached the highest levels of the Bush administration. There were deep concerns within the administration that the president had authorized what amounted to an illegal usurpation of power. The image we'd been presented a year earlier in our meetings with the administration of a united front—with unflinching support for the program and its legality—was largely a facade. The administration, it seemed clear to me, had lied to us. And we were coming closer to understanding the cracks. The tensions over the program—and the perception that the NSA program was veering "out of control"—became so great in 2004 that it was on the verge of collapse. There seemed to be little in the way of formal checks and balances that would stand up to judicial scrutiny, and as the prospect of a John Kerry presidency looked increasingly plausible that fall, there were real fears among NSA officials at Fort Meade and elsewhere that a Democratic administration would mean an end to the program and, worse yet, possible congressional or even criminal investigations into what had transpired. Some officials, I was told, even began lining up defense lawyers to brace for the worst.

With Rebecca as the line editor with her hands on the keyboard, we retrieved the now musty drafts of our original story from a year earlier and began revising and updating them. There was still no decision to run the story, but we were hopeful. We needed to get the story into shape. Rebecca toned down portions of the original version that played up some of the dramatic, far-reaching, and more controversial aspects of the program; there had to be no question about the story's balance, she insisted. Tell exactly what we knew—fairly, accurately, and completely. We strengthened sections we were now more certain about, and we deleted portions that now seemed less clear. "We need to be bulletproof on this," Jim would often say as we combed through the story line by line. We spent hours and days in Rebecca's office overlooking Farragut Square in Washington, empty soda cans littering the floor and printouts of story drafts scattered on the desk. Other reporters began to ask what was going on, but we couldn't say. We still didn't know if there would ever be a story in the paper, and we didn't want to risk letting word get out for nothing.

WITH THE FATE of the NSA story still unclear, I left the office one evening and headed south down Interstate 395 toward Alexandria and parked outside the city jail. I had an 8 p.m. appointment to visit an inmate there. Behind a glass partition sat Judy Miller, the reporter for the *Times* who had been jailed on contempt charges for refusing to reveal a source in the FBI's investigation into the leak of CIA operative Valerie Plame's name. I had worked with Judy on a number of stories on terrorism and al Qaeda, and I considered her a friend. Whatever the shortcomings of her coverage on Iraq's purported weapons of mass destruction in the run-up to the war, I thought she had been unfairly vilified by her critics on the left for supposedly pushing the country to war, and I respected the stand she had taken in refusing to break a pledge of confidentiality to a source. Judy sat behind the partition with a phone receiver in each ear; she was getting so many visitors that she had to book them two at a time, and another *Times* reporter and I were sharing a fifteen-minute slot after I'd gotten bumped by a U.S. senator the week before. Judy was smiling and upbeat as she greeted us; she was excited about maneuvering a transfer to something called the "women's empowerment unit" at the jail, where she was able to get her nails done regularly by fellow inmates training to be beauticians.

She never let on that she was thinking of cutting a deal for her release just days later. But the stress of more than two and a half months in jail had clearly taken a toll. Normally a fireball of unrestrained energy, she seemed drained. She'd been sleeping on a yoga mat because there weren't enough beds in her cell block, and the skin seemed to sag from her face from all the weight she'd lost eating the miserable jail food. As she sat behind the partition in her jail jumpsuit and ticked through the litany of her daily routine, I couldn't help but think of the NSA story now sitting in draft form back at Rebecca's desk. When the story was published, *if* it was published, it could conceivably generate another FBI leak investigation, with the looming threat that prosecutors would come after the newspaper again at a time when it was already weakened by a string of court rulings in Judy's case.

The circumstances were markedly different: Judy, as we would learn, was protecting the confidentiality of Cheney aide Scooter Libby in the efforts by the White House to discredit a critic of the Iraq war; we were relying on people who believed they were witnesses to an illegal abuse of power by the White House. But circumstances and motives might not matter much for a reporter facing a contempt of court citation for refusing to reveal a confidential source. If we pushed ahead with this story, would Jim and I be faced with the same decision Judy had to make? Could I find myself sitting on the other side of that Plexiglas partition and taking jailhouse visitors, a phone in each ear? The possibility was sobering.

Weeks later, the editors let the Bush administration know that we were once again considering running the NSA story, a year after our initial foray. Again, Bush's senior advisors wanted to meet with us to plead their case. This time, I think, they realized they faced a tougher sell. At one meeting in early December of 2005, Bill Keller, Phil Taubman, and I checked in at the security gate at the White House and were led to a waiting area. This was it: the White House's last best chance to tell us why we shouldn't run the story. An escort came for us. We still weren't sure who would be making the case for the White House, but as we made our way into a small, elegantly appointed sitting room, the line of White House VIPs waiting to shake our hands wrapped around the corner and out of sight: Condi Rice, the new secretary of state; Stephen Hadley, now the national security advisor; John Negroponte, the director of national intelligence; Harriet Miers, the White House counsel; and General Hayden. (Cheney had thought about attending the administration's meetings with us as well. He was the main advocate for the program and, in different times, would have been the natural pick to defend it. But the vice president decided to sit out the meetings because he figured, with some justification, that the tensions between him and the newspaper might distract from the White House's efforts to kill the story.)

After a few brief pleasantries, the meeting began with Keller telling the principals that we were once again considering running the NSA story. This time, he made clear, he was leaning toward publication. He then turned to me to lay out what we knew about the program. For five minutes or so, I outlined our understanding of the program—the need to use the NSA's technical capabilities to capture international communications, the need to work quickly in tracing dirty numbers from Afghanistan and elsewhere, the legal tensions and disagreements the program had caused within the administration, the questions about its controls and oversight. Most of my remarks were directed at General Hayden, sitting quietly to my immediate right in a comfortable armchair, in his usual military dress. He's an imposing adversary, and he clearly was unimpressed by my presentation. Parts of my narrative, he said as I wrapped up, were simply unrecognizable. When I said we believed that up to five hundred Americans at a time had been wiretapped under the program, he strongly suggested that the number was inflated but would not give an estimate of his own. (In fact, the administration has refused to this day to say how many people in the United States were wiretapped without warrants under the program, and later reporting by us and other news outlets indicated that our initial estimate may have been far too low. The actual total remains unknown.)

The Bush team urged us to consider the calamity of publishing the story. The telecommunications companies would face pressure from their corporate boards and financial damages if their cooperation was disclosed, one official said. (Months later, in fact, the administration would push for legislation to give immunity to the telecom companies, protecting them from civil lawsuits and from criminal prosecution.)

More important, the alert we would be sending the terrorists would force the White House to shut down the program immediately because it would cease to be effective. The story would "shut down the game," a second official said. "It's all the marbles." This official made clear that shutting down the program risked another attack. "The enemy is inside the gates," he said. The message was clear from the long, grave faces around the room and the stern words of warning: if the story was published and the United States was attacked again, *The New York Times* would share the blame for the next attack.

I circled back to the concerns within the administration about the program's legal footing and the operational controls, which I knew had played a part in the program being suspended for a period of time in 2004. Were they concerned about the underpinnings of the program? I asked. The response was dramatically different from the response I'd gotten to that same question a year earlier. One by one, the Bush advisors raised their hands to say that, yes, sure, they had all had their concerns about a program of this magnitude. I couldn't help but smile at the odd sight of the president's top advisors with their hands all raised in the air like students in a classroom. Then I asked what seemed like the obvious follow-up question: Did the president share those concerns? Harriet Miers, who had been silent the entire meeting, leaned forward in her chair to my right, clearly agitated. "Why would you ask that?" she interrupted. "I don't even know why that is relevant." The president, under his personal signature, had been authorizing the NSA to operate outside the normal boundaries for wiretapping Americans amid concerns from his own lawyers about the legality, but any questions about his own level of confidence or concerns were, in the view of his one-time Supreme Court nominee, irrelevant. It was an illuminating moment, and I suspect the other advisors in the room quickly picked up on the irony. "He's very comfortable with the program," another official interjected.

The short walk back to the office, a few blocks through Lafayette Park on a bright December day, made me more hopeful than I'd ever been that we were going to run the story. The final decision would be made by others, but I'd heard no surprises in the room to derail the story, and Bill Keller and Phil Taubman both seemed of a mind to publish. With the lineup of luminaries they had thrown at us, we figured that the White House had played its last card. We were wrong. Hours after the meeting had wrapped up, the editors got word that the White House was requesting one final meeting. This time, President Bush wanted to meet personally with the publisher, Arthur Sulzberger. They weren't done yet.

Bush is an impassioned man who often seems most comfortable in one-on-one settings, and he was ready to use all his powers of persuasion on the publisher as he met with Sulzberger, Keller, and Taubman. If there was another attack, Bush told him in their meeting, Sulzberger would be sitting up there at the hearing room table alongside the president, explaining to Congress why it had happened and how they had missed it. Bush's message, as Keller said later in recounting the episode, was clear: If there's another attack, "there'll be blood on your hands." It was fire-and-brimstone stuff from the president, but Keller was famously unflappable, and he had all but decided that the story should be published. Afterward, he and Sulzberger stood outside the White House together comparing notes. "Nothing I heard in there changed my mind," Keller told the publisher. Sulzberger agreed.

With the story on what seemed like a clear track to publication, we were hopeful that it would run in the next day or two. Instead, there was the promise of still more meetings set up by the White House— meetings that could, conceivably, produce substantive information about the program and its evolution. The editors thought it was worth waiting out the White House. Days passed. In the meantime, the clock was ticking on the Patriot Act. Passage of the legislation extending the law before parts of it expired was clearly one of the White House's major legislative initiatives for the year. Another top priority—the Social Security reform initiative trumpeted by the president—had died a quiet death, and the White House was clinging to the Patriot Act as its last chance for a major legislative triumph. But support was teetering. I worried that the White House was stringing us along with the promise of more meetings, hoping to buy enough time to get the Patriot Act approved before disclosure of the NSA program changed the equation. By holding the story out of the paper until the bill was passed, we might be playing right into their agenda—and we risked getting hammered for it if the story were then to run days after the passage of the legislation. "We're going to get attacked either way," Phil said. In a story this complex and this politically sensitive, there were no easy solutions. But Keller made clear that the timing of the

Patriot Act would not push the story into the paper. "We should publish when we're ready to publish," he told me in one e-mail as we waited for a final decision.

For twelve long days, we awaited word from the White House on whether the promised new rounds of meetings would materialize. As we bided our time, I tried to firm up some gaps in the story. I'd heard rumblings that one PR strategy the White House was considering if the story ran was the "blame Ashcroft" approach—a tried-and-true tactic over Ashcroft's four years that had served to put distance between Bush and some of his more controversial policies by laying them off on his lightning rod of an attorney general. I put in a call to one of Ashcroft's senior aides. Ashcroft had been out of office more than a year at that point, and the aide seemed surprised to hear from me. Although our once friendly relations had become strained by the end of Ashcroft's term, I told him I'd like to buy him a cup of coffee. "What about?" he asked. "There's an issue that I understand Ashcroft was involved in," I responded. "I won't discuss anything classified," the aide said. I hadn't said anything about classified material. I hadn't even said what the topic was. "I don't think this was something you were read into," I said, trying to ease his mind. We tentatively agreed to meet, but he canceled on me. Instead, the aide notified the White House about my call and, within a matter of hours, I had gotten word from the editors that the White House was upset by my continuing inquiries. We had never agreed to stop reporting the story, but the White House apparently felt that reaching out to former government officials who already knew about the program could somehow jeopardize national security. The decision was made for Jim and me to "stand down" for the weekend in our reporting.

That weekend was a particularly agonizing one. The waiting game had made us all edgy. The editors, we realized, remained under intense pressure from the administration not to publish the story, and we didn't know what else the White House would do to plead its case. In my mind, it seemed more a question of when we would run the story, not if. But Jim was still worried that the story wouldn't run at all. Keller and Taubman were clearly leaning toward publishing the story, but Jim felt he needed to make one final push, so he went to Jill Abramson, the managing editor of the newspaper, who had been our boss in Washington and was a strong and unflinching ally on sensitive stories. Jim realized that all the internal angst over his book's upcoming publication had complicated the decision, and he wanted to make sure that distraction didn't stand in the way of publishing a story that he thought was critically important. Jill had already been pushing behind the scenes to see the story published, but after fourteen months of waiting, Jim wasn't convinced that it would actually happen. So he sent her an e-mail from home that Sunday, making a final, impassioned plea. "I am not a religious person," Jim wrote, "but I have prayed about this. I do believe that there are a few points in our lives when we must make moral choices. Sometimes, we don't recognize those moments until they have passed. To me, this moment has hit me in a very clear and painful way. To me, this story has been like a stone in my shoe. I can't walk away from it. . . . But all I want is this story to be told, so the American people can decide what they think about it."

The waiting game continued for four more days—until a chance conversation that week all but made the decision on the timing for us. I learned, almost in passing, that the administration had apparently discussed seeking a Pentagon Papers–type injunction against the paper to stop publication of the NSA story. Senior administration officials had reviewed the legal options for possibly seeking an injunction, but they had not moved on it. The tidbit was a bombshell. Few episodes in the history of the *Times*, or for that matter in all of journalism, had left as indelible a mark as the courtroom battle over the Pentagon Papers. The case had proven perhaps the ultimate test of the tense balance between the government's claims of national security and the public's right to know, and the Supreme Court had clearly tipped the scales on the side of the press.

Now, we were learning that the Bush administration had dusted off a Nixon-era tactic to consider coming after us again. I rushed to tell Phil and Rebecca what I had heard. At the very least, I figured that our corporate lawyers should know about it in case they wanted to retrieve their thirty-four-year-old briefs from the Pentagon Papers matter. But the tip, it turned out, did more than prompt a legal review. By the time word about the injunction had been relayed to the editors in New York some hours later, it had an effect I hadn't envisioned. The editors had already run out of patience with the White House and were ready to move ahead with the story, but talk of an injunction helped seal the decision. We had a tool that wasn't available three decades earlier during the Pentagon Papers clash—the Internet—and the paper wanted to use it to our advantage. The story would be printed in Friday's paper, the editors decided, but it would go on our Web site the night before. The editors figured that once we had notified the administration of our intention to publish the story, a court injunction might, in theory, be able to shut down the presses in the hours it took to get an edition printed and on the streets. But there was no way to stop the near-instant ability to post a story on the Internet.

Phil called us into his office to hear the news from Keller via the squawk box on a corner table. We were publishing the story, Keller told us. Smiles washed over the room. Rebecca inquired about the "play" of the story. There'd been talk of a modest, one-column-wide headline on the front page to display the story, and she wanted to know if we might be able to get at least a two-column headline, maybe even three columns. This seemed like a big story. Keller demurred. We didn't know it at the time, but Keller had been quietly discussing the NSA matter with his old boss and mentor, former editor Joe Lelyveld, and Keller had decided he didn't want it to look like we were poking the White House in the eye with a big, screaming headline about NSA spying; we wanted to be discreet, he said, and the story would speak for itself. Jim, Rebecca, and I smiled at one another. This wasn't the moment to quibble over the size of a headline. After all this time, we were just relieved to see the story in the newspaper at all; in the back of the paper among the bra ads would have been fine.

CHAPTER SEVEN

High-Level Confirmation

THIRTY-SIX HOURS after our NSA story broke on the newspaper's Web site, I was rummaging through some moving boxes at home and trying to escape all the recent tumult for a few hours when Jim's caller ID popped up on my phone. Jim is a notorious night owl, and a Saturday morning call signaled that something was up. "Turn on CNN," he said. "Why, what's going on?" I asked. "Just turn on the TV," he repeated. "Bush just confirmed the program." "Holy shit" was all I could think to say.

I scrambled to find the remote for the TV. It was true. The president, at the last minute, had scrapped the canned Saturday morning radio address that he had taped a few days earlier. In its place, he was delivering a live talk about the NSA on national television. A day earlier, Bush had publicly dismissed our story about the NSA program as "speculation" and refused to discuss it when confronted by an interviewer. Now, after arguing for more than a year that our story should not be published, a grim-faced Bush sat in the Roosevelt Room next to the Oval Office, confirming the existence of perhaps his administration's most tightly held secret. "This is a highly classified program that is crucial to our national security," said Bush. Now I could see why Jim was so excited. I'd had big breaks before as a reporter, but in the journalistic coarseness made famous by *The Washington Post*'s Ben Bradlee during Watergate, this qualified as a true "holy shit" moment for me.

It was a startling scene; reminiscent, as my colleague David Sanger noted in the newspaper the next day, of President Dwight Eisenhower's famous acknowledgment in 1960 that he had authorized U-2 flights over the Soviet Union after Francis Gary Powers was shot down in one on a reconnaissance mission. Just as Eisenhower had declared that "no one wants another Pearl Harbor," Bush was declaring forty-five years later that no one wanted another 9/11. With the threat of al Qaeda still looming, Bush said that the American people expected him to "do everything in my power, under our laws and Constitution, to protect them." The president was acknowledging that he had authorized the NSA to conduct wiretaps on international communications outside the courts in furtherance of that end, and he made no apologies for it. At the same time, he made clear his anger and disgust over the fact that he was discussing the program publicly on live television, and he sent a clear message to the FBI leak investigators who just a few weeks later would begin to interview scores of witnesses to try to plug the leak. Details about the program, the president said testily, had been "improperly" leaked to the media. "Our enemies have learned information they should not have, and the unauthorized disclosure of this effort damages our national security and puts our citizens at risk. Revealing classified information is illegal, alerts our enemies and endangers our country."

While he attacked the decision to publish the story, Bush didn't dispute anything in it. Confirmation didn't come any better than this. Competition and fear are what drive most reporters to keep asking questions again and again—the competition to get the story first; the fear of getting it wrong. Before running our story, we'd gone back to anyone we could find to double- and triple-check our facts as best we could, and Rebecca Corbett and Phil Taubman had scrubbed every line word by word to look for possible problem spots. But as confident as we were about the basics, there were doubts until the end. It was a long and complicated story, with lots of moving parts and technical details. Did we get it all right? Were there elements we'd misunderstood, technical issues we'd garbled? Now, on live TV, the president himself was providing about as good an answer as we ever could have envisioned. The president was confirming our story.

The last two days had been a blur. Worried about the threat of another Pentagon Papers injunction by the White House, we posted the story on our Web site at about 8 p.m. that Thursday night, December 15, 2005—a half-hour after the editors notified the White House that we would be running the piece. The quick turnaround infuriated White House officials, leading to expletive-filled phone calls of complaint to the top editors. Indeed, a year later, administration officials were still upset about the timing, saying they felt sandbagged by the newspaper's decision to post the story so quickly after informing the White House of its decision. After succeeding in getting a fourteen-month delay, the White House apparently wanted even more time to brace for the public fallout.

Indeed, the fallout was fierce. The first domino to fall was the Patriot Act. Already wobbling, the reauthorization of the antiterrorism law by Congress—seen by the administration as the critical legislative piece in its national security agenda—was knocked clear off its legs as the Senate blocked the measure just hours after our story ran; lawmakers said they felt duped by having spent months debating the intricacies of the government's antiterrorism powers even as the NSA program was still being kept a secret from them. Cheney made a hurried trip to Capitol Hill to try to staunch the bleeding, but he was met by angry recriminations. Senator Chuck Schumer, who had positioned himself as a centrist on national security issues to the dismay of some of his more liberal colleagues, said the disclosure of the NSA program was the death knell for the Patriot Act as he decided to vote against the measure. Democrats and even some Republicans denounced the NSA program as illegal and promised formal congressional investigations. A few congressmen called for an immediate end to the operation; others demanded Bush's censure, or even his impeachment. Bush "doesn't need the Patriot Act because he can just make it up as he goes along," said an exasperated Senator Russ Feingold, ten months after his "hypothetical" colloquy with Alberto Gonzales about the prospect of warrantless wiretapping. "He's *President* George Bush, not *King* George Bush. This is not the system of government we have and that we fought for." FISA, he said, had been rendered meaningless, and the public debate over added safeguards in the Patriot Act was "a cruel hoax." The existence of the NSA program, Senator Pat Leahy said in what would become a familiar refrain from him and his fellow Democrats, showed that the Bush White House believed it was "above the law."

We always figured that the NSA story, if and when it was published, would cause major reverberations inside Washington. What I was unprepared for were the tremors it triggered in the rest of the country as well. Within hours and days of the story's publication, Big Brother images of the NSA's spying had become almost ubiquitous, the topic of endless riffs on late-night comedy shows, political cartoons, and headlines around the world. "Bush in 'Ear' of Storm" read the headline in the *Kuwait Times* the day after our story ran. A Canadian network called Bush's public acknowledgment of the program "a rare and stunning admission from a sitting American President." For many, the story—read at its most sinister level—seemed to confirm their worst fears about the secret power grab that they suspected the Bush administration had plotted after 9/11. Talking heads on TV who didn't know what the Foreign Intelligence Surveillance Act was just a week before were now on talk shows debating whether Bush had violated it and could be criminally prosecuted. Callers were jamming radio call-in shows, and political satirists produced so many cartoons on the eavesdropping program that Rebecca nearly ran out of room on her bulletin board to display them all.

For weeks, it seemed as if everyone in the county who suspected the government was eavesdropping on them—or, on occasion, had implanted microchips in their heads—was now calling or e-mailing me and Jim to plead for help and get us to somehow validate their suspicions. We became the dumping ground for the distressed. One distraught woman drove most of the night from West Virginia to Washington and somehow talked the security guard in our building into letting her into the bureau one morning at 7 a.m.; when I arrived at my desk, she was waiting for me, still dressed in her nurse's garb from her shift the night before, to report that the NSA had installed a camera in her shower and was spying on her and her teenage daughter. "I don't think I can help you," I said. I suggested she call the Justice Department inspector general as I showed her to the door.

Other leads seemed harder to dismiss out of hand. A few weeks after the NSA story broke, I got an intriguing call from a lawyer in Philadelphia named Madeleine Sann. FBI agents from the local Joint Terrorism Task Force had shown up at her door in 2004—not once, but twice. They were looking for her father, then in his late eighties, because they wanted to talk to him about a suspicious e-mail they thought he'd sent to India that talked about parking garages in Manhattan. Somehow, the e-mail had piqued the FBI's curiosity. It turned out that it was not the woman's father who'd sent the e-mail, but her nephew, a high schooler at Manhattan's prestigious Horace Mann School who shared his name and an e-mail address. The young entrepreneur had come up with a business plan to rent out Manhattan parking spots to out-of-towners and overseas visitors, and he was e-mailing it around.

So how had the e-mail ended up in the hands of the FBI? After our story broke, the family was convinced: the NSA's computers must have been sucking up international communications and trolling through e-mails to look for key words like "Manhattan" and "garage." The episode left the family frazzled. "They're reading everything," Madeleine Sann warned her relatives as she related the FBI visits. "It's pretty disturbing," the teenager told me when I reached him. "I didn't suspect this was public information, and here they were looking at private, confidential information."

Was their theory true? It was plausible enough. The first World Trade Center bombing in 1993, after all, had ripped through an underground garage in Manhattan. I called an official at the FBI, who agreed to research the history of the teenager's case for me. After a few days, word came back from the FBI: no, this hadn't come from the NSA program. The FBI had gotten on to the e-mail through some other means, the official insisted. Exactly how, the FBI wouldn't say. I was still suspicious despite the FBI's denials, but I knew from my past reporting that tracing the NSA fingerprints to any particular case was an all but futile pursuit. With the trail gone cold, we never put the teenager's experience in the newspaper. Several dozen litigants after them would go to court to try to show the NSA had wiretapped them, but they all ran into the same near-impossible problem as the Sann family: proving that they had been caught up in a secret, inscrutable program that the public wasn't even supposed to know about.

On the FISA court, meanwhile, judges on the secret panel were as surprised as anyone to learn in the newspaper about what had been going on at the NSA. One even resigned from the court in protest over it. Judge James Robertson, appointed to the federal bench by President Clinton in 1994, had taken the spot on the spy court left vacant by Judge Lamberth's departure in 2002. Like Lamberth, Judge Robertson was a big believer in the courts as an essential backstop against government abuses and an advocate for the protection of individual liberties.

He kept on his desk at the courthouse a novelty coffee mug with the Bill of Rights written on it; when the hot coffee was poured in, the First and Fourth Amendments would disappear. A few days after our story ran, he sent a short, curt note to Chief Justice John Roberts at the Supreme Court informing him that he hereby resigned his seat on the foreign intelligence court. No other explanation was given, and none was needed. The idea that the Bush administration was simply bypassing the court altogether, he told associates in his pique, made the court look like a Potemkin court, an elaborately designed cover story meant to hide a blatant end run around the judicial system. Robertson wasn't a well-known jurist outside Washington, but when his resignation was disclosed publicly the next day, he received a flood of mail from laymen and lawyers around the country; some lauded him as a courageous hero, others condemned him with vitriol for his stance. Like almost everyone the NSA program affected, the judge had become a touchstone of sorts for determining where people stood on whether President Bush was justified in acting outside the law.

We became high-profile targets ourselves. Conservative commentators, following the lead of Bush and Cheney, denounced the newspaper for running the story, calling it a treasonous and traitorous act. Some sources who had been helpful before simply stopped returning phone calls because they were so upset by the publication of the story. "Who the hell elected *The New York Times* to decide when national security information should be declassified?" a veteran Justice Department prosecutor, whom I had lunched with just a few months earlier, yelled at me in a phone call after our story ran. Hate mail and occasional threats arrived by the day, filling my in-box. The leakers, one blogger wrote in a posting titled "High Treason and the New York Times," were "21st Century Julius Rosenbergs" who needed to be found and prosecuted, and "when they are found guilty, we should then hang them by the neck until [they] are dead, dead, dead."

Our story had clearly agitated people in ways that were impossible to fully predict when the paper was debating whether to run the story. To those on the right, the story was the product of a liberal media that was accountable to no one and was willing to put American lives at risk in its hell-bent pursuit of George Bush. To those on the left, it was evidence of an imperial presidency that placed itself above the law in creating a Big Brother state to fight its much hyped "war on terror." (And the *Times*, some of these same critics were quick to add, was complicit in Bush's 2004 reelection by delaying the NSA story for more than a year.)

As Phil Taubman had warned, this was a story so sensitive that we were bound to get hammered from all sides no matter what we did. These were heady and harrowing times, as we were lionized by the left and vilified by the right. But there was little chance for self-reflection; there was still a lot of reporting left to do in a story that had now gone very public. Hours after the story was published, I filed Freedom of Information Act requests that I'd prepared weeks earlier seeking access to a long list of government records on the program. As much as we now knew about the program, there were a million unanswered questions, and we were determined to try to stay out in front on the story. We had a running head start on our competition, and that allowed us to break more stories in the controversy's first days. Some sources dried up completely for fear of getting drawn into an FBI leak investigation, but others became more willing to talk about what had now become such a public scandal.

Doors once shut in our faces were now starting to open a crack. One big break came, ironically enough, with the aid of our competitors in the media. Within hours of the story's publication, some lawmakers were on national TV news shows discussing technical details of the NSA operation—including some of the same details that the newspaper had decided to leave out of our initial story at the request of the administration. It was not commonly known to al Qaeda or anyone else, the White House had argued to us for weeks, that much of the world's communications traffic—even non-U.S. calls from, say, Riyadh to Jakarta—happened to flow through American telecommunications switches. This was the "home field advantage" that the NSA was seeking to exploit.

But now here was Senator Bob Graham, the former chairman of the Senate Intelligence Committee, appearing on *Nightline* and CNN and discussing that very fact. A briefing he had attended with Cheney, the senator told CNN's Wolf Blitzer, "focused on the fact that there were telephone communications from one foreign site to another that were now being sent, transited through the United States." Other members of Congress made similar points on television. Some of the technical details of the operation were now being discussed publicly, and we saw the chance to probe more deeply into areas that were regarded as off-limits just a few days earlier.

The international "transit traffic" was critical to the NSA's efforts to target what it believed were suspected al Qaeda calls; by combing through the vast volumes of communications, it could help identify the ones it considered most urgent and troubling. The White House had gone to great lengths in the first days of the controversy to cast the NSA program as a narrowly targeted, tightly controlled operation. We had reason to suspect otherwise, and with the technical details of the operation now being debated on national television, we had a chance to tell that broader story too. We spoke with more government and industry sources and prepared a story that would run on the front page eight days after the initial piece. "Spy Agency Mined Vast Data Trove," the headline read.

The story discussed how the NSA had been able to trace and analyze huge streams of phone and Internet traffic by securing the cooperation of the telecom giants and tapping into the country's international switches. We reported: "The volume of information harvested from telecommunication data and voice networks, without court-approved warrants, is much larger than the White House has acknowledged, the officials said. It was collected by tapping directly into some of the American telecommunication system's main arteries, they said." Without actually listening to phone calls or reading e-mails, the NSA was able to pinpoint the ones of interest by combining the call records with other data like travel records and credit card information housed in its vast databases.

The data-mining operations appeared to cut dangerously close to another congressional ban—this one imposed on John Poindexter's Total Information Awareness program. But the White House wasn't willing to talk about data-mining operations conducted by the NSA or anyone else. The eavesdropping program that Bush had confirmed a week before, a White House spokesman said in response to our data-mining story, "is a limited program. This is not about monitoring phone calls designed to arrange Little League practice or what to bring to a potluck dinner. These are designed to monitor calls from very bad people to very bad people who have a history of blowing up commuter trains, weddings, and churches." It would be another nineteen months before the White House, under pressure, acknowledged that the "targeted" eavesdropping program that Bush had confirmed from the Roosevelt Room was only part of a much broader intelligence operation approved by the president almost immediately after 9/11.

The publication of the data-mining story, which began to peel back some of the technical details of the NSA's operations, angered intelligence officials almost as much as our initial piece. Publicly, the story caused barely a ripple, as it was subsumed by the still thundering debate over whether the president had the power to eavesdrop without warrants. We wrote off the tepid response to the hazards of putting a complicated story in the Saturday paper on Christmas Eve. Six months later, however, *USA Today* took another cut at the NSA data-mining story in a piece that paralleled the same basic disclosures as our December 2005 piece and offered a few intriguing and important new details about the role played by specific telecommunications companies. This time, the response to what CNN termed a "bombshell" was enormous, with renewed calls for investigation, public denouncements, the threat of subpoenas, and the usual harrumphing from Washington politicians. In the fickle world of media and politics, timing is everything.

Another big break came just a week after the data-mining story, and it would lead us to uncover the most dramatic episode in the whole tangled NSA saga. Like everything with the eavesdropping story, Jim and I stumbled our way through a good bit of misdirection and wrong turns to get there. Months earlier, in talking to people about the NSA program at a time when it was still secret, we had gotten a cryptic lead urging us to look more closely at John Ashcroft's hospital stay in 2004 and a possible connection to the eavesdropping operation. By now, we had grown accustomed to cryptic leads on the story; everyone associated with the program seemed committed to speaking in code.

The source wouldn't say anything more about the hospital stay or its significance, and I misread the smoke signals. I already had a sense of the strain the NSA program had caused for Ashcroft and the Justice Department. I had covered Ashcroft's emergency hospitalization, sitting through briefings at the hospital with his doctors, and I figured the source was suggesting that the stress of the program had somehow put the attorney general in the hospital.

The lead led nowhere, and we made no mention of Ashcroft's hospital stay in our initial story. But as we tried to chase down new leads and double back on old ones after our initial story ran, the topic of Ashcroft's hospital stay and the NSA program came up again in a conversation with another government official. "Well," the official said, "you know Gonzales and Card were at the hospital with Ashcroft." No, I didn't know that. What were they doing there? The official wouldn't say. But the tip we had gotten months earlier was starting to make a little more sense. We knew that aspects of the NSA program had been shut down temporarily around the time of Ashcroft's hospital stay. From other conversations, it appeared that the hospital visit had something to do with the reauthorization of the NSA program ·during Ashcroft's absence and questions about its legal framework. But what exactly happened in the hospital room was unclear. With intense interest in any scrap of information involving the burgeoning NSA controversy, I suggested writing a story saying that Gonzales and Card had made a mysterious visit to Ashcroft in the hospital to talk about the future of the program but that what exactly happened in the room was unclear. Jim and Rebecca both thought that was a dumb idea. "How can we write a story?" Jim asked me. "We don't even know what happened."

With the New Year's Eve holiday weekend approaching, we figured we would wait until the next week to try to flesh out the rest of the story. As it turned out, we couldn't afford to wait. A chance conversation that I had over the weekend made clear that *Newsweek* was working on essentially the same story. The magazine knew about the visit to Ashcroft's hospital room too, and its reporters appeared ready to pop something in the edition coming out the next Tuesday, if not earlier on their Web site. We were at risk of getting beaten on our own story. I called Jim and Rebecca that afternoon and told them what I'd heard. We figured we needed to get something in the next day's Sunday newspaper if we wanted to beat *Newsweek*, but we still weren't sure we knew enough to make any sense of what had happened in the hospital room. We had to do more reporting. The timing wasn't good: I'd been sick with a stomach bug all day, my two young sons were demanding my undivided attention for another multiround game of hide-and-seek, and I was still hoping to make it to a couple of New Year's Eve parties that night. We kept trying people to get a better sense of what had actually happened in that hospital room. Finally, over the course of the next few hours, a couple of the key pieces fell into place.

It became clear from talking to more people who had learned of the dramatic episode that Ashcroft's deputy, James Comey, acting as attorney general during his boss's illness, had refused to sign off on the NSA program because of all the questions about its legality, and Gonzales and Card had gone to the hospital to get Ashcroft to overrule him so that President Bush could continue the operation. The president's men were there for Ashcroft's signature on the NSA program because they hadn't been able to get Comey to budge. As I heard the details, I imagined a scene straight out of *The Godfather*, with Gonzales playing the part of Robert Duvall as the soft-spoken, trusted consigliere, Ashcroft as the bedridden capo, and Bush as an off-screen Marlon Brando: *General Ashcroft, please know that Don Corleone would greatly appreciate your help on this sensitive matter; lives are at stake if you don't help us.*

Finally, we had enough for a story. The deadline to get a story in the next day's newspaper was fast approaching, so I tried to file our piece in takes from home, writing up a few hundred words or so at a time to send to the news desk. Midway through the process, my laptop crashed, and I ended up having to dictate most of the story over the phone. It was a disjointed and rushed effort, completed after 10 p.m. that night—far past our normal deadline. Somehow, from all the gibberish and butchered dictation, Rebecca and our Washington weekend editor, Adrianne Goodman, were able to cobble together a fairly coherent, 1,100-word story that read with surprising ease. "A top Justice Department official objected in 2004 to aspects of the National Security Agency's domestic surveillance program and refused to sign on to its continued use amid concerns about its legality and oversight, according to officials with knowledge of the tense internal debate. The concerns appear to have played a part in the temporary suspension of the secret program," the lead paragraph of the story read. The second paragraph continued: "The concerns prompted two of President Bush's most senior aides—Andrew H. Card Jr., his chief of staff, and Alberto R. Gonzales, then White House counsel and now attorney general—to make an emergency visit to a Washington hospital in March 2004 to discuss the program's future and try to win the needed approval from Attorney General John Ashcroft, who was hospitalized for gallbladder surgery, the officials said."

Despite the late hour, the editors in New York realized the significance of the story and managed to rip up the front page of the Sunday newspaper and run it at the top. As I picked up the blue-bagged newspaper from the driveway the next morning, I prayed that the story was right. There were still many unknowns about what had happened in the hospital room, and this was about as uncertain as I'd ever felt about something I'd written for the newspaper. Not until nearly a year and a half later, when Comey himself was asked about the hospital visit at a Senate hearing, would we realize that the New Year's Eve piece, while accurate as far as it went, told only half the story of that dramatic episode. We would have to wait sixteen months for the rest of the details to emerge. But at least we had something in the newspaper, two days ahead of *Newsweek* or anyone else. The story was still ours.

NAMED FOR A ONETIME RIVAL to Franklin Delano Roosevelt, Kansas State University's Landon Lecture Series has provided an unlikely but powerful platform allowing world leaders, from Ronald Reagan and Mikhail Gorbachev to Jimmy Carter and Henry Kissinger, to expound on the critical public policy issues of the day. In 1970, a battle-weary Richard Nixon used the stage to defend an unpopular war in Vietnam and to bemoan the ability of a "small minority" of war protesters to "drown out the responsible majority." Thirty-six years later, in January 2006, President George W. Bush came to the same friendly Republican environs of Kansas State to confront growing protests over twin crises of his own: one overseas in Iraq, the other at home in Fort Meade, Maryland, at the NSA. Bush was there, he told thousands of college students, cattle ranchers, Army soldiers, and other cheering supporters, "to tell you how I see the world, and how I have made some of the decisions I've made, and why I made them." For Bush, the war in Iraq and the month-old controversy over the NSA's eavesdropping program were bookends to the same story: aggressive, essential operations aimed at making America safe again in the post-9/11 age.

Halfway through his talk, Bush brought up "something that you've been reading about in the news lately. It's what I would call a terrorist surveillance program." It was a telling choice of words because the term itself—terrorist surveillance program—did not exist just a few weeks earlier. There was no such thing. It was a creation of what would become a full-scale media blitz by the Bush White House to defend intelligence activities that many were now charging were illegal. Soon, the terrorist surveillance program would become the Terrorist Surveillance Program, mentioned prominently by Bush and all of his advisors at every public appearance on national security matters. Then, it would become simply the TSP, in the White House's shorthand. Semantics is a powerful weapon in politics, and the difference between calling an activist "pro-life" versus "anti-choice," or between calling a legislative proposal an "inheritance tax" rather than a "death tax," inevitably helps tilt the public debate in one direction or the other. The White House, adept at the game, realized just how critical the name game would be in the debate over the NSA's operation.

In the days after the story broke, shorthand media descriptions of the program let fly from newspaper headlines and TV news bulletins, referring to the NSA's "warrantless wiretapping" program, or its "eavesdropping" program, or its "domestic spying" program. The labels grated at White House officials. Bush would come to mock the labels; in a tongue-in-cheek nod to his critics, he even briefly redubbed the program the "IEP"—"the illegal eavesdropping program." But it was the "domestic surveillance" label that most grated at senior administration officials like Cheney and Hayden. How can you call this a "domestic surveillance" program, an administration official asked me, if one end of the wiretapped communication is outside the United States? "I don't think 'domestic spying' makes it" as an apt description for the program, Hayden complained in one speech in Washington a month after the story broke. "I've taken literally hundreds of 'domestic' flights. I have never boarded a 'domestic' flight in the United States of America and landed in Waziristan."

That very day in Kansas, Bush rolled out the White House's new name, and over the next week, the White House would build its media blitz around the moniker. For more than a month since the program's disclosure, the White House had found itself in an unusual position: back on its heels. Lawyers were attacking the program as illegal, stories were emerging by the day that questioned its operations and effectiveness, and some polls showed a slight majority of Americans opposed to the idea of the president wiretapping without a warrant. Andy Card,

Karl Rove, and Bush's other senior White House aides all thought the administration needed to be "working feverishly" to tilt back public opinion on the wiretapping furor, according to internal memoranda. Even conservative commentators like George Will were beating up on the president over the NSA program. In one column that caused particular nervousness in the West Wing, Will wrote that times of war give rise to "the danger of arbitrary power" by an emboldened executive branch. "It is not good," senior Bush aide Brett Kavanaugh wrote in an internal White House e-mail just five days after our story ran, "if Americans or Members of Congress think we did something that is a good thing but stretched the law in doing it, so we need to fight back hard on that legal part in the court of public opinion and the court of Congress."

And fight back they did. Alberto Gonzales, greeted by student protesters in black who turned their backs on him in silence at a speech at Georgetown Law School, cited the historical precedent for Bush's wartime authority. His Justice Department put out a forty-two-page white paper defending the legal rationale for the NSA program and recruited conservative commentators to speak out about its legality. Rove told the stalwarts at the Republican National Committee that Democrats' attacks on the program reflected their wrongheaded "pre-9/11 view of the world." General Hayden peeled back the curtain on the NSA's operations in his first-of-its-kind speech before the National Press Club. And the NSA provided a helpful set of talking points to members of the congressional intelligence committees who complained that they were uncertain what they were allowed to say publicly about the growing controversy.

One suggested response from the NSA's general counsel, Alonzo Robertson, in a memo to intelligence committee members was this: "I have been briefed on the Program and stood on the operations floor at NSA to see first-hand how vital it is to the security of our country and how carefully it is being run." Or, perhaps this: "I have personally met the dedicated men and women of NSA. The country owes them an enormous debt of gratitude for their superb efforts to keep us all secure." Democrats were livid when they got the memo; they were now reduced to playing Charlie McCarthy to the NSA's Edgar Bergen. What's more, the carefully scripted suggestions didn't seem to comport with the limited information the members were getting in their closed-door briefings. "They claim the program has done all sorts of wonderful things," one congressional aide grumbled to me, "but we'd like to see some evidence of that."

But that evidence was hard to come by, because the White House was refusing to say much of substance about what the NSA was actually doing. This was the second prong in the White House's carefully calculated response to the NSA controversy: shutting down the flow of information. Disclosure of the program gave rise to a host of questions, not only from congressmen, but from judges, from national security lawyers, from litigants, from the media, and from the public itself. For months after the story broke, even members of a new, quasi-independent office located in the White House, known as the Privacy and Civil Rights Oversight Board, were refused the security clearance needed to learn about the NSA program and examine its workings, much to their anger and chagrin. "Why are we not read into a program that we can read about in *The New York Times*?" Lanny Davis, a member of the board, demanded at one particularly testy, private meeting with General Hayden and other intelligence officials. Hayden claimed that he wanted to let members of the White House panel look behind the NSA curtain, but he was being blocked by higher-ups at the White House—presumably Cheney. Even Ted Olson, a legal icon in the conservative community who served on the privacy panel, found himself shut out. "If we're not read in," he told Hayden, "we might as well disband, because we're useless."

How did the NSA go about actually determining the targets of its eavesdropping operations? How many people in the United States had come under its reach? What were the successes and failures of the program? What was its legal rationale?

These were questions that would go largely unanswered by the administration. Even the tough-minded Glenn Fine, the Justice Department inspector general who had become one of the administration's most tenacious internal critics on matters of 9/11 policy, was forced to back off. More than three dozen members of Congress pressed him to open an investigation, wanting to know whether Justice Department lawyers were complicit in giving legal advice about what the lawmakers viewed as a potentially illegal program. They knew Fine's reputation: he had pried open the window into the post-9/11 roundups two years earlier, and he had been a relentless provocateur in calling for change in the stodgy bureaucracy of the FBI. This time, however, Fine was stymied. The review, he said, "falls outside the jurisdiction" of the Office of the Inspector General.

BUT INSIDE THE HALLS of Justice there was one man agitating from the start: Marshall Jarrett, a former prosecutor who led the department's Office of Professional Responsibility. Although the office's clout had waned a bit in recent years, it had a long history of making life uncomfortable for lawyers and politicos at the department who may have crossed the line between good behavior and bad. A call from OPR was the last thing any Justice Department lawyer wanted to see in the morning's in-box. Particularly under the long reign of Michael Shaheen, an unflinching former prosecutor who built the ethics office up from nothing in the late 1970s, the place was a much feared powerhouse within the department. Under Shaheen, OPR had gone after FBI directors (its investigation into William Sessions' travel habits cost him his job), attorneys general (it produced a blistering report on Edwin Meese's financial dealings), and even presidents (Jimmy Carter's brother got caught in Shaheen's crosshairs over his Libya dealings in an investigation that touched on both the president and his attorney general, Benjamin Civiletti). And OPR had routinely investigated sensitive and classified intelligence matters, making life miserable for prosecutors and FBI agents accused of skirting FISA in their investigations. So when Jarrett told Democrats that January, weeks after the NSA story broke, that his hallowed office was opening an investigation into the NSA program, there was reason for encouragement among Capitol Hill lawmakers who complained they were being stonewalled. The optimism, however, proved short-lived.

Jarrett's inquiries were friendly enough at the outset. In a letter to a senior Justice Department official in the deputy's office a month after the story broke, he noted that his office was opening an investigation into the program and asked, as a routine matter, that he and six of his people be given "the necessary security clearances" to do their work. "Thank you for your assistance in this matter," he concluded blandly.

The request went nowhere. So a month later, Jarrett took pen in hand again, sending his request higher up the Justice Department hierarchy to Paul McNulty, the deputy attorney general to Gonzales.

His plea became more urgent: "OPR cannot proceed with its investigation if the clearances we have requested are not approved." This time, he noted that a large team of lawyers and agents in the Justice Department's Criminal Division—responsible for investigating possible leakers connected to our story two months earlier—had already been read into the program. Those clearances, Jarrett noted sardonically, were "promptly granted, and that investigation is moving forward." Also getting clearance at that same time were the lawyers in the Justice Department's Civil Division tasked with defending the program against what was already becoming a flood of civil lawsuits challenging the program as illegal.

The irony was unmistakable: the investigation into the public disclosure of the administration's NSA secret was allowed to proceed full throttle; lawyers were given clearance to review the operation's top secret details to defend the program in court and prop up its questionable legal rationale; but when it came time for the parallel inquiry into whether the program itself violated legal or ethical guidelines, the wheels of justice had ground to a halt.

Jarrett didn't let up. Even as Gonzales was telling senators on Capitol Hill that the OPR investigation was progressing, Jarrett was complaining directly to Gonzales' deputy chief of staff about the failure to get clearances approved. And a month after his first try with McNulty, Jarrett sent the deputy attorney general another letter, his frustration growing more evident with each plea. As a result of the failure to grant clearances, Jarrett told McNulty, "this Office, which is charged with monitoring the integrity of the Department's attorneys and with ensuring that the highest standards of professional ethics are maintained, has been precluded from performing our duties." The result was the same: no clearance.

Jarrett had run out the string. On April 21, three months after he had first appealed to let the ethics investigation move forward, he went directly to Gonzales to inform him that he had no choice but to shut down his investigation because the department would not grant him the security clearances needed to review it. It was a move without precedent in the long history of the Justice Department's now toothless ethics watchdog. "Since its creation some 31 years ago," Jarrett finally wrote to Gonzales, "OPR has conducted many highly sensitive investigations involving Executive Branch programs and has obtained access to information classified at the highest levels. In all those years, OPR has never been prevented from initiating or pursuing an investigation."

So it was over. What started as perhaps the government's most dogged effort to explore the legal underpinnings for the NSA program ended before it even really began, buried under a stack of increasingly desperate pleas with the Justice Department's letterhead at the top and H. Marshall Jarrett's signature below them. The only question that lingered was this: Who shut down the investigation, and how high did it go?

The answer, startling as it was, came three months later from Attorney General Gonzales himself at a hearing before Senator Arlen Specter's Judiciary Committee. Always irascible, Specter was in a particularly prickly mood as he grilled the attorney general about the Justice Department's refusal to give OPR access to the program so it could investigate possible ethical wrongdoing. Who had made that decision, Specter wanted to know. Gonzales' answer: Bush himself. "The president of the United States," Gonzales said, "makes decisions about who is ultimately given access" to the NSA program.

Gonzales and his aides insisted that the refusal to allow OPR to look at the program was justified by national security demands and the need for secrecy surrounding the operation. Democrats had another word for the decision. "The president's latest action," said Zoe Lofgren, a Democratic congresswoman from California, "shows that he is willing to be personally involved in the cover-up of suspected illegal activity."

THE JUSTICE DEPARTMENT'S ETHICS investigation was now shut down, and the fortress walls that the White House had erected around the eavesdropping program meant that even senior lawmakers in Congress were left to guess what the NSA was really doing on the other side. By the summer of 2006, the furor surrounding the eavesdropping program was quieting—until one typically sweltering August day in the capital. I was spending the afternoon meeting with the newspaper's lawyers in a back office at the bureau. This was the less glamorous side of our newfound notoriety. Jim and I were still fielding plenty of TV invitations and "attaboy" congratulatory messages from colleagues, but with them came hours spent cloistered in musty offices with our well-heeled lawyers, mapping out where the FBI's leak investigation might lead and how the newspaper might respond. As I listened to the lawyers talk about the threat of subpoenas and the string of setbacks the media had suffered in court of late, all I could think about was that image of my colleague Judy Miller, a phone in each ear as she greeted me through the Plexiglas partition.

All the dispiriting talk from the lawyers was interrupted by an excited knock at the door, as Phil Taubman came bounding into the office. He was waving a single sheet of paper in his hand. "Have you seen this Detroit ruling?" he asked. In a bygone era, a generation or two before, we would all now have been huddled around the Associated Press teletype machine, the *rattattat-tat* banging out the breaking news line by line like a scene from *The Front Page*. But what we had lost in nostalgia we gained in immediacy. Just minutes before, a federal court in Michigan had released a long-awaited ruling in a case brought against the government over the NSA program. "URGENT" read the top line of the Associated Press bulletin that Phil handed me. The wire service only had time to get out a single line to its subscribers describing the ruling, but that line told enough of the story to know it was big: a federal judge had declared the eavesdropping program illegal and unconstitutional and had ordered it shut down.

We knew we had a front-page story for the next day's paper. Whether you agreed with the court's decision or not—and there would be those on either side—it would be much tougher now for even the fiercest critic of the *Times'* publication of the NSA story to argue that there was no compelling public interest in knowing about a program that a federal judge determined was illegal. The language of the ruling by Judge Anna Diggs Taylor was both sweeping and incendiary, as she summoned the lessons of American history in declaring that the NSA program was both illegal under the 1978 intelligence framework established by Congress and unconstitutional under the Fourth Amendment. "There are no hereditary Kings in America and no powers not created by the Constitution," Taylor wrote in her forty-four-page ruling. The president, she said, cannot escape judicial scrutiny simply by declaring his powers as commander-in-chief. "It was never the intent of the framers," she said, "to give the president such unfettered control, particularly when his actions blatantly disregard the parameters clearly enumerated in the Bill of Rights. The three separate branches of government were developed as a check and balance for one another."

It was fiery rhetoric, not the kind of dispassionate legal discourse normally heard from the federal bench. But the NSA program and the power grab it represented seemed to bring out that kind of anger even from federal judges. A year later, when a Justice Department lawyer in another NSA lawsuit argued that the courts weren't the right place to be arguing about the government's wiretapping powers and that "other avenues" were preferable, an appellate judge, in a decidedly un-judicial rebuke, shot back from the bench: "What is that? Impeachment?"

Judge Taylor closed out her ruling by quoting a 1967 Supreme Court opinion from then–chief justice Earl Warren in a decision rejecting a "guilt by association" approach to barring avowed Communists from working at defense facilities. Warren's message seemed particularly apt four decades later. "Implicit in the term 'national defense' is the notion of defending those values and ideas which set this Nation apart," the chief justice had written. "It would indeed be ironic if, in the name of national defense, we would sanction the subversion of . . . those liberties . . . which makes the defense of this nation worthwhile."

Within hours of Judge Taylor's ruling, even supporters who agreed with her conclusion were predicting it wouldn't stand up. Her rhetoric was too impassioned, legal scholars maintained; her legal logic too reaching. Taylor would come under attack from critics on the right as a liberal Jimmy Carter appointee who served with a group that had given money to a branch of the ACLU, one of the plaintiffs in the case. And, as predicted, the appellate court above her in Cincinnati struck down the ruling a year later—not on substantive grounds, but on purely technical ones. The divided appeals court reached no conclusion about the legality of the eavesdropping program itself, but it said that the lawyers, journalists, and other plaintiffs in the case didn't have legal standing to sue the government because they couldn't prove they were actually wiretapped. Without evidence that they were caught up in the program or harmed by it, the plaintiffs had no ability to sue, but the great catch-22 was that government's wall of secrecy made proving that all but impossible. No one knew who was actually wiretapped. Somewhere, Joseph Heller must have been chuckling.

CHAPTER EIGHT

Swift-Boated (Round Two)

I N THE BOWELS of the West Wing, the White House Situation
Room serves as the nerve center for the president and his senior
advisors in gaming out the country's most sensitive national security matters. Few visitors, even the most vaunted VIPs, ever get to lay
eyes on the place. But the Belgian banking industry executives who visited the Situation Room one spring day in 2003 weren't like most
White House visitors. They were the silent partners in the Bush
administration's war on terror, an essential cog in a far-reaching and
risky intelligence operation that was, at that moment, on the verge of
collapse. A red-carpet treatment awaited the small overseas delegation
for their secret visit: a classified CIA briefing on terrorism in the Situation Room with a surprise appearance by National Security Advisor
Condoleezza Rice, then a private meeting with Fed chairman Alan
Greenspan and other officials at the Treasury Department, then
another session at the FBI with Bob Mueller, with the bureau's fine
china laid out on the director's conference table for coffee, tea, and
chocolate chip cookies. "This," one government official remarked on
the high-level guest list, "is a full-court press." With all the accou-
trements came an urgent and unmistakable plea from Rice,
Greenspan, Mueller, and the rest: *Don't leave us now. The threat is too
great, and we need you on the team.*

For a year and a half, the Belgian visitors had been key players on
that team. Soon after the September 11 attacks, their outfit—an
obscure but enormously powerful banking consortium in Brussels

known as SWIFT that routes the bulk of the world's major financial transactions—began turning over millions of records from its vast repository to American intelligence officials. Matching the data against their own lists of suspected terrorist financiers and operatives, analysts at the CIA pored through the records looking for any hints of dirty terrorist money. Was that $10,000 wire transfer from the Saudi British Bank in Riyadh to the Bank of America branch in Manhattan a legitimate charitable donation, as advertised, or was it seed money for another 9/11? The financial patterns gleaned from the international records, Treasury Secretary John Snow would say, "don't lie; they tell a story." And that story, he said, could "lead to the terrorists themselves." There were a few notable hits. But far more often, there were dead ends, trails that led nowhere, and as the program wore on, the executives at SWIFT were getting more and more nervous about the legal peril created by their involvement.

At the outset, few people involved in the tightly held program thought this would be a permanent arrangement. It was designed as an emergency document dump, many U.S. officials figured, to try to trace how al Qaeda had funded the September 11 attacks and what other terrorist money might be corroding the pipeline. SWIFT's exposure was enormous. Officially, it was complying with a legally binding mega-subpoena from the U.S. government for its records. In reality, American officials saw the company as eager to turn over everything it could—even more than the Americans had sought, in fact—to help follow the money that brought down the World Trade Center. This, in the eyes of grateful American officials, was an act of true patriotism. But it was patriotism at significant peril to the company. Hundreds of the world's biggest banks and financial institutions used SWIFT to route their money in large part because of the consortium's promises of tight controls on their encrypted financial information to guard against economic espionage; their customers had no idea SWIFT was routinely sharing their information with the spooks at the CIA. Neither did many members of the European Union or the host countries where SWIFT was authorized to operate. The idea of the U.S. government sweeping up many millions of sensitive banking records with a single piece of paper was an extraordinary legal departure. In normal times, a government subpoena would be narrowly tailored to zero in on those financial records—dozens, maybe hundreds, sometimes thousands—that it could show might actually be relevant to an investigation. But these were not normal times. President Bush was invoking his emergency wartime powers under a broadly worded, 1970s-era statute known as the International Emergency Economic Powers Act, or IEEPA, to gather everything the Treasury Department and the CIA could grab. In the United States, the legality of the wide-ranging operation appeared to sit within a gray area of American banking and privacy laws that gave the government wide maneuvering room to troll for financial data if it could show a national security need. But in Europe, the program seemed to fall more clearly on the wrong side of the line—in violation of tight data-privacy laws enacted by the European Union, the United Nations, and other groups to protect consumers. The legal risks were substantial. Just about everyone involved in the operation worried about the potential for abuse from housing a database of sensitive financial information inside an off-site CIA facility, and everyone realized the downside, especially if it were ever to become public. Privately, a couple of foreign intelligence services were beginning to squawk because they had come to suspect that the United States was somehow tapping into SWIFT, and some foreign officials feared that the United States could turn the giant database against them. The longer the program wore on, the greater chance there was of the whole thing blowing up. What was once seen as a temporary, emergency response to 9/11 had now become a permanent part of the Bush administration's unending war on terror.

In April 2003, word reached senior counterterrorism officials in Washington: The company was refusing to turn over its monthly data in response to the latest subpoena from the U.S. government. SWIFT wanted out. "Oh, shit," one counterterrorism official moaned to colleagues when first learning of the company's sudden skittishness. U.S. officials were panicked. The Brussels consortium, they realized, was too important to lose as a partner. Quickly, officials scrambled to set up a day-long series of emergency meetings in Washington to plead their case directly to SWIFT's executives. Lenny Schrank, the Brooklyn-born, MIT-educated CEO at the company, who had been instrumental in creating the program, flew to Washington. So did Jaap Kamp, the Dutch banker who was chairman of the board, and Yawar Shah, the company director in line to succeed Kamp as chairman. Kamp made the case for the company, laying out the company's concerns and the reasons it was considering pulling out. The company was turning over too much data with too few controls on how it was used. The few European banking regulators who even knew about the program had offered only tepid support for such an extraordinary operation. And perhaps most important, Kamp told his FBI hosts, this was supposed to be a short-term, emergency operation that was now in its second year. "How long can this go on?" he asked Mueller as they sat around the director's long wooden conference table. Kamp seemed eager to answer his own question. "This has been going on for a while, and it's become institutionalized. It's time," he said. "It's time."

WITHIN DAYS of the September 11 attacks, U.S. officials had a new mantra that would become a visible if ultimately futile flank in the war on terror: *Cut off the money.* The strategy of the 9/11 hijackers was to hide in plain sight, living nondescript lives in places like San Diego, Ft. Lauderdale, and Laurel, Maryland, and hoping that no one would notice them. Hardly anyone did. They opened bank accounts in their real names at places like SunTrust Bank in Florida, they used credit cards, they withdrew cash from ATMs, and they used wire transfers to move tens of thousands of dollars from people overseas with known links to al Qaeda to pay for things like flight training, travel, housing, and auto insurance. The transactions were so innocuous that none of the banks they dealt with noticed anything remarkable enough to trigger a "suspicious activity report" with the federal government. The hijackers worked on the cheap. Remarkably, a shoestring budget of just $400,000 or so to finance the brazen, years-long international plot would sow billions of dollars in economic devastation. So minimal were the hijackers' financial needs, in fact, that they ran a surplus; days before their deadly attacks, they returned $26,000 in unspent funds to a handler in the United Arab Emirates. Where they were going, they wouldn't need it.

Quickly, Bush and his senior advisors vowed to "shut down the money pipeline" that was funding al Qaeda. Twelve days after the attacks, Bush signed Executive Order 13224 giving the Treasury Department broad new powers to crack down on terrorist financing and shut down American businesses and charities that it suspected were funneling money to al Qaeda; it was, the White House said, "the first strike in the war on terror." The FBI set up a new unit to trace the 9/11 money. At the Treasury Department, the Customs Service set up its own shop—named Green Quest—to do essentially the same thing. The CIA, which had two of the hijackers in its sights and missed the chance to trace their banking transactions into the United States through traditional procedures, beefed up its own terror-financing operations. Within weeks, in a high-profile blitz, federal officials froze more than $30 million in funds from U.S. Islamic charities, Middle Eastern money transmittal businesses, and other groups with suspected ties to terrorist financing, groups that formed the financial and cultural backbone of many Muslim communities inside the United States. American charities that were fixtures in Islamic communities—groups like Holy Land, Global Relief, and Benevolence International—were forced to shut their doors after the feds moved in, seized their money, and linked them to al Qaeda, sometimes with the scantest evidence of actual terrorist ties. The seizures shuttered lives as well. One businessman in Minneapolis, a U.S. citizen from the Middle East whose money transmittal business was shut down and his assets frozen, "couldn't buy a cup of coffee" without violating Bush's new economic sanctions, his lawyer complained; the man's money was ultimately returned and, like many of the Americans swept up in the early seizures, he was never shown to have any link to financing terrorism.

As aggressive as the strategy was in the weeks and months after 9/11, and as low as the bar had dropped for shutting down suspect businesses and charities, some of Bush's top advisors wanted to go after bin Laden's purported financiers even harder. At one White House briefing a few months after the attacks, Don Rumsfeld was outraged over the frustrating lack of any coherent strategy for going after the terrorists' money, castigating Attorney General Ashcroft and Treasury Secretary Paul O'Neill for what Rumsfeld saw as the lack of aggression by his colleagues in targeting the supposed financiers on American soil, according to people privy to the heated confrontation. "He called them on the carpet," one government official said. "He wanted a scorched-earth policy. He didn't think enough was being done." Rumsfeld was "throwing grenades" at his counterparts in other agencies, a second official within the administration said, to push them to go even harder and even faster after the terrorists' money. But intelligence officials at the Justice and Treasury departments saw Rumsfeld's bluster and bravado as a transparent way for the Pentagon to flex its own muscle and grab more authority over terrorist financing to add to its already growing portfolio. The message from the Pentagon was clear: push harder against al Qaeda's bankrollers, or get out of the way.

Not that Ashcroft needed much of a push. In a briefing of his own at the Justice Department not long after 9/11, Justice Department and FBI officials were updating the attorney general on the status of the fast-moving Penttbom investigation and the hunt for the terrorists' money. Ashcroft listened quietly, a bit detached, until an FBI briefer mentioned almost in passing that investigators had found an ATM bank card apparently linked to one of the hijackers. The card's PIN was 6-7-2-6-2; by one formulation, it spelled out O-S-A-M-A. Now Ashcroft jumped to attention. "They're mocking us!" he yelled. "These guys are mocking us!" Ashcroft was outraged: Find out who else in the United States had that PIN, he said, and go after them hard; arrest them. He was so agitated that his briefers couldn't tell just how serious he was about the idea, but an FBI official dutifully jotted down the attorney general's directive at the bottom of a to-do list and even mentioned it to colleagues at FBI headquarters, with some astonishment, after returning across the street from Main Justice. The FBI never acted on it; this was one directive from the attorney general that the bureau thought best to let lie.

The frustrations were widespread within the government. Even as the Bush administration was publicly touting its successes in shutting down the terrorist money pipeline, the internal grousing grew louder. Fourteen months after the 9/11 attacks, a senior Treasury Department official in charge of coordinating terror-financing matters across the administration had this dour assessment of the progress in finding al Qaeda's money in an internal e-mail he sent:

> *Sometime in the next 3 months a Congressional committee is rightfully going to haul us up to the Hill (or the President is going to call us into the Oval office) and ask us 4 questions:*
>
> *1. Who finances al Qaeda?*
> *2. How?*
> *3. Where is [the money]?*
> *4. Why don't you have it (and stop it)?*

Treasury Secretary O'Neill, the official wrote, "could not answer [those questions] today."

At the root of the frustration was that old demon of government—the turf battle. Bureaucratic infighting plagued terrorist-financing operations in the months and early years after 9/11, and no one had a more heated rivalry than the FBI and the newly minted Green Quest team at the Treasury Department's Customs Service. Both agencies now had, on paper, the urgent job of tracing terrorists' money and were supposed to be working together, but they came at the task from opposite vantage points, looking through opposite ends of the telescope: customs' investigators would examine "dirty," laundered money and try to trace it forward to determine if it was being used to finance terrorism; the FBI would target suspected terrorists and try to trace the money backward to try to determine what financial schemes were generating it. In the end, both approaches proved hair-pullingly frustrating, and the clashes between the two warring agencies, though largely hidden from public view, laid bare for policy-makers the pitfalls of trying to join different agencies and mindsets under a single wartime footing. Distrust and feuding permeated the relationship. Each would mock the other's cases, question rival agents' credentials, and refuse to share documents and leads. Rival officials at the two agencies were barely on speaking terms, and when they did speak, the conversations were often laced with profanity.

The tensions reached a peak in early 2002, as the Treasury Department's customs agents were stepping up their investigation into a mysterious network of Islamic cultural, business, and charitable institutions in Northern Virginia, known as the Saar group. The investigation into possible international terrorist-financing ties by the group had largely languished in the 1990s, but after 9/11, customs investigators attacked it with renewed zeal. Though they had little hard evidence to back it up, they suspected that the Islamic network's complex, almost indecipherable financial structure was a way of cleverly masking its ties to Middle Eastern militants. At the FBI, however, officials thought the case was garbage, and they were doubly skeptical about plans by their counterparts at the customs agency to get a search warrant and raid the businesses. Some prosecutors had doubts as well. "Unless I see a plan, my guys aren't going out there," the FBI's Dennis Lormel, a salty, blunt-spoken agent who headed the bureau's terrorist-financing unit, told a rival counterpart at Customs as plans for the raid accelerated. Lormel went to Bob Mueller, urging that the FBI stay out of the operation. "The search is going to be a disaster and we don't want the FBI anywhere near it," Lormel told the director. "You're putting guys on the line. We don't want any part of it." Mueller agreed: this was a customs operation from the start, and the FBI wouldn't be involved.

Finally, on March 20, 2002, customs agents led raids on sixteen businesses and homes in Northern Virginia linked to the mysterious Islamic network, carting away box-loads of documents and potential evidence in a U-Haul truck. At his FBI office, Lormel turned on the TV to see local news footage from the well-publicized raid, and there, in the middle of the swarm, were agents with the familiar FBI logo embossed on the backs of their jackets, helping to carry out the search warrants. Customs officials, in what Lormel suspected was a deliberate end run, had apparently enlisted the help of line-level FBI agents from the field who were unaware of the edict from on high at their own headquarters. Lormel was livid. So was Mueller. At a briefing soon after the raid, Mueller pulled Lormel aside. "I thought there weren't going to be any FBI there? What the hell happened? What were our guys doing there?" Lormel had no good explanation. He was as surprised as Mueller. In the new war on terror, it seemed, sometimes it was tough to tell where the enemy fire was actually coming from. (Six years later, the case remains open, with none of the central groups or individuals targeted in the Virginia raids charged with funding terrorism or any other crime.)

By May of 2003, the feuding between the FBI and Green Quest, now moved from the Treasury Department to the newly created Department of Homeland Security, had become so acidic that President Bush himself had to intervene. The president signed off on an agreement that had been drafted by the Justice Department with the Department of Homeland Security that would put Green Quest out of business and establish, once and for all, that the FBI was the lead dog in charge of terrorist-financing investigations; customs investigators could still chase money-laundering cases, but if the trail led them to possible terrorism, they had to turn it over to the FBI to take the lead. Tom Ridge, the homeland security secretary, knew he would face fire from his own department about the perception that he was caving to the bullying tactics from the Justice Department and the FBI, but he was inclined to go ahead with the agreement anyway in the interests of peace and pragmatism. Just before it was finalized, he talked over the deal one day with two of his senior aides, Asa Hutchinson and Michael Garcia. "If we sign the memo," Ridge asked Garcia, who oversaw Green Quest, "you think your relationship with the FBI will be any different than it was today?" Garcia didn't hesitate. "Governor, I don't think so." "Fine, then sign the damn memo," Ridge said. "If they need a security blanket to make them feel they're protecting their turf, give it to them. We've got plenty of other things to worry about. Linus needed a security blanket to make him feel better too."

AS DESTRUCTIVE as the turf battles had become, the administration's efforts to combat terrorist-financing faced an even bigger problem: the strategy for "shutting down the money pipeline" was built, in large part, on a myth of the administration's own making. The bold pronouncements from Bush and his top advisors fueled the idea that al Qaeda was getting significant amounts of money from Muslim extremists in the United States and that closing suspect Islamic charities and freezing their assets would help shut down the money pipeline. Ashcroft had talked of the Al-Farooq mosque in Brooklyn being used to help raise $20 million that was hand-delivered to bin Laden. Treasury Secretary O'Neill had closed the U.S. offices of a Somalia-tied financial group known as Al-Barakaat two months after 9/11, calling the organization and its local affiliates "quartermasters of terror." "Millions of dollars have moved through these U.S. offices of Al-Barakaat," he said. "This organization is now exposed for what it is, a pariah in the civilized world. U.S. businesses and individuals are now forewarned and prohibited from doing business with this company."

The reality was very different. Al-Barakaat, the supposed "quartermaster of terror," was never shown to have any established links to al Qaeda or any other terrorist group; with much less fanfare the Treasury Department gave back the money it had seized from the group's U.S. outlets, and the FBI closed down its terrorism investigation without bringing any charges. Likewise, investigations into numerous other Islamic groups and charities in the United States failed to turn up the long-sought links to al Qaeda either. What was one to make of the notorious U.S. pipeline that Bush and his advisors had warned was funding al Qaeda? "The pipeline," a law enforcement official told me one day over coffee a few years after 9/11, "never really existed." There was little doubt that American Muslims, for years, had been responsible for sending large sums of money overseas to extremist Palestinian causes like Hamas, Hezbollah, and Palestinian Islamic Jihad, both before and after such contributions were banned. But there was little sign that any significant amount was going to al Qaeda. Intelligence officials believed that bin Laden and his cohorts got the bulk of their money from groups in Middle Eastern nations like the United Arab Emirates and Saudi Arabia, financial juggernauts that U.S. officials found hard to pry open.

Four years after the 9/11 attacks, staff investigators for the 9/11 Commission confirmed publicly what Bush administration officials had long ago concluded privately: "The United States is not, and has not been, a substantial source of al Qaeda funding." While some money originally raised in the United States may have made its way to al Qaeda and its affiliates, "there is little hard evidence of substantial funds from the United States actually going to al Qaeda," said the report, which drew virtually no public attention despite its startling conclusions. This was not just the perspective of a bunch of Monday morning quarterbacks from the 9/11 Commission; one CIA expert on al Qaeda financing dismissed as "minuscule" any U.S. money going to the terrorist organization. Then there was this: for all the talk by U.S. officials after 9/11 about shutting down the money pipeline, "in reality," the staff report concluded, "completely choking off the money to al Qaeda and affiliated terrorist groups has been essentially impossible."

That was where SWIFT came into play. The rising importance of the secret Belgian banking operation in the minds of American policymakers was, by one measure, a reflection of the very failure of Bush's much touted strategy to "choke off the money." Soon after 9/11, U.S. officials began to realize that the idea of cutting off the money was largely a pipe dream; often, they were hapless in even identifying the terrorists' money, much less stopping and seizing it. From that grudging realization was born a subtle but significant policy shift: *follow* the money as best they could. Collect as much intelligence as possible on the world's financial systems, trace it and analyze it to death, and try to get a better understanding of the patterns that linked Islamic charities, businesses, and other groups suspected of funding terrorism. The administration didn't advertise the important shift, but it did allude to it obliquely at times in public even while the SWIFT banking program was still a closely guarded secret. "Where necessary," the Treasury Department's David Aufhauser told a congressional committee in 2005, "we have a pretty deep understanding of what happens in the documented banking world today."

SWIFT's vast repository of financial data was the envy of American intelligence officials long before 9/11. In the early 1990s, the Justice Department in the administration of George W. Bush's father had pushed the consortium to pack more financial data into their messaging traffic and give the United States greater access to it to help them in investigations. It was left to Bob Mueller, then a senior Justice Department official who was active in money-laundering operations a decade before he took over as FBI director, to plead the government's case with SWIFT. He was part of a Justice Department delegation that visited Brussels to lobby company officials on the issue. Mueller "pushed them very hard," according to one participant. With terrorism still a second-tier issue in the 1990s, the chief target for Mueller and the Justice Department then in lobbying SWIFT was drug-traffickers. U.S. officials wanted to be able to trace international banking transactions more easily to determine how and when Colombian drug lords and narco-traffickers were moving their money; terrorism wasn't even mentioned.

Executives at SWIFT were polite but firm with Mueller: they weren't ready to commit to anything. The banking consortium had logistical problems with what Mueller and the Justice Department were proposing, but more important were their legal and philosophical worries: with Europe's tough banking secrecy laws and cultural mindset, SWIFT didn't want to be seen as a clandestine partner of the U.S. government in giving away access to sensitive banking data and putting itself in legal jeopardy in the process. So deep were their reservations that the company's executives warned U.S. officials that if they tried to subpoena its banking information, SWIFT would pull its U.S. outlets off American soil so it couldn't be forced to comply with the demand. Mueller and company went home empty-handed.

Then came 9/11. With orders from the White House to choke off the money, SWIFT once again became the subject of intense interest from American policy-makers. Within weeks of the attacks, officials at the Treasury Department—designated by Bush to take the lead on terrorist-financing—were hearing from one of the CIA's terrorist-financing gurus, a jittery intelligence official nicknamed "Nervous Phil," about how valuable the data from this little known Belgian cooperative could prove in fighting terrorism. A few Wall Street executives—the target of such devastation on 9/11—were gently making the same suggestion to their government colleagues in Washington. SWIFT, to those few who even knew of its existence, was "the mother lode, the Rosetta stone" for financial data. It routed some $6 trillion a day between banks, brokerages, stock exchanges, and other financial institutions, and the routing instructions that the company used to move money around the globe often included much more detailed data than any other system: passport information, phone numbers and local addresses, critical identifying information about the senders and the recipients, the purpose of the transaction, and more. A government investigator with that kind of data in his hands could skip past what would ordinarily be many levels of bureaucratic mazes to get key records. For years, in fact, officials at the CIA had eyed SWIFT's database so enviously that they had apparently been trying to tap into the firm's system on their own, without the company's knowledge, but they couldn't figure out how to break the complicated encryptions that the company used to guard the privacy of its customers. Now, with 9/11 as a catalyst, the CIA wanted to push anew to break into SWIFT's system and get at the data. Officials at the Treasury Department balked at the idea of what amounted to a black bag job. "Let's go in the front door," said David Aufhauser, the general counsel at the Treasury Department.

So a few weeks after 9/11, Treasury officials called over to Brussels to pitch SWIFT on the idea: the U.S. government wanted to find a way to leverage the company's data to get at the terrorists' money. "I was wondering when you were going to call," came the response from Schrank, the chief executive at SWIFT. "What took you so long?"

There were still many details of the novel arrangement left to be worked out. The most important centered on SWIFT's legal liability. The company's lawyers wanted protection—a subpoena, a piece of paper, something to make clear if and when the program was exposed that the company was *obligated* to cooperate. And the company wanted controls: the operation had to be limited strictly to finding terrorists, and there had to be other measures put in place to make sure that the U.S. government wasn't just rummaging willy-nilly through the most sensitive financial records in the world.

For their part, Bush administration lawyers at the Treasury Department did a hurried review of the legal issues surrounding the extraordinary prospect of accessing large chunks of SWIFT's database. Was this legal? They concluded that the idea appeared to fall within the president's emergency economic powers invoked just a week after the September 11 attacks and did not violate the Right to Financial Privacy Act protecting banking records, in part because the consortium was not considered a "financial institution" under the meaning of the statute. It was "a gray area," one official conceded; technically within the letter of American banking privacy law, if not the spirit. "People were trying to do things," another official told me, "that had never been done before." With the legality seemingly assured, officials at the Treasury Department drafted an administrative subpoena from the Office of Foreign Assets Control, or OFAC, that would seek financial records from the company for U.S. transactions involving more than thirty countries thought to be affiliated with terrorist financing— Saudi Arabia, Pakistan, United Arab Emirates, and on down the list. The idea, in theory, was to craft a subpoena that would extract the information from the company's database considered most relevant to terrorism. But SWIFT had no way of separating out its data in such a fine-tuned way, so the company, according to the account of John Snow, who succeeded O'Neill as treasury secretary, came back to the United States with an even better proposal: "We'll give you all the data." That was an offer the Bush administration couldn't refuse.

The extraordinary access allowed officials at the CIA, the Treasury Department, and the FBI to conduct hundreds of thousands of searches of SWIFT's data against their own terrorist watch lists; thousands, perhaps more, involved the international transactions of Americans inside the United States. The system, Treasury Secretary Snow said, was "government at its best." Indeed, at its best, the system could point analysts to money trails they never knew existed, as appears to have happened in the 2003 capture of an al Qaeda operative in Thailand, known as Hambali, who was believed to be the mastermind of the

2002 bombings at a Bali resort. Although a number of intelligence methods appear to have been combined to lead officials to Hambali, data from SWIFT helped to identify a suspicious money transfer between a suspected terrorist operative in the Middle East and an official with an NGO—a nongovernmental organization—in Thailand. The group hadn't appeared on anyone's list of terrorist suspects, so the transaction caught the attention of U.S. analysts once it showed up as a hit on the SWIFT database. A second transaction then helped lead officials to Hambali himself. His capture was a major coup and, in the view of terrorist-financing officials, an important validation of the SWIFT program.

But far more often, the searches led to the inevitable dead ends; there was smoke, but no fire, and Americans' private banking records had been examined by the CIA based on suspicions that often proved unfounded. At its worst, everyone involved in the program acknowledged the huge potential for abuse in an operation so far-reaching. "The capability here is awesome or, depending on where you're sitting, troubling," one official said. "The potential for abuse is enormous." The CIA, after all, was sitting on a gold mine containing reams of the most sensitive financial information in the world, with little in the way of outside checks or scrutiny. So it was that one government official early on in the program used SWIFT's data for "inappropriate" purposes. By one account, the employee was checking the finances of someone he had a grudge against; another version was that he was using the data to follow a money-laundering investigation unconnected to terrorism—in violation of the rules set by SWIFT's executives. Whatever the truth, the employee was soon removed from the team. "In any enterprise where it's being conducted by human beings, there's going to be some mistake that may get made," the Treasury Department's Stuart Levey acknowledged. The episode underscored for government officials the need for tight controls in the operation—including the use of an outside auditing firm, Booz Allen, to do occasional audits of the financial searches conducted by the CIA to establish whether analysts had a legitimate reason to believe a transaction might actually be connected to terrorism.

From the beginning, there was intense nervousness over the program. The government was now sweeping up reams of private financial data in record numbers—with little input or knowledge by regulatory banking officials in Europe or by members of Congress, much less their express approval. Some counterterrorism officials wanted to make sure they were on sound legal footing and, in 2002, the Treasury Department proposed giving full briefings to all the relevant banking and financial services committees, beyond the few lawmakers who knew of the program, to make sure they were on board with the program. The White House quickly rejected the move. This was a secret program that had to be held to a small group. As if to ease any doubts, Vice President Cheney himself would speak with SWIFT officials, tour the CIA facility that housed the banking operation, and get occasional reports on its progress. Word soon come back to officials at Treasury and the FBI that the vice president was "very impressed" by the program—a clear sign that it had the explicit backing of the White House.

SWIFT executives knew the priority attached to their secret program, but it did little to ease their own nervousness. Executives in Brussels were frustrated by the slow pace of security clearances for their own people and other bureaucratic problems. Concerns were running so high by April of 2003 that the company was withholding the records that the Treasury Department was seeking in its standard monthly subpoena. Treasury officials were flustered; without the banking data, Treasury's Aufhauser told his counterparts in Brussels, the United States was "running blind" and was risking another attack. SWIFT held firm. Without greater assurance that it was on solid legal ground and without greater protections built into the process, the company would walk.

It was left mainly to Fed chairman Greenspan and the FBI's Mueller to persuade the company officials to stay on, as they hosted the Brussels delegation for their high-level visits in Washington on May 8, 2003. From Greenspan, the Brussels delegation wanted peace of mind—an assurance from the wise old man of America's financial markets that the consortium was on solid ground before it committed to going forward. Greenspan began the soft sell. He understood the company's misgivings, he told SWIFT's executives while meeting with them at the Treasury Department. If the world's financiers were to find out how their sensitive internal data was being used, he acknowledged, it could hurt the stability of the global banking systems. But, he continued, the secret banking program was vital to national security, and that outweighed the risks. Greenspan quoted the famous admonition from former secretary of state Henry Stimson, in shutting down a code-breaking unit in the late 1920s, that "gentlemen do not read each other's mail." But sometimes, Greenspan said with a twist, if you want to keep the postal system in operation in the first place, "it's *necessary* to read other people's mail." The implication was clear: this was such a time.

Then it was Mueller's turn at the FBI to woo his Belgian visitors. Mueller was a prosecutor by training, not a firefighter, but putting out brushfires seemed to have become de rigueur for him in his job as FBI director. Usually, he was putting out fires started by someone else. After the dramatic showdown at John Ashcroft's hospital room over the NSA eavesdropping program, it was Mueller who played the part of peacemaker sent in by Bush himself to help put the pieces of the program back together. After the 9/11 Commission began exploring the FBI's many failures prior to the 9/11 attacks on his predecessor's watch, it was Mueller's calming, dispassionate assurances about reinventing the FBI that helped convince many commission members not to recommend tearing the bureau apart altogether. And after FBI agents reported that they were witnessing abusive interrogation tactics by the CIA on prisoners at Guantánamo Bay and elsewhere, it was Mueller who ordered his agents to stay out of the interviews for fear of acquiescing in possibly criminal acts of torture. Mueller was never one to buck the system altogether, but he was adept at working within it and sealing the cracks that appeared before they ruptured completely.

Now, it was the threat of another rupture over the CIA's secret banking program that Mueller had to fix as he met with Jaap Kamp and SWIFT's other leaders in the FBI director's suite. This was Mueller at his best. He thanked his visitors for their cooperation, and he told them how grateful he was and how valuable their contribution to the war on terror had been. He pointed to specific cases where their financial data had proven helpful in identifying people the FBI might never have known about otherwise. He understood their discomfort over the sensitive position they were in, Mueller told his guests, but the banking program they had made possible was simply too vital to national security to abandon now.

"The risk," Mueller told them, "is worth the reward."

The pitch seemed to work. Kamp and his colleagues weren't ready to commit to sticking with the program yet, but their resistance was clearly softening. Administration officials at the FBI and the Treasury Department saw an opening: if SWIFT was given greater control over the operation, greater assurance that the spies at the CIA weren't misusing their private data for sundry intelligence operations that had nothing to do with fighting terrorism, then maybe, just maybe, they could keep the Belgians on board. The Treasury Department went to work drafting new procedures and, within a few weeks of the Washington meetings with SWIFT, they sent them on to Brussels. The key element of the new plan ensured that the CIA would not have unfettered access to the data. Executives in Brussels would be able to put their own employees at the CIA to sit next to the analysts, peek over their shoulders, and make sure that whatever they were doing with the company's data was proper and authorized. "The scrutineers," SWIFT's new watchdogs would be dubbed. If they saw something they didn't like—a CIA analyst looking up his ex-wife's financial transactions or, worse yet, delving into corporate trade secrets of overseas companies—he could literally hit a button and bring the operation to an immediate halt. Early on, in fact, the "scrutineers" were hitting the button rapid-fire because of what they saw as a slew of poorly documented searches, forcing American analysts to put more and more information into their requests to show why they thought someone's records might be tied to terrorism. With the added level of insulation now built into the system, SWIFT's executives were sold. Their exposure was scaled back just enough to ease their nerves and put them back in a comfort zone of sorts. They would stay on the Bush team, and the administration's secret banking operation was still safe.

THE PUBLIC OUTCRY generated by our disclosure of the NSA wiretapping program in December 2005 gave rise to the obvious follow-up question from congressmen, the media, and the public itself: What else was the Bush White House doing that it didn't want the public, or congressional committees for that matter, to know about? The Bush administration itself only fanned the flames of wild speculation through its ardent refusal to say what else, if anything, the president had authorized the government to do outside normal judicial channels in taking the fight to al Qaeda. At a Senate hearing less than two months after the NSA story broke, Attorney General Gonzales was asked repeatedly what else the president could claim the power to do under his emergency wartime authorities; repeatedly, Gonzales sidestepped the questions. Such "hypotheticals," the attorney general said in his usual soft-spoken, passionless monotone, went beyond the scope of the NSA wiretapping program that the president had publicly acknowledged in December. Gonzales' evasiveness only fueled more questions. The public was clamoring for answers, and we were anxious to try to provide them as best we could.

Soon after we broke the NSA story, Jim Risen and I began hearing vague rumblings about parallel efforts in the realm of terrorist-financing. It made perfect sense: if e-mails and phone calls were the essential arteries for terrorist networks, money was the lifeblood that kept them pumping, and the government would be anxious to tap that vein as well. In fact, Bush had made no secret of his intense desire to shut down the money pipeline to al Qaeda. It was a frequent applause line for him and his top advisors, especially in the early months of the war on terror. Most people assumed that the administration was using its many publicly touted tools—the expanded powers granted under the Patriot Act, the seizures of suspect money by the Treasury Department, and the like—to combat terrorist-financing. Government reports, in fact, reinforced that notion. The 9/11 Commission's staff report on terrorist-financing, for instance, talked about the FBI's aggressive use of traditional subpoenas and other tried-and-true legal mechanisms to get relevant data from financial institutions in emergencies "at any time, including nights, weekends, and holidays." But was there more going on behind the scenes?

Soon, we had an answer. No one had to tell us that the government was tapping into SWIFT's database in Brussels. It became clear from our reporting that if the government wanted to get at vast volumes of financial data all at once, there were two likely sources: SWIFT and a domestic counterpart known as CHIPS, a New York–based clearinghouse that settles banking and financial transactions in the United States. As we began asking people in the know about CHIPS and whether the government was tapping into it, we were met with staunch denials. When we asked about SWIFT, we got mostly silence and unreturned phone calls. We figured we were on to something.

As details of the program came into sharper focus, the broad-brush parallels to the NSA program were striking. As in the NSA program, the SWIFT operation relied on a broad reading of the president's emergency powers and a largely untested legal theory to gather counterterrorism intelligence. As in the NSA program, the government was getting access to huge streams of information that inevitably touched on the privacy of Americans who had no known connection to terrorism. As in the NSA program, the White House had insisted on extraordinary secrecy surrounding the program and, with a go-it-alone muscularity, had shunned oversight by relevant congressional committees and by international banking officials. And as in the NSA program, the SWIFT operation had led to such nervousness that there were efforts to shut it down long before it threatened to become public.

In trying to follow the various strands of the story, I talked to a former administration official involved in the operation and asked about the SWIFT program. He wouldn't discuss it. But he did contact his old colleagues in the administration to pass on word: *The New York Times* knows about the banking program. Soon, the editors and I began getting phone calls from the Treasury Department asking what we were working on. They already knew the answer. The NSA spying controversy was now in full scandal mode, and the administration was anxious to avoid another brouhaha over the president's use of his emergency wartime powers. Whenever we wanted to talk about the SWIFT story and why it shouldn't be published, Treasury Department officials told us, the front door on Pennsylvania Avenue was wide open. We were about to begin Round Two in the battle between national security and the public's right to know.

The arguments from administration officials, made over the course of two months in a series of lengthy meetings, had a déjà vu feeling to them after our experience with the NSA wiretapping program: the SWIFT operation was a vital program in the war on terror, it was built on a firm legal foundation, its disclosure was sure to aid the terrorists and do grave harm to national security. Some of the desperate pleadings from the administration and its allies had a sky-is-falling feel to them as well. If the story was published, we were warned, SWIFT's complex in Brussels might be attacked by the terrorists. Or, all the negative publicity and pressure from the firm's customers were sure to shut the place down. And if that happened, the stability of the entire global economy might be imperiled.

Despite the occasional over-the-top histrionics from the administration, the question of whether or not to publish the story was, in my mind at least, a closer call than the one we faced six months earlier over the NSA wiretapping program. While a strong case could be made that the NSA program was, on its face, illegal, the SWIFT program fell within a grayer area of the law. And while we were careful in the NSA story to skirt the role played by any particular telecommunications company, that was impossible to do with the SWIFT program because the company itself was such a singular part of the story. Here, we would in effect be outing a partner that the White House considered vital to the war on terror. Was that a step the newspaper was willing to take?

Our critics liked to charge that the *Times* would run anything, no matter the harm to national security. "Washington Planning Surprise Attack Across the Delaware" read the headline on a mock newspaper on a political cartoon skewering us, with the caption: "If the New York Times Had Covered the Revolutionary War." It provided us with more head-shaking material for our bulletin boards, as ludicrous as the charge was. It was tough to imagine that anyone levying the accusation had actually followed the painstaking debate over the newspaper's decision to hold the NSA story for more than a year. For the editors to even consider running a piece, we knew that there had to be a legitimate public interest that outweighed any potential harm to national security. After the NSA story was published, in fact, Jim and I learned of two additional programs launched as part of the Bush administration's "war on terror." One involved a particular, and particularly clever, method of accessing the communications of suspected terrorists; the other involved a particular, and equally clever, method of tracking the movement of their money. Both programs appeared narrowly focused on targets overseas, with no obvious conflict with U.S. law or Americans' privacy interests. The White House never had to ask us not to run the stories; in our early discussions, Jim, Rebecca Corbett, and I all agreed that each of these operations, at least from the limited amount we knew about them, seemed to fall well below the threshold of what we would even consider publishing. Our reporting ended there.

Had it not been for the public furor over the NSA program, the editors might have decided not to publish the story on the SWIFT program either. In a different time, it might have been considered too sensitive, too close to the "sources and methods" that editors are sometimes willing to help protect. But news decisions aren't made in a vacuum. The context of the NSA story was tough to ignore in weighing the banking program. Treasury Department officials realized that as they lobbied us. They knew they were caught in an unfortunate circumstance of timing, swept up in the NSA's backdraft, and they did their best to distance the SWIFT operation from the mess over Bush's wiretapping program. "I understand how it may look," one senior official told me insistently in urging us not to publish the story, "but you have to understand: this is *not* the NSA program."

He had a point. The banking program had not, as far as we could tell, triggered the same level of angst and protest seen within the administration over the NSA program. But the editors believed, as did I, that to withhold a story so central to the raging public debate over the government's antiterrorism powers and the balance against civil liberties would be to effectively abdicate our role as journalists. As with the NSA program, our aim was never to declare the program legal or illegal, effective or ineffective. The SWIFT program was, above all else, an interesting yarn about the administration's extraordinary efforts since 9/11 to stop another attack. Many readers, if they knew about the program, would no doubt cheer the administration's aggressive efforts to track the terrorists' money; others would no doubt question just how far the administration was willing to stretch the legal system in taking the fight to al Qaeda. Our job was to lay out the facts of the program and let people decide for themselves what they thought of it. Long before Fox News turned the concept into a jingle ("We report. You decide."), that's what newspapers had always done. An old mentor of mine once put it well: newspapers don't determine what people think, they determine what they think *about*.

Just as important, the potential harm to national security cited by the Bush administration appeared oblique at best. Treasury Secretary John Snow himself had led reporters from major media organizations on a six-day tour to trumpet the administration's supposed success in tracking terrorist-financing and going after their dirty money. The government's efforts were so loudly trumpeted, in fact, that a whole slew of high-profile stories in the media from 2002 through the spring of 2006 noted that terrorist financiers for al Qaeda and other terror groups were actively moving their money out of traditional banking systems and moving it to places like informal "hawala" money exchanges or the rare minerals trade; many financiers were already afraid of getting caught up in the U.S. dragnet if they moved their money through traditional financial institutions because they were so aware of the government scrutiny they faced. That the U.S. government was actively monitoring terrorist-financing was no secret. That it was doing so through its extraordinary and arguably extralegal access to the nerve center of the global banking industry, however, was.

Any doubts in my own mind about running the story were put to rest in a conversation that, ironically, was set up by the Bush administration in an effort to dissuade the editors from publishing the story. The White House realized that its own credibility might be suspect after its failed lobbying over the publication of the NSA story, so in making the case against publishing the SWIFT story, it sent emissaries on its behalf. One of them was Lee Hamilton, the much respected former Democratic congressman from Indiana who was co-chairman of the 9/11 Commission. Once the story ran, the Bush administration would cite the supposedly fervent "pleas" of Hamilton and its other liaisons in pummeling the newspaper for our purported disregard for national security. Even a prominent Democrat like Lee Hamilton, administration ally William Bennett proclaimed on one talk show, had "begged *The New York Times* not to run this piece." It made for good television. If only it were true. I was at the meeting with Hamilton, who met for nearly an hour with Phil Taubman, Rebecca Corbett, Jim, and myself. From the little he knew about the SWIFT program, Hamilton told us, it appeared to be valuable. But as he sank into the couch in Phil's office, Hamilton was clearly uncomfortable with his role as its proxy defender. Whatever its value, Hamilton said, the program relied on an expansive reading of the law, it intruded on civil liberties, and, in his mind, it fit a pattern of what appeared to be the trappings of an "imperial presidency." We weren't sure what to say after that. Finally, Jim asked Hamilton haltingly why he felt the paper shouldn't run the story. Hamilton interjected. "I'm not telling you not to run the story," he said. It was a startling moment: here was the man sent by the White House to persuade the newspaper not to run the story, and he was telling us just the opposite.

The administration's damage control efforts extended beyond the newspaper. Even as administration officials were urging us not to run the SWIFT story that spring of 2006, they were also reaching out to members of Congress who knew nothing about the program. This was a step that some Treasury Department officials had urged years before, without success, as knowledge of the program was kept to a small circle at the insistence of the White House. Now, with the possibility of a big national story hitting the newspapers, there was little choice but to widen the circle. The Treasury Department began quietly putting out calls to nearly two dozen lawmakers who sat on the relevant banking and financial services committee. These were people who, by all rights, should have been briefed on the program from the outset.

Barney Frank, the ranking member on the House Financial Services Committee, was one of them. Normally, his committee would have had clear jurisdiction for oversight of a program like this. But no one on the committee was told about this one. One day in June, the Treasury Department summoned Frank to a secure conference in the Capitol for some sort of hush-hush briefing. He couldn't remember ever getting an invitation like this. He had to go to the conference room alone, and he had to leave his cell phone outside. A pair of young Treasury Department officials greeted him and ushered him inside. A couple of folders sat on a conference room table. One of them, he noticed, said "SWIFT." He didn't know what SWIFT was.

"We want to brief you on something that's going to be in the newspaper," one of the Treasury officials told him. "Why, is it something you're going to announce?" Frank asked, now a bit confused. No, came the response; Treasury wasn't planning to announce anything. "So this is something that's going to be leaked?" the congressman said. "And you'd rather *not* see in the newspaper?" Now the picture was becoming a little clearer. Frank figured he would have to sign something to accept this classified briefing, the equivalent of an administration gag order. So, he asked, if he signed the form, listened to the briefing, and read the briefing materials on this classified program, would he still be able to publicly discuss whatever the issue was once it hit the newspapers? "Not unless we give you permission," the Treasury official responded. Frank had heard enough. He turned for the door.

"Thank you. Goodbye. If you ever want to tell me something that's not going to be in the newspapers, call me."

OUR STORY on the SWIFT program hit the *Times* Web site on June 23, 2006, just an hour or so ahead of the competition. Late into our weeks of discussions with the Bush administration about whether to run the story, a couple of old colleagues from the *Los Angeles Times* had heard what we were working on, and they began following the money trail to Brussels themselves. They had almost caught us by the time the newspaper let the administration know we were planning to move ahead with the story. Making one last plea for us not to publish the piece, the Treasury Department hurriedly cut short a European trip by one of its senior counterterrorism officials, Stuart Levey, and flew him back to Washington to pitch the administration's case; we met one last time in Levey's spacious office a block from the White House, but the editors were unmoved. The story, they decided, would run. Even as Rebecca Corbett and the editors were giving the story one last review the next day and preparing to hit the "send" button, the *L.A. Times* was at the Treasury Department meeting with the same officials we had met the day before to hear the same pitch. As they met, BlackBerries went off at the Treasury Department with e-mails alerting Levey's aides to the news: *The New York Times* had just posted its SWIFT story on the Internet. The story was out.

The *L.A. Times* posted its own story not long after, and, by night-fall, the Treasury Department had disclosed the existence of the still classified program to *The Wall Street Journal* and *The Washington Post* as well in an effort to put their own spin on it and contain the damage. This was one time I didn't mind the competition catching up to us at the finish line. We knew we were in for another pounding from the political right, and the fact that the *Times* had company in deciding to publish the story might, at least in theory, help cushion the blow.

At a time of such bitter partisan divisions, the fallout from the story was intense from both the left and the right. In Europe, banking regulators were outraged to learn that the CIA had been trolling through sensitive banking records and quickly declared the program an illegal violation of Europe's tight data-privacy laws. The denunciations set in motion months of negotiations with SWIFT that would lead to new oversight and restrictions for the operation. The wave of unrest in Europe caused such headaches for Lenny Schrank, the SWIFT chief executive, that when he bumped into Arthur Sulzberger, the *Times* publisher, at an executives' conference some months later, he demanded thirty bottles of aspirin for all the grief he said the newspaper had caused him. (Sulzberger sent Schrank a bottle of Bayer aspirin, which Schrank declared twenty-nine short of the requisite.)

In the United States, meanwhile, civil rights advocates called for formal investigations, and privacy lawyers and banking customers quickly sued SWIFT on Fourth Amendment grounds, claiming an invasion of privacy. Some members of Congress, Republicans and Democrats alike, were angry to learn that the administration had once again been keeping secrets from them about vital intelligence programs. "Many people in Congress who should have been briefed by the administration were not," an exasperated Sue Kelly, the Republican chairwoman of a House banking subcommittee, told the Treasury Department's Levey. "What else is it that we don't know?"

Days after our SWIFT story appeared, I spoke about the furor with Arlen Specter, the Pennsylvania senator who was chairman of the Senate Judiciary Committee. Specter had been the GOP's biggest agitator over the NSA wiretapping program, blasting the White House for cutting Congress out of its oversight role, and the disclosure of the SWIFT program found him nearly as exercised. Again, his main beef was over the White House's apparent disdain for Congress and its constitutional function as a check on the executive branch. "They may have the authority to do this," he told me. "I don't know until I look more. But my point is, why does it take a newspaper investigation to get them to comply with the law? That's a big, important point. What else don't we know is going on until we read it in *The New York Times*?" Maybe, Specter suggested to me with a chuckle, he'd offer up a constitutional amendment giving the *Times* a formal oversight function over the executive branch. Months later, after a colleague and I wrote another lengthy story breaking new ground on the Pentagon's expanded role in domestic intelligence issues, Specter's Democratic counterpart on the Judiciary Committee, Pat Leahy, provided another mock suggestion aimed at speeding Congress's access to information being held so tightly by the White House. "Sometimes I wish they would just mark *The New York Times* 'Top Secret,' " Leahy said as an aside in the middle of a Judiciary Committee hearing, "and we'd get the information quicker, in more detail, and the wonderful crossword puzzle at the same time."

THE BUSH WHITE HOUSE'S zealous devotion to secrecy and its circumvention of congressional checks were strong undercurrents in the newspaper's decision to publish the SWIFT story. Even as we were readying the final version for the newspaper, Jim and I learned of a remarkable private letter to President Bush on that very point written by the most unlikely of critics: Congressman Peter Hoekstra, the Republican leader of the House Intelligence Committee and one of the administration's most dependable allies on national security matters. Hoekstra was steaming over the White House's failure to tell his committee about yet another, still undisclosed intelligence program that the administration was conducting in the war on terror. "I have learned of some alleged intelligence community activities about which our committee has not been briefed," Mr. Hoekstra wrote to the president in his letter of May 18, 2006. "If these allegations are true, they may represent a breach of responsibility by the administration, a violation of the law, and, just as importantly, a direct affront to me and the members of this committee who have so ardently supported efforts to collect information on our enemies." These were strong words from a normally unflinching supporter. Congressional oversight had become an oxymoron. If lawmakers with the highest security clearances in the government wanted to know what the executive branch was actually doing, they might indeed have to rely on the media to tell them.

Many Republicans, of course, didn't see an aggressive press as a solution to their oversight problems, and the concerns raised in the United States and Europe about the banking program were quickly drowned out by the thunderous denunciation from the right over the *Times'* decision to run the story. Although other newspapers had printed the story the same day that we had, the crowded field didn't matter much. We were clearly the target. To our critics on the right, *The New York Times* was red meat, a reliable piñata to rally the base in times of political trouble. The White House's strategy was to single out the *Times* as loudly and as often as possible. "If *The New York Times* decides that it is going to try to assume responsibility for determining which classified secrets remain classified and which don't, it ought to accept some of the obligations of that responsibility; it ought to be able to take the heat as well," White House spokesman Tony Snow declared. "*The New York Times* and other news organizations ought to think long and hard about whether a public's right to know, in some cases, might override somebody's right to live, and whether, in fact, the publications of these could place in jeopardy the safety of fellow Americans."

Bush himself called the publication of the SWIFT program "disgraceful." Vice President Cheney did too, saying it was "doubly disturbing" that we had been awarded a Pulitzer Prize two months earlier for our story on the NSA wiretapping program. A conservative publication demanded that the newspaper be stripped of its White House press credentials. Picketers demonstrated in front of our building, and our e-mail in-boxes again filled with hate mail and invectives. A right-wing talk show host suggested that Bill Keller should be sent to the gas chamber for running the SWIFT story. Republican congressmen called for the newspaper to be prosecuted for treason. And the Republican-controlled House of Representatives passed a symbolic resolution denouncing the media for disclosing the program; Jim and I talked about getting an official copy of the resolution to have it autographed and framed, but we thought better of it.

We had our defenders. Fellow journalists, media commentators, open-government advocates, and civil rights leaders all rallied to our defense. We'd been "SWIFT-boated," declared MSNBC commentator Keith Olbermann, a clever nod to the sharp-elbowed political tactics employed against John Kerry and his Vietnam service in the 2004 campaign. Many commentators and legal analysts were unimpressed by the administration's claim that the story gave the enemy any tactical edge, charging that the White House was again playing the national security card to distract from the program's obvious legal and political perils and discourage aggressive reporting. At the Minneapolis *Star Tribune*, the readers' representative framed the issue in bold brushstrokes in one column: "For those who enjoy a summer blockbuster, the dust-up between the Bush Administration and *The New York Times* has been a real clash of the Titans, a bare-knuckle brawl between the press and the White House. We haven't seen the likes of this since Spiro Agnew labeled the press 'nattering nabobs of negativism' back in the Nixon Administration. It's a controversy that defies easy answers or a safe harbor to decision makers. Should a free press wait patiently for government officials to spoon-feed information only when officials deem it time for the public to know what they've been up to? There are countries that operate that way, but they're not democracies."

To find myself again in the middle of the cacophony was dizzying stuff. When the NSA wiretapping story had broken six months earlier, Jim—with his new book out in bookstores—did the bulk of our TV and radio appearances. Now, the roles were reversed, and I was the one usually playing the part of public front man on the SWIFT story. The *Times'* PR office seemed to call me twice a day with media invitations: ABC's *Good Morning America*, CNN, PBS, National Public Radio. I was anxious to talk about the banking program itself and how it fit into the war on terror, but it seemed all anyone wanted to discuss was the *Times'* decision to run the story in the first place and the feud it had festered between the newspaper and the White House. In the who-can-shout-louder echo chamber of the Washington media, our critics clearly drowned out our supporters, with the White House again leading the way. "The whole thing seems uglier this time around," I said to Jim a few days after the story broke, as we grabbed a sandwich. Jim laughed. "Yeah," he said, "that's only because you're the one out there now on TV all the time. Trust me," he said, "it was just as ugly the first time around."

We were both growing a bit tired of all the notoriety. Amid the din that followed the SWIFT story, Jim even declared to me and Rebecca that he had decided he was getting out of the classified reporting business altogether to write about less sensitive and controversial topics (if the NSA eavesdroppers were listening, there must have been champagne corks popping at Fort Meade), and he threatened to turn over his Rolodex of sources to me. "I've decided what else I want to write about," Jim told me one morning as he arrived at the office, an air of certainty in his voice that I hadn't heard for a while. "I'm gonna write about the civil war." I looked up from my computer terminal, a little surprised. "The civil war in Iraq? You're going to Baghdad?" "No, the *American* Civil War," said Jim, a big history buff. It took me a moment to realize he wasn't joking. "I'll go write the untold story of the Battle of Spotsylvania Court House or something. There's nothing classified about that," he said. "Don't be so sure," I told him. Luckily, he reconsidered his self-imposed exile; the White House couldn't get rid of him that easily.

It became all but impossible to avoid all the clamor. Gonzales had recently floated the idea on *Face the Nation* that reporters could be prosecuted under the 1917 Espionage Act for writing stories on classified programs like the NSA operation. The remark was no idle slip of the tongue; internal Justice Department documents that I obtained showed that Gonzales and department aides had been talking about that very idea within weeks of our NSA story. Gonzales quickly backtracked after an onslaught of criticism over the once unthinkable idea of prosecuting reporters for espionage ("A shot across journalism's bow," the *Boston Herald* called Gonzales' remarks), but GOP supporters picked up the rallying cry. The FBI, with a leak investigation already started on the NSA story, was now sending in more investigators to look for the purported "leakers" on the SWIFT story, and the threat of another subpoena like the one that had put Judy Miller in jail hung over our heads. The FBI was almost certainly tracing phone records to determine which government officials had been in contact with me and Jim, along with other reporters in Washington who had done stories on sensitive topics like the CIA's black site prisons in Europe. Some sources began to shut down and stopped returning calls, not out of any animus but simply out of fear of being unfairly drawn into an FBI investigation. I called up a former official one day to ask if I could buy her a cup of coffee. "Does that come with a subpoena?" she asked, dead serious. Every time I spoke with Valerie Caproni, the FBI's general counsel, she would jokingly suggest that our conversations were being monitored, and when we spoke on one panel together at a judicial conference in California, she used me as an example of what intelligence officials would do if they wanted to monitor someone. I leaned toward my microphone and interrupted her. "You *are* speaking hypothetically, right?" I asked. The judges in the audience erupted in laughter at the vaudeville act starring the FBI and *The New York Times*, but all the jokes couldn't mask the real predicament that Jim and I found ourselves in. We were living the old saying: You're not paranoid if they're really after you. Jim and I became more careful about how we contacted people, we avoided discussing sensitive topics altogether, and we talked about using counterespionage methods like throw-away cell phones and coded messages hidden in potted plants, just like in *All the President's Men*. It all seemed a little pointless; if the FBI and the NSA wanted to find us, we figured they'd know where to look.

All the while, we realized that the legal protections we had once all taken for granted as reporters in Washington were now crumbling around us. Reporters in San Francisco were facing the prospect of jail time from federal authorities for writing about Giants slugger Barry Bonds' ties to illegal steroids. The FBI was seeking to comb through the years-old files of legendary Washington investigative reporter Jack Anderson—dead for two years—to look for classified material that might be buried in some 188 boxes of archives. Jim and I were now looking at the threat of subpoenas over two stories, and every new reporting road we ventured down now first required a gut check of sorts: Could this get us in more trouble? Was it worth the risk—not only to us, but to the people we interviewed? Investigative reporting, it seemed, had now become a crime.

Nearly all states have shield laws protecting the confidentiality of the relationship between reporters and their sources. California has an especially strong one that is incorporated into the state constitution; two decades before, as a cub reporter at the *Los Angeles Times*, I had to take the witness stand for all of about two minutes in a lurid murder trial in Orange County before it became clear that, under the state's shield law, I could not be forced to divulge the identity of a source who had provided me with a set of audiotapes containing jailhouse confessions by a man who'd set up his daughter to kill his wife. The federal government has no such shield law. Just a few weeks before the SWIFT story ran, in fact, Jim was part of the latest retreat for press freedoms.

In an extraordinary settlement, the *Times* and four other major news organizations reluctantly agreed to pay $750,000 between them to nuclear scientist Wen Ho Lee to help settle invasion-of-privacy claims he had made against the government over the publicity surrounding the spying investigation against him seven years earlier. Jim and four other reporters had been held in contempt of court—and were facing fines of $500 a day from their own pockets—for refusing to give up the names of the confidential sources who had discussed the Wen Ho Lee investigation. With the legal appeals exhausted, lawyers for the media companies saw little choice but to settle the case. In an uncomfortable turn of events, newspapers now had to pay for the press freedoms we had once taken for granted.

In the midst of the SWIFT imbroglio, I was scheduled to be interviewed about the story on PBS's *NewsHour.* The show was taping my end of the segment live from the *Times'* makeshift studio tucked in a small alcove at the back of our bureau. Curt Weldon, a Republican congressman from Pennsylvania, would also be appearing on the show from another location to talk about the banking story and the newspaper's decision to publish it. I could guess where Weldon stood on the question of publishing our latest story. Cultivating a tough-on-terrorism reputation, Weldon was Congress's biggest backer of data-mining and of the discredited notion that the Pentagon's Able Danger data-mining program had identified several 9/11 hijackers long before the attacks.

Less than five months later, Weldon would be voted out of Congress after it was disclosed that the FBI was investigating allegations that he had traded political favors for consulting fees for his daughter from a Russian oil firm. But now, as he took the air on PBS, Weldon was urging that prosecutors go after the leakers on the SWIFT story and bring criminal charges. The press, he suggested, was complicit when it "encourages that kind of activity" by supposed lawbreakers. "This is outrageous!" Weldon shouted repeatedly, so loudly that I had to pull the earpiece away from my ear. "*The New York Times*, a profit-making entity, designed to improve their bottom line to make a profit, has decided that they can supersede members of Congress from both parties who are briefed on these important programs for our national security," he thundered. That *The New York Times* would impose its own independent judgment in deciding when the public should know classified information, he repeated, "is absolutely outrageous!"

I wasn't going to try to outshout the congressman from Pennsylvania on national TV. We obviously held fundamentally different views on what the role of the press was supposed to be in America. Mine was something modeled after the independent press corps envisioned by Justice Hugo Black in the Pentagon Papers case, when he wrote that the rights of a free press were protected in the Constitution "so that it could bare the secrets of the government and inform the people." Weldon's perception of the press as part lapdog, part stenographer was one I barely recognized. I did manage to get in a few brief rejoinders on the air. The press, I said, "obviously has a fundamental role as a watchdog over government." That was a notion, I reminded him, "that's deeply embedded in our Constitution, and it's not a responsibility that the paper takes lightly." Another thought came to mind too, but I didn't bother voicing it to the faceless congressman still shouting at me on the other end of my earpiece. If the Curt Weldons and Alberto Gonzaleses of the world got to decide what the public had a right to know, I thought, we were all in trouble.

CHAPTER NINE

A Loyal Bushie

THE ATTORNEY GENERAL'S AGENDA for the day listed terrorism and Internet piracy, but Alberto Gonzales' mind was on baseball. In just a few days, Gonzales would be throwing out the ceremonial first pitch at a Washington Nationals baseball game early in the 2005 season, and he was nervous. "Whatever you do," former Texas Rangers co-owner George W. Bush had advised his new attorney general in prepping him for the debut, "don't throw short." Gonzales, as always, didn't want to let his boss down. Hoping to get in some practice time, he'd even thrown his baseball mitt in his bag for a business trip he was taking to Los Angeles. He had visions of breaking away from all the mundane official meetings with prosecutors, FBI agents, and Hollywood movie executives to get in a few practice tosses at Dodger Stadium—throwing off the same mound where a Mexican phenom, Fernando Valenzuela, had wowed the crowds at Chavez Ravine with his wicked screwball a quarter-century earlier.

The problem was, Gonzales' FBI security detail didn't think he had time for a side trip all the way up to Dodger Stadium in between his scheduled appointments. I was tagging along with the new attorney general on his L.A. trip to research a story I was writing about him, and in between his appearances at UCLA, Gonzales was telling me how disappointed he was that he wouldn't be able to make the trip to Dodger Stadium after all. If he wanted any practice time at all, his security people had insisted, it would have to be done at the UCLA baseball park nearby. It was that or nothing. "But you're the boss now," I said, goading him a bit. "Don't you get to tell them where you want to go?" His eyes lit with a determination that you rarely saw in Gonzales. He'd make another run at the Dodger Stadium idea, he decided. He marched away to find his security person. A short while later, Gonzales' caravan headed out for his next stop. "Dodger Stadium?" I asked Gonzales. He shook his head, his lip furled in disappointment. I had to stop myself from laughing. I knew what John Ashcroft would have done in the same situation. After all his famous run-ins with his own security detail, Ashcroft would no doubt have told them: "*I'm* the attorney general, and you do what I tell you." Then again, Gonzales' main mission at the Justice Department as the fledgling attorney general seemed to be to prove to everyone—to his security detail, to Congress, to the press, to the public, and, most critically, to George Bush—that Alberto Gonzales was *not* John Ashcroft.

So there we were a few minutes later at UCLA's Jackie Robinson Stadium. In the dugout were a handful of Gonzales' aides, hurriedly eating take-out lunches they had picked up on the way. Off to the side was the FBI security detail. On the field were a few coaches from the UCLA baseball team. And on the pitcher's mound was the odd sight of the attorney general, short and squat, dressed in shirt sleeves, a Washington power tie, and pinstriped suit sans jacket, trying to find his fastball. He was struggling. The first few pitches were in the dirt, bouncing away from the UCLA coach perched hopefully behind the plate sixty feet six inches away. "Don't want to do that," Gonzales mumbled to himself. Must be a case of pregame jitters. He remembered his mentor's advice: *Whatever you do, don't throw short.* Gonzales was never one to disobey George Bush's instructions.

The last few months had been difficult ones for Gonzales after a bruising confirmation battle, and there were already questions about whether Bush had made the wrong decision in tapping his old Austin statehouse lawyer to serve as the highest law enforcement official in the land. Much of the internecine warfare between the White House and the Justice Department had not yet become public, but what had leaked out—Gonzales' characterization of parts of the Geneva Conventions as "quaint" and "obsolete," the torture memos, and more—had not put him in a flattering light. The Democrats had pummeled him with the torture memos in his confirmation hearings, with thirty-six senators ultimately voting against him.

Four months later, it was clear that the wounds were still raw for Gonzales, as we shared a quick breakfast of muffins and juice that morning at a café in a Century City hotel. Gonzales always had a bit of a chip on his shoulder—the poor immigrant's son forever proving that he deserved the high place he'd earned—and it emerged in plain view now. "I was disappointed by the fact that I did not garner support from the Democrats," he told me as he nibbled on a muffin. "But that's now history. They did what they felt like they had to do. Now I'm going to work as hard as I can to show they made the wrong decision in not supporting me."

We chatted about his confirmation, about his agenda at the Justice Department, about his experience in the White House after 9/11, but I wanted to ask him more. I wanted to ask him about that NSA eavesdropping program. Five months before, he and I had sat ten feet across from one another at the Justice Department as he urged the newspaper's editors not to run the story. The program remained secret as we sat at the hotel café with an aide to Gonzales. The aide knew nothing about the eavesdropping operation, so I made an oblique reference to it to gauge Gonzales' reaction. If Gonzales got the allusion, he didn't let on, and I didn't press it. I figured it would wait for another day.

On the pitcher's mound, Gonzales dug his dress leather shoes into the dirt. Off near the dugout, Kyle Sampson, the deputy chief of staff to Gonzales and a trusted political advisor, was critiquing the attorney general's delivery. Sure enough, Gonzales finally hit his stride, throwing a string of fastballs through the strike zone and even a decent curveball or two. The UCLA coach behind the plate cheered on Gonzales. The attorney general smiled. A few days later, Gonzales was back in Washington for the real thing at the Nationals game. A smattering of boos didn't faze him as he sailed the opening pitch across the plate. Just the way the president would have wanted it.

WITH THE Justice Department's official seal at the top of the page, the neat, cursive handwriting seemed to wind its way off the right side of the page.

Dear Mr. President:
    Nothing in my life compares to the high honor of serving America as Attorney General in your administration.
    The cause of justice is indeed a serious calling. Americans have been

spared the violence and savagery of terrorist attack on our soil since
September 11, 2001 . . .

So began John Ashcroft's handwritten resignation letter to President Bush on November 2, 2004, the day of Bush's reelection to a second term in the White House. Ashcroft was the first of Bush's cabinet members to leave, but his resignation would not be announced for another week. Indeed, even after Ashcroft had quietly turned in his resignation to Bush, aides would float the idea in the media that he might stay on for a second term. There was no truth to the idea, but Ashcroft's people didn't want it to look like he had been forced out; Ashcroft would leave, as he always did, on his own terms. No one at the White House had told him it was time to go, Ashcroft always insisted. Perhaps no one had to state the obvious. To the White House, Ashcroft had become too much of a distraction, both publicly and privately, and it was clear that the White House wanted its own man at the Justice Department. The White House valued cabinet members who stayed on message; too often, it seemed, Ashcroft had his own agenda. The joke at the White House was that Ashcroft, the former senator from Missouri, still thought he was running for political office after all this time as a presidential appointee. The perception of him as a public grandstander—and the suspicions that he was putting his own interests ahead of the White House agenda—were key reasons in the view of administration insiders that he did not stay on for Bush's second term.

The tension and mistrust between the White House and the Ashcroft Justice Department had run deep for four years, although few realized just how abrasive the relationship had become. One of the first major flare-ups between Ashcroft and the White House had come just nine months after 9/11, as Ashcroft broke from his itinerary on an official diplomatic visit to Moscow and scheduled an urgent announcement from a Russian TV studio carried live on U.S. television one Monday morning. The live feed began airing on MSNBC even before Ashcroft realized he was on the air. "We have captured a known terrorist," Ashcroft began, clearing his throat. "Let's try that again," he said, his handlers brushing off his shoulders and applying hair spray. With the rehearsal over, the real announcement began. "We have disrupted an unfolding terrorist plot to attack the United States by exploding a radioactive 'dirty bomb,' " Ashcroft said, his tone made all the more ominous by an eerie orange glow that enveloped him on the air. Five times Ashcroft mentioned the "dirty bomb" that he said Jose Padilla, aka Abdullah Al Mujahir, a convert to Islam from the hard-scrabble streets of Chicago, was planning to detonate on U.S. soil on his return from Pakistan. Padilla, he said, "poses a serious and continuing threat to the American people and our national security."

Viewers were alarmed. The White House was furious. A live hookup from Moscow? A seething Dan Bartlett, the White House communications director, got a senior Justice Department official back in Washington on the phone within minutes for an explanation. "What the fuck are you guys doing?" Bartlett demanded. He ordered the FBI's Bob Mueller and Larry Thompson, the deputy attorney general, to do another press conference with the Pentagon in Washington to tamp down the story. The plot was in the discussion stages, officials at the follow-up stressed in more sober tones. "I don't think there was actually a plot beyond some fairly loose talk and his coming in here obviously to plan further deeds," said Paul Wolfowitz, the deputy defense secretary. By the time Padilla was charged in the criminal courts three years later with aiding al Qaeda after being held as an enemy combatant in a military brig, there was no mention by prosecutors of any dirty bombs.

Ashcroft had become, in the words of *The Washington Post*, "the de facto minister of fear." But for all the grumbling at the White House about getting Ashcroft to lower his profile, he remained a constant and often foreboding public presence in the critical early years after 9/11 in helping to shape public opinion about the war on terror. Ashcroft proved a useful tool for the White House: he got the word out, loudly and often, about the ongoing threat the country faced and the dangers of national disunity, and he allowed the White House, in a classic bit of good-cop, bad-cop, to distance itself from its vitriolic attorney general by adopting, at least in comparison to Ashcroft, a more measured tone. By design or not, both Bush and his attorney general profited from the arrangement, at least for a while.

In a career built on political showmanship, Ashcroft took his trade-craft to a new level in April of 2004 as he prepared to testify before the 9/11 Commission in the most critical phase of its investigation. The attorney general had endured several bruising rounds of verbal fisticuffs with the media in recent months, but now, with the historical telling of 9/11 itself at stake, he was intent on getting his message out to the public unfiltered—without the media in the way to distort the message. The Bush administration was under fire for its failings in the eight months leading up to the 9/11 attacks and, in Ashcroft's view, the commission's investigation had become a show trial, a political circus aimed at assigning blame. He felt the commission had treated Condoleezza Rice shabbily in her testimony a few days earlier, and he figured they were now out for a pound of his flesh too.

Ashcroft was never one to run from a fight. Under commission protocol, witnesses were expected to give the panel their prepared testimony a day ahead of time. Ashcroft, still stinging from testimony unearthed by the commission about his apparent inattentiveness to terrorism before 9/11, was in no mood to comply. In fact, as Ashcroft walked into the hearing room that day, an aide was sitting atop the prepared copies of his testimony, guarding them until the last minute. Commission staffers were left to wonder what was so explosive that the attorney general couldn't share it with them in advance like everyone else. One of the commissioners, Jamie Gorelick, who had been the deputy attorney general for Janet Reno for three years, walked over to Ashcroft in a side waiting area to greet him, one former Justice Department leader saying hello to a current one. Ashcroft's greeting seemed unusually terse. A few minutes later, as the tense hearing began, she discovered why.

"The single greatest structural cause for the September 11th problem," Ashcroft said at the start of his testimony, was the so-called wall—the set of bureaucratic, Byzantine regulations that restricted how and when intelligence officers and criminal investigators could share counterterrorism information. The government, he said, "had blinded itself to its enemies." Had the wall not been in place on September 11, Ashcroft suggested, the authorities might have known enough to move against Zacarias Moussaoui in Minneapolis and two of the 9/11 hijackers in San Diego. It was a sensational charge, but Ashcroft was just laying the mortar. The impediments were not a mere accident of bureaucratic ineptitude. "Somebody built this wall," he said. The foundation was laid, he said, in a classified Justice Department memo from 1995. "Although you understand the debilitating impact of the wall, I cannot imagine that the commission knew about the memorandum. So, I have had it declassified for you and the public to review." Ashcroft paused for dramatic effect. "Full disclosure compels me to inform you," he said, "that the author of this memorandum is a member of the commission."

On the dais a few dozen yards away, Gorelick sat stunned. Ashcroft didn't utter her name, but he didn't have to; everyone on the panel knew which of the ten commissioners Ashcroft was talking about. Gorelick was fuming. The one who built the wall, the one who was responsible for creating the bureaucratic impediments that had cost American lives, was sitting right there in the room. She had been attacked, on live television, with what she thought was a gross distortion of the historical record, and she wanted to return fire. She began scribbling notes on what she might say to Bush's attorney general. Slade Gorton, a Republican commissioner sitting next to Gorelick, nudged her on the arm. "Don't do it," he whispered. "Let me do it."

Gorton was almost as angry as his seatmate. He had worked with Ashcroft for six years in the Senate, and he considered him a friend. Sure, Ashcroft always had impassioned views on issues like abortion and social policy, but Gorton considered Ashcroft a man who spoke from principle, from truth and conviction. That is, at least until the moment Ashcroft let loose on Gorelick. "I was so shocked," Gorton recounted to me later, "because it seemed so out of character and so unprincipled. That's what outraged me so." Gorton faced off against his old Senate colleague for cross-examination. Why had Ashcroft's own deputy issued a memo just a month before the 9/11 attacks affirming that the Reno-era procedures on information-sharing "remain in effect today," Gorton wanted to know. And, he demanded, "if that wall was so disabling, why was it not destroyed during the course of those eight months?"

The dramatic episode—the witness on live television, the radioactive charge against an unnamed target, the secret evidence suddenly made public—had a certain McCarthyesque feel to it. And like the Wisconsin senator's accusations of communists in the government's midst a half-century before, most in the media could do little but parrot Ashcroft's whopper of a charge against Gorelick. What had been a civil if simmering controversy over which administration bore the blame for 9/11—Bush's or Clinton's—had now erupted into an all-out political slugfest. Ashcroft claimed victory. Commissioners who had once attacked him "now sat back in their chairs," he later wrote, and "necessary truths had been revealed." Few others, however, were ready to chalk up a win for Bush or his embattled attorney general. Far from intimidated, most of the ten commissioners were infuriated. "One ought to be careful about attacking a woman who has nine brothers," commissioner Richard Ben-Veniste muttered to another member of the male-dominated panel as they made their way out. On the commission, the episode became known simply as "Ashcroft's assault." Commission staffers and Ashcroft's people were barely on speaking terms for the remainder of the investigation. Before the mud-slinging, Gorelick was a typical Washington insider: well known and well respected inside the Beltway, virtually invisible outside it. That ended with Ashcroft's public attack.

Almost immediately, Republican leaders in Congress like Jim Sensenbrenner and Tom DeLay demanded Gorelick's resignation from the commission. Radio talk show hosts, op-ed columnists, and letter writers from Phoenix, Arizona, to Bangor, Maine, vilified her, blaming her for 9/11 and citing the conflict of interest posed by her continued role on the commission. Hate mail filled her in-box. And somewhere in New England, one man was so outraged by Gorelick's alleged complicity in the September 11 attacks that he phoned her home in suburban Washington. "You tell that bitch I'm going to blow up her and her family," the caller told the housekeeper who looked after Gorelick's two young children. The FBI sent in bomb-sniffing dogs to the home and traced the call to a pay phone in Boston before the trail went dead.

But like Senator McCarthy's thunderous accusations a half-century earlier, the charges rang hollow. Ashcroft's accusation—that Gorelick's 1995 memo was somehow to blame for erecting the "wall" that contributed to 9/11—was belied by the record. To blame Gorelick for erecting the infamous "wall" was a bit like blaming the ship steward for the sinking of the *Titanic*; she had laid, at most, one brick in the wall, and perhaps not even that. Gorelick's directive dealt with the sharing of intelligence information in a narrow and unprecedented situation— suspicions that defendants already indicted in the 1993 attacks on the World Trade Center might be involved in plotting attacks on witnesses and others. It established procedures for how intelligence information arising from that criminal case should be treated to avoid tainting the criminal process, and it had no bearing on the handling of terrorist information beyond that single case. Indeed, a detailed, sixty-two-page analysis prepared by the 9/11 Commission staff but never released publicly concluded that Gorelick's 1995 memo "had no role in the events of the summer of 2001."

It was the bureaucratic culture at the FBI and the Justice Department and the misinterpretation of years of guidelines—rather than any single memo or directive—that produced the communication breakdowns within the government that preceded the 9/11 attacks, the review said. The legal morass over how intelligence information could be shared spanned presidential administrations both Republican and Democratic, up through George W. Bush's, and as Gorton noted in his icy exchange with Ashcroft, the system was kept largely in place by Ashcroft's own deputy just a month before the September 11 attacks. Ashcroft's testimony, the review concluded, "did not fairly or accurately reflect the significance of the 1995 documents."

But Ashcroft wasn't done. Two weeks after his dramatic appearance before the 9/11 Commission, the Justice Department again suddenly declassified decade-old national security documents with Gorelick's signature on them and posted them on the department's Web site. It was the latest salvo in the Justice Department's public relations effort to paint the Clinton administration as culpable for the intelligence failures that led to 9/11. The 9/11 Commissioners were flying back from interviews they had conducted with military officials at the U.S. Southern Command in Florida when Gorelick got word on her Black-Berry about the Justice Department's latest document dump. Aside from penning a fairly understated op-ed piece in *The Washington Post* defending her record and vowing to finish her work on the commission, Gorelick had largely maintained her silence in the face of the onslaught of the last two weeks, even as the FBI investigated the bomb threat against her family. Now, she was even more livid than she had been during Ashcroft's initial attack at the hearing. "This is really outrageous," she told her fellow commissioners on board, shaking her BlackBerry. "The Justice Department has just declared war on me and the commission, and we've got to deal with this."

To her fellow commissioners, the tactic of declassifying the memos and posting them online rather than giving them to the commission as part of its work smacked of rank politics. Tom Kean, the Republican co-chairman of the 9/11 Commission, called Andy Card, Bush's chief of staff, from Andrews Air Force Base soon after they'd landed. "Andy, I'm mad, and this is going to be the first thing I ask about tomorrow," Kean said. Card knew what tomorrow was. The next morning, all ten commissioners were scheduled to interview Bush and Cheney about 9/11 in a meeting the commission had sought for weeks. The meeting began promptly at 9:30 a.m. in the Roosevelt Room, with Bush and Cheney seated in high-back chairs by a fireplace to greet their visitors. At the very start of the historic session, Bush went off script. "I want you to know," he told Gorelick and the other commissioners before taking any of their questions, "that I do not approve of the conduct of my attorney general, and I'm going to direct that that be known." Hours later, White House spokesman Scott McClellan delivered the same message publicly. The White House was not involved in the public release of the documents by the Justice Department, he assured reporters. The president was "disappointed" by the very public finger-pointing, McClellan said, and "it's been communicated to the Justice Department."

But if Bush's public rebuke was aimed at reining in his attorney general and getting him to lower his public profile, the gesture proved short-lived. Less than a month after the Gorelick dustup, in May of 2004, another confrontation was brewing with Ashcroft at the center, this time pitting one Bush advisor against another. Department of Homeland Security secretary Tom Ridge got word one Tuesday evening that Ashcroft was planning some sort of public announcement the next day on the rising threat of al Qaeda. That was usually Homeland Security's turf. Ridge's staff tried to raise someone at the Justice Department to find out what exactly Ashcroft was going to be announcing. They couldn't get any answers. That worried Ridge. He could only guess what was coming.

By now, the government's public warnings and ever-changing threat levels about al Qaeda—packaged in the form of ornately produced, color-coded bar charts—were becoming a growing embarrassment for Ridge and the Bush administration. Warnings that were once a source of public alarm in the months after 9/11 were instead now the stuff of public ridicule and punch lines. Ashcroft himself seemed to mock the warnings at times. In early 2003, he met with his senior U.S. attorneys in his private dining room, just as Ridge and his colleagues at

Homeland Security were enduring endless public needling over the new department's suggestion that Americans keep a supply of duct tape in their homes to seal off windows in the event of a chemical or biological attack by al Qaeda. As they sat around the long dining room table, Ashcroft told his prosecutors over bowls of ice cream how he had given a speech a few nights earlier at a black-tie event and was just about to walk out to the podium when he realized his bow tie was broken. He saw a piece of duct tape stuck to the wall, Ashcroft recounted, and used it to reattach his bow tie. "I'm convinced," Ashcroft said, "that God left that duct tape for me as a sign!" His prosecutors all guffawed at the odd post-9/11 imagery, but for Ridge, the gap in public credibility had become a serious worry.

The color-coded warnings were "awful, just awful," Ridge acknowledged in an interview I did with him after he left office. "Ashcroft and Mueller and Ridge getting up there and saying, 'Well, today there's a little bit more of a threat. But have a nice day. Go on about your business. Have a nice July 4th,' or Christmas or whatever it was—that just didn't fly." With each spike in the threat level, there was always the vague suspicion among many Americans that the White House was timing its dire warnings to gain political leverage or distract Americans from the damaging news of the moment from Iraq and elsewhere. When I asked Ridge directly whether political considerations had ever influenced the administration's decisions on the threat warnings, the perennial grin disappeared from his face, and he thrust both of his beefy forearms onto the conference table in front of him, offering himself up for a mock lie-detector test. "Wire me up," he demanded. "Not a chance. Politics played no part."

But members of the public weren't the only ones growing skeptical about the credibility of the threat reports. Some of Bush's senior advisors were having doubts of their own. A critical turning point had come in December of 2003, when U.S. intelligence officials began reporting dire concerns that al Qaeda was targeting specific flights to the United States from London and Paris. Ridge put the country on Code Orange—"high risk"—to brace for what he said was perhaps the greatest threat of a terrorist attack since 9/11. Bush gathered his national security team at the White House Situation Room to decide what they should do, with particular worry over an upcoming Christmas Eve flight from Paris to Los Angeles that U.S. intelligence officials had flagged as a possible target. Some of his advisors were already voicing doubts about how seriously to take the alarming new intelligence, but Bush was a president who often relied less on cold, sober analysis than on gut instinct to guide his decisions. "Would you let your son or daughter fly on that plane?" the president asked Ridge and his other senior advisors at the meeting. Around the table, heads shook. No, several answered, they wouldn't. "Well," Bush said, "neither would I." The flight, the president decided, had to be grounded. At the urging of the United States, the French grudgingly did just that, stranding holiday travelers, and American transportation officials ordered a slew of other flights grounded or even turned around in midair before they could enter American airspace. They scurried to deploy biohazard detectors and bomb-sniffing dogs around American airports and demanded that foreign allies post armed marshals aboard suspicious flights. America's newly created homeland security apparatus was now in full panic mode. No one was taking any chances.

Only weeks later would the whispers of skepticism among Bush's national security officials give voice to an unavoidable reality: the whole thing was a false alarm. One trigger for the scare, it turned out, was secret intelligence from U.S. code-breakers indicating that al Qaeda had managed to encrypt information on terror plots into reports on the Al Jazeera TV network; the flight numbers for targeted planes were purportedly hidden in code in the crawl lettering in Arabic at the bottom of the screen, some intelligence officials believed. There was nothing to it; just a series of unfortunate "overlays and coincidences," as Ridge put it, suggesting, wrongly, that certain flights were targeted. And the names of suspicious passengers on flight manifests scrubbed by intelligence officials turned out to have no known terrorist connections at all. One passenger on an Air France flight suspected of being an extremist Tunisian pilot, in fact, was just a little boy.

While the 2003 flare-up proved baseless, it created long-lasting tensions with European allies and air carriers. The Europeans, long accustomed to living with the threat of terrorism, believed America had gone jittery on them. And it left senior U.S. officials like Asa Hutchinson, who headed the massive Transportation Security Administration within DHS, to deal with the messy fallout. For Hutchinson, who had spent most of that Christmas week having to personally clear flights for take-off based on the cryptic information that the CIA was giving his agency, the episode was a sobering moment that left him increasingly skeptical about the filtered intelligence he was getting. He had to deal with the CIA's mess. It wasn't that he suspected politics was at play in the information he was getting from Langley; he just wasn't sure the CIA knew what it was doing. The next time, he decided, he wouldn't be made to fly blind. The next time, he would want to know for himself why exactly he and his agency were being asked to ground passengers, turn around planes, and screw up everyone's holiday plans.

The next time came a few months later, when Hutchinson and other Homeland Security officials began seeing a spike in classified reports from U.S. intelligence officials about possible plots and airline targets, much of it apparently culled from new CIA interrogations of "high-value" al Qaeda detainees like Khalid Sheikh Mohammed, the 9/11 mastermind captured in Pakistan the year before. The nervousness and chatter were rising once again, but this time, Hutchinson told a CIA staffer assigned to his agency at Homeland Security that he wanted to go over to CIA headquarters at Langley and examine the intelligence reports himself. "Why do you want to do that?" the surprised CIA staffer asked. That just wasn't done. The CIA and other intelligence agencies were zealous guardians of the sources and methods they used in collecting intelligence. In the climate after 9/11, intelligence officials were passing along to other agencies more classified information on terrorist threats than ever before, but it usually came in a "laundered" or cleansed format that left the reader guessing where the classified information was coming from and how solid it really was. After the embarrassment of the Christmas flight scares, that arrangement was no longer good enough for Hutchinson. He wanted to see for himself.

He cleared an afternoon on his calendar and drove across the Potomac River to CIA headquarters, where the agency agreed to set him up alone in a secure conference room, with a set of thick binders stacked on the conference table. For more than two hours, Hutchinson read line by line through the CIA interrogation reports on the debriefings of "KSM" and other detainees at secret CIA "black sites" as they talked of al Qaeda's operations and plots yet to be hatched. Operatives like KSM were notorious for trying to pass on disinformation to their captors, and it was impossible for Hutchinson to know as he sat there in the bug-proof room just how much of what he was reading reflected actual al Qaeda plots and, just as important, what rough methods the CIA interrogators had used to extract the information. Still, there was a certain comfort level for Hutchinson in getting the intelligence unfiltered, in seeing it with his own eyes. This wasn't based on some magic formula to decrypt Al Jazeera messages; this, he thought, was real.

Hutchinson's boss, Tom Ridge, knew better than almost anyone just how sketchy the intelligence could be—and just how much fear it could cause once it was put out publicly. That was one reason Ridge was so anxious that Tuesday evening in May of 2004 to find out what exactly Ashcroft was planning to announce on his own. The answer came the next morning in a leaked report on the front page of *The Washington Post*; citing unnamed officials, the piece said that Ashcroft and Mueller would be seeking the public's help to find al Qaeda operatives who might already "be in the country" to plot another attack. Ridge's department was supposed to be the one making pubic announcements about possible terror threats and attacks, but this episode, in Ashcroft's view, was a law enforcement matter. Sure enough, Ashcroft went before live TV cameras and a jam-packed press gallery at the FBI that Wednesday afternoon to make an urgent announcement. "Credible intelligence from multiple sources," Ashcroft said, "indicates that al Qaeda plans to attempt an attack on the United States in the next few months. The disturbing intelligence indicates al Qaeda's specific intentions to hit the United States hard," he said. With Mueller at his side, the attorney general stood ramrod straight in front of a display with the blown-up mug shots of seven suspected terrorists and the words "Seeking information: ALERT" in large block letters at the top. Officials had no details about an actual plot, Ashcroft acknowledged, but he said al Qaeda's preparations for another attack could be as much as 90 percent complete. The upcoming 2004 political conventions and other big summer events could prove "especially attractive targets for such an al Qaeda attack," the attorney general said.

Ashcroft took a few questions from reporters about the nature of these possible attacks. Then, a reporter asked the question that, in one form or another, came up at almost every press conference Ashcroft held on the threat of al Qaeda: How did he balance the need to keep the public informed about serious threats against "the inevitable criticisms that you're scaring people unnecessarily?" Ashcroft wasn't buying the premise. "We plan to make announcements whenever they would be in the national interest to make announcements," he said. "I just don't think my job is to worry about what skeptics say. My job is to do everything I can to protect the American people and to help the American people protect themselves."

Some of the skeptics, however, included his senior colleagues in the Bush administration. At Homeland Security, Ridge cringed when he heard Ashcroft's ominous forecast. The attorney general, Ridge said later, was working off "old intelligence." Inevitably, Ridge knew that the administration's critics would accuse Bush's team of trying to scare the bejeezus out of the public just as the presidential campaign was hitting its stride. Even as Ashcroft spoke before the TV cameras, Ridge was just completing a round of TV interviews that carried a very different message. Intelligence analysts were picking up "general, nonspecific threats against the United States," he said on CNN. "There is absolutely nothing specific enough or that rises to the level where we would presently, today as we speak, make a recommendation to the president to raise the threat level."

If the public was confused by the maddeningly mixed signals, so was the White House. At the next morning's White House intelligence briefing, Bush dressed down Ashcroft and Ridge in private, playing the part of schoolteacher scolding two unruly students in the hallway. Conflicting messages from two cabinet secretaries were simply unacceptable, Bush told them. "That will not happen again. Do I make myself clear?" Bush said. Ridge was chagrined. "The president was not happy with either one of us," Ridge said. "We both should have been singing off the same song sheet."

Ashcroft would serve another eight months as attorney general before turning in his resignation. Yet as rival officials at the Homeland Security Department liked to point out with no small measure of satisfaction, Ashcroft's warnings in May 2004 would be the last time he faced the cameras to announce a possible al Qaeda attack. Just two months later, when Ridge announced the threat of possible attacks against financial targets along the eastern seaboard—only to generate criticism himself for using old intelligence—Ashcroft was nowhere to be seen. The "minister of fear" had gone to ground.

. . .

A Loyal Bushie

WITH ASHCROFT GONE, Bush and his White House advisors wanted someone at the Justice Department who could execute the president's agenda without promoting his own. They wanted someone who could carry out the president's policies with the utmost discretion without creating the kind of public distractions that Ashcroft invariably created. They wanted someone who could keep his own lawyers at the Justice Department in tow without nibbling away at the legality of the central planks in the war on terror like the NSA's eavesdropping operation, the CIA's interrogation practices, or the Pentagon's terrorist tribunals. They wanted someone who would sign off on the White House's most extreme policies without having to send Bush's top aides over to the hospital for an emergency bedside visit. They wanted someone low-key and loyal, someone discreet, someone like Alberto Gonzales. And Gonzales, in turn, wanted to become the first Hispanic attorney general in history. In fact, his only real regret about taking the job, he would tell colleagues, was that he didn't get to see as much of Bush as he did in his days at the White House.

Gonzales knew the criticism he was bound to face when he was named for the job: that he was the president's lackey, a yes-man who would do whatever Bush, Cheney, and Addington asked of him without regard for the law. For hour upon hour at his so-called murder boards before his Senate confirmation hearing, administration officials playing the part of hostile Democrats prepared him by throwing every question they could imagine at him on all the dirty laundry just then starting to spill out of the White House. Then, before a skeptical Senate Judiciary Committee at his confirmation hearing in early January of 2005, he tried to address the rap on him head-on. Never a gifted orator, the soft-spoken Gonzales managed to strike at least a few of the right chords in making his case. "I will no longer represent only the White House, I will represent the United States of America and its people," Gonzales declared at the outset. "I understand the differences between the two roles. In the former, I have been privileged to advise the president and his staff. In the latter, I would have a far broader responsibility to pursue justice for all the people of our great nation; to see that the laws are enforced in a fair and impartial manner for all Americans. Wherever we pursue justice—from the war on terror to corporate fraud to civil rights—we must always be faithful to the rule of law. And I want to make very clear that I am deeply committed to

279

the rule of law. I have a deep and abiding commitment to the fundamental American principle that we are a nation of laws and not of men. I would not have the audacity to appear before this committee today if that commitment were not the core principle that has guided all of my professional endeavors."

Strong words—audacious, even—from a man whose job for the last four years in the White House had been, ever so quietly, to rein in the rebels at Justice Department. Now, he was being sent down Pennsylvania Avenue to run the asylum. In his first few months on the job in early 2005, Gonzales used his famously subdued demeanor to his advantage, positioning himself in the eyes of lawmakers as the anti-Ashcroft. The message was clear: in style and tone, at least, this would be a very different Justice Department with Judge Gonzales, as he liked to be called from his Texas days, on the fifth floor. Where Ashcroft often seemed impervious to his old colleagues in Congress, if he agreed to testify before them at all, Gonzales sat patiently and politely at Capitol Hill hearings, taking copious notes with a furrowed brow and promising to work with lawmakers in a new spirit of cooperation. Where Ashcroft derided the "phantoms of lost liberty" and mocked civil liberties groups, a smiling Gonzales invited them over to the Justice Department to sit down and chat over coffee and crumb cake. Where Ashcroft led the full-throated battle cry of the war on terror from his bully pulpit at the Justice Department, Gonzales preached conciliation and compromise with the administration's growing legion of critics. And for a while, it worked. "A sea change," Senator Russ Feingold called the new attorney general's attitude toward working with Congress to meet concerns about the government's antiterrorism powers. Just three months earlier, at Gonzales' confirmation hearing before the Judiciary Committee, Feingold himself had questioned Gonzales' "commitment to the rule of law." Now here he was singing from the "anyone but Ashcroft" hymnal in support of Alberto Gonzales.

But behind the wooden double doors of the attorney general's suite, Gonzales' policies were even more severe and unyielding than those of Ashcroft—and even less transparent. For all the public relations wizardry, his mandate from the president was clear: carry out Bush's agenda with a minimum of distractions.

Within his first month on the job, in February of 2005, Gonzales had the chance to prove to the White House his ability to do just that on a critical issue: the interrogations of suspected al Qaeda leaders like Khalid Sheikh Mohammed and Abu Zubayda. Months earlier, after the torture memos started leaking out, the administration had publicly rolled back some of the most extreme legal opinions of the Justice Department's Office of Legal Counsel, declaring the concept of torture "abhorrent." One of the authors of the restrictive new legal opinion, Daniel Levin, had even gone to a military base in 2004 to be water-boarded himself to find out just how abhorrent the practice really was before it could be used again on American prisoners. But with Gonzales now in charge at the Justice Department, the White House was privately angling for a way to get the advantage back and reassert the legality of the CIA's tough tactics.

Without legal cover, the CIA and its officers worried that they could face criminal prosecution for some of the tactics they were employing on their black site prisoners—things like head-slapping, frigid temperatures, and simulated drowning. The techniques might be okay one at a time, but could they use them *together* to exert maximum pressure on a prisoner to talk, perhaps dozens of times as in the case of 9/11 mastermind Khalid Sheikh Mohammed? With Gonzales at the helm, the Justice Department began drafting a secret legal opinion that would authorize the CIA to use many of the same old tactics en masse—a panoply of all its weapons. Now, Gonzales just needed to make sure someone would sign the authorization. His deputy, James Comey, always the agitator ever since he had led the hospital coup at Ashcroft's bedside the year before, made clear that he was dead-set against the latest torture memo. When the world eventually learned of it, he told colleagues angrily, they would be ashamed they had ever approved it.

But Gonzales had a willing partner in Steven Bradbury, the new acting chief of the Office of Legal Counsel. Often disengaged on day-to-day matters, Gonzales began meeting frequently with Bradbury on national security issues. Bradbury was on an odd tryout of sorts as head of the powerful legal office. After the internal fiasco the year before over the former head of OLC—Jack Goldsmith, the once trusted conservative who would go on to repudiate some of the White House's most important legal policies—Harriet Miers and other top Bush aides wanted Bradbury to prove his chops before he was nominated for the job. They didn't want another Jack Goldsmith. There were no conditions attached, no strings, administration officials would insist. No one was trying to dictate to Bradbury just what his legal opinions should look like, and Bradbury insisted he would never soft-pedal his legal conclusions to give the White House what it wanted. But there it was: Bradbury signed off on the opinion authorizing the CIA to use the extreme interrogation techniques en masse in May of 2005 and, a month later, the White House nominated him for the prestigious Office of Legal Council job. He'd passed the audition. Was the job a nicely timed coincidence, or a bone from the White House in exchange for his good work on the new torture opinion? Others in the building were left to decide for themselves, but they figured they knew the answer.

IN NOVEMBER OF 2006, as Alberto Gonzales was finishing up his second year as attorney general, there was plenty to keep him and his top aides busy. The administration was worried about another terrorist attack after the discovery three months earlier of an alleged British plot to blow up airliners bound for America. Justice Department appellate lawyers were trying to overturn the ruling from U.S. District Judge Anna Diggs Taylor in Detroit that the NSA eavesdropping program was illegal and unconstitutional. Democrats, after retaking both the Senate and the House that month, were promising tough oversight of Bush's war on terror after six years of Republican rule. Gonzales was directing a law enforcement roundup aimed at what aides described as his one true passion: going after sexual predators who preyed on children. Murder rates in many big cities were on the rise, congressmen were calling on the attorney general to do something about the growing violence at the Mexican border, and Gonzales and his people were preparing National Methamphetamine Awareness Day that November as their way of combating the drug's rising scourge across middle America.

Somehow, amid all that, Gonzales and his aides managed to find time to move ahead with an off-the-books plan that was many months in the making: a purge of United States attorneys around the country who were not considered "loyal Bushies." On November 15, Kyle Sampson—who by then had risen from critiquing Gonzales' fastball to serving as his chief of staff—sent an e-mail to Harriet Miers, the

White House counsel, along with her aide William Kelly and Deputy Attorney General Paul McNulty. The distribution list was intentionally small, and the contents were so closely held that even top officials at the Justice Department didn't know about it. Sampson, at the behest of the White House, had been secretly conducting a review to determine which of the ninety-three U.S. attorneys around the country should be let go.

At the outset of the process nearly two years earlier, Miers had pushed to fire them all. Even Gonzales thought it was a bad idea. Administration officials quickly backed away from the radical proposal, but they were determined to dismiss those they considered the weakest performers. But this was not a formal performance review. In the rough evaluation process used by Sampson, it meant ranking the prosecutors based in part on their "loyalty to the President and the Attorney General." Loyalty to the rule of law, it seemed, was secondary. Sampson was the keeper of the list, and some two dozen prosecutors had appeared on it at one time or another for possible firing. At one meeting at the White House, Sampson had even suggested getting rid of Patrick Fitzgerald—the widely respected federal prosecutor in Chicago whose investigation into the CIA leak case led to the conviction of Cheney aide Scooter Libby. Miers and others in the room gave him an "are you crazy?" look—the idea was apparently too politically radioactive even for them—and the idea quickly died.

By November of 2006, the list had been whittled down to eight prosecutors, and the administration was ready to move on it. Nothing like this had been done before. United States attorneys are political appointees who serve at the pleasure of the president, and during changeovers in administration, they are replaced as a matter of standard practice. But in the past quarter-century, only ten U.S. attorneys in total had been removed from office unwillingly by the administration that put them there, and those were usually for clear offenses like criminal or ethics violations. None of the eight U.S. attorneys slated for firing faced any accusations like that; their worst offense, it seemed, was that they didn't follow the Bush-Gonzales playbook. Sampson prepared a multistep plan on how the firings should be carried out, who should tell the prosecutors and the local senators, what should be said if questions were asked; every detail was synchronized to avoid possible disruption. In his November 15 e-mail to Miers, he sent along the plan.

Gonzales and his aides, in hindsight, misread almost everything connected to the purge and its political impact, but Sampson did get one part right. "I am concerned that to execute this plan properly we must all be on the same page and be steeled to withstand any political upheaval that might result," Sampson wrote in the e-mail. "If we start caving to complaining US Attorneys or Senators then we shouldn't do it—it'll be more trouble than it's worth. We'll stand by for a green light from you." Quickly, Miers gave it, with one question: What should the president be told?

Two weeks later, on November 27, 2006, Sampson, McNulty, and other top Justice Department officials met for an hour with Gonzales himself for his final sign-off. There was some debate about who had made it onto the final purge list. McNulty, the deputy attorney general, wanted to know about David Ogden, the U.S. attorney in Las Vegas. How had he gotten on the list? He seemed like one of the good guys. After some brief discussion, it was agreed that Ogden would stay on the firing list. There were other details to discuss: the eight U.S. attorneys would have to be told over the phone of their abrupt dismissals. Face-to-face meetings would invite a discussion of how and why this had happened, and no one wanted that. As the meeting neared a close, Gonzales' aides turned to their boss. As usual, Gonzales had sat quietly throughout much of the meeting, saying little of note. "What do you want to do?" someone asked him. He nodded to signal his agreement with the plan. "Okay," he said simply. The plan was on.

It was, for Gonzales, a typically understated command. But it would set in motion a purge that laid bare what Nancy Pelosi, the newly empowered House speaker, called the "rampant politicization" of the U.S. Justice Department. And it would ultimately empty the top ranks of the department's political appointees and cost Gonzales his own job after eight months of turmoil in a descent not seen at the Justice Department since Watergate.

Politicization. It's a tough word to pronounce, tougher still to define. Reagan's attorney general, Edwin Meese, faced accusations of it for much of his term, as he sought to impose a conservative cultural and legal agenda on the Justice Department. His Justice Department, one columnist in *Newsweek* maintained, was "little more than an agency to service the needs of President Reagan and, occasionally, the A.G. himself. His four-year reign was the archetype of politics over conscience, ideology over law." Clinton's attorney general, Janet Reno, faced the charge too over her refusal to appoint an independent counsel to investigate alleged campaign finance violations by Clinton and Al Gore, most famously centering on Gore's California fundraiser at a Buddhist temple. But what did the charge mean exactly? Even the hallowed Justice Department is not meant to be free of political influence altogether; the mantle of the presidency, the argument goes, brings with it the political perks of picking judicial nominees of a like ideological bent and leaving the standard-bearer's stamp on a range of legal policies, from affirmative action to abortion, so long as the existing law is followed. But where does shaping legal policy cross the line into blind political loyalty and disregard for the law? Ask Justice Department lawyers and historians, and the answer, much like Supreme Court Justice Potter Stewart's famous observation regarding obscenity four decades earlier, is that they know it when they see it. In the view of many career lawyers at the Justice Department, they saw it in the Bush Justice Department to a degree rarely noticed before in federal law enforcement, and it started long before Alberto Gonzales arrived as attorney general in 2005. "I understand you can never sweep politics completely away," said Mark Posner, who worked in the civil rights division of the Justice Department from 1980 until 2003, leaving before Gonzales' arrival. "But it was much more explicit, pronounced, and consciously done in this administration."

Indeed, the scandal that would come to engulf Gonzales had a certain "gambling in Casablanca" feel to it for anyone who had followed the workings of the Justice Department for the first six years of the Bush administration. Except that now, it was members of Congress playing the part of Captain Renault as they declared with a wink and a nod that they were "shocked, shocked to find that politics is going on here!" For others, the revelations of 2007 didn't come as much of a surprise.

Was it politics or policy when the Justice Department overrode the recommendations of career lawyers in a series of voting rights cases— including Texas, Georgia, and Mississippi—in ways that seemed to dilute the voting power of blacks and other minorities? From the very start of the Bush administration, the civil rights division had seen a marked shift in its priorities. What had been bread-and-butter priorities for decades, like bringing cases against employers or government officials who discriminated against minorities, were quickly seen by career lawyers as less pressing in the Bush administration's new paradigm. And issues that were rarely raised before, like bringing claims of religious-based bias on behalf of groups like the Salvation Army, were suddenly at the fore. With their mission turned on its head, career civil rights lawyers began fleeing the department. In 2003, during Ashcroft's tenure, eight staff members in the voting rights sections unanimously concluded that a Texas redistricting plan would violate federal voting rights law by weakening the electoral power of blacks and Hispanics, but they were overruled by the division's political appointees. "We're not going to politicize decisions within the department. We're going to make decisions based on what the law requires," Attorney General Gonzales told reporters after *The Washington Post* first disclosed the internal rift over the Texas decision. Whatever the motive, it did not escape notice that the decision to overturn the voting rights decision helped House Majority Leader Tom DeLay consolidate his power in Texas and, in turn, helped the Republicans keep control of the House of Representatives.

Was it politics or policy when the Justice Department's political appointees buried the findings of a statistical report on the aggressive treatment of black and Hispanic drivers by police? The numbers were sure to make a big splash if publicized, but the Justice Department never announced the findings because of a rift between the department's statisticians and the political appointees who oversaw them. The research study found that police in traffic stops nationwide were two and three times more likely to search the vehicles of blacks and Hispanics—and to use force against them—than they were with white drivers. The head statistician who ran the bureau, Lawrence Greenfeld, thought that was important data that belonged in the public announcement of the findings. His boss, a political appointee who was a close aide to Ashcroft, disagreed and ordered it taken out. Greenfeld, a twenty-three-year veteran of the statistics bureau, refused on principle, and the announcement never went out. A few months later, Greenfeld was called to the White House and, with just six months left until he was to get his pension, was informed that he was being removed as head of the bureau. The episode was a flashpoint in more than three years of simmering tensions between the statistics agency and the political appointees who oversaw it, and I first heard about

Greenfeld's dismissal from sources close to the agency who were fed up with what they saw as political meddling in their work. Greenfeld, for his part, remained a loyal soldier to the end. When I called and asked him about the episode, he seemed stunned to hear from a reporter, and he clearly wasn't comfortable with the idea of seeing his name in the media. This was a man used to generating numbers, not controversy. He'd clearly been mistreated in the whole episode by the political appointees at the Justice Department, but he wouldn't talk about any of the details. "I serve at the pleasure of the president and can be removed at any time" was all he would say at first. "There's always a natural and healthy tension between the people who make the policy and the people who do the statistics." When I asked him whether that tension had become worse in the last few years under the current administration, he grew quiet. "I'm not going to comment on that. It's just a fact of life."

Was it politics or policy when political appointees at Main Justice began overturning prosecutors' recommendations in record numbers beginning in 2001 in ordering them to seek the death penalty in capital cases? Beginning in the 1990s, the trend line in nearly all states and in the federal government had moved away from imposing the death penalty, but Ashcroft was a fervent believer in capital punishment, spurred in part by his Christian fundamentalism; "Because our lives have meaning, there are consequences to our actions, and we must learn to accept them," he wrote in explaining his views on the death penalty. He and his aides in Washington would seek to impose death in high-profile cases like the Zacarias Moussaoui terror trial and the prosecution of the Washington area sniper shootings in 2002, along with a bevy of smaller cases that few had ever heard of. Privately, federal prosecutors grumbled. In many cases, they believed the facts behind a routine gang slaying, a drug deal gone bad, or other murder prosecutions didn't justify seeking the ultimate penalty, and they had recommended against it. But many United States attorneys felt that the push for a "national agenda" at the Justice Department in the wake of the September 11 attacks had robbed them of their authority to decide local priorities and policies without meddling from Washington. The war on terror had emboldened Main Justice to consolidate its power in Washington as never before. In a carefully worded memo to senior Justice Department officials in Washington in early 2002 that was never made public, Patrick Fitzgerald, the veteran prosecutor in Chicago, gave voice to the concerns of many prosecutors about the way Washington officials were imposing the death penalty in local cases. No one was afraid to seek the death penalty when it was warranted, Fitzgerald wrote, but in many districts "there is a concern about our ability to have any meaningful input into the death penalty process." Washington's push to seek the death penalty in a wide assortment of cases threatened to tie up lawyers' time on marginal cases and swallow up the limited resources of the U.S. Attorney's Offices, he wrote, and defense attorneys were already reluctant to negotiate with prosecutors because of a sense that the real decisions were being made in Washington and that "our recommendation will not matter." Now, decisions on life or death were being made by the politicos in Washington.

Was it politics or policy when the Justice Department moved to jettison a landmark civil lawsuit brought by the Clinton administration against Big Tobacco? Bush had never liked the multibillion-dollar lawsuit, seeing it as a symptom of a "litigious society." And when Ashcroft came into office, he promptly declared his department's own case weak and tried to cut the funding for the litigation team that was preparing it. The case moved ahead anyway, but at the close of a lengthy trial in 2005 that exposed some of the tobacco industry's fraudulent and dangerous marketing practices, the Justice Department stunned the courtroom by slashing the damages it was seeking for its own case by $120 billion. What had happened? Political appointees at the department, it turned out, had ordered the career staff on the case to dramatically scale back their own case. The issue had come to a head at a Sunday afternoon meeting just prior to the closing arguments, as the career staff lawyers met with Robert McCallum, the number three official at the Justice Department and an old friend of the president's from their days together in Yale's Skull and Bones society, to discuss how the case would proceed. McCallum was adamant that the damages sought by the government had to be lowered drastically in light of a recent appellate ruling against the government. But Stephen Brody, the deputy on the tobacco team, wasn't backing down. "You're going to do it this way," McCallum ordered sternly as the two men sat across from each other at a long conference table. "This isn't going to work," Brody shot back. "It makes no sense, and we'll get torn apart. We'll get laughed out of court." "No," McCallum said. "Do it your way and you'll get laughed out of court." By now, the two men were leaning toward each other, voices rising. They looked like they might come to blows as Sharon Eubanks, the head of the tobacco team, moved to separate them. "Guys, guys, guys, stop." Brody clearly wasn't willing to prepare the closing argument that McCallum wanted to see delivered in court, so Eubanks offered a grudging compromise. "You write it," she told McCallum, "and I'll do it." The scaling back of the case had caused such distress at the Justice Department that one source provided me with a memo that the tobacco team leaders wrote in protest over the decision by McCallum and the political higher-ups. "We do not want politics to be seen as the underlying motivation" for slashing the damages sought in the case, the team leaders wrote, "and that is certainly a risk if we make adjustments in our remedies presentation that are not based on evidence." Their appeal went nowhere; the politicos won out.

Was it politics or policy when the Justice Department, soon after Ashcroft took over in 2001, began revamping its recruitment program for young law school graduates to give the attorney general more direct control over the hiring process? Applications for the prestigious program were once reviewed by nonpartisan section chiefs at the Justice Department, but Ashcroft and his aides complained that the process lent itself to a narrow selection of Ivy League graduates. They wanted to broaden the mix. In practice, liberal-leaning career lawyers complained, that meant hiring more young lawyers from conservative schools with Federalist Society credentials on their résumés. "If they're seen as Democrats," said Phil Heymann, a Harvard law professor who served as a senior Justice Department official in the Clinton administration, "they'll be out of the running."

It was this politicized climate that allowed the acting head of the Civil Rights Division, Bradley Schlozman, to boast of bringing more conservative lawyers into his division and to recruit more like-minded Federalist Society members to staff its ranks. And it was this climate that allowed an aggressive young lawyer named Monica Goodling, brought in to the Justice Department during Ashcroft's tenure from the Republican National Committee, to try to block the hiring of lawyers and prosecutors she considered "liberal" and to populate the department with those who were sufficiently conservative-minded. I'd first met Goodling in 2002, when she was a lowly public affairs person in the press office, and even then she had a sharp, mistrustful edge about her. We in the press, it seemed clear, were regarded as the enemy. She was my "chaperone" for one trip I took to rural Pennsylvania with a senior Justice Department official, Viet Dinh, the author of the Patriot Act, for a profile I was writing on Dinh, and she shadowed my every move, maneuvering her way in between Dinh and me whenever I would try to speak with him. I was writing a standard profile on an up-and-comer in the administration. What, I wondered, didn't she want me to see?

Within a few years, Goodling had risen to senior positions at the Justice Department, working as its White House liaison and as an aide to Gonzales. She soon acquired an influence over hiring decisions that belied her youth and inexperience, and at interviews with prospective employees at the department, Goodling, the product of a small Christian law school founded by evangelist Pat Robertson, would ask applicants what presidents they admired, what judges they liked, and even whether they had ever committed adultery. "Holy hires," the old-timers called the newcomers who passed the test. Quizzing candidates for top political appointments at the department about their political or cultural views was not altogether uncommon, but for career lawyers—nonpartisan employees hired to make sure the notion of equal justice applied to everyone—it was strictly verboten. Ultimately, a contrite Goodling admitted before Congress: "I know I took political considerations into account on some occasions. . . . I know I crossed the line."

FOR ALL THE VITRIOL that infects Washington, it is a place that usually lets its public servants die in peace. Even the most mediocre among them are allowed to leave office with a bit of their dignity intact. In the decorum of the capital, they are ushered out of town with carefully worded goodbyes from many of the same well-wishers who had helped banish them. All of which makes it even more remarkable that Alberto Gonzales, the most private of men, died such a public and agonizing death in Washington—a tortured symbol of all that had gone wrong with the Bush administration's notions of justice. With each public appearance on national television in the last months of his abbreviated tenure, with each misstatement and retraction he made before Congress, with each dubious assertion he tossed out, his credibility shriveled away to nothing. And Gonzales himself seemed to grow smaller with each barb thrown his way as he sank behind the blood-red felt tablecloth at the witness table. Even the president couldn't save him now.

Before anyone had ever heard of David Iglesias or Carol Lam or any of the other ousted United States attorneys, there was a sense among Justice Department officials that Judge Gonzales didn't have much of a grasp over the 110,000-employee Justice Department. He was struggling. That old Peter Sellers imagery from *Being There* kept coming up. It was the kind of unease felt but rarely spoken. Ashcroft had inspired passions in his underlings—intense loyalty from his defenders; thinly veiled contempt from his detractors. Gonzales inspired, well, nothing.

At one congressional hearing in July of 2006, Gonzales fumbled his way through questions about the NSA eavesdropping program, gun control, voting rights, and any number of other topics that he had to know he would be asked. Where Ashcroft appeared fearsome, Gonzales seemed simply ineffectual. "Ashcroft Nostalgia," read the headline on *The Washington Post* opinion page the next week over a column by Ruth Marcus. "Alberto Gonzales is achieving something remarkable, even miraculous, as attorney general: He is making John Ashcroft look good," she began. "I was no fan of President Bush's first attorney general, who may be best remembered for holding prayer breakfasts with department brass, hiding the bare-breasted statue in the Great Hall of Justice behind an $8,000 set of drapes, and warning darkly that those who differed with administration policy were giving aid to terrorists. But as I watched Gonzales testify before the Senate Judiciary Committee last week, it struck me: In terms of competence (the skill with which he handles the job) and character (willingness to stand up to the president), Gonzales is enough to make you yearn for the good old Ashcroft days."

Could we really be seeing a "Bring Back Ashcroft" movement in Washington? This was the kind of political commentary that would never make it into the news pages of a newspaper, but even tongue-in-cheek, it was an idea that I heard people at the Justice Department talking about for days. No one was endorsing the thesis outright, but

Marcus' column was a talker, always mentioned with a "Hey, did you read that?" look of intrigue. Remarkably, Ashcroft had his old rival Gonzales to thank for his renaissance.

Then, six months later, came the U.S. attorneys' purge. It was nothing at first. As Kyle Sampson had planned it, the firings—executed on Pearl Harbor Day, December 7, 2006—landed softly, with few people even noticing. Gone was David Iglesias in New Mexico, a military reservist who was once a favorite son in the Republican Party but had fallen out of favor in part because Republicans now saw him as too unwilling to go after voter fraud cases and corruption charges against Democrats; the head of the New Mexico Republican Party had even gone to Karl Rove at the White House to complain. Gone too was John McKay in Washington, who, like Iglesias, was seen by Republicans as tepid in investigating voter fraud charges that could have impacted the hotly contested 2004 governor's race in his state. And Carol Lam in San Diego, who was in the midst of one of the biggest public corruption cases in the country: the investigation surrounding the bribery conviction of Republican congressman Randy "Duke" Cunningham. And Bud Cummins, the Arkansas prosecutor who was moved out of the way simply because Karl Rove wanted to make room for a protégé. Then there was Paul Charlton in Phoenix, who'd raised a fuss internally at the Justice Department over Washington's insistence that he seek the death penalty in a capital case with no dead body and little forensic evidence to tie the crime to the defendant.

The prosecutors themselves were stunned by their abrupt dismissals. On word of her ouster, Margaret Chiara, the sixty-three-year-old prosecutor for western Michigan, pleaded with Justice Department officials in Washington to help her find another federal job for fear that "I will lose everything I have been working toward for the past five years." She begged for an explanation for her dismissal, anything to make sense of what had happened. "This makes me so sad. Why have I been asked to resign?" she asked McNulty, the top deputy to Gonzales, in one particularly plaintive e-mail. But publicly, Chiara and the other fired prosecutors kept silent. (She even joked in one e-mail to officials in Washington that she had started "an informal version of a 'witness protection program' to elude reporters!")

Little was made of the personnel moves, as dressed-up press releases were put out announcing the prosecutors' "resignations" and praising their many accomplishments and service to their country in the war on terror. U.S. attorneys come and go all the time—for better-paying jobs at tony private law firms, or just to reclaim their private lives. It wasn't even clear at first that anyone had been fired. There were a few stories in the local papers. Then the rumblings began. "I guarantee politics is involved," the head of the FBI's San Diego office, Dan Dzwilewski, told the local newspaper in regards to Carol Lam's unexplained resignation. (FBI officials in Washington later scolded Dzwilewski for making what they felt were "inappropriate" comments. Such matters, even if true, were best left unspoken.) Then Senator Dianne Feinstein of California brought up questions about the resignations on the Senate floor. It was a floor that Democrats, swept back into office two months before over public opposition to the Iraq war, now controlled. Had Republicans still been in power, there would have been no controversy, no investigation. But Chuck Schumer and the newly empowered Democrats saw a scandal in the making that they could seize, and seize it they did.

"How many United States attorneys have been asked to resign in the past year?" Senator Feinstein asked Gonzales at one January hearing as the controversy—barely a controversy—was still in its infancy.

"Senator, you know, you're asking me to get into a public discussion about personnel," the attorney general answered, squirming a bit in his seat.

"No, I'm just asking you to give me a number," Feinstein said. "That's all. I'm asking you to give me a number."

"You know, I don't know the answer to that question. But we have been very forthcoming . . ."

"You didn't know it on Tuesday when I spoke with you. [You] said you would find out and tell me."

"I'm not sure I said that, but . . . "

"Yes, you did, Mr. Attorney General."

"Well, if that's what I said, then that's what I will do."

It would only get worse for Gonzales. Soon it would emerge that the Bush administration, without anyone noticing, had managed to slip a key change into the Patriot Act that allowed it to appoint replacement prosecutors indefinitely without having to go through the courts. Then came the firestorm created by Gonzales' own deputy, Paul McNulty, when he acknowledged to the Senate Judiciary Committee in February that Bud Cummins in Arkansas had been let go simply to make way for a former aide to Karl Rove named Timothy Griffin. Gonzales was traveling in South America when word of McNulty's comments reached him. "The attorney general is extremely upset with the stories on US attys this morning," Brian Roehrkasse, a top press aide traveling with him, told officials in Washington in an e-mail. "He also thought some of [McNulty's] statements were inaccurate." Roehrkasse suggested some PR strategies for containing the damage, but added: "I think from a straight news perspective we just want the stories to die."

Gonzales' reaction to McNulty's testimony showed a tin political ear that would hasten his undoing. He was upset that McNulty had suggested that Cummins was removed in Arkansas for political reasons unconnected to his performance. What would ultimately prove much more damaging to Gonzales, however, was the *rest* of what McNulty told Congress: that the other fired U.S. attorneys had been let go for "performance-related" issues. The implication was that these were deadwood prosecutors who deserved to be fired. For weeks, the prosecutors had stayed largely silent as the controversy unfolded. But with McNulty's broadside, one by one, they returned fire. Their professional reputations were now on the line. All but one of the fired prosecutors had positive performance evaluations, and few of them were ever told of any concerns about their performance before their sacking. "Now that the record is out there in black and white for the rest of the country to see, the argument that we were fired for 'performance-related' reasons (in the words of Deputy Attorney General Paul McNulty) is starting to look more than a little wobbly," David Iglesias, the Navy reservist who was one of the first to start fighting back publicly, wrote in *The New York Times*. Politics, he said, clearly played a part in the dismissals.

Then came evidence of a series of unsolicited phone calls that Michael Elston, a top aide to McNulty, had made to at least four of the ousted prosecutors in January and February as the publicity was growing. Elston's tone was "sinister," John McKay, the fired prosecutor in Seattle, said in handwritten notes he turned over to Congress, and it was clear to McKay that Washington wanted him to stop saying things publicly about his dismissal in defending his reputation. The message, McKay said, was unmistakable: Elston was trying to "buy my silence by promising that the attorney general would not demean me in his Senate testimony." Paul Charlton, fired in Phoenix, related a remarkably similar conversation with Elston. He called the proposal "a quid pro quo: my silence in exchange for the attorney general's." Sinister threats and quid pro quos? These were the kinds of charges usually levied against gangsters in racketeering trials, except that now it was a group of fired federal prosecutors making the charge of witness intimidation against senior Justice Department officials in the Bush administration.

In the view of even his senior aides, Gonzales himself seemed oblivious at times to the potential damage the scandal might cause him as it was unfolding. "There was no wrongdoing here," Gonzales told aides huffily in one private Justice Department meeting. "I don't even understand what the issue is." Kyle Sampson, despite his clear mishandling of the U.S. attorneys' purge, was seen within the Justice Department as a workaholic chief of staff who managed to keep things moving for Gonzales. When Sampson resigned in March and became the first in a string of casualties in the U.S. attorneys affair, Gonzales was left even more rudderless than he had been before. The department proved unable to navigate the barrage of document demands from congressional Democrats, ensuring a *drip, drip, drip* of embarrassing releases of thousands of documents and internal e-mails that became fodder for many weeks of damning headlines. As Democrats demanded more answers, Gonzales seemed reluctant to prep for the congressional hearings, telling staffers that he could handle the testimony on his own. And his own aides were at odds over the best strategy for dealing with the rampaging Democrats. Some aides wanted Gonzales to become more aggressive in confronting his accusers, but the more lawyerly minded aides in the room—apparently fearing a perjury trap if Gonzales misspoke again—favored a conservative approach, advising the attorney general to point to his faulty memory when pressed for details.

The "I don't recall" strategy won out, and it was a disaster. In one congressional appearance after another, Gonzales gave muddled or even contradictory responses about key issues in the controversy: how the firing list was developed, who weighed in, his own level of personal involvement, the role of Karl Rove and the White House, the impact that sensitive political corruption investigations had in determining who was ousted, and more. Sixty-four times at one particularly painful Senate Judiciary Committee appearance in April, Gonzales said he couldn't remember key details. One protester in the audience even put aside his antiwar poster and replaced it with a running "I don't recall" tally. It was a remarkable scene even in the view of normally stalwart Republican allies. Senator Jeff Sessions, an Alabama Republican and a former federal prosecutor himself, wanted to know why Gonzales had initially denied any involvement in discussions about the firings, when his own aides testified he was briefed on the final purge list at the critical November 27 meeting and green-lighted the plan.

"Senator, I have searched my memory," Gonzales said haltingly. "I have no recollection of the meeting. My schedule shows a meeting for 9 o'clock on November 27th, but I have no recollection of that meeting."

"This was not that long ago," the white-haired senator said in his thick Alabama drawl. "This was in November of last year?"

"According to my calendar, November 27th," Gonzales answered.

"And Mr. Sampson seemed to indicate that he really, he understood it was a momentous decision, that there would probably be political backlash," Sessions said with some measure of amazement. "He even performed some outline about how that should be managed. And you don't recall any of that?"

The attorney general hemmed and hawed a bit more before an exasperated Sessions told him: "Well, I guess I'm concerned about your recollection, really, because it's not that long ago. It was an important issue. And that's troubling to me, I've got to tell you."

With Gonzales' disastrous performance, he had lost whatever meager support he could once claim from congressional Republicans. The attorney general had always counted a constituency of one—President Bush—and that was now about all he had left. Less than a month later, however, even that bond would be tested by a fresh round of damning accusations from Gonzales' own former deputy.

This was Jim Comey's payback. Ostensibly, the former deputy attorney general was called to testify before the Senate Judiciary Committee on May 15 about the firings of the U.S. attorneys. But in a carefully scripted bit of theatrics, Chuck Schumer, leading the assault on Gonzales, had one small piece of business he wanted to address first. He wanted to know about that visit that Gonzales had paid to Ashcroft's hospital room over the NSA's secret eavesdropping program.

"Can you remember the date and the day?" Schumer began.

"Yes, sir, very well, it was Wednesday, March the 10th, 2004," Comey answered.

"And how do you remember that date so well?"

"This was a very memorable period in my life, probably the most difficult time in my entire professional life. And that night was probably the most difficult night of my professional life, so it's not something I'd forget."

Was he troubled by the conduct of Gonzales and Andy Card at the hospital that night? "Yes," Comey answered. Reporters started to perk up in their seats in the audience, their notepads and laptops now out. This was getting good. Why, Schumer asked, had he gone to the hospital that night?

Comey hesitated for a few long seconds, all eyes in the Senate hearing room on him. "I've actually thought quite a bit over the last three years about how I would answer that question if it was ever asked," Comey answered finally, "because I assumed that at some point I would have to testify about it." So began one of the most dramatic mornings of testimony that anyone on Capitol Hill could remember. In a minute-by-minute narrative, Comey filled out in vivid hues the rough outline of the hospital episode that we had put on the front page of the newspaper that New Year's Eve sixteen months earlier, and he added dimensions to it that we had never even imagined. With Hollywood bravado, he recounted racing up the stairs of the hospital to beat Gonzales and Andy Card to Ashcroft's bedside; watching the ailing Ashcroft lift his head from his pillow to refuse Gonzales' pleas to sign off on a program that the Justice Department now thought might be illegal; threatening to resign, along with virtually all his aides, over the showdown with the White House; and appealing personally to President Bush to try to break the impasse over executive power.

"I was very upset. I was angry," Comey said of Gonzales' bedside visit. "I thought I had just witnessed an effort to take advantage of a very sick man."

For once, even the always loquacious Chuck Schumer seemed at a loss for words. "The story makes me gulp," the senator said as Comey finished the narrative. By noon, video of Comey's testimony from C-SPAN would begin caroming around the Internet courtesy of YouTube. By afternoon, congressmen would begin calling for a perjury investigation against Gonzales over his repeated claims that there had never been any serious legal disagreement over the NSA's eavesdropping program. And by nightfall, the calls for his resignation would only accelerate.

The Democrats could now sit back and watch as their colleagues across the aisle lambasted Gonzales. The attorney general was back two months later at his old battleground—the Senate Judiciary Committee—and Senator Arlen Specter, the ranking Republican who had struggled unsuccessfully for more than a year to come up with new legislation governing the NSA's wiretapping powers, didn't try to hide his disgust. "First of all, Mr. Attorney General," Specter demanded, "what credibility is left for you when you say there's no disagreement and you're party to going to the hospital to see Attorney General Ashcroft under sedation to try to get him to approve the program?" When Gonzales insisted that the hospital disagreement centered on "other intelligence activities" unrelated to the NSA eavesdropping, Specter was incredulous. "Mr. Attorney General," Specter said, "do you expect us to believe that?"

The pressure for Gonzales to resign was now intense from all quarters. Some aides suspected that even Gonzales' wife, Rebecca, who was as outgoing as he was introverted, was pushing him to step down. She would read his negative press clippings and contact Justice Department aides in a huff to find out why they weren't doing more to defend the honor of a man she thought was being unfairly pilloried in the media. No doubt the scandal was taking a toll on the couple and their teenage sons, but Gonzales, for his part, remained mostly silent as always about his plans. Publicly, he showed no sign of backing down to the Democrats, and Bush was unqualified in his support for his attorney general, dismissing the attacks on him as "political theater" by the Democrats. He even praised Gonzales' testimony before Congress, leaving Senate aides to wonder if the president had watched the same performances as they had. For aides at the Justice Department, there was a growing sense that Gonzales' continued presence was bogging down some of the department's key initiatives, including its most pressing legislative priority: getting Congress to change the foreign intelligence law to essentially legitimize what the president and the NSA had done in their secret eavesdropping program. With Gonzales still atop the department, aides realized, the debate would be inexorably clouded by the role of the attorney general himself. Despite the misgivings, Gonzales gave no indication to other senior officials that he was thinking of leaving. Just the opposite: he would talk with his aides about law enforcement initiatives many months down the road, as if he'd be around to shepherd them through.

Then, one Saturday night in late August, another reporter in the *Times'* Washington bureau, Eric Lipton, who had been tracking the U.S. attorneys scandal for months, got an urgent message from a source on Capitol Hill. Still sweating from a quick workout at his Dupont Circle gym, Lipton called back the source from the locker room to find out what was happening. "The attorney general is going to resign," the source said. "It is going to happen in the next couple of days. We have this from an extremely reliable source. It is going to happen." Lipton let the weekend editor on our Washington desk know what he'd heard, then hurried home on his bike to try to figure out if it was true. This was an all-hands-on-deck tip, a huge scoop if true, so the night editor called several other reporters in the bureau to see if they could help confirm the story. I was among them. I had only been back from my book leave for a few weeks when I got the 9 p.m. call from the news desk with the tip. "Lipton heard Gonzales is resigning," the night editor told me.

I started making some calls to see if I could find out anything, but in the meantime, Lipton had managed to reach Brian Roehrkasse, the top spokesman at the Justice Department, who was on vacation on the West Coast. Roehrkasse didn't think there was anything to the rumor, but he promised to check it out. Minutes later, Roehrkasse got Gonzales himself on the phone. No, Gonzales assured his press aide, there was nothing to the rumor; tell the *Times* he's not resigning. Roehrkasse passed on the word from Gonzales. "The Attorney General is not resigning," he told Lipton in an e-mail. "So it is a rumor." It was a strong denial. When public officials are confronted by reporters with news that they don't want out, they usually rely on the timeworn "no comment," but here was the Justice Department denying the story outright. With the White House soon denying the story too, Lipton decided to meet up with his girlfriend, late for a Saturday night dinner because of a lead that had fizzled out. Something told him the tip was probably accurate, but without a second source to confirm it, there was nothing he could write. The next day, the *Times'* Phil Shenon got the same response from Roehrkasse: the attorney general was not leaving.

The day after that, we found out the truth. The White House, early that Monday morning, announced that Gonzales was stepping down. "After months of unfair treatment that has created a harmful distraction at the Justice Department," President Bush said from his home in Crawford, Texas, "Judge Gonzales decided to submit his resignation, and I have accepted his decision." In fact, the decision had been made on Friday, the day before Lipton started canvassing the Justice Department. By the time Gonzales and the Justice Department were busy knocking down Lipton's purported rumor on Saturday night, it was a fait accompli: the bedraggled attorney general had already turned in his resignation, and Bush had already accepted it. It made for the perfect coda to the attorney general's downfall. After all the bobs and weaves the newspaper had seen from the Bush White House these last two tumultuous years, after all the accusations about Gonzales' honesty these last eight months, it seemed only fitting that his final act was to deceive *The New York Times* one last time. As farce, Oscar Wilde himself couldn't have written a better ending.

EPILOGUE

Toward the end of his term as the country's first-ever secretary for homeland security, Tom Ridge was visiting with a senior European dignitary during an overseas diplomatic trip. The talk between the two men turned to America's standing in the world in the age of terrorism, and Ridge's friend grew somber. America's indefinite detention of hundreds of men at Guantánamo Bay, its harsh treatment of prisoners, its overall prosecution of the war on terror—all had left a stain on America's once-proud place in the world community, Ridge's friend told him in sober terms. "The rest of the world looks at you differently than you look at yourselves," the diplomat told Ridge. "You project yourselves internationally as a unique nation of law and due process and transparency, yet you conduct your affairs in a way very different from the rest of the world."

Ridge sat silent for a moment, then nodded his head. He might quibble with some of his friend's harsh rhetoric, but the overall sentiment seemed inescapable. America, in the eyes of its allies, was losing its moral authority as a nation of laws. "I agreed with him," Ridge said as he related the scene to me some two years later. His friend's words still stuck with him that long afterward. "The notion that we would detain all those individuals at Guantánamo indefinitely never made a hell of a lot of sense to me," Ridge said, shaking his head. This, from the man President Bush had installed to defend the homeland. Ridge and his colleagues weren't just fighting al Qaeda; they were fighting world opinion, and all the resentments that America's extralegal policies brought with them as well.

As the years passed after 9/11, echoes of this theme emerged more and more frequently in my interviews with government officials— from senior policy-makers like Ridge on down to street-level agents. America had started out fighting the good fight after 9/11, making good on Bush's promise, as he stood atop that wrecked fire truck at Ground Zero in September of 2001, that "the people who knocked down these buildings will hear all of us soon." But somewhere on the road to retribution, there was a sense that America had lost her way.

Yes, the nation had avoided another attack. Whether it was the result of smarter defense, or stronger offense, or luck, or patience by al Qaeda, or some combination of all these factors, no one was quite certain. But everyone was thankful for it, even as they prayed that it held true. In the months after the attacks, Bush and his aides were given wide berth to do whatever it took to stop the much-feared "second wave" of attacks, and many of the changes put in place to fortify the country were no doubt essential and overdue. Few blinked at the beginning when Bush declared the country was in a state of emergency, a wartime footing. The problem, even in the view of many counterterrorism officials in Bush's own administration, was that the state of emergency never ended and that the modus operandi—the extralegal measures; the obvious disdain for oversight from Congress, the courts and international allies; the intense secrecy and lack of transparency—all continued unabated as part of that wartime footing. There was little attempt to go back to Congress to get clear authority for some of the secret programs the administration had been running. There was little attempt to take a breath, to step back a year or two after the attacks and say: What now? As Ridge put it to me: "Shouldn't we be talking about adjusting the adjustments? Or do we want to operate in this new world permanently?"

The answer, in the view of Bush, Cheney, and senior national security advisors like David Addington, was a clear yes. Their war on terror was indeed an unending one. "I have never said we could win it in four years," Bush told NBC's Matt Lauer in 2004, just days before accepting the GOP nomination for his second term as president. "I don't think you can *win* it." What you can do, he said, was to keep al Qaeda on the run through every means possible. "The country must never yield," Bush said, "must never show weakness."

As the end of President Bush's term neared four years later, the shards left by the implosion of his administration's saber-rattling terrorism policies lay strewn everywhere.

At the Justice Department, the ghosts of the administration's war on terror shadowed Michael Mukasey even before his first day as attorney general. Alberto Gonzales was gone in disgrace, off to give speeches about Bush's war on terror for a reported $40,000 an appearance. Mukasey, a man with a reputation as a sober, fair-minded judge and prosecutor in New York, was Bush's safe pick to replace him and try to right the Justice Department. It wouldn't be easy. Mukasey saw his own nomination nearly scuttled in the Senate by his dogged refusal to say whether he thought the CIA's past practice of water-boarding senior al Qaeda leaders amounted to torture. The judge was a caretaker, inheriting a mess that was created on someone else's watch, but now it was Mukasey's mess too, and he couldn't run from it.

Only three weeks into his new job, in December 2007, Mukasey would find that out. The administration was already bracing for the results of what promised to be bruising internal investigations at the Justice Department into both the NSA wiretapping program and the firings of the U.S. attorneys when another bombshell hit. The *Times* discovered that the CIA had destroyed hundreds of hours of videotaped interrogations of two al Qaeda prisoners, showing the rough and possibly illegal tactics used to get them to talk. General Hayden, the former NSA director who oversaw the agency's wiretapping program and was now running the CIA, said the tapes were destroyed for the safety of the agency interrogators pictured in them, but even normally supportive Republicans scoffed at the explanation. Critics demanded the appointment of an independent counsel to investigate the destruction of tapes that contained possible evidence of torture and criminality, but Mukasey balked from the outset. His Justice Department, he said, could investigate the Bush administration's actions itself. When Mukasey and the Justice Department refused initially to turn over material to Congress on the destruction of the tapes because he said it would impede the department's own investigation, Republican congressman like Pete Hoekstra accused Mukasey's department of "obstruction."

There would be no honeymoon for the new attorney general, not with the Bush administration's counterterrorism tactics under such sharp scrutiny. It seemed that anyone associated with the administration's policies, even a newcomer held in high regard, risked being tainted by its legacy. By the time Mukasey made his first appearance before the Senate Judiciary Committee in January of 2008, his tap-dancing on sensitive topics like the CIA's use of tough interrogation tactics looked little different to lawmakers than the two-step they had seen from Gonzales a few months earlier. Whipsawed officials at the Justice Department had to wonder whether a "Bring Back Alberto" campaign could be far behind.

THE SUMMER OF 2007 brought a sobering report from U.S. intelligence officials, concluding that America was losing ground to al Qaeda on a number of key fronts, most notably in Pakistan, where Osama bin Laden was still believed to be in hiding along the rugged Afghan border six years after the September 11 attacks.

The finding echoed the stark conclusions of another formal intelligence assessment less than a year earlier, which made clear what many critics of the Iraq war had long feared: that the U.S. invasion there—predicated in part on the false link between Saddam Hussein and the 9/11 attacks—was helping to breed more anti-American hatred and extremism among violent strains of Islam. "The Iraq conflict," the intelligence agencies' own formal assessment concluded, "has become the 'cause celebre' for jihadists, breeding a deep resentment of U.S. involvement in the Muslim world and cultivating supporters for the global jihadist movement." Bush, who had argued for much of the last three and a half years that the war in Iraq had made America safer, rejected the core conclusion that his war had in fact helped breed another generation of terrorists. "Does being on the offense mean we create terrorists?" he scoffed. "My judgment is the only way to defend the country is to stay on the offense."

At home, meanwhile, opposition to the war in Iraq continued to surge to a record high by 2008, with sporadic protests in Washington and elsewhere around the country drawing large numbers of demonstrators. Now, however, government officials seemed less intent than they once were about keeping an eye on the protesters—or at least they were more discreet about it. After the embarrassing stories in the *Times* and other media outlets a few years earlier about the government's interest in seemingly peaceful protests, there were fewer complaints about the FBI's tactics. And the Pentagon in 2007 dropped its controversial Talon database altogether after the public disclosures that it had been used to collect information on war protests at churches, college campuses, Quaker meeting houses, and the like. The program, military officials acknowledged, had become too discredited to be of much use. James Clapper, the first intelligence chief at the Pentagon in the post-Rumsfeld era, made the dismantling of Talon one of his first acts in the new job, an important symbolic gesture meant to move past the tumult of the last few years. Whatever new system the Pentagon would put in place to analyze actual threats to its military installations, Clapper said, "must lay to rest the distrust and concern about the department's commitment to civil rights."

IN THE COURTROOM, the Bush Justice Department struggled as well. As a rule, federal prosecutors win nearly all the cases they bring in court. That had long been true even in the notoriously complicated realm of prosecuting terrorism and national security cases—at least until 9/11 and the new "preemptive" strategy of moving against terrorist suspects before they could strike. Now, for every much-trumpeted conviction, there was an embarrassing defeat at the hands of a skeptical jury.

In Miami, prosecutors failed to get a conviction in December 2007 against any of seven immigrants accused of plotting to blow up the Sears Towers in Chicago, with jurors clearing one defendant and deadlocking on the six others.

In Dallas, prosecutors failed to get a single guilty verdict on any of 197 counts brought against five leaders of the Holy Land charity accused of funneling money to Palestinian terrorism. The case was once seen as perhaps the administration's flagship prosecution of terrorist-financing. Secretly, investigators had been using financial data from the SWIFT database to track the charity's money, but the prosecution collapsed once the jury began to consider the allegations. "There were so many gaps in the evidence," said one juror afterward, "I could drive a truck through it."

In Tampa, the much-ballyhooed case against Sami al-Arian, a university professor accused by John Ashcroft of being the clandestine North American leader of Palestinian Islamic Jihad, ended without a single guilty verdict against al-Arian or three codefendants after an elaborate five-month trial. Prosecutors ultimately had to work out a plea deal with al-Arian on a much lesser charge, as they sought the ex-professor's deportation.

Even Zacarias Moussaoui, an admitted member of al Qaeda who had become a poster boy for violent jihad and bragged about wanting to fly a plane into the White House on September 11, escaped the death penalty. The government's high-profile case was hobbled by charges of witness tampering against one of its own lawyers. The jury rejected the death penalty in favor of a life sentence for Moussaoui, but even that verdict appeared imperiled by the discovery that the CIA had destroyed the tapes of its al Qaeda interrogations—tapes that Moussaoui's lawyers maintained should have been turned over to them to aid in his defense.

Then there was Rick Convertino, the black-sheep prosecutor who brought the case against the four Detroit men accused of operating an al Qaeda sleeper cell in the first terrorism case after the September 11 attacks. Six years after Convertino climbed that rickety ladder up to the roof of the warehouse in Turkey in search of al Qaeda's next target, the ex-prosecutor was back in court on the case in 2007—this time as a defendant accused of covering up evidence to win a conviction. Again, the Justice Department failed to prove its case, and Convertino walked out of court a free man after a jury took less than a day to declare him not guilty. Suddenly, there was a newfound credence to Convertino's claims that the Justice Department had brought the charges against him in retaliation for his speaking out publicly about the mismanagement of the war on terror. The department's case against him, Convertino declared outside the federal courthouse, was "a politically motivated prosecution that never should have been brought."

ONE BY ONE, the cornerstones of the administration's legal policies were being knocked away. And by 2008, federal judges seemed locked in battle to see who could summon the most fire and verve in condemning the government's extralegal tactics in waging war on al Qaeda.

"For over 200 years, this nation has adhered to the rule of law—with unparalleled success," U.S. District Judge Anne L. Aiken of Oregon wrote in September 2007 in ruling on the tangled case of Brandon Mayfield, the Portland lawyer who was mistakenly locked up three years earlier in connection with the Madrid bombings. "A shift to a nation based on extraconstitutional authority is prohibited, as well as ill advised," she said. Mayfield, as part of his two-million-dollar settlement with the government, had extracted one unusual condition: the right to continue suing the government over its use of the Patriot Act against him. With Aiken's ruling, he got what he wanted: a judge's determination that the expanded power given to the government under the Patriot Act—allowing the FBI to secretly search his home and bug his family's conversations—was unconstitutional.

That same month, across the country in Manhattan, U.S. District Judge Victor Marrero struck down as unconstitutional a separate part of the Patriot Act governing the FBI's expanded use of national security letters to demand records. The judge blanched at the undue secrecy surrounding the FBI's records demands, and he warned ominously about "the hijacking of constitutional values."

And even the appellate court renowned as the most conservative in the country—the Fourth District Court of Appeals in Richmond, Virginia—was unwilling to give Bush the type of unchecked wartime authority that he and his aides had claimed. The court dealt the administration a crushing defeat in June of 2007 when it found that an immigrant from Qatar named Ali al-Marri had been wrongly detained by the military as an "enemy combatant" for four years and denied the writ of habeas corpus to challenge his detention.

Al-Marri, unlike other suspected al Qaeda operatives held as enemy combatants, was captured on American soil, not overseas, and he was in this country legally with his wife and children on a student visa. The appeals panel that heard the case was scathing in ordering that al-Marri be freed from military detention. "To sanction such presidential authority to order the military to seize and indefinitely detain civilians, even if the President calls them 'enemy combatants,' would have disastrous consequences for the Constitution—and the country," the appeals court wrote. "For a court to uphold a claim to such extraordinary power would do more than render lifeless" the rights to due process guaranteed under the Constitution, the court said; "it would effectively undermine all of the freedoms guaranteed by the Constitution. It is that power—were a court to recognize it—that could lead all our laws 'to go unexecuted, and the government itself to go to pieces.' We refuse to recognize a claim to power that would so alter the constitutional foundations of our Republic."

FOR ALL ITS MANY SETBACKS, the Bush administration did have one victory to savor, and it was a critical one. Nearly six years after Bush first launched the NSA's secret wiretapping program, the White

House got Congress to put into law a new legal framework that, in many respects, mirrored Bush's once-secret operation. The "Protect America Act," it was called, and it handed over to the executive branch many of the broad decisions about wiretapping orders that had once been governed by the FISA court. The court, already accused by its critics of being a rubber stamp for government wiretapping, saw its role diminished even further in an eleventh-hour push by the administration to get the legislation passed before Congress went into its 2007 summer recess. The administration had made a passionate plea for its expanded wiretapping powers, citing an "intelligence gap" overseas that it said had left even American soldiers vulnerable to attack. Democrats called it something else: a fear-mongering strategy. But the strategy succeeded in luring the votes of enough wobbling Democrats afraid of being cast as weak on terrorism. The White House, Senator Russ Feingold grumbled to me after the vote, "has identified the one major remaining weakness in the Democratic Party, and that's its unwillingness to stand up to the administration when it's making a power grab regarding terrorism and national security."

As Congress reconvened in 2008, the White House was poised to win an extension of the broadened wiretapping powers. House Democrats, suddenly displaying a backbone, temporarily stalled the legislation in February of 2008, but a frustrated Bush was already warning of another terror attack "that will make September 11 pale in comparison." Successful or not, this was a debate the Bush White House never wanted to have. The NSA program was never supposed to become public, and there was never supposed to be any public schism over whether the president had the legal authority to do what he did. That the country was still immersed so deeply in the topic two years after we disclosed the NSA program was, in the view of the White House, doing more harm to national security.

"The fact we're doing it this way," Mike McConnell, Bush's new director of national intelligence, told one interviewer in the midst of the debate, "means that some Americans are going to die, because we do this mission unknown to the bad guys."

The reporter interviewing McConnell wanted to make sure he'd heard him right. "So you're saying that the reporting and the debate in Congress means that some Americans are going to die?" he asked him. "That's what I mean," McConnell answered. "Because we have made it so public. We used to do these things very differently, but for whatever reason, you know, it's a democratic process and sunshine's a good thing. We need to have the debate."

It was a startling assertion: the fact that the media, the Congress, and the public were talking about the federal government's wiretapping powers meant that Americans would die. Reporting on the story, I had to read the transcript of McConnell's remarks two or three times to make sure he was really saying what he seemed to be saying. I called up Steven Aftergood, an open-government advocate who runs the Project on Government Secrecy for the Federation of American Scientists, to see if he found McConnell's comments as striking as I did. "He's basically saying," Aftergood remarked with a sense of wonderment in his voice, "that democracy is going to kill Americans."

Perhaps we shouldn't have been so surprised. For seven years, the administration had craved secrecy, and it had sought to effectively muzzle journalists who would compromise that secrecy and "endanger" national security in the war on terror. If democracy was killing Americans, the First Amendment must be too. I thought about all the stories that the public wouldn't have known about were it not for the media, all the stories the administration had tried to keep quiet in the name of national security: NSA wiretapping, the monitoring of banking records, the CIA's black site prisons, the water-boarding of al Qaeda prisoners, classified memos on torture, the treatment of Iraqi prisoners in Abu Ghraib. The list went on and on. By McConnell's reasoning, Americans were going to die because these stories were told.

It was a philosophy antithetical not only to a free press, but to a free country. Luckily, not everyone shared it. By the end of Bush's term, even conservatives in Congress were growing tired of the refrain. From that frustration grew the Free Flow of Information Act of 2007. The measure, a strong affirmation of the First Amendment, would do at the federal level what most states had done long ago: put in place a shield law to recognize the confidentiality of reporters' anonymous sources in informing the public about vital matters of public interest.

For years, dozens of similar measures had gotten nowhere in Congress, but the 2007 proposal made it further in the legislative process than any shield law proposal in thirty years. Although it didn't make it into law, the measure passed the full House of Representatives in October of 2007 by an overwhelming vote of 398–21 in the face of a veto threat from Bush, with conservative Republicans among its champions. Its prospects for ultimate passage looked more promising than ever.

"What's a conservative like me doing passing a bill that helps reporters?" asked Congressman Mike Pence, an Indiana Republican who sponsored the legislation. On most pivotal issues, Pence was a down-the-line Republican: he voted for Bush's tax cuts, he supported a ban on so-called partial birth abortion, and he pushed for tougher immigration enforcement. But he also had a soft spot for the First Amendment. He was struck by a newspaper editorial he'd read that discussed all the reporters around the country facing subpoenas or jail time for refusing to disclose the sources of their stories on important public matters, so he took up their cause. "As a conservative who believes in limited government, I believe the only check on government power in real time is a free and independent press," he said.

The rabble-rousing defense of the First Amendment sounded like it could have come straight from one of our meetings at the *Times* about our NSA story, except that now it was being delivered on the floor of the House of Representatives by a conservative Republican. Without a strong press to hold the government accountable, Pence told his fellow lawmakers, the integrity of the government itself is in jeopardy. This, he said, "is not about protecting reporters; it's about protecting the public's right to know."

AUTHOR'S NOTE

THIS BOOK is drawn in large part from more than 120 interviews that I conducted with current and former government officials, lawyers, academics, human rights activists, and others who witnessed the remarkable events that have transformed and tested this nation and its notion of justice since 9/11. When possible, I have named the sources who were interviewed in the endnotes that follow. Full disclosure was often impossible, however, because, during the bulk of my research, the FBI was conducting two very active and wide-ranging leak investigations into stories I co-authored for *The New York Times* on secret government programs: the NSA's eavesdropping program and the CIA's bank monitoring program. As a result of those investigations, many of the government officials whom I interviewed were, quite understandably, unwilling to discuss sensitive internal matters if the material was attributed to them by name. The use of anonymous background sources and the lack of transparency that comes with it are the price that we all pay for the recent crackdown on aggressive investigative reporting. But confidential sources, protected by almost all states through reporters' shield laws, are also essential to producing what Bob Woodward once called "the best obtainable version of the truth." Without them, this story could not have been told.

Many of the recurring figures in this narrative, including Alberto Gonzales, John Ashcroft, Robert Mueller, Michael Hayden, David Addington, Dick Cheney, and President Bush himself, declined to be interviewed for this project. (A White House aide said my request for an interview with Bush "took my breath away!") Where possible, I have used available public accounts to reflect their perspectives on critical events.

Despite the recent obstacles faced by reporters, or perhaps because of them, the historic events since the September 11 attacks have generated some of the finest journalism of this or any other generation. In researching this book, I was fortunate to be able to fall back on the outstanding reporting of a number of media organizations, particularly *The Washington Post*, the *Los Angeles Times, USA Today, The Wall Street Journal, Newsweek, The New Yorker, Time*, and, of course, *The New York Times*.

I have also relied on many thousands of pages of government reports, congressional testimony, court records, and internal government memoranda from both public and confidential sources. The investigative reports produced by the office of Justice Department Inspector General Glenn A. Fine were a particularly rich vein that I tapped frequently in my research.

I was also lucky to be able to rely on colleagues, family, and friends whose insight and counsel helped transform this project from the roughest of rough drafts into something more readable. My many thanks go to Lenny Bernstein, Richard Brunell, Rebecca Corbett, Bob Elston, Thuan Elston, Kevin Johnson, Marc Lacey, Matt Lait, Anita Lichtblau, Bernice Lichtblau, Jim Risen, Scott Shane, and Leslie Zirkin. They were blunt in their criticism and inspiring in their encouragement. My editor at Pantheon Books, Dan Frank, and my literary agent, Ron Goldfarb, guided a novice through a difficult project with patience and grace. Barclay Walsh provided both invaluable research assistance and equally invaluable comic relief through her steady diet of political cartoons. And lastly, my editors at *The New York Times*—Bill Keller, Jill Abramson, Rick Berke, Phil Taubman, Dean Baquet, and Rebecca Corbett—provided the support and encouragement to do the kind of important reporting both for the newspaper and for this book that seemed unimaginable back when I was covering fires for the *Cornell Daily Sun*. I am grateful for that. As the dean of University of Oregon's journalism school said in honoring the *Times* with the 2007 Payne Award for our story on the SWIFT program, the *Times* has come down squarely on the side of "the public's right to know when faced with substantial government pressure to not publish." In today's climate, that is no small achievement.

NOTES

PROLOGUE

ix **Step by rickety step:** This account of the scene at the roof of the Turkish warehouse and the arrests in Detroit that led up to it is based primarily on author interviews with a number of government officials involved in the case. It is supplemented in part by court filings in *United States v. Hannan, Koubriti et al.*, in United States District Court, Eastern District of Michigan, including the testimony of FBI agent Mike Thomas regarding the trip with Rick Convertino to Incirlik Air Base.

ix **From his pocket:** Author interviews.

xi **"This is a terrorist sketch":** Author interviews.

xiii **critical busts that had "thwarted terrorists":** Danny Hakim and Eric Lichtblau, "The Detroit Terror Case; After Convictions, the Undoing of a U.S. Terror Prosecution," *New York Times*, Oct. 7, 2004, p. A-1.

xiii **advance knowledge of the attacks on 9/11:** Justice Department press conference on Oct. 31, 2001, by Attorney General Ashcroft, at which Ashcroft said, "Three Michigan men suspected of having knowledge of the September 11 attacks, for example, were arrested on charges of possessing false documents." No evidence emerged to support this claim, and a judge later censured Ashcroft for it.

xiii **"the higher-ups in D.C. are pleased":** Hakim and Lichtblau, "The Detroit Terror Case; After Convictions, the Undoing of a U.S. Terror Prosecution."

xiv **Ashcroft himself was reprimanded:** Order of United States District Court Judge Gerald Rosen, Eastern District of Michigan, on Dec. 16, 2003, in *United States v. Hannan, Koubriti et al.*

xiv **lifted language for the indictment:** Hakim and Lichtblau, "The Detroit Terror Case; After Convictions, the Undoing of a U.S. Terror Prosecution."

xiv **would be indicted:** As discussed in the Epilogue, Convertino and the State Department witness, Harry R. Smith III, were acquitted of criminal charges in Detroit on Oct. 31, 2001.

xv **"a fine kettle of fish":** Hakim and Lichtblau, "The Detroit Terror Case; After Convictions, the Undoing of a U.S. Terror Prosecution."

xvi **"restless voyeurs who see the warts":** Gay Talese, *The Kingdom and the Power* (New York: Dell, 1966), p. 1.

CHAPTER ONE: "This Thing Called the Constitution"

3 **a tangled web of sixty miles of fiber-optic cables:** FBI fact sheet on the Strategic Information and Operations Center, or SIOC (pronounced SIGH-ock).

4 **code-named Penttbom:** The code name is an FBI amalgamation combining abbreviations for the buildings struck by the hijackers—the Pentagon ("Pen") and the Twin Towers ("tt")—with bureau shorthand for bomb ("bom"). Although there were no bombs involved, the FBI has used this construction for past terrorist attacks, such as the "Unabom" investigation.

4 **"Don't ever let this happen again":** John Ashcroft, *Never Again* (New York: Center Street, 2006), p. 130.

4 **all were eyed:** Author interviews and news accounts.

5 **"sorting through the outbound international mail":** Internal FBI report on status of Penttbom investigation obtained by author. References to mirroring library computers and capturing "all fugitives of Arab descent" are from the same document.

6 **"I know you're not a lawyer":** Author interviews with administration officials who participated in the 9/11 meeting at SIOC. Part of this scene was first referenced in a story in *The Philadelphia Inquirer*, June 16, 2003, "Government's Efforts to Thwart Terrorism Go Too Far, Critics Say," by Thomas Ginsberg.

7 **"Who does this asshole think he is?":** Author interview with former FBI official.

7 **"Think outside the box":** Author interviews with Justice Department officials.

10 **"They don't help us":** Author interview with Justice Department official.

11 **"People were screaming":** Geraldine Baum and Paul Lieberman, "America Attacked," *Los Angeles Times*, Sept. 12, 2001, p. A-1.

12 **The front-page scoop:** Eric Lichtblau, "Aboard Flight 11, a Chilling Voice," *Los Angeles Times*, Sept. 20, 2001, p. A-1.

13 **unusual arrangements that the Secret Service had made:** Author interviews.

13 **A photo of the jaunt:** *Del Rio News-Herald*, July 21, 2001, p. A-1.

14 **"Al Qaeda may favor spectacular attacks":** David Johnston and Eric Lichtblau, "Little Headway in Terror War, Democrats Say," *New York Times*, Nov. 15, 2002, p. A-1.

15 **"The United States is winning the war":** John Ashcroft appearance before Senate Judiciary Committee, March 4, 2003. Transcript from Federal Document Clearing House.

16 **the story ran the next day:** Eric Lichtblau and William Glaberson, "Millions Raised for Qaeda in Brooklyn, U.S. Says," *New York Times*, March 5, 2003, p. A-1.

17 **"That is an imaginary number":** Andy Newman and Daryl Khan, "Brooklyn Mosque Becomes Terror Icon, but Federal Case Is Unclear," *New York Times*, March 9, 2003, p. A-29.

17 **Several jurors, in fact:** William Glaberson, "Federal Court Jury Finds Sheik Guilty of Conspiracy and Financing Terrorism," *New York Times*, March 11, 2005, p. B-1.

18 **And the suggestion of a link:** In his memoir, Ashcroft repeated the claim from Al-Moayad that he raised money for jihad from the mosque in Brooklyn, and Ashcroft pointed to the case as a prime example of the improved international cooperation by the FBI and the CIA (*Never Again*, p. 286).

CHAPTER TWO: Collateral Damage

19 **The neighbors at the Royal Oak Apartments:** This account of the arrest and incarceration of Taj Bhatti is based on the author's interviews with numerous family members, neighbors, law enforcement officials, human rights activists, and others with knowledge of the case. Dr. Bhatti himself, who left Virginia not long after his release from jail, declined to be interviewed because he said the case had taken too great an emotional toll on him. The FBI and the United States Attorney's Office for the Western District of Virginia also declined to discuss the case.

19 **"he was just a really strange fellow":** Author interview with G. C. Jennings.

20 **Jennings was watching TV:** Author interview with G. C. Jennings.

21 **She was out on her front porch:** Author interview with Nancy McNey.

22 **some 2,700 men:** Author's estimate of the total number of people locked up worldwide by American officials since 9/11 on terrorism suspicions, based on government data, media accounts, and reports from human rights groups. This estimate includes, in approximate numbers, at least 1,200 people incarcerated on immigration violations immediately after 9/11, 70 arrested as material witnesses to terrorism, 525 charged in the criminal courts with terrorism-related offenses, 100 held in CIA prisons, 775 held at Guantánamo Bay after 9/11, and 50 who were incarcerated and taken to foreign countries in U.S. "renditions." Because of the absence of reliable government data, the 2,700 figure is an imprecise estimate and is probably far too low. For instance, David Cole, a law professor at Georgetown University and co-author of the book *Less Safe, Less Free* (New York: New Press, 2007), puts the number of foreign nationals detained in terrorism-related investigations since 9/11 at 5,191. Many of those people who were incarcerated—perhaps a large majority, in fact—were ultimately never found to have any proven links to terrorism, according to a number of academic and media studies. (See, for instance: Dan Eggen and Julie Tate, "US Campaign Produces Few Convictions on Terrorism Charges," *Washington Post*, June 12, 2005, p. A-1.)

22 **Add to the club's membership the tens of thousands:** Ellen Nakashima, "Terror Suspect List Yields Few Arrests; 20,000 Detentions in '06 Rile Critics," *Washington Post*, Aug. 25, 2007, p. A-1.

22 **"Who is this Kafka":** Deborah Sontag, "Who Is This Kafka That People Keep Mentioning?," *New York Times Magazine*, Oct. 21, 2001, p. 54.

23 **fourteen men ultimately exonerated:** Data compiled by the Innocence Project at the Benjamin N. Cardozo School of Law at Yeshiva University.

24 **"It's very important":** Author interview with former Attorney General Janet Reno.

24 **a Latin-American man was locked up:** Author interview with former Justice Department official.

25 **"In a war like this":** Remarks by Bradford Berenson, former associate White House counsel, in panel discussion on terrorism and civil liberties at the Center for American Progress in Washington, D.C., Sept. 25, 2007.

25 **The One-Percent Doctrine:** Ron Suskind, *The One Percent Doctrine* (New York: Simon & Schuster, 2006), p. 62.

26 **For Taj Bhatti, the great adventure:** Author interviews with Munir Bhatti, son of Taj Bhatti.

27 **Bush administration officials would credit:** Author interviews with administration officials.

27 **"The material witness law has been twisted":** Report of Human Rights Watch and American Civil Liberties Union, *Witness to Abuse: Human Rights Abuses Under the Material Witness Law Since September 11*, June 2005.

27 **Bhatti was brought:** Author interviews with Munir Bhatti and Nancy McNey.

28 **"The impression I got":** Human Rights Watch/ACLU, *Witness to Abuse.*

28 **Three thousand miles away:** Author interview with Munir Bhatti.

29 **Dumond was a bit skeptical:** Author interview with Chris Dumond.

30 **The story ran on the front page:** Chris Dumond, June 26, 2002, *Bristol Herald Courier,* "Retired Doctor Held Under Sealed Warrant," p. A-1.

31 **"I wouldn't have even known":** Author interview with Munir Bhatti.

31 **"This is why we have a system":** Brief author interview with Judge Pamela M. Sargent. She declined to discuss any details of the case, citing her order sealing the records six years earlier.

31 **"As far as an individual's liberty":** Author interview with Dennis Jones. Citing the judge's gag order, he also declined to discuss any details of the case.

32 **Who was your source?:** Author interview with Chris Dumond.

33 **They hadn't spoken:** Author interviews with Chris Dumond and Nancy McNey.

34 **were warning privately:** Author interviews with administration officials.

34 **"We're just trying to learn the facts":** George W. Bush interview with ABC News' *20/20,* aired Dec. 5, 2001.

34 **"He chose to embrace fanatics":** John Ashcroft press conference at Justice Department, Jan. 15, 2002. Transcript from Federal Document Clearing House.

35 **In a heated phone conversation:** Author interviews with administration officials.

37 **"My charge is to make sure":** *Los Angeles Times* interview with Alberto Gonzales, March 25, 2001.

37 **compared him to Peter Sellers:** Author interview with administration official.

37 **he refused to meet with him:** Thomas Kean and Lee Hamilton, *Without Precedent*, p. 36.

38 **"I'll take that back to my client":** Author interview with commission official.

38–39 **"She is a very good bowler":** Todd Purdum, "Plenty of Praise for a Nominee, but Few Details," *New York Times*, Oct. 16, 2005, p. A-1.

40 **He was seated at the dais:** Author interview with Suzanne Spaulding of the American Bar Association.

41 **former Secretary of State Warren Christopher confronted:** Adam Liptak, Neil A. Lewis, and Benjamin Weiser, "After Sept. 11, a Legal Battle on the Limits of Civil Liberty," *New York Times*, Aug. 4, 2002, p. A-1.

41 **"Difficult times such as these":** Opinion of Judge Gladys Kessler, U.S. District Court for the District of Columbia, in *Center for National Security Studies et al. v. U.S. Department of Justice* (CIV.A.01–2500-GK), Aug. 2, 2002.

42 **a Chihuahua on the outside:** Sonja Barisic, "Ex-Guantánamo Officer Accused of Passing Detainee Information in Valentine's Card on Trial," Associated Press, May 14, 2007.

42 **"it was really Matt's patriotism":** Kate Wiltrout, "Navy Lawyer Who Shared Detainee List Found Guilty," *Virginian Pilot & The Ledger-Star*, May 18, 2007, p. A-11.

43 **"we may initiate some type":** Remarks by Alberto Gonzales before the American Bar Association Standing Committee on Law and National Security, Washington, D.C., Feb. 24, 2004.

44 **"A state of war":** U.S. Supreme Court decision in *Hamdi v. Rumsfeld* (03–6696) 542 U.S., June 28, 2004.

44 **an ill-fated plan called Operation Tips:** Eric Lichtblau, "Terrorism Tip Network Scaled Back," *Los Angeles Times*, Aug. 10, 2002, p. A-1.

45 **Of some 1,200 people:** This account of the arrests and treatment of the September 11 detainees is based primarily on the June 2, 2003, report from the Office of the Inspector General of the Justice Department, *The September 11 Detainees: A Review of the Treatment of Aliens Held on Immigration Charges in Connection with the Investigation of the September 11 Attacks*. This account is supplemented in part by author interviews.

45 **"THESE COLORS DON'T RUN":** Inspector general's report, *The September 11 Detainees*.

46–47 **"We have to hold these people":** This and other internal communications at the Justice Department about the September 11 detainees were included in the inspector general's report.

48 **Finally, Ziglar put in a personal call:** Author interview with administration officials.

49 **"If the report's only achievement":** Eric Lichtblau, "Report on Detainees Shines a Brighter Spotlight on an Inspector General," *New York Times*, July 5, 2003, p. A-9.

50 **"for which we do not apologize":** John Ashcroft testimony before House Judiciary Committee, June 5, 2003.

50 **"links to the September 11th investigation":** Ashcroft speech in Durham, North Carolina, in support of the Patriot Act, Sept. 6, 2003.

50 **"We make no apologies"**: Eric Lichtblau, "U.S. Report Faults the Roundup of Illegal Immigrants After 9/11," *New York Times*, June 3, 2003, p. A-1.

50 **"I apologize for nothing"**: Sanford J. Ungar, *FBI: An Uncensored Look Behind the Walls* (Boston: Atlantic-Little, Brown, 1975), p. 44.

51 **Bush wanted to meet**: Ashcroft, *Never Again*, p. 40.

51 **"I like Ashcroft a lot"**: David Kirkpatrick, "In Secretly Taped Conversations, Glimpses of the Future President," *New York Times*, Feb. 20, 2005, p. A-1.

52 **"a marked man"**: Ashcroft, *Never Again*, p. 39.

53 **"We don't water flowers"**: Ibid., pp. 90–91.

53 **Crisco oil**: John Ashcroft, *Lessons from a Father to His Son* (Nashville: Thomas Nelson, 1998), p. 199.

53 **"Blessed are you"**: Ibid., p. 57.

53 **met only once**: Author interview with Janet Reno.

54 **They were copies of memos**: This account of the Janet Reno–John Ashcroft lunch and of Reno giving the FBI memos to Ashcroft is based on author interviews with Reno. The existence of the memos themselves was first publicly disclosed in a story written by Eric Lichtblau and Charles Piller in the *Los Angeles Times*: "War on Terrorism Highlights FBI's Computer Woes," July 28, 2002, p. A-1.

54 **Pickard briefed Ashcroft**: Testimony and staff reports of 9/11 Commission.

55 **notice soon filtered down**: Author interviews with intelligence officials.

55 **"almost fell out of his chair"**: 9/11 Commission staff report #9, *Law Enforcement, Counterterrorism, and Intelligence Collection in the United States Prior to 9/11*, issued April 13, 2004, p. 7

56 **As his plane was passing**: Eric Lichtblau and Adam Liptak, "On Terror, Spying and Guns, Ashcroft Expands Reach," *New York Times*, March 15, 2003, p. A-1; and account in Ashcroft, *Never Again*.

56 **"There has been an insistence"**: John Ashcroft statement at Senate Judiciary Committee hearing on encryption, March 17, 1998.

57 **"The rules of engagement had changed"**: Ashcroft, *Never Again*, p. 134.

57 **One Sunday a few weeks after**: This account of the Sunday meeting is based entirely on author interviews with administration officials.

59 **carved out a gaping exemption**: Eric Lichtblau, "Bush Issues Racial Profiling Ban but Exempts Security Inquiries," *New York Times*, June 18, 2003, p. A-1.

60 **"We have decided"**: Matthew Purdy, "Bush's New Rules to Fight Terror Transform the Legal Landscape," *New York Times*, Nov. 25, 2001, p. A-1.

60 **"Do they really believe"**: David Sanger, "On High-Speed Trip, Bush Glimpses a Perception Gap," *New York Times*, October 24, 2003, p. A-6.

60 **a "scorched earth" policy**: Author interviews with government officials.

61 **A new version landed**: Author interviews with government officials.

62 **the new legal opinion had become final**: The Justice Department fought to keep secret the opinion from the Office of Legal Counsel, issued in April,

2002 but it was publicly disclosed as part of federal litigation in *National Council of La Raza et al. v. Department of Justice.*

62 **"How many people":** Author interviews with government officials.

62 **summoned Ziglar at the last minute:** Author interviews with government officials.

63 **"Good afternoon":** John Ashcroft press conference at Justice Department, June 5, 2002.

65 **Then came Brandon Mayfield:** This account of the arrest and release of Brandon Mayfield is based primarily on author interviews with Mayfield and others. It is supplemented in parts by the investigation of the Justice Department's Office of the Inspector General, *A Review of the FBI's Handling of the Brandon Mayfield Case*, issued in March 2006, and by media accounts.

65 **he became the unofficial:** Author interview with Brandon Mayfield.

66 **"Did you leave":** Author interview with Brandon Mayfield.

68 **maybe even get him to cooperate:** Inspector general's report on Brandon Mayfield, *A Review of the FBI's Handling.*

70 **had warned the FBI's lab people:** Sarah Kershaw, Eric Lichtblau, Dale Fuchs, and Lowell Bergman, "Spain and U.S. at Odds on Mistaken Terror Arrest," *New York Times*, June 5, 2004, p. A-1.

73 **his public defender, Steve Wax, walked in:** Author interviews with Brandon Mayfield and Steve Wax.

73 **"I want to thank my family and friends":** Wire service reports, May 21, 2004.

74 **"couldn't be ignored":** Inspector General's report on Brandon Mayfield, *A Review of the FBI's Handling.*

74 **"turned out not to be true":** Deposition of Gary Bald in *Youssef v. FBI*, United States District Court for the District of Columbia, p. 86.

CHAPTER THREE: "Don't Embarrass the Bureau"

75 **Bassem Youssef was sitting:** This account of Bassem Youssef's experience after 9/11 is based primarily on author interviews with Youssef, his attorney Stephen Kohn, and other participants, as well as court depositions and other documents in *Youssef v. FBI*. It is supplemented in part by author interviews with other government officials. FBI director Robert Mueller declined to be interviewed, as did Congressman Frank Wolf.

78 **still a lingering perception:** Nov. 26, 2002, letter to Mueller from Senators Patrick Leahy and Chuck Grassley, regarding alleged retaliation against an FBI unit chief, John Roberts, after Roberts spoke out about a perceived double standard in FBI disciplining procedures.

78 **"the director was truly appalled":** Deposition of John Lewis in *Youssef v. FBI*, May 17, 2005, p. 181.

79 **OPR investigators found:** OPR memorandum of July 3, 2006, from H. Marshall Jarrett.

80 **Years later, the dearth:** Eric Lichtblau, "F.B.I. Said to Lag on Translations of Terror Tapes," *New York Times*, Sept. 28, 2004, p. A-1. Two days later, John Kerry used the issue at a presidential debate to attack President Bush's terrorism response.

81 **"whether any director":** March 27, 2007, hearing of Senate Judiciary Committee.

82 **"I'd like to come work":** Eric Lichtblau, "Mueller Brings Platoon Leader Instincts to Job," *Los Angeles Times*, July 6, 2001, p. A-1.

82 **"Prosecution cannot be":** Bob Woodward, *Bush at War* (New York: Simon & Schuster, 2002), p. 42; and Ashcroft, *Never Again*, p. 133.

83 **"Dear Asa":** Ron Suskind, *The One-Percent Doctrine*, p. 287.

85 **For agents like Brad Doucette:** This account of Brad Doucette's suicide is based on a poignant May 3, 2005, front-page story in the *Los Angeles Times*, "After 9/11, a Fatal 24/7," by Greg Krikorian, as well as on subsequent author interviews with Doucette's widow, Suzanne Doucette, a former FBI agent.

85 **"We're spinning":** Author interview with Suzanne Doucette.

86 **"He was not one":** Krikorian, "After 9/11, a Fatal 24/7."

87 **Kris described the dire mood:** Author interview with David Kris.

89 **Gebhardt's frustration:** Internal FBI memo obtained by author. Portions of the memo first appeared in *The New York Times* (Eric Lichtblau, "F.B.I. Officials Say Some Agents Lack a Focus on Terror," Nov. 21, 2002, p. A-1).

91 **again, the editors played the story on the front page:** Eric Lichtblau, "F.B.I., Under Outside Pressure, Gets Internal Push," *New York Times*, Dec. 2, 2002, p. A-1.

92 **"given out like candy":** Author interview with FBI agent.

94 **Woods said the path:** Author interview with Michael Woods.

94 **"You've got seven hundred district judges":** Speech by Judge Royce Lamberth before American Library Association, June 23, 2007, Washington, D.C.

95 **I did a modest story:** Eric Lichtblau, "F.B.I., Using Patriot Act, Demands Library's Records," *New York Times*, Aug. 26, 2005, p. A-11.

95 **But public court filings:** Alison Leigh Cowan, "Hartford Libraries Watch as U.S. Makes Demands," *New York Times*, Sept. 2, 2005, p. B-5.

95 **"What are you celebrating":** Alison Leigh Cowan, "U.S. Ends a Yearlong Effort to Obtain Library Records Amid Secrecy in Connecticut," *New York Times*, June 27, 2006, p. B-6.

95 **A few months after:** Barton Gellman, "The FBI's Secret Scrutiny; In Hunt for Terrorists, Bureau Examines Records of Ordinary Americans," *Washington Post*, Nov. 6, 2005, p. A-1.

96 **in a blistering report:** Justice Department Office of the Inspector General, *A Review of the Federal Bureau of Investigation's Use of National Security Letters*, released June 9, 2007.

97 **Youssef had a knack:** Author interview with Bassem Youssef.

98 **So it was that:** Author interviews with Bassem Youssef and Stephen Kohn; congressional testimony; and Edmund Andrews, "Official Alerted F.B.I. to

Rules Abuse 2 Years Ago, Lawyer Says," *New York Times*, March 19, 2007, p. A-10.

98 **Wouldn't it be essential:** Gary Bald deposition, *Youssef v. FBI*, p. 77.

99 **The idea that:** Ed Curran deposition, *Youssef v. FBI*, p. 71.

100 **there was little incentive:** R. Jeffrey Smith and John Solomon, "Amid Concerns, FBI Lapses Went On," *Washington Post*, March 18, 2007, p. A-1.

101 **there was close to consensus:** Author interviews with commission officials.

102 **"He really got it":** Author interviews with commission officials.

102 **"Our recommendations to leave":** *The 9/11 Commission Report* (Washington, D.C.: U.S. Government Printing Office, 2004), pp. 424–25.

103 **made it next to impossible:** Lichtblau and Piller, "War on Terrorism Highlights FBI's Computer Woes Security."

103 **In one unpublicized episode:** Author interviews with law enforcement officials.

103 **was expected to cost $425 million:** Justice Department Inspector General, "Sentinel Audit II: Status of the FBI's Case Management System." December 2006; and inspector general updates.

104 **"slow and uneven":** Justice Department inspector general's report, *Follow-up Audit of the Federal Bureau of Investigation's Efforts to Hire, Train, and Retain Intelligence Analysts*, April 2007, p. ii.

105 **Mike German got the message too:** This account of Mike German's experience at the FBI is based primarily on author interviews with German. It is supplemented in part by the findings of the Justice Department inspector general's investigation into the case, which was completed in December 2005, and by the records of Senate investigators, as well as by earlier reporting by the author for *The New York Times*.

106 **as he read the transcript:** A redacted FBI transcript, obtained by Senate investigators, was reviewed by the author and is quoted from extensively here.

108 **"The risk of waiting":** Eric Lichtblau, "Trying to Thwart Possible Terrorists Quickly, F.B.I. Agents Are Often Playing Them," *New York Times*, May 30, 2005, p. A-10.

110 **"Hang him":** E-mail from Bassem Youssef to Robert Mueller, Aug. 7, 2007.

112 **As he reflected back:** Author interview with Mike German.

CHAPTER FOUR: Threats, Pronouncements, and the Media Wars

113 **It was a routine request:** This account of the origins of the military's anti-war files is drawn primarily from author interviews. It is supplemented in part by reporting by Eric Lichtblau and Mark Mazzetti, "Military Expands Intelligence Role in U.S.," *New York Times*, Jan. 14, 2007, p. A-1.

114 **"didn't want to have to noodle":** Author interview with former administration official.

114 **"Is there an organization":** Author interview with military official.

115 **Hersh's concerns:** Author interview with Rich Hersh.

116 **A later review:** Pentagon inspector general's report "The Threat and Local Observation Notice (TALON) Report Program," released June 27, 2007. The report found that among Talon's database of some 13,000 entries, more than 1,100 were deleted as outdated or improper, including 263 involving war protests and demonstrations.

116 **"Why do we have this stuff":** Author interview with military official.

117 **"I don't want it":** Eric Lichtblau and Mark Mazzetti, "Military Documents Hold Tips on Antiwar Activities," *New York Times*, Nov. 21, 2006, p. A-18.

117 **The collection:** Pentagon inspector general's report, "The Threat and Local Observation Notice (TALON) Report Program."

119 **Teams of New York City Police Department:** Jim Dwyer, "City Police Spied Broadly Before G.O.P. Convention," *New York Times*, March 25, 2007, p. A-1.

119 **an editorial in the Dubuque paper:** Editorial, *Dubuque Telegraph Herald*, Feb. 13, 2004.

119 **"The message I took":** Eric Lichtblau, "F.B.I. Goes Knocking for Political Troublemakers," *New York Times*, Aug. 16, 2004, p. A-1.

119 **As Pentagon officials had feared:** *NBC Nightly News with Brian Williams*, "Is the Pentagon Spying on America," Dec. 14, 2005.

120 **forcing the Democrats:** An unofficial House hearing was held by the Democrats on Jan. 20, 2006, with Rich Hersh as one of several witnesses to testify.

120 **men like William "Crazy Bill" Sullivan:** Ungar, *FBI*, p. 296.

121 **"I think we have been conducting":** Ibid., p. 650.

121 **That was why:** Author interview with Coleen Rowley.

123 **"Given the limited nature":** Lichtblau, "F.B.I. Goes Knocking for Political Troublemakers."

124 **"might have a chilling effect":** Justice Department inspector general's report, *A Review of the FBI's Investigative Activities Concerning Potential Protesters at the 2004 Democratic and Republican National Political Conventions*, April 2006, p. 15.

124 **the inspector general ultimately concluded:** Ibid., p. 3.

125 **It was a balanced piece:** Eric Lichtblau, "F.B.I. Scrutinizes Anti-war Rallies," *New York Times*, Nov. 23, 2003, p. A-1.

125 **"A strange thing happened":** Eric Lichtblau, "A Surprising Civil Rights About-Face for Ashcroft," *Los Angeles Times*, May 13, 2001, p. A-1.

127 **what role Mike Chertoff:** Eric Lichtblau, "Dispute over Legal Advice Costs a Job and Complicates a Nomination," *New York Times*, May 22, 2003, p. A-15.

132 **Andy Card, told one interviewer:** Ken Auletta, "Fortress Bush," *The New Yorker*, Jan. 19, 2004.

133 **he even went so far:** Documents released by House Committee on Oversight and Government Reform, June 21, 2007.

133 **The steps they sought:** Author interviews with administration officials.

134 **"We need the criminal penalties":** Author interviews with administration officials.

135 **a 2004 report:** Reporters Committee for Freedom of the Press, *Evaluation of the Likely Impact of Attorney General Nominee Alberto Gonzales on Press Freedoms and the Public's Right to Know*, Nov. 2004.

135 **librarians at public universities:** Eric Lichtblau, "Rising Fears That What We Do Know Can Hurt Us," *Los Angeles Times*, Nov. 18, 2001, p. A-1.

135 **And page after page:** Eric Lichtblau, "Judge Scolds U.S. Officials over Barring Jet Travelers," *New York Times*, June 16, 2004, p. A-19.

136 **One open government group catalogued:** Report by openthegovern ment.org, "Secrecy Report Card," Aug. 26, 2004.

136 **"a wartime environment":** Eric Lichtblau, " 'Wartime Environment'; Government by, for and Secret From the People," *New York Times*, *Week in Review*, Sept. 5, 2004.

CHAPTER FIVE: Sworn to Secrecy

137 **By accident:** Author interviews with intelligence officials.

137 **"What the hell's":** Author interviews with intelligence officials.

138 **The vice president's office:** Jack Goldsmith, *The Terror Presidency* (New York: Norton, 2007), p. 182.

139 **even Tom Ridge:** Author interview with Tom Ridge.

139 **At an AT&T facility:** Author interview with Mark Klein.

140 **At the nation's secret intelligence court:** Author interviews with government officials.

140 **At the FBI command center:** Author interview with Michael Woods.

140 **And at the Justice Department:** Author interviews with government officials.

142 **Within hours and days:** Eric Lichtblau and James Risen, "Eavesdropping Effort Began Soon After Sept. 11 Attacks," *New York Times*, Dec. 18, 2005, p. A-44.

143 **"not up to the job":** PBS' *Frontline* Documentary, *Spying on the Homefront*, May 2007, transcript of John Yoo interview.

144 **An intelligence lawyer tried:** Author interview with government official.

144 **"Blindly following":** John Yoo, *War by Other Means* (New York: Atlantic Monthly Press, 2006), p. 107.

144 **David Addington:** Goldsmith, *The Terror Presidency*, p. 181.

145 **The War Powers Act:** Dick Cheney's comments to reporters en route to Muscat, Oman, Dec. 20, 2005. Official White House Transcript.

146 **From Cheney, there came only silence:** Barton Gellman and Jo Becker, "A Different Understanding with the President," *Washington Post*, June 24, 2007, p. A-1.

146 **"The president of the United States":** Dick Cheney comments en route to Oman.

147 **Cheney posed a question:** George Tenet, *At the Center of the Storm* (New York: HarperCollins, 2007), p. 237.

147 **Tenet phoned Michael Hayden:** Testimony of Michael Hayden at his

confirmation hearing for director of the CIA, Senate Intelligence Committee, May 18, 2006.

147 **"We don't get involved":** Author interview with Connie Vilhauer.

149 **Even before Bush took office:** Eric Lichtblau, James Risen, and Scott Shane, *New York Times*, "Wider Spying Fuels Aid Plan For Telecoms," Dec. 16, 2007, p. A-1.

150 **"Tomorrow is zero hour":** General Hayden and the NSA always bristled at the publicity generated by the two warnings. He told the joint House and Senate intelligence committees on Oct. 17, 2002, that the information collected by the NSA did not indicate an attack was to occur that day, nor did it indicate the place or nature of the attack. "Because of the processing involved, we were not able to report the information until September 12th," Hayden said.

150 **Two days after:** Remarks of Michael Hayden at National Press Club on Jan. 23, 2006.

151 **unwilling to share:** CIA inspector general's report, *Report on CIA Accountability with Respect to 9/11 Attacks*, released in redacted form on Aug. 21, 2007, p. xxiii of executive summary.

151 **In a classified, closed-door briefing:** Letter from Nancy Pelosi to Michael Hayden sent Oct. 11, 2001, cited in Eric Lichtblau and Scott Shane, "Files Say Agency Initiated Growth of Spying Effort," *New York Times*, Jan. 4, 2006, p. A-1.

152 **"I am concerned whether":** Nancy Pelosi letter, Oct. 11, 2001.

152 **the CIA director went to see Cheney:** Tenet, *Into the Storm*, p. 237.

152 **As Tenet recounted:** Ibid.

153 **75 percent by one estimate:** Author interview with government official.

154 **"There's not a computer":** Author interview with senior intelligence official.

154 **Cheney, by all indications:** Scott Shane and Eric Lichtblau, "Cheney Pushed U.S. to Widen Eavesdropping," *New York Times*, May 14, 2006, p. A-1.

154 **NSA officials were hesitant:** Without ever actually denying it, General Hayden took issue with our May 14, 2006, story about Cheney's efforts to broaden the program and the NSA's resistance. "I could recognize a thin vein of my experience inside the story, but I would not characterize how you described the *Times* story as being accurate," Hayden said at his confirmation as CIA director on May 18, 2006, when asked about the article.

154 **"I made the decision":** George W. Bush interview with *CBS Evening News*, Jan. 27, 2006. Although the administration always insisted that the NSA program was limited to international communications, some conflicting accounts have emerged. When Alberto Gonzales was asked at a Senate Judiciary Committee hearing on Feb. 6, 2007, whether the government could eavesdrop on purely domestic communications without a warrant, he answered: "Sir, it is beyond the bound of the program which I'm testifying about today."

155 **But the decision to authorize:** George W. Bush, *CBS Evening News* interview.

155   **no serious discussion:** Author interviews with government officials.

156   **"President Addington":** Author interview with administration official.

156   **a tattered copy of the Constitution:** Jane Mayer, "The Hidden Power," *The New Yorker*, July 3, 2006; and Goldsmith, *The Terror Presidency*, p. 88.

156   **"We're going to push":** Goldsmith, *The Terror Presidency*, p. 126.

156   **In wartime:** John Yoo, *Frontline*, "Spying on the Home Front," interview.

157   **"It will take fifty years":** Author interview with Justice Department official.

157   **"air of sufficiency":** Michael Hayden, National Press Club remarks.

158   **He went separately:** Michael Hayden, Senate confirmation hearing.

158   **"good to go":** Ibid.

158   **Days later, Hayden gathered:** Ibid.

158   **they heard Bush defend:** George W. Bush, "A Conversation About the USA Patriot Act," April 20, 2004, Buffalo, N.Y. Transcript from Federal Document Clearing House.

159   **"anytime you hear":** Ibid.

159   **Bush would insist later:** "I was talking about roving wiretaps, I believe, involved in the Patriot Act. This is different from the NSA program," Bush said when pressed on the apparent contradiction on Dec. 31, 2005.

161   **That was a difficult conversation:** At Michael Hayden's confirmation hearing for the CIA in 2006, Senator Russ Feingold asked Hayden about the apparent discrepancy between Hayden's assurances in 2002 and his acknowledgment of the NSA program in 2005. "If my language could have been more precise, I apologize," Hayden said of his 2002 statements. "But it was not an intent to mislead; it was to describe the limitations under which the agency worked and continued to work inside the United States."

163   **Baker said in a rare interview:** Jim Baker, *Frontline* PBS documentary, "Spying on the Homefront," interview transcript.

164   **"Every deepest, darkest":** Royce Lamberth speech, American Library Association.

165   **"We sent a message":** Ibid.

165   **When Ashcroft took over:** Author interviews with administration officials.

165   **"What we found":** Royce Lamberth speech, American Library Association.

166   **when Lamberth was summoned:** Author interview with administration officials.

167   **Lamberth "wasn't being asked":** Author interview with administration official.

168   **Hitting with a count:** Michael Hayden, CIA confirmation hearing.

169   **There were "omissions of consequence":** Evan Thomas and Daniel Klaidman, "Full Speed Ahead," *Newsweek*, Jan. 9, 2006, p. 22.

169   **Jane Harman joked:** Panel discussion at the Center for American Progress, Washington D.C., March 30, 2007.

169   **he talked of Armaggedon:** Michael Grunwald, "Running Scared; Bob Graham's Message to the Voters Is Simple: However Frightened We Are, It Isn't Nearly Frightened Enough," *Washington Post Magazine*, May 4, 2003, p. 8.

169 **It wasn't even clear:** Douglas Jehl, "Spy Briefings Failed to Meet Legal Test, Lawmakers Say," *New York Times*, Dec. 21, 2005, p. A-36.

170 **So Rockefeller . . . composed a letter:** Eric Lichtblau and David Sanger, "Administration Cites War Vote in Spying Case," *New York Times*, Dec. 20, 2005, p. A-1.

171 **by one official's estimate:** Author interview with administration official.

171 **"If anything was presented":** Royce Lamberth remarks to reporters after American Library Association talk, as reflected in wire service story by Greg Gordon, McClatchy Newspapers, June 24, 2007.

173 **"There was an ongoing concern":** Author interview with government official.

174 **Too often, Goldsmith believed:** Goldsmith, *The Terror Presidency*, p. 161.

175 **When Justice Department lawyers:** Author interview.

175 **"Since you've withdrawn":** Daniel Klaidman, Stuart Taylor Jr., and Evan Thomas, "Palace Revolt," *Newsweek*, Feb. 6, 2006, p. 34. This episode was later repeated, with slightly different wording attributed to David Addington, in Goldsmith's *The Terror Presidency*.

175 **they were shocked:** Author interviews with government officials.

176 **In November of 2003:** Documents produced as part of Freedom of Information Act lawsuit in *New York Times v. Justice Department*.

176 **Goldsmith saw it as his mission:** Goldsmith, *The Terror Presidency*, p. 182.

176 **Ashcroft's people liked Comey:** Author interviews.

176 **"Nothing about Mr. Comey's tenure":** Benjamin Weiser and Eric Lichtblau, "Manhattan U.S. Attorney in Line to Be Ashcroft Aide," *New York Times*, Oct. 4, 2003, p. B-2.

177 **"This is not":** James Comey press briefing at Justice Department, Aug. 5, 2004.

177 **Comey did not even know:** Author interviews with government officials.

177 **By the accounts of several officials:** Author interviews with government officials.

178 **Ashcroft told associates:** Author interview with administration official.

179 **"We all saw agents":** Author interview with government official.

179 **Ashcroft began having stomach pains:** Author interviews with government officials; and Ashcroft, *Never Again*, p. 231.

179 **he was the first to admit:** Ashcroft, *Never Again*, p. 234.

180 **Gonzales insisted that the "consensus":** Testimony of Alberto Gonzales before Senate Judiciary Committee, July 24, 2007.

180 **That night, Comey:** This account of the visit to John Ashcroft's hospital bedside and the events surrounding it is based primarily on James Comey's testimony before the Senate Judiciary Committee on May 15, 2007, except where noted otherwise.

182 **"I've been told":** Alberto Gonzales testimony, July 24, 2007.

182 **He looked so ill:** Jeffrey Rosen, *New York Times Magazine* profile of Jack Goldsmith, Sept. 9, 2007, p. 40.

184 **"You've been poorly served":** Author interview with government official familiar with the account of the White House meeting.

184 **it appears to involve several:** Author interviews with intelligence officials.
184 **"Imagine you're doing":** Author interview with intelligence official.
185 **he bade farewell:** Klaidman, Taylor Jr. and Thomas, "Palace Revolt."

CHAPTER SIX: Blood on Our Hands

193 **"Nothing gave us more trouble":** James Reston, *Deadline* (New York: Random House, 1992), p. 322.
198 **When the Patriot Act was first approved:** George W. Bush remarks on signing of Patriot Act, Oct. 26, 2001, White House transcript.
205 **At one meeting in early December of 2005:** The meetings between the newspaper and the Bush administration over the question of whether the NSA story should run were originally held off the record. Since the publication of the story, both the White House and the newspaper have spoken publicly about different elements of the meetings, discussing their existence as well as the substance and arguments conveyed at them, and I have done so here as well. I have continued to withhold from publication certain technical details about the NSA program that the newspaper felt could realistically compromise national security, and I have paraphrased some comments or quoted them only on background, without including the names of administration officials who made the comments.
206 **Cheney had thought about attending:** Stephen F. Hayes, *Cheney: The Untold Story of America's Most Powerful and Controversial Vice President* (New York: HarperCollins Publishers, 2007), p. 483.
208 **"Nothing I heard in there":** Joe Hagan, "The United States of America vs. Bill Keller," *New York Magazine*, Sept. 10, 2006.

CHAPTER SEVEN: High-Level Confirmation

212 **"This is a highly classified program":** George W. Bush, presidential address, Dec. 17, 2005, White House transcript.
213 **Just as Eisenhower had declared:** David Sanger, "In Address, Bush Says He Ordered Domestic Spying," *New York Times*, Dec. 18, 2005, p. A-1.
214 **death knell for the Patriot Act:** The Senate blocked reauthorization of the Patriot Act the day the NSA story appeared, forcing the White House to agree to a series of short-term extensions to keep it alive temporarily. Three months later, Congress reauthorized the act as a whole after the White House agreed to include greater civil rights protections in it.
216 **One even resigned from the court:** Author interviews with government officials; and Carol D. Leonnig and Dafna Linzer, "Spy Court Judge Quits in Protest," *Washington Post*, Dec. 21, 2005, p. A-1.
218 **Hours after the story was published:** After several of the Freedom of Information Act requests were denied, *The New York Times* brought suit in federal court; the litigation is still pending as of this writing.

218 **A briefing he had attended with Cheney:** *CNN Situation Room*, Dec. 20, 2005. Senator Bob Graham made the point about the foreign transit traffic passing through the United States in asserting that the administration never told him it would be conducting wiretaps on Americans without a court warrant.

219 **It would be another nineteen months:** Letter from Mike McConnell, director of national intelligence, to Senator Arlen Specter, July 31, 2007, acknowledging the existence of "other" NSA intelligence activities after 9/11 beyond the eavesdropping program that the president had acknowledged.

220 *USA Today* **took another cut:** Leslie Cauley, "NSA Has Massive Database of Americans' Phone Calls," *USA Today*, May 11, 2006, p. A-1.

224 **Bush would come to mock the labels:** George W. Bush, presidential press conference, Sept. 15, 2006, White House transcript.

224 **"I don't think 'domestic spying' ":** Michael Hayden, National Press Club speech.

224–25 **Andy Card, Karl Rove and Bush's other senior aides:** Internal e-mail sent December 21, 2005, from White House lawyer William Kelley to Justice Department assistant attorney general Steven Bradbury about the "urgency" of effective public-relations on the wiretapping issue. The e-mail includes excerpts from an earlier e-mail Kelley had received on the same issue from Bush aide Brett Kavanaugh.

225 **In one column:** George F. Will, "Why Didn't He Ask Congress," *Washington Post*, December 20, 2005, p. A-31.

225 **"It is not good":** Kelley e-mail, December 21, 2005.

226 **"Why are we not read in":** Author interview with board officials.

226 **"If we're not read in":** After months of pressure, the White House finally agreed to allow the privacy board to review the program, and panel members concluded, after what some saw as a cursory review, that the NSA program included adequate checks and balances to prevent abuses. Lanny Davis, a Democrat who served in the Clinton administration, eventually quit the panel in 2007 because of what he charged was political meddling by the White House that had robbed the panel of any semblance of independence.

227 **This time, however, Fine was stymied:** Glenn Fine's office later reversed course and opened an investigation into the NSA program and the Justice Department's handling of it. That investigation is still pending as of this writing.

228 **So it was over:** Nearly two years later, OPR was allowed to open its own investigation after President Bush agreed to give its investigators the needed security clearances to examine the program. The move came just days after the new attorney general, Michael Mukasey, was sworn into office in November 2007. That investigation is also pending at this writing.

231 **"What is that?":** Karl Vick, "Judges Skeptical of State-Secrets Claim," *Washington Post*, Aug. 16, 2007, p. A-4.

CHAPTER EIGHT: Swift-Boated (Round Two)

232 **But the Belgian banking industry executives:** This scene at the White House, as well as the description of the SWIFT program and the tensions surrounding its secret operations, is based primarily on author interviews with numerous government and industry officials. It is supplemented in part by reporting first conducted by the author for *The New York Times,* as well as by other government and public accounts as noted.

233 **known as SWIFT:** The full name of the consortium is the Society for Worldwide Interbank Financial Telecommunication.

233 **The financial patterns gleaned:** Remarks by Treasury Secretary John Snow and Undersecretary Stuart Levey at a press briefing at the Treasury Department, June 23, 2006.

233 **At the outset:** Author interviews with government officials.

234 **The company was refusing:** Author interviews.

235 **"How long can this go on?":** Author interviews.

235 **So minimal were the hijackers' financial needs:** John Roth, Douglas Greenburg, and Serena Wille, staff report to the 9/11 Commission, *Monograph on Terrorist Financing,* (2004), p. 3.

236 **sometimes with the scantest evidence of actual terrorist ties:** A number of the highest profile terrorist-financing cases fizzled out in court. For instance, when Enaam Arnaout, the head of Benevolence International Foundation in the Chicago area, was sentenced on a racketeering count in 2003, the federal judge refused to tack on an extra ten years for what the government claimed were his ties to al Qaeda. "Arnaout does not stand convicted of a terrorism offense," U.S. District Judge Suzanne Conlon wrote in rejecting the terrorism enhancement. "Nor does the record reflect that he attempted, participated in, or conspired to commit any act of terrorism." (Matt O'Connor, "Charity Leader Wins Round; Judge Tosses a Request for Longer Sentence," *Chicago Tribune,* July 18, 2003, p. A-1.)

236 **One businessman:** Roth, Greenburg, and Wille, *Monograph on Terrorist Financing,* p. 81.

236 **At one White House briefing:** Author interview with government official.

237 **The card's PIN:** Author interview with government official.

237 **"Sometime in the next 3 months":** Roth, Greenburg, and Wille, *Monograph on Terrorist Financing,* p. 81.

238 **"Unless I see a plan":** Author interviews with federal officials.

239 **"I thought there wasn't":** Author interviews with federal officials.

239 **none of the central groups or individuals:** The investigation did yield convictions in two offshoot cases that were peripheral to the Virginia investigation: A New Jersey businessman, Soliman S. Biheiri, whose investment firm received money from the Northern Virginia charities, was convicted in 2003 on federal immigration charges; and a leading Muslim activist, Abdul Rahman al-Amoudi, who worked at the charities in the early 1990s, was convicted and sentenced to twenty-three years in 2004 for illegally moving money out of Libya as part of a purported murder-for-hire plot involving

the Saudi crown prince. But as of this writing, no one has been charged or convicted in connection with the terrorist-financing allegations against Northern Virginia's Saar group itself.

240 **"If we sign the memo"**: Author interview with Tom Ridge.

240 **"Millions of dollars"**: Press conference of Treasury Secretary Paul O'Neill, Nov. 7, 2001. Transcript from Federal Document Clearing House.

240 **Treasury Department gave back the money**: Roth, Greenburg and Wille, *Monograph on Terrorist Financing*, case study on Al-Barakaat, p. 67.

241 **staff investigators for the 9/11 Commission**: Roth, Greenburg, and Wille, *Monograph on Terrorist Financing*, p. 24.

242 **"Where necessary"**: David Aufhauser, testimony before Senate Banking Committee, Sept. 25, 2005. Transcript from Federal Document Clearing House.

242 **It was left to Bob Mueller**: Author interview with former government official.

243 **For years, in fact**: Author interviews with government officials.

243 **"Let's go in the front door"**: Author interviews with government officials.

243 **"I was wondering"**: Author interviews with government officials.

244 **It was "a gray area"**: Eric Lichtblau and James Risen, "Bank Data Sifted in Secret by U.S. to Block Terror," *New York Times*, June 23, 2006, p. A-1.

244 **an even better proposal**: John Snow press conference, June 23, 2006.

244 **the 2003 capture of an al Qaeda operative**: Author interviews; and Lichtblau and Risen, "Bank Data Sifted in Secret by U.S. to Block Terror." Numerous accounts, some conflicting, have emerged from the American government itself of how exactly Hambali was captured.

245 **"The capability here"**: Lichtblau and Risen, "Bank Data Sifted in Secret by U.S. to Block Terror."

245 **"In any enterprise"**: John Snow press conference, June 23, 2006.

246 **without the banking data**: Author interviews.

248 **Early on, in fact, the "scrutineers"**: Author interviews.

253 **I was at the meeting with Hamilton**: This meeting was originally held off the record. Hamilton subsequently allowed me to use his name and the substance of the meeting for this book.

254 **the Treasury Department summoned Frank**: Author interview with Barney Frank.

256 **he demanded thirty bottles**: Author interview with Lenny Schrank.

256 **quickly sued SWIFT**: The main case, *Walker v. SWIFT*, is still pending as of this writing in United States District Court for the Eastern District of Virginia. Two judges have refused to throw it out, citing constitutional issues.

256 **"Many people in Congress"**: Edmund Andrews, " Republicans Criticize Lack of Briefings on Bank Data," *New York Times*, July 12, 2006, p. A-10.

257 **"I have learned"**: Pete Hoekstra said he was told about the intelligence activities by a government whistle-blower, but the nature of the program has not been disclosed publicly as of this writing.

257 **These were strong words**: Eric Lichtblau and Scott Shane, "Ally Told Bush Project Secrecy Might Be Illegal," *New York Times*, July 9, 2006, p. A-1.

257 **"If *The New York Times*":** White House press briefing by Tony Snow, June 26, 2006.
258 **At the Minneapolis *Star Tribune*:** Kate Parry, "Press, President Collide over Secrecy," *Minneapolis Star Tribune*, July 9, 2006, p. 2AA.
260 **The remark was no idle slip:** Justice Department talking points memo released to *The New York Times* in its Freedom of Information Act lawsuit.
261 **The federal government has no such shield law:** Although there remains no federal shield law in place as of this writing, the idea has gained significant traction in Congress with the House's passage of the Free Flow of Information Act in October 2007, as discussed in the Epilogue.
262 **I was scheduled to be interviewed:** PBS's *NewsHour*, June 26, 2006.
262 **the FBI was investigating allegations:** Weldon's former chief of staff, Russell J. Case, pleaded guilty in December 2007 to conspiracy charges connected to his dealings with a nonprofit with ties to Weldon. The FBI investigation is still ongoing at this writing.

CHAPTER NINE: A Loyal Bushie

267 **Ashcroft always insisted:** Ashcroft, *Never Again*, p. 282.
267 **too often, it seemed, Ashcroft had his own agenda:** Author interviews with administration officials.
267 **The live feed:** Laura Sullivan, "Ashcroft's Faith, Persona Inspire Split Sentiments," *Baltimore Sun*, July 8, 2002, p. A-1.
268 **"What the fuck":** Author interview with administration official.
268 **no mention by prosecutors of any dirty bombs:** Padilla was convicted on terrorism conspiracy charges in federal court in Miami in August 2007. In January 2008, Padilla was sentenced to seventeen years in prison. The judge rejected the life sentence sought by the Justice Department and questioned both Padilla's links to any actual acts of terrorism and the "harsh" conditions of his prolonged confinement.
268 **"minister of fear":** Dan Eggen, "Ashcroft's High Profile, Motives Raise White House Concerns," *Washington Post*, June 17, 2002, p. A-4.
268 **In a career built:** This account of Ashcroft's run-in with the 9/11 Commission is based primarily on author interviews with government and commission officials, except where noted.
269 **He felt the commission:** Ashcroft, *Never Again*, p. 243.
269 **an aide was sitting atop:** Author interviews with commission officials.
270 **"I was so shocked":** Author interview with Slade Gorton.
270 **Ashcroft claimed victory:** Ashcroft, *Never Again*, p. 249.
272 **a detailed, sixty-two-page analysis:** Internal commission report obtained by author. The commission's final report included a brief footnote concluding that Jamie Gorelick's memo had no connection to the events of 9/11, but the unreleased analysis gave a much more detailed and expansive reading of the reasons behind that conclusion.
272 **smacked of rank politics:** Kean and Hamilton, *Without Precedent*, p. 207.
273 **"Andy, I'm mad":** Ibid.

273 **"I want you to know":** Author interviews with commission officials.

273 **Tom Ridge got word one Tuesday evening:** Author interview with Tom Ridge.

274 **As they sat around the long dining room table:** Author observations at Justice Department.

274 **The color-coded warnings were "awful":** Author interview with Tom Ridge.

275 **"Would you let":** Author interviews with administration officials.

276 **Hutchinson told a CIA staffer:** Author interview with Asa Hutchinson.

278 **working off "old intelligence":** Author interview with Tom Ridge.

278 **Conflicting messages from two cabinet secretaries:** Author interview with Tom Ridge.

279 **he didn't get to see:** Scott Shane, David Johnston and James Risen, "Secret U.S. Endorsement of Severe Interrogations," *New York Times*, Oct. 4, 2007, p. A-1.

280 **Within his first month on the job:** This account of the Justice Department's secret torture memo in 2005 under Alberto Gonzales is drawn from the account in *The New York Times* of Oct. 4, 2007: "Secret U.S. Endorsement of Severe Interrogations."

281 **One of the authors:** *ABC World News with Charles Gibson*, Nov. 2, 2007.

282 **On November 15:** This account of the internal deliberations at the Justice Department and the White House over the firing of the U.S. attorneys is drawn primarily from several thousand pages of e-mails and documents obtained by the House Judiciary Committee and released publicly in March, April, and May of 2007. It is supplemented in parts by author interviews with administration officials, congressional testimony, and media accounts as noted.

283 **only ten U.S. attorneys in total:** Congressional Research Service report, *US Attorneys Who Have Served Less than Full Four-Year Terms, 1981–2006*, released Feb. 22, 2007.

284 **"What do you want to do?":** Testimony of Monica Goodling, House Judiciary Committee, May 23, 2007.

285 **"I understand you can never":** Eric Lipton and Ian Urbina, "In 5-Year Effort, Scant Evidence of Voter Fraud," *New York Times*, April 12, 2007, p. A-1.

286 **issues that were rarely raised before:** Neil Lewis, "Justice Dept. Reshapes Its Civil Rights Mission," *New York Times*, June 14, 2007, p. A-1.

286 **eight staff members:** Dan Eggen, "Justice Staff Saw Texas Districting as Illegal," *Washington Post*, Dec. 2, 2005. p. A-1.

286 **buried the findings of a statistical report:** Eric Lichtblau, "Profiling Report Leads to a Clash and a Demotion," *New York Times*, Aug. 24, 2005, p. A-1.

287 **"there are consequences":** Ashcroft, *Lessons from a Father to His Son*, p. 136.

287 **In a carefully worded memo:** Internal memo from Patrick Fitzgerald to Attorney General's Advisory Committee regarding the application of the death penalty, Feb. 12, 2002, obtained by author.

288 **The issue had come to a head:** Author interviews with government officials.

289 **"We do not want politics":** Eric Lichtblau, "Lawyers Fought U.S. Move to Curb Tobacco Penalty," *New York Times,* June 16, 2005, p. A-1.

289 **the politicos won out:** The Justice Department's Office of Professional Responsibility investigated accusations of political meddling against Robert McCallum and others but found no ethical violations in their oversight of the case.

289 **"If they're seen":** Dan Eggen, "Justice Dept. Hiring Changes Draw Fire; Law Grads Chosen Based on Politics, Say Critics," *Washington Post,* Jan. 12, 2003, p. A-8.

289 **prosecutors she considered "liberal":** Eric Lipton, "Colleagues Cite Partisan Focus by Justice Official," *New York Times,* May 12, 2007, p. A-1.

290 **"Holy hires":** Lewis, "Justice Dept. Reshapes Its Civil Rights Mission."

290 **Ultimately, a contrite Goodling:** Testimony of Monica Goodling before House Judiciary Committee, May 23, 2007. An ethics investigation into the accusations against Goodling is still pending as of this writing.

292 **in a capital case with no dead body:** Testimony of Paul Charlton before Senate Judiciary subcommittee, June 27, 2007. The case involved murder charges against a drug dealer suspected of killing his supplier. Charlton testified that investigators believed the body was buried in a landfill and he sought funding of $500,000 to $1 million to dig up the body and develop more evidence that might bolster capital charges. The Justice Department refused the request.

292 **On word of her ouster:** Justice Department e-mails released by House Judiciary Committee.

293 **"I guarantee politics":** Kelly Thornton and Onell R. Soto, "Lam Stays Silent About Losing Job," *San Diego Union-Tribune,* Jan. 13, 2007, p. B-1.

293 **"How many United States attorneys":** Testimony before Senate Judiciary Committee, Jan. 18, 2007.

294 **Gonzales was traveling:** E-mails released by House Judiciary Committee.

294 **series of unsolicited phone calls:** E-mails released by House Judiciary Committee. Michael Elston, who resigned amid the scandal, told Congress that he "certainly had no intention" of threatening anyone and was not trying to influence anyone's testimony.

295 **"There was no wrongdoing here":** Author interviews with administration officials.

295 **Some aides wanted:** Author interviews with administration officials.

296 **Sixty-four times:** Dana Milbank, "Maybe Gonzales Won't Recall His Painful Day on the Hill," *Washington Post,* April 20, 2007, p. A-2.

296 **One protester:** Ibid.

296 **"Senator, I have searched":** Alberto Gonzales testimony before Senate Judiciary Committee, April 19, 2007.

297 **begin calling for a perjury investigation:** The Justice Department inspector general's office would widen its investigation into the NSA affair to include an examination of Gonzales' apparent misstatements about the program. That investigation is still pending as of this writing.

298 **She would read:** Author interviews with administration officials.

299 **one Saturday night in late August:** Author interviews with Eric Lipton and with administration officials.

EPILOGUE

301 **Tom Ridge was visiting:** Author interview with Tom Ridge. Ridge declined to identify the European dignitary by name out of concern for his privacy.

302 **"I have never said":** Interview with President Bush on NBC's *Today* show, Sept. 2, 2004.

303 **bracing for the results:** Neither investigation by the Justice Department inspector general's office has been released as of this writing.

304 **"Does being on the offense":** Bush press conference at the East Room of the White House, Sept. 26, 2006.

304 **had become too discredited:** Author interviews with Pentagon officials.

305 **Whatever new system:** Reuters, "Pentagon Considers Ending Threat Report System," April 24, 2007.

305 **secretly, investigators had been using financial data:** Author interviews with government officials.

305 **"There were so many gaps":** Jason Trahan, "Defendants Celebrate as U.S. Vows to Retry Case," *Dallas Morning News*, Oct. 23, 2007, p. A-1.

307 **The appeals panel that heard the case:** The Justice Department appealed the ruling, and the full Fourth Circuit court heard oral argument in the case on Oct. 31, 2007. A decision is still pending at this writing.

308 **Senator Russ Feingold grumbled:** Eric Lichtblau, James Risen, and Mark Mazzetti, "Reported Drop in Surveillance Spurred a Law," *New York Times*, Aug. 11, 2007, p. A-1.

308 **"The fact we're doing it this way":** Interview with Mike McConnell by Chris Roberts, *El Paso Times*, Aug. 22, 2007, online edition.

309 **"He's basically saying":** Eric Lichtblau, "Role of Telecom Firms in Wiretaps Is Confirmed," *New York Times*, Aug. 24, 2007, p. A-13.

310 **"What's a conservative like me":** Remarks by Congressman Mike Pence on House floor, Oct. 16, 2007.

INDEX

Index

international transit traffic monitored
by, 218–19
Jarrett's attempted investigation of,
227–29
judicial ruling on constitutionality of,
230–31, 282
Justice Department concerns about,
160–61, 162–63, 167, 173, 174–76
Justice Department investigation of,
303
Lichtblau and Risen's stories on,
191–211
Protect America Act and, 307–8
reaction to *New York Times* story on,
214–18, 248
recertification of, 154, 180–83
Rockefeller's concerns about, 168–71
secret rooms at AT&T of, 139–40
telecoms and, 139–40, 149–50, 153,
206, 219
tighter controls imposed on, 184–85
Yoo's justifications of, 174–76
National Security Council, 82
Native Americans, 164
Naval Academy, 133
NBC News, 119, 120
Negroponte, John, 206
New Left, 121
Newman, Andy, 16–17
NewsHour, 262
Newsweek, 69, 70, 221, 223, 284
New York Police Department, 119
New York Times, 14, 16, 29, 32, 38, 48,
70, 90, 91, 125–26, 127, 129, 130,
132, 133, 190, 226, 230, 294, 299,
300, 303, 304, 310
Ashcroft sickbed story of, 220–23
Bush administration attacks on,
xvi–xvii, 257–58
and Bush administration pressure not
to run NSA story, 194–96, 205–11
NSA wiretapping stories in, 191–98,
202–11, 212, 219–20
public's right to know vs. national
security considerations of, 193–95,
199–200, 251, 252, 258
right wing attacks on, 217, 257
SWIFT story in, 249–63
threat of injunction against, 210–11
and Treasury Department pressure
not to run SWIFT story, 250, 252
Web site of, 211, 255
Wen Ho Lee suit against, 261–62
Nicaragua, 145
Nightline, 12, 218

9/11 Commission, 4, 12, 15, 64, 241,
247, 249, 253, 273
Ashcroft's testimony to, 268–71
Gonzales' resistance to requests of,
37–38, 135
intelligence failures blamed on
bureaucratic culture by, 272
separate counterterrorism agency
considered by, 101–2
9/11 Commission Report, 102, 112
1984 (Orwell), 139
Nixon, Richard, 5, 133, 134, 194, 210,
223, 258
No Fly List, 118, 136
NORTHCOM, *see* USNORTHCOM
Novak, Robert, 177
NSA, *see* National Security Agency
NSLs (national security letters), 92–93,
99, 118
FBI's overuse of, 96–97
Fine's report on, 96
secrecy provisions in, 94–95

O'Connor, Kevin, 95
O'Connor, Sandra Day, 44
Office of Foreign Assets Control
(OFAC), 244
Office of Intelligence Policy and Review
(OIPR), 140
Office of Legal Counsel (OLC), 61, 123,
178, 179
NSA wiretapping program and,
174–76
torture memos of, 173, 174–75,
281–82, 309
Official Secrets Act, 133
Ogden, David, 284
Oklahoma City bombing, 82
Olbermann, Keith, 258
Olson, Barbara, 7, 34
Olson, Ted, 7, 34, 182–83, 226
O'Neill, John, 7
O'Neill, Paul, 236, 238, 240, 244
"One Percent Doctrine," 25
Ong, Betty, 12
Operation Tips, 44–45
Orlando, Fla., jihadist-white supremacist
meeting in, 105–7
Orwell, George, 139
Oscar Madison (char.), 191

Padilla, Jose, 41, 43, 126, 268
Paine, Thomas, 117
Pakistan, 30, 244, 268, 276, 304
Palestine, 107, 305

A NOTE ABOUT THE AUTHOR

Eric Lichtblau received the 2006 Pulitzer Prize for national reporting. He has worked in the Washington bureau of *The New York
Times* covering the Justice Department and national security issues
since 2002. From 1999 to 2002 he covered the Justice Department
for *The Los Angeles Times,* and he worked for the newspaper for ten
years before that. He is a graduate of Cornell University and currently lives in the Washington area with his two sons, Matthew and
Andrew.

A NOTE ON THE TYPE

THIS BOOK was set in Janson, a typeface long thought to have
been made by the Dutchman Anton Janson, who was a practicing
typefounder in Leipzig during the years 1668–1687. However, it
has been conclusively demonstrated that these types are actually
the work of Nicholas Kis (1650–1702), a Hungarian, who most
probably learned his trade from the master Dutch typefounder
Dirk Vostens. The type is an excellent example of the influential
and sturdy Dutch types that prevailed in England up to the time
William Caslon (1692–1766) developed his own incomparable
designs from them.

Composed by North Market Street Graphics,
Lancaster, Pennsylvania
Printed and bound by Berryville Graphics,
Berryville, Virginia
Designed by Virginia Tan